Alistair
Cooke
Reporting
America

'I am a reporter of the facts and the feelings
that go into the American life I happen to
observe. I mention "the feelings" if only to
stress a belief that there is no such thing as
an objective reporter. But the way to be as
fair as possible is to notice that no fact of
human life comes to you uncoloured by what
people feel it means.'

Letter From America No. 831, 9 August 1964

Alistair Cooke Reporting America

The Life of the Nation 1946-2004

Introduction and commentaries by
Susan Cooke Kittredge

ALLEN LANE
an imprint of
PENGUIN BOOKS

ALLEN LANE

Published by the Penguin Group
Penguin Books Ltd, 80 Strand, London WC2R 0RL, England
Penguin Group (USA) Inc., 375 Hudson Street, New York, New York 10014, USA
Penguin Group (Canada), 90 Eglinton Avenue East, Suite 700, Toronto, Ontario, Canada M4P 2Y3
    (a division of Pearson Penguin Canada Inc.)
Penguin Ireland, 25 St Stephen's Green, Dublin 2, Ireland (a division of Penguin Books Ltd)
Penguin Group (Australia), 250 Camberwell Road, Camberwell, Victoria 3124, Australia
    (a division of Pearson Australia Group Pty Ltd)
Penguin Books India Pvt Ltd, 11 Community Centre, Panchsheel Park, New Delhi – 110 017, India
Penguin Group (NZ), 67 Apollo Drive, Rosedale, North Shore 0632, New Zealand
    (a division of Pearson New Zealand Ltd)
Penguin Books (South Africa) (Pty) Ltd, 24 Sturdee Avenue, Rosebank, Johannesburg 2196, South Africa

Penguin Books Ltd, Registered Offices: 80 Strand, London WC2R 0RL, England

www.penguin.com

This collection first published by Allen Lane 2008
2

Introductions and all 'Letters from America' copyright © The Estate of Alistair Cooke, 2008
All *Guardian* reports © Guardian News and Media Ltd.

The moral right of the author has been asserted

Created and produced by
Palazzo Editions Ltd
2 Wood Street
Bath, BA1 2JQ

www.palazzoeditions.com

Printed in Malaysia

A CIP catalogue record for this book is available from the British Library

ISBN: 978–1–846–14047–1

Previous Page: A.C. with a giant redwood tree on
location in California in 1970 for *Alistair Cooke's
America*, photograph by Penny Tweedie.

Contents

Introduction

I HAVE OFTEN been asked what it was like to grow up surrounded by 'famous' people. It is a question that leaves me dumb. Four-year-olds haven't the faintest idea what it means to be famous or infamous; they either like someone or they don't and judge people with uncanny clarity on their warmth, friendliness and approachability. I have found that, with allowances for circumstance and history, most people are pretty much alike, driven to greater and lesser degrees by fear, longing, ambition and desire.

As a child, this is how I viewed the adults who flowed through our house and my world: as nice or not so nice, fun or distant. My view of my father is, therefore, much the same: seen through my own very personal lens. Regardless of whatever else pulled on his coattails, when I was little, like all children, I just cared about how much attention he was paying to me.

When my father died, accolades flowed and many an erudite observer sought to delineate, once and for all, if not the role he played in furthering international understanding, then at least his influence on broadcasting and reporting in the twentieth century. Because that was what he was, first and foremost: a reporter. It was how he described himself, often with a marked vehemence: 'I am not a "television personality," I am a *reporter*. A *reporter*!' The more refined title of 'journalist' never sat as well with him as the simple, descriptive term of 'reporter'. 'I don't comment, I don't judge, I report.'

This book seeks to honour what he valued most, reports filed in print and broadcast over the air about what he observed in his assigned and chosen territory: the United States of America. It begins as the Second World War ends, with the sun rising on the second half of the twentieth century. It is divided chronologically into decades, each section presenting pieces from that time. In keeping with this somewhat arbitrary though useful framework, I will loosely also look back by decades to my life with my father, relating, as best I can, not the events and facts – I shall leave that to the reporter – but what was going on at home. Though I would not presume to know with certainty what Daddy was feeling or thinking, I feel comfortable in sharing my impressions. They are offered as just that, for in the end I can speak for no one else.

As my reflections in this book are primarily about my life with my father, I have not addressed our broader family life. My parents had each been married before and had children from their first marriages; my mother's children are Holly and Stephen and my father's son is John. Holly and Stephen lived with us, and John with his mother, Ruth. It may seem from the stories I tell that I was an only child; this was in some ways true and in others decidedly not. But Holly was eleven years older than I, and Stephen and Johnny both, coincidentally, eight, a span of years that seemed enormous when we were young. Stephen went away to boarding school when I was 3 and Holly to college when I was 11, and although I couldn't wait for their return for holidays, for most of my childhood I was the only kid at home. So many of my early memories relate to stories I have been told, making it difficult to know exactly if I really remember the event myself or if it simply has been implanted time and again by others and by familiar photographs.

One of the earliest memories I have of my father was of Sunday nights. In the early 1950s his star was rising; he was a regular correspondent for *The Manchester Guardian*, his radio broadcast, *Letter From America*, seemed pretty secure, and he was the host of a television programme called *Omnibus*. My impression that his feet seemed rarely to touch the ground was probably correct. He was a tightly strung, lean, energetic and engaged man at the time, whose focus, ambition, and intelligence had secured for him a stronghold in New York City. Though his commitments were certainly demanding, taking him away from home a considerable amount of time, what I recall was that when he was home the air was charged with vitality.

At no other time was this more true than on Sunday nights. *Omnibus* was broadcast live, and after each show a slew of the crew came to our house for dinner, always the same fare: chili and beer. High on the excitement of the show, elated that it was over, and not yet under the weight of the next week's production, they were a very merry and raucous group. My bedroom at the time was a maid's room just off the pantry. The pantry led to the dining room, and if I lay at the end of my bed, opened my door just a crack, and made sure that the door to the dining room was also open, I could watch a section of the table and feel part of the gaiety. Generally I was in bed before the crew even arrived at the apartment, and I remember Daddy coming in to kiss me goodnight and ask if I had seen the show. His entrance into my dark slice of a bedroom was like a thunderbolt strike, and I would jump on the bed with excitement. Later I would drift off to sleep on the waves of laughter and camaraderie, the smell of chili, the sound of my mother bustling in and out of the kitchen. To this day several people from *Omnibus* remain close friends of our family.

During the 1950s it seems to me that the initial elation my father felt at his rising good fortune began to give way a bit to the sobering reality of all he had taken on. As one of the first real television personalities, he was often asked to speak about the evolving medium. As *Omnibus* struggled for survival and sponsorship, his impatience with the hard realities of its financing grew. He was barraged with offers to lecture on a variety of topics, play parts in films, and write for various periodicals and magazines. He was in great demand, and there pervaded in the household an understanding that we cut him a wide berth. This was essential since he worked in the apartment, the doors to his study remaining closed from the moment he awoke until he shut up shop in the evening. We were keenly aware that what was happening within his study was none of our concern. This work routine would remain intact until he gave up *Letter From America* in February 2004, a week after he was diagnosed with cancer and only a month before he died at the age of ninety-five.

Though he was very busy in those years, he was also capable of putting aside his professional demands. During the summer months he went out to our summer beach cottage on the North Fork of Long Island every weekend and was, for the most part, able to leave work behind. I do, however, recall a few times when he drove up the driveway on Friday afternoon to the phone ringing from Manhattan. Some event had occurred during his three-hour drive that rendered irrelevant his freshly recorded *Letter From America*, which would be broadcast over the weekend. On those occasions he would simply go into the kitchen, pour himself a glass of milk, get in the car and head back to the city.

Before he became obsessed with golf, he fished. Fishing is an early morning endeavour, and the fact that Daddy even considered this pastime is staggering to me. Being a night owl, he went to bed around 2 a.m. and, generally, rarely rose before 10 a.m. I, on the other hand, am an early bird. How clearly I recall tiptoeing into my parents' bedroom and waking him on our fishing days. He would ceremoniously make us a lunch of bologna sandwiches, and we'd go off to Captain Jim's to rent a tiny boat with a 10-horsepower motor.

Fishing from a small boat, afloat on the changing tide in a small bay, is all about waiting. Perhaps that is why those trips made such an impression on me. Daddy, for all his flurry, energy, verbosity and dynamism could sit, silently, at the end of a fishing pole like no one else I've ever seen. Maybe it was a relief for him not to talk. He was always shushing me, telling me the fish could hear us speaking, that we had to be quiet or they wouldn't bite.

Another thing that was surprising about the fishing trips was that, for a pretty squeamish person, he never flinched at baiting the hooks or handling and cleaning the fish. When I was eleven I caught an especially large kingfish, the record that season for Peconic Bay. The catch made it into the local paper, and Daddy preened and waxed eloquent about the lucky day. I was delightfully surprised at his reaction to the catch; he was as excited as I had ever seen him.

His uncensored and ready expression of emotion was as infectious as it could be unnerving. Though he had been raised in a strict Methodist household in Blackpool, his passionate nature was not subdued by that restrictive environment. When he was happy you knew it instantly, and when he was not, well, you knew that too. In one of the prayers I wrote for his memorial service at Westminster Abbey, I called him a man of 'tender heart'. I did not mean that he wished none of God's creatures ill or that he was a softy in any sentimental sense. On the contrary, he often remarked that one of the great bonds he and my mother shared was that together they had not a single ounce of sentimentality. He had a tender heart because it was always exposed, as if he were so busy dashing hither and yon that he couldn't be bothered to cover it. This made him receptive to the person on the street, available, if you will, to hear a story. When he was happy, he whistled and danced, his joy a welcome contagion that spread through the house. But he was just as easily wounded, developing, I believe, the art of ready dismissal as a result. It was not that he didn't feel the slight, the reproof, the judgment, he just learned to sweep it from his emotional desk top with alacrity and, on occasion, no small measure of reciprocal reproof. The one feeling he could not dismiss, the one emotion that flattened him, was fear. For a man of great intelligence, remarkable knowledge and accomplishment, he was a scaredy cat.

The first time I sensed his being profoundly afraid was during the Cuban Missile Crisis in 1962. I say this with the valued perspective that comes only with time and years of looking back. Like many who grew up in the early 1960s in the United States, I was terrified of the Russians and nuclear war. But I was keenly aware that I was more frightened than my friends were and took it as a sign of weakness. In that tense week in October 1962, I looked to him for assurance, asking if we were going to war. I think that actually what I asked was that he tell me we weren't going to war. 'I can't tell you that,' he said. I now realize that my fear was weighted by his.

I have wondered over time if his grave concern might not have been the result of more information than he could ever have shared. Though he was not *The Manchester Guardian*'s Washington, D.C., correspondent at the time, his connection with men at the front of the situation was very real. His first friend in the United States, Gene Rostow, was the brother of Walt Rostow, President Kennedy's National Security Advisor. Adlai Stevenson, United States Ambassador to the United Nations, was a close friend. Although during the Bay of Pigs disaster, earlier that year, Stevenson had been humiliated and used by the Kennedy Administration, his bequeathal and anointing as the spokesperson in October had an air of righteous vindication to it. It has recently become public knowledge that the situation in October of 1962 was every bit as dire as even our wildest nightmares might have suggested.

Until he died, Daddy remained ever watchful and fearful of 'the trembling of the fingers on the nuclear bomb', fearful not so much of the bombs as of the frailty of the humans who controlled them. Whenever some international fracas sparked hot and wild, he would say with an air of resignation, 'This may be it'. He passed to me the ability, the practiced skill, of being good and scared, or at least on occasion appropriately anxious while on other occasions inappropriately so. This is not to be confused with what is now termed an anxiety disorder; we just shared a ready fear of international calamity.

Against the backdrop of the international Cold War, a certain cold war was going on at the time in our house as well. Though I believe my parents' marriage to have been remarkably solid, all marriages experience times of stress, and theirs was no exception. During the 1950s and 1960s, they travelled a bumpy road, though they definitely travelled it together. They stayed together through difficult times because they quite simply never lost their love for one another. My mother often remarked how fortunate she felt to be married to her best friend. A painter all her life, she lived with her greatest fan and her eye and artistic sense were never lost on my father. 'One of the most important things I have learned from my wife', he would observe, 'is an appreciation for dirty colours.' Ever conscious of the pressure on reporters to clarify, delineate, perhaps even rush to simplicity in black and white, he took this new way of seeing as a cautionary and enriching lesson. Though Daddy could be impatient and dismissive towards her at times, after fifty-seven years she still inspired his puppy-love adoration.

During the last weeks of his life, the apartment that was normally their quiet haven was occupied, aside from me, by round-the-clock hospice and nursing care and all the mechanical support required by one who is bedridden. At ninety-one the management of Daddy's routine was beyond Mummy; she felt a bit superfluous as a result and one afternoon expressed this to him. Lifting himself up on his pillows, with a clarity and strength of voice he had not had for weeks, he looked her straight in the eye and said, 'Don't you understand that the only person I want in the world is you? I long to be here, just the two of us, as it's always been. But it can't be like that now, we both need more help.' Throughout their marriage, regardless of ups and downs, he was always clear about his feelings for her.

During the rough patch in the fifties and sixties, a symptom of their established marital diplomacy was that my mother travelled to Europe every spring by herself. Several weeks later my father would sometimes join her, but when I was growing up, spring in the city meant bubble gum, baseball cards, roller skates, and my father's earnest forays into single parenthood. Because we had a live-in maid, it did not fall upon him to tend to my daily schedule of school, riding lessons, laundry and meals, but he did enjoy on occasion stepping into the role of the indulgent parent.

The most memorable of such times was when he took me to Kentucky the first weekend in May to stay with some friends on a lavish farm outside Louisville and go to the Derby. I was ten at the time, horse mad and wild about the country. But this was not just country; this was heaven. I arose at dawn and ran with woolly sheep and wobbly lambs through fields flecked with buttercups and daisies. I was taken horseback riding down lanes that smelled of magnolias and galloped over grass that really was blue. The grandeur of the estate on which we stayed was unlike anything I had ever imagined, and Daddy took great pleasure in my total happiness. In keeping with the fairy-tale adventure, our seats at Churchill Downs were directly over the finish line. Flying back to New York, he felt compelled to bring me back to earth, to remind me that what we had enjoyed over the weekend was not real life. My recollection is that I was not interested in his wet blanket, preferring to savour the scent of a dream come true.

There were times during these intermingling cold wars when my worry manifested itself in insomnia. My mother would ask me what the matter was, what was troubling me; I had no neat answer. Daddy, as if knowing too well the complexity of a racing spirit, simply sat on my bed and stroked my forehead, if not easing the turmoil within

Daddy reading to me.

at least the furrowed brow without. He was not a man overly disposed toward expressions of affection (in this he reflected his age and upbringing), but he was deeply loving toward those to whom he had lost his heart, and that list was long.

I have always felt I am pretty much the same person now that I was in eighth grade. My world view, my assessment of my own failings and capabilities, has not changed or altered substantially in the intervening fifty years. Whether this was due to a genetic predisposition to early maturity or to events that occurred from 1962 to 1963 – or to both – I have no idea, but for whatever reason, my personality seems to have been cast then.

On Friday afternoon, 22 November 1963, dressed in my cheerleader's uniform, I waited with the basketball team in the lobby of the Dalton School for the bus that would take us across town to the scheduled game. But instead of being ushered out in a single line to the buses coughing plumes in the chill fall air, we who crowded the lobby – students looking forward to a game or a party that night or a weekend overnight date with a friend or a night in front of the television – were told by a weeping teacher that President Kennedy had been shot. Dazed, a friend and I walked repeatedly around the block, trying in vain to march some sense into what had happened. In the end everyone just dispersed, falling away from the searing news like ashes drifting into the air from a raging fire.

What I recall most of my walk home from school that grey, cold November afternoon was the silence of the streets. Were there no cars, buses or taxis? Surely people were crying, for they were staggering as though gravity were no longer a steady pull but an erratic pulse on their bodies, but I can't remember the sound of shock and sorrow. Perhaps my head was so filled with incomprehension that nothing else could get in, and I was simply struck deaf.

But not for long. If the streets were a daze of surreal incredulity, the atmosphere inside our apartment had all the focused energy the outside world lacked. On opening the front door that afternoon, I was slapped back to consciousness. The phones were ringing, the television on, the radio crackling. Smoke was pouring from Daddy's study, and he was alone in the apartment frantically trying to get off the phone so he could get back to the urgent work of figuring out what was going on and what to report.

Jolted from the oppressive weight of shock and its accompanying sense of ineffectualness, I realized that, in fact, I might actually be able to do something after all. We had two televisions in our apartment, one in my father's study and another in a back room. The three major networks were scrambling to keep up with events, scooping one another from time to time, conjecturing, retracting, and surmising. In no time it was clear that I could monitor two stations in the other room and report back to the study with developments. What was tricky was figuring out what was potentially significant and, consequently, when it was all right to interrupt Daddy's frantic hammering at the typewriter. And still the phone never stopped ringing, with demands that he file his piece, his broadcast, immediately. At one point late in the night when I was still in my little navy-blue, pleated cheerleader's skirt and he was rumpled and wild and we were both hungry and tired, he exclaimed to some impatient editor, 'Listen, we are doing the best we can.'

'We.' And that was it for me. It was such an affirmation, such a declaration of both worth and appreciation, that there dropped from my psyche layers of cumbersome adolescent insecurity. Later when I heard him relate to friends and colleagues his appreciation of my help over that long weekend, I flushed with delight.

Was this a turning point in our relationship? I think not so much a turning point as a cementing and a cherished affirmation for me that I was not just little Susie anymore. The dawning of this altered view had begun a year or so earlier when Daddy had expressed admiration for some short stories I had written for a class assignment at school. He had been so enthusiastic that he had given the stories to his friend Bennett Cerf who was then head of Random House. Naturally I was thrilled, but not so much at Bennett's praise as at Daddy's, since he was the real taskmaster when it came to language and words.

Sometimes I think it's a miracle I dare even open my mouth, having been raised by someone who never, ever let the slightest grammatical imperfection go uncorrected. Brendan Gill, theatre critic for *The New Yorker*, on one of the several occasions he introduced my father at a speaking engagement dubbed him 'the Corrector'. When it came to the English language, Daddy was a fanatic, a man possessed of a passion. He loved the language, its sound and meaning, its cultural reflection and heritage.

Nothing got his goat like newly created idiomatic obfuscations. The word 'area', as in 'We are now approaching the Philadelphia area', drove him crazy. 'We are now approaching Philadelphia!' he would shout. Another, 'on a daily basis', evoked a classic response. 'My doctor asked me if I have a bowel movement on a daily basis. I told him that I do not; I have it on the toilet.' He enjoyed corresponding about language with people similarly afflicted with his passion, notably H. L. Mencken, William Safire, and Nunnally Johnson. When he became concerned that his memory might be slipping – a ridiculous worry for someone who could recall details, dates and events like few others – he decided to put himself to sleep at night by reciting Shakespeare's plays. The English language, beautifully presented, was a balm to his soul.

As is so well known and endlessly documented, the 1960s were pivotal in the United States. Changes were being effected in the structure, the thinking, and the functioning of American life, predominantly as a result of the Civil Rights movement and the Vietnam War.

Daddy suffered neither fools nor change gladly. His feelings about the Vietnam War and the protest movement it sparked stemmed, I think, in large part from his law- abiding nature, deep respect for authority and, if not a particular president, surely the office of the presidency itself. To those who would judge administrative policy, he would proclaim, 'You don't know the facts!' He didn't claim that he did either, but in the absence of such he was always willing to defer to those in authority. In light of this, the tactics employed by the more radical leaders of the anti-war movement were anathema to him.

My parents' differing views about the Vietnam War would prove a constant irritant during the course of that engagement. My mother was against the war from the start and her position only became more vehement as time went on. The simple fact that one of their inviolate traditions was to watch the news together each evening meant that they argued about the war most nights. Loosened by the 'twilight wine of Scotland', their tongues slashed like daggers in the small study. This time in the evening became known in our family from then on as 'The Jane and Alistair Show'.

Unlike many of my contemporaries, I was not a dedicated protester of the war, though I was definitely against it. Working at a publishing house in New York, I was more engaged in the Manhattan literary scene than campus riots.

My job kept me in the city the summer of 1968 while my mother was out at our beach cottage on Long Island. As it was an election year my father did a lot of travelling, so it was perfectly normal for him to be at the California Primary in Los Angeles on 4 June of that year. But it was not a normal night, and when news first broke that Senator Robert Kennedy had been shot, I somehow knew that Daddy was close to it, though I would not know until later that he had actually been in the pantry.

Waking early to the shattering news, I waited by the phone for him to call. He didn't call, however, until late on the afternoon of 5 June, by which time I was frayed. But not as frayed as him. His voice was a grave rubbing of its original; it was bumpy, unclear, with jagged edges and none of its usual forthright clarity. Only in the last days

Family portrait. Daddy playing the piano; Johnny on the left
and Stephen more towards centre, playing their guitars; Holly
looking regal; me dreaming; our dog Pompey being pampered and Mum
capturing it all on canvas as reflected in the mirror.

of his own life would I hear that gravelled tone again. Certainly he was shattered, but
he also had a job to do, and as he has said, 'A professional is someone who can do his
best work when he doesn't feel like it.' So he did his job and came home to collapse.

During the 1960s he worked very hard at what he did best, reporting. *Omnibus*
had ended and he was not an especially recognizable celebrity in the United States.
Therefore, I did not grow up with a 'famous' father. I was married in 1968, and it
wasn't until the early 1970s that his career in television brought him the recognition
he had until he died. With the *America* series and then *Masterpiece Theatre* he became,
once again, a celebrity. But by that time I was married, living in Vermont, and raising
a family.

Although my father never mentioned it, my getting married at the age of nineteen
was difficult for him. Late in December of 1968, the wedding ceremony was to take
place at 5 p.m. and at 3:30 he was still in bed. I kept asking my mother what was the
matter with him, and she replied, 'His little girl is getting married.' Finally, at close
to 4 p.m., she and I went into their bedroom, and with great command and authority
she said, 'Alistair, your daughter is getting married in an hour and you have to get up
NOW!'

Nine years later when that marriage ended in divorce, he was, as my mother said,

'Acting like a canary let out of a cage.' It wasn't that he hadn't liked my first husband, he just preferred my undivided attention and was shameless in his delight at thinking he'd have it again. When shortly after my divorce we went to England to spend Christmas with my sister, I recall his saying to my mother one night as we drove across London in a cab, 'Hey, sweetie, isn't this great; we've got Susie back.' Which, of course, was not the case, as I had two small boys and a busy life in Vermont. In a couple of years my second husband, Charlie, and I were married, and my father came to accept and even delight in the increasingly full life I was living in the wilds of Vermont.

During the 1970s, for the first time, Daddy started to make more money than he needed for his and my mother's normal living expenses. His feelings about money, however, were deeply entwined with his strict Methodist upbringing. My grandfather had been a Methodist lay preacher, and though not the powerhouse in the family – my grandmother amply filled that role – he instilled in my father the iron rod of ethical behaviour, based first and foremost on scripture. Hence, interest was usury; to get something for nothing, immoral. The fact that he kept his money in a checking account was not only a result of his financial naiveté; it was intentional as well. He also believed that money was the root of all evil. When first *America* and then *Masterpiece Theatre* started looking as though they might make him some money, he retreated into a minor depression. My mother observed that he was far more frightened of having money than of not having it.

And this is where we came to blows about the war. Exasperated, idealistic and strident, I accused him of funding the bombing of Cambodia by donating the interest his money generated to the Federal government's war chest. He was cursory and sharp in his dismissal of my stupidity, and I didn't bring it up again, knowing a blind spot when I saw one.

Religion in our house was pretty much a taboo subject. In order to know why, it is helpful to understand both of my parents' religious upbringings. As mentioned, my father grew up in Blackpool in a deeply faithful culture. Methodism in the early part of the twentieth century in northern England was about as strict as any religious teaching could be. When Daddy received a scholarship to Cambridge University, he essentially left God before God could leave him. And leave him he was sure God would, for three specific reasons. First, he had a cowlick in his hair that required a liberal application of hair tonic to control. Surely God would punish him for such a display of vanity. Second, he was crazy about music, especially American jazz. He suspected God would look harshly on such frivolity and judge him accordingly. Third, he thought girls terrific. Surely he would be sent to the fires of hell for what he longed to do. Part of his leaving Blackpool and his upbringing was to cast aside the restraints of the church.

My mother's experience was similar. She grew up in Montclair, New Jersey, and was raised an Episcopalian. Like my father's, her view of God was of a harsh and judgmental deity. She told of playing hide and seek as a child one day and of finding herself neatly hidden away beneath a bed chewing on some gum that had lost its flavour. She stuck the gum to the bed slats over her head. But no sooner had she done so than she knew God was watching, so she peeled the gum from the board, taking layers of varnish with it, and placed it back in her mouth. When she was fifteen she went to the rector of her church to ask him a nagging question. 'The bread and wine,' she said, 'are they symbols or do they really turn into flesh and blood?'

'They really turn into flesh and blood,' the rector replied.

'They don't taste like that to me,' she said and was gone for good.

Coming together from different though surprisingly similar theological backgrounds, my parents vowed that they would never inflict upon their children the oppressive, repressive religious upbringing they had endured.

Whether it is simply indicative that all parents are doomed to failure or that the forbidden fruit always has the sweetest aroma, in 1987, at the age of thirty-eight, I decided that I wanted to go into the ministry. Having worked in publishing directly after high school, I had not received a bachelor's degree and quickly – and sinkingly – realized that I would have to go to college before seminary. I told my parents only that I wanted to go to college after all, not daring to mention my real intentions. Only two years later, as I was approaching my final year and applications to graduate school, did I muster the courage to tell them my plan. I anticipated that they might well be the only parents in America who, upon hearing of their child's intention to enter the ministry, would hang their heads and wonder what they had done wrong.

But they surprised me. My mother was admittedly baffled but very supportive. As an ardent pragmatist and believer in science, her refrain would always be, 'But how can you believe in God and in science?!' Her curiosity was real, and she was intrigued to have a member of the enemy camp in her midst.

My father's reaction was first shock that gave way to a growing sense of intrigue and perhaps even pride. Oddly enough, I think he subconsciously felt there might be hope for him yet, that my affiliation might stand him in good stead at the Pearly Gates.

It took ten years for me to complete my training for the ministry, and during that time my father talked more openly about his own beliefs and musings. When he was around eighty he said to me, 'A day does not go by that I do not recall a piece of scripture that I learned by rote at the age of eight. And more and more, I see that it is the foundation of who I am.'

I have wondered if his late reconsideration of religion still carried with it the weight of Judgment and if this might not have contributed to the turmoil he experienced upon turning eighty. Though he was in good health, he was increasingly frail and his life was changing. The schedule of *Masterpiece Theatre*, his speaking engagements, preparing books for publication, and his ever beloved *Letter* all put a great deal of pressure on him. As a result, he was often grumpy and crotchety.

In 1988 he and my mother came to Vermont for Thanksgiving. He was always a little uneasy about visiting Vermont; he had a deep angst about going to the wilderness, as he called it, going to the land I had chosen as home. He was a city person at heart, and too much green – unless on a golf course – made him nervous. A houseplant was often enough to bring on an anxiety attack. Until he settled in, he was a little on

Although he never learned to read music, Daddy enjoyed playing the piano throughout his life. Twenty minutes' practice at the end of the day marked the transition from work to play.

edge in the country, but on this particular trip he never did settle down. It seemed to me that we could do nothing right. I didn't remember his saying one nice thing all weekend; the kids were too boisterous, the cake wasn't sweet enough, the turkey dry, the house cold, the dog too affectionate, the TV reception pathetic, the roads icy, and on and on. He and my mother flew back to New York City on Saturday, and I brooded for a day. I felt that I had lost him, that he was dead to me, that there was no sense in his coming again if he was going to be so disagreeable. Right at the start of Advent I was in a foul place, a wilderness; I was cross and hurt and sad. Had it not been Advent, I might not have heard the call to hope, the call to courage and honesty, the small voice crying in the wilderness. So on Sunday afternoon I called my mother – I have only so much courage – and told her through my tears how I was feeling.

Early on Monday morning, around seven, she called back. She said that she'd told him what I'd said and that he'd been completely shocked. He had no idea that he'd been behaving that way, no idea that he had hurt the most important people in his life. Mother said that he had wanted to call on Sunday night but was crying so hard he couldn't. She said that he hadn't slept much and would probably be calling soon. Around nine o'clock the phone rang. It was Daddy. He said he was very sorry, that he had had a lovely time and that the last thing in the world he wanted to do was to hurt us. Please believe me, he said, his voice cracking. I told him the truth; I told him that I did believe him. What I didn't do was brush it off as I might normally have done and say, 'It's okay, it's nothing.' It *was* something, but what was more was what was happening right then. I told him, I think, that I loved him and that I didn't want to lose him, and I knew in that moment I wouldn't.

My father was not an egotist, one inclined to exaggerate one's self-worth, but he was by nature egocentric, wrapped up in himself. Compounding his natural inclination, he had a lot going on and a great deal of attention and admiration flowing his way. So my mother and I took it upon ourselves to shake him down every once in a while and bring him back to reality. These radical wake up calls were never easy, they involved tears and trauma and rants of varying degrees, but they always cleared the air and brought him back to us.

Aside from the intense calls to attention, I must admit that my mother and I – and my sister to a lesser degree – did see it as our job to make sure he didn't get too swelled a head. To this end we were, in hindsight, perhaps a bit ruthless in our kidding, but he took it in good humour, throwing up his hands and complaining, 'I get no respect!' A frequent source of jibbing followed his having been voted in the 1970s one of the 'Ten Best Dressed Men in America'. Though he cut a dapper figure and managed to portray a certain elegance, his clothes themselves were more threadbare than anyone would imagine. He didn't have time to fuss over his attire most of the time; but his magnetic personality commanded attention, making him appear well turned out and dashing. As he aged, his rumpled appearance was a result, I'm certain, of elderly, failing eyesight; he simply did not see the spills of Ovaltine that decorated his clothes.

My husband, Charlie, often called us brutal in our teasing of my father. I wonder if this happens in other families where one member is the recipient of a certain amount of public acclaim or admiration. It is almost as though, in an effort to hold on to the one whom the fans would happily eat alive, the family has to recast the individual as less tasty than might be presumed. The teasing was all in good fun, and he was surprisingly tolerant of our barbs.

His sense of humour, his delight in good jokes – or 'stories' as he called them – was with him until the last difficult weeks of his life. He applied the same intensity to enjoyment as he did to work, cultivating laughter the way others dote over African violets. Certain friends were great sources of stories, and as soon as he heard a good one, he'd call me. 'I've got one for you,' he'd say. Though he loved a good story, what enthralled him more were the real-life turns of fortune or the phrase that surprised and shocked. One of his favourites actually happened to him.

As he told it, he had by necessity developed a quick response to people who approached him saying, 'I know who you are!' or 'Are you who I think you are?' Flippantly, he would simply say, 'Yes, I'm Bob Hope,' and, smiling, continue on his way.

One afternoon, while staying at The Huntington in San Francisco, Daddy was headed out of the hotel. Going down the steps from the main entrance, he came upon an elderly woman ascending the same stone stairs. She stopped, looked at him, and said, 'Are you who I think you are?'

'Yes,' he replied, 'I'm Bob Hope.'

To which she replied, 'Isn't that interesting. I'm Mrs Bob Hope.'

'And she was!' Daddy exclaimed as he fell over laughing. The joke was on him, and far from being embarrassed or shy about it, he loved it. His love of a good laugh balanced, I think, the very serious daily dose of hard reality he was forced to swallow in his job as a reporter. His weekly *Letter* had much the same effect, allowing, as it did, a look not at the headlines of the news but rather at the people and context, their lives and idiosyncrasies.

As he grew older, he became naturally less resilient, suffering as he did from arthritis and a gut with a proclivity to inflammation. The total knee replacement he received when he was days shy of his eighty-fourth birthday gave him a new lease on life, but his heart was increasingly troublesome, requiring a pacemaker and careful monitoring.

The decline in health that he experienced in the last five years of his life was, I believe, exacerbated by the events of 11 September, 2001. Fuelling his lifelong fear of nuclear war or some sort of major world calamity, it was as though his nightmare had come true, and he would remain haunted by it for the rest of his life.

Since my mother was on Long Island, Daddy was alone in the apartment that Tuesday morning in September. I tried calling him as soon as the news came of the planes crashing into the Twin Towers, but neither my mother nor I could reach him as the phone lines were down in the city. We both were worried that he had heard the news and collapsed of a heart attack. It wasn't until the next day that we heard from my cousin in England, who for some reason had been able to get a call through to him, that he was fine and doing what the situation required: reporting.

Far from paralyzing him by anxiety, the crisis summoned in him a strength and determination recently dimmed by infirmity. Once again he was the observer, out looking for the human interest stories as well as the big news. Though he was still able at the age of ninety-two to go around the block for a quart of milk, he rarely did so despite my mother's urging that he 'stir his stumps'. That week in September he was padding the streets more than he had been in the previous six months.

'I went looking for milk,' he said. 'There's no milk in this city! Only a warm, chalky white liquid called "diary creamer" that makes your cereal taste foul.'

He told of going out to dinner at the local restaurant because, unlike in his own icebox, theirs still had food. 'It's not like New York,' he said, 'it's a small town now. People don't sit at their tables and mind their own business; everyone talks together, because everyone's business is the same.' In a matter of days, though, as the practical aspects of procuring food and drink eased and supplies once again were trucked into the city, his apprehension about the future grew and would remain a cloud over his head for the rest of his days.

He continued to visit us in Vermont for Christmas until a couple of years before he died, when all travel became impossible for him. He enjoyed reading scripture at the Christmas Eve Service at the church I serve, The Old Meeting House, and delighted in the family traditions of food, music, and revelry.

I like to think that my ministry allowed him to revisit, and in some way perhaps reconcile, his feelings about – if not religion – God. I will never forget a frightening night in Manhattan in the fall of 2003 when one of our daughters then attending college in the city was gravely ill and was rushed to the hospital. I was at my parents' apartment at the time, and when the call came telling me of the crisis, shaking and undone I grabbed my coat to leave. But Daddy held my shoulders firmly in his frail arthritic hands, looked me fiercely in the eye and said with a command and intensity, 'You must trust in the Lord!' And I cried harder, not only for his acknowledgment of the severity of the situation but that he could say that out loud, though exactly what it said of his own faith I am not certain.

An especially nice offshoot of my ministry was his meeting Frederick Buechner, a renowned writer and theologian, at my ordination where they both spoke. A friendship was immediately ignited, based so thoroughly on mutual admiration. If my path had opened the door to Daddy's reconsideration of his own beliefs, Fred Buechner blew the spirit into his heart. Always on his bedside table would be a dictionary, whatever three books he was reading at the time, and a couple of Buechner's theological gems, *Wishful Thinking* and *Whistling in the Dark*. Daddy's insistence on referring to him as 'Dr Buechner', though I repeatedly told him Fred was not a PhD, reflected only, I think, his feeling that Buechner had healed something in his heart.

It had long been my feeling that my father would either die because he stopped doing his *Letter* or stop doing the *Letter* because he died. As it turned out, both were in part true. In the last few years of his life, researching, writing, and recording *Letter From America* became his *raison d'être*. His weekly rhythm and moods were driven by his preparation and completion of the task. Should I have something important to discuss with him, I would never call on Tuesday, Wednesday or Thursday. His intention was to record on Thursday, but more often than not it was postponed until Friday. Wondering about his availability, I would call my mother and ask if the *Letter* were done, and only upon assurance that it was would I call. I confess that I too am affected by an inclination to become preoccupied with the immediate deadline before me. Often we would speak at the end of a particular week; he would gloat that he had finished his talk and wonder if I'd done mine. Inevitably, since my sermon would not be delivered until Sunday, it was not completed, and I would kid him, lamenting that he could not operate a fax machine and send me his piece to use.

In February 2004 when he was diagnosed with lung cancer that had already metastasized to his bones, he knew immediately that he would stop the *Letter*. He experienced in those first weeks after the fateful news an odd exhilaration of sorts. As one who had certainly enjoyed a fair measure of success in his life, there was one area in which he had failed: though a lifelong hypochondriac, he had never been gravely ill. There was a certain satisfaction, morbid to be sure, in finally having a severe diagnosis. On top of that, when his retirement was announced, the tributes and accolades poured in. It was as though he were attending his own laudatory funeral. But the thing that lifted his spirits the most was not having to pay attention to the news. He would say,

'It's great, I don't have to worry about Iraq or what the Security Council is doing or not doing.' Not only was he freed from having to worry about the world, he no longer had to make sense of it.

Originally told he had between three and six months to live, it turned out that his demise was far more swift. I overheard my mother speaking on the phone shortly after he died, 'They gave him three months and he only used one.' Ever frugal by nature and upbringing, this seemed to her an honourable course to have taken.

Though swift, his dying was rough. He reacted adversely to the medications given him and essentially lost two of his last four weeks to drug-induced confusion, nausea, and misery. My routine those last weeks was to spend most of the weekdays in Manhattan and then fly home to Vermont for services on the weekend, returning Sunday night. Every time I left him, I feared I would not see him again, and the partings were wrenching for us both.

Though it was a gruelling time, there were moments of grace as well. Listening in the kitchen via the baby monitor, I heard my parents, then aged ninety-five and ninety-one, working together on the *New York Times* crossword puzzle as he lay on his death bed. The hospice nurse observed with amazement that this was not standard entertainment in such circumstances.

As they die many people look back over their lives, recalling and then releasing memories, people and events. This was to prove a daunting task for my father. Because he was endowed with an astonishing memory and because world history was his fascination, he had a lot to remember and let go. My husband Charlie called one morning from Vermont to ask how he was and where he was on his travel through time. 'The Boer Wars,' I replied; 'we have a long way to go.'

In the end, however, it wasn't that long at all. He was able to rally in the last week a few times, once to see his dear friend Bill Buckley, another to meet with his literary executor, and a third time simply to leave his bedroom and try to regain normalcy by going into his study to watch the evening news. The last was especially moving because when my mother walked into the study as she had for fifty-five years, Daddy lit up and said, 'Look who's here! Hi Tootsie.' Sadly, just ten minutes later, he would feel too ill and return to his bedroom.

In his will Daddy asked that, if possible, his ashes be scattered in Central Park. In a discreet, quiet ceremony ten members of my family, my brother John, and my father's secretary Patti Yasek gathered around a patch of grass as my mother watched from her window in the apartment. John sang a haunting ballad, I recited a psalm, we prayed, and set him to rest in the Park he so loved. It seemed a fitting and appropriate end.

The subsequent service the following October at Westminster Abbey was as spectacular as the sprinkling of his ashes was simple; two appropriate reflections of a man both ordinary and extraordinary.

As it turned out, however, what we thought had been an end was, unfortunately, the beginning of another chapter in a long life. Eighteen months after his death, I was informed that the night he died his body had been stolen and his bones illegally sold. I have been asked what I think he would have made of this turn of events, of the ghastly ring of modern-day grave robbers that was uncovered. Undoubtedly, he would have appreciated the Dickensian nature of the crime and the complicated cultural forces that allowed it to happen. He would probably have researched the scandal and done a talk on it. But he would have been horrified to think such a thing might happen to him. The subject of willed body donation was not foreign to our family, as my mother had long since made the decision to donate hers. Daddy did not like the idea and chose instead to be cremated.

The discovery of this travesty was understandably difficult as it temporarily unravelled the healing process of grief that comes, one hopes, after any death. Suddenly I was thrown back to that dark midnight in 2004, to a dead body and not to the life I fondly remembered. Time has dimmed the impact of the situation, though its resurfacing in the news has proved a jolting reminder again and again. Nothing has been more restorative, however, than the writing of this simple introduction and the chance to think about his life and not his death, to remember that he could whistle and hum two parts of a tune simultaneously; the sight of his making banana splits for his grandchildren – and eating two himself; his adoration of my mother; his asking me, at the age of eighty, why my dog wagged her tail when he walked into the room. To which I replied, 'Daddy, don't tell me that at the age of eighty you still don't know why dogs wag their tails!' He was either pulling my leg or had been honestly otherwise engaged for some time.

This book shows exactly how engaged he was with the major events in the United States in the latter part of the twentieth century. It is the witness of a great writer with a keen eye, extraordinary memory, seasoned perspective, and tender heart.

Susan Cooke Kittredge

Overleaf, Daddy in the study, clearly on top form, having just poured himself a little twilight wine of Scotland. His study was his haven, housing his treasures: books, antiques, drawings, statuaries, art and music.

1946–1959

MY FATHER'S AFFINITY for interviewing ordinary people on the street was fed by his assignment in 1942–43 to crisscross the United States to find out how the war was affecting its citizens. This journey, the record of which was later published as *The American Home Front* in the US and as *Alistair Cooke's American Journey* in the UK, connected him with shopkeepers, farmers, mechanics and waitresses, in a way that would never be broken. Those car and rail rides across the continent subtly and permanently shaped his particular kind of reporting. He would forever after be interested not in the flashy headline but in what generated it, how it came to be, and how some grand event played out in the kitchens and barnyards of America and in the consciences of its leaders.

I think that an especially formative experience for my father was his dogged reporting of the Alger Hiss trial between 1948 and 1950. In the book that followed, *A Generation on Trial*, one clearly sees his expertise as an objective reporter, his willingness to put aside any preconceived notion of whether Hiss was guilty of perjury or not, to become, in effect, a member of the jury, hearing first this side and then the other. This was a landmark in his reportorial style, his avid aversion to a rush to judgment, and he received both acclaim and attack for it.

What he sensed throughout the Hiss trial was a growing witch-hunt in the country. Clearly this was borne out during the McCarthy era as anticommunist fever swept the US and Klaus Fuchs was sentenced in England for selling nuclear intelligence to the Russians. Daddy's lifelong fear of nuclear war was entrenched in these years as was his scepticism of any stance overly dogmatic or strident.

On occasion he was criticized for not taking seriously enough the racial unrest in the 1950s and 60s. I think whatever reluctance he exhibited to joining in the righteous indignation of Northern liberals was born not of denial but of honest incomprehension. He had such a fundamental belief in the equality of all people that he could not fully comprehend racial prejudice. Perhaps it was his love of American jazz that made him feel bound in soul and rhythm to the spirit and heart of blacks in this country. His

A.C. always obsessed with the news from the printed dailies
and from the always informed man on the street.

Waiting for action outside the Plaza Hotel in Manhattan.

aversion to violence contributed to his dismay over the simmering unrest in the South. (As the pieces in this book are printed using terms that were specific to the period in history, we have retained them as written. Hence we have not changed the designation of 'negro' for the now more acceptable term black, or African American.)

His gift for getting beneath the surface of a story, for revealing its underpinnings and nuances, was both a blessing and a curse. It made him an excellent reporter, but it took its toll on his spirit; he felt genuine unease and apprehension about the state of the world a lot of the time. His saving grace was his ability to have a good time, to find relief in writing about light subjects and in playing with his friends and family.

S.C.K.

Coming Home

Letter No. 1, 24 March 1946

I want to tell you what it's like to come back to the United States after a sobering month or more in Britain, and what daily life here feels and looks like in comparison. I came back with a couple of thousand GI brides. The first shock came shortly after the liner thundered its great horn as we slipped away from the dock at Southampton. All the mothers clung to the rail, and all the babies clung to their mothers and watched England slide away. Along the entire main deck of the ship the handkerchiefs fluttered in an unbroken line, like washing day in Manchester or Leeds; and then a small Coast Guard cutter came scuttering alongside the liner like a playful puppy. An American soldier stood at the cutter's bow, cupped his hands, and yelled, 'You don't want to go back, do you?' And the young mothers and wives, weeping like mad, yelled, 'No.' The ship turned about, we headed into the Channel, night began to fall, and we moved below deck. And then came the first surprise. There was a meal, with meat and a vegetable that was not easy to recognize right away. It was not, you see, Brussels sprouts. It was lima beans and corn. I say *it*, because in combination they constitute a favourite American vegetable known as 'succotash', and the British brides had their first practical encounter with an American Indian word. Succotash means 'the grains are whole'. Well, the grains were whole, the corn was green, the butter was fresh and plentiful, and the oranges were to take away. This went on for five days, though few ironies of peace are so delicate as the sight of a GI bride on the very rolling waves refusing to touch butter, plum pudding, French beans or even a steak and kidney pie – for reasons too agonizing to go into. In other words, there were days on the ocean waves when many of them regarded the whole food problem as very academic.

The fifth day out we sighted land, way off on our left. Away ahead there, rising like a rim of mist was the almost dewy coast of New Jersey. On the right was the flat, twinkling line of the south shore of Long Island, and then for a half day, with the blue sky swooping all over us, we came slowly up New York Harbor. And then we saw the towering cluster of the downtown skyscrapers, crowned with a small cloud of smoke and mist. Somebody asked why this should be so, when all around was sparkling sun and blue sky, which recalled that New York is in one minor way a war casualty. Before the war there was a soft-coal law in New York City that forbid any office building or factory to burn soft coal – or let's just say smoky coal – for more than ten minutes a day. Before that, it was banned altogether. But in 1940, when war factories were cooking on sites in the boroughs of New York, the law was suspended, and it has not been put back yet.

Well, scores of little freighters and tugs would pipe out three toots as we went by, and each time the *Queen Mary* would terrify the children by roaring back three thunderous blasts. A specially chartered ferryboat tagged along by the *Mary*'s side, playing jazzed-up versions of 'Why Did I Kiss That Girl?' and 'Here Comes the Bride'. And the captains of tugboats would look up and wave at the brides, and soon we saw great signs painted on the ends of docks, and on the roofs of pier buildings that said 'Welcome Home' and 'Well Done'. A soldier friend of mine told me about the lump that came in his throat when he heard the bands and saw these signs. Full of pride and bounce, he came down the gangplank to meet New York and its grateful citizens, and then he started to look for a hotel room. Then just a room. He wound up begging a man who ran a Turkish bath to rig up a cot for him just for the night. That was the due of fame. That was his welcome home.

And that's a normal thing to happen to you these days. My own disillusionment started the moment I was off the ship. I made a telephone call and noticed how much more tinny and battered our telephones were than those in Britain, though I should add that the New York ones work like a charm: that is to say, like an American telephone. The taxi cab I rode in had one door tied on with string. The other door stayed in a droopy sort of balance, somewhere between the door frame and the running-board. That night I was in another cab. The driver couldn't use his first gear, which had given up shortly before VE Day, and he couldn't go in third, which had been out of condition since the Battle of the Bulge. He also couldn't go in reverse. If he went too far past the address you wanted, he had to go right round the block again to land just right. This is a useful money-making device that I offer without patent.

And I thought back to the London cabs, those solid almost luxurious blue boxes that turn in small alleys like trick bicycle riders do on one wheel. The next morning I went to my office. At intervals of possibly six or eight blocks, buildings that I knew quite well only six weeks before were now in powdered ruins, or in their place was an empty lot boarded up at the corner. It was very much like London, except that cranes and concrete mixers were busy in some of them, building the skeletons of new shops and office buildings that would be up by next autumn.

Outside the building that contains my office, along with those for about thirty-thousand others, was a long queue about eighty yards long, mostly of women, but there was a sprinkling of men reading newspapers and shifting wearily from foot to foot. It was a queue for nylon stockings. At several places the queue had to be broken and patrolled by policemen to allow workers to have a smooth right-of-way into the building. I have seen this queue, sometimes a hundred yards long, every day since, and

GI war brides arrive in New York on the S.S. Queen Mary in 1946. A.C. returned home on the same boat.

yesterday I saw two others in midtown New York. Now here is a situation that is quite typical of what happens when it is announced in this country that you'll soon be able to get all you want of something that you want very much. Before nylons could be legitimately released, they could be bought at exorbitant prices in the Black Market. Then the big stores sent letters to all their customers with charge accounts, and, in America, mostly good-class housewives have charge accounts at lots of stores, even ones they never use. This may be a convenience for when you're passing by sometime. These letters gave you a certificate, asking you to appear on a certain day to pick up a pair or two of nylons that they would save for you. When the day came, the ladies discovered that the stockings were not fully fashioned, and the American housewife in disgust would not claim her pair, deciding to wait a month or two till the genuine article was available. Now this time, there are in theory enough nylons to provide most women with a single pair, but at this point starts what might be called 'Operation Greed'. People get so afraid they'll miss their pair that they queue up for one pair and get their husbands to queue up for another. There are also standing in these queues very smooth-looking gentlemen and swarthy-looking youths in leather jackets, prob-ably with faked certificates, who have no personal use for nylons and no wife to be a hero for. They are doing the rounds of the queues and running their own modest Black Market on the side.

Now nylons are not a unique case by any means. Since I got back I have only once had butter offered me in a restaurant. The other times it has been marmalade or noth-ing at all. I was irritated to recall that in Britain, with your strict controls, there was not much butter, but at least everybody got his little share. Here again, a wholesaler in the Black Market hears that there's going to be a natural shortage of butter in the New York area, or the Chicago area, or wherever – not a serious shortage. New York for instance is still trying to catch up on supplies that didn't come in when there was a tugboat strike last month. And remember that New York, Manhattan, is an island, and most of its food must come in by ferry cross-river. Now, this is the insidious thing that happens. There is a natural brief shortage, maybe only for a day or two. The Black Market cannot depend these days on long shortages, so it has to make hay while the sun shines; so it corners the market and forces along the shortage and knows there are plenty of people who will pay a little extra to get some butter. Mind you, I think it's very important to point out that 90 percent of the people who deal with the Black Market, people like my friends, are unaware of that fact; they just notice when they get home that butter costs two cents more this week than last. The big hotels and fancy restaurants, many of them simply will not go for two days without butter. They are busy laying the foundations for their prosperous, peacetime patronage, so they lay in extra supplies. And in the end, in a week or two weeks, almost everybody is the loser. Two weeks ago a strike of dairy distributors was the last straw; last week you could roam the stores of Manhattan and not find any butter to buy. And now we've been told we shall soon be eating 'grey bread'. The fact that what you call black bread (what we call grey) is far more nutritious and also tastes better has not been well enough publicized – you know what I'm talking about, bread with more of the wheat kernel. But in this country, the mere fact that somebody puts his finger beside his nose and says, 'You're not going to have much more white bread,' doesn't cause, as you might expect, loud and prolonged cheering; for I should tell you that the ordinary store bread in America looks like dehydrated snow and tastes like blown-up blind paper. This announcement causes a panic among housewives, who fear they're going to go short of something vital, so they've been rushing around buying up stacks of white flour. This of course produces an even worse shortage of flour, and will lead to further reductions of grain to the farmer for his feed, and to the brewers for their beer.

The artificial panic is based on chronic fear, the constant absurdity in a land of plenty of fearing that you may go short and become like Europe. The result of this fear was that, during the war, Americans ate more meat than ever before in their history, all because they were chronically afraid that they might be forced to eat less. And now, because several hundred thousand housewives make a rush for the white flour they should have been glad to let go of, it's still the farmer who will have to make up for this sudden drain on the market, and add to this the fact that the new wheat extraction process leaves less what they call 'mule feed'. That's the residue from milling that farmers feed their cows and chickens. And this will mean in another month, or maybe less, fewer chickens, perhaps a big and unnecessary egg shortage, and a beer shortage, the likes of which the United States has not seen since Prohibition.

So, when you're inclined to grumble at your drastic ration controls, think on these things, as the prophet says, and consider how hectic and unpredictable it is to be a housewife in a country where the government does not buy food in the first place, and where controls start mainly with the rather bewildered retailer. I thought you'd like to know how it feels to get back to the Land of the Free and the Home of the Brave.

The GI Bill

Letter No. 30, 6 October 1946

You may have seen that a famous American university has recently been celebrating the two-hundredth anniversary of its founding. Princeton is in New Jersey, which is not one of the six New England states. But I say that because it is unique in being – as are many towns in New England and a few in Virginia – a lovely relic of Colonial America and a complete image of a way of life that declined at the turn of the century and died after a few decades of the nineteenth.

Princeton inevitably recalls New England, because it is a small country town where you can walk along many long streets whose houses are all variations on the exquisite Colonial style, graceful wooden monuments in white to the exciting period of American domestic architecture known here as the Greek Revival. In this place a great university was born, and here today in a small Colonial house lives the wise old man who on a fateful day sat down and wrote a letter to Franklin Roosevelt, assuring him that an atomic bomb was more than a possibility, and urging him to do something about it, because the word was confirmed that the Germans had already started. His name is Albert Einstein.

If we owe a dreadful debt to Einstein, there are many other men around to whom we owe something too; I mean men around Princeton. Some ex-servicemen especially may already have wondered who lives in those other beautiful and simple houses that Americans built at a time that was like ours in being full of national pride, but unlike ours in being proud and graceful at the same time. I'm afraid the answer to that question is: not ex-servicemen. If there are any, they are freaks.

If you were at Princeton during these anniversary celebrations, I don't think you could help noticing any vigorous and handsome young men around more anxious-looking than any Princeton students for a quarter century. To their wives they are unappreciated heroes, and to politicians they are the headache that begins at home: they are the Vets, the ex-GIs.

This fall there will be 2,080,000 young men and women applying to enroll in American universities and colleges. Just short of a million of them are ex-servicemen

A twenty-five-year-old war veteran pickets the
Philadelphia City Hall in search of a job.

and women. At most of the big universities, and especially at the Catholic universities, between three-quarters and four-fifths of all the freshmen will be ex-servicemen, veterans as we call them. Of the whole 970,000 veterans who applied for college, 480,000 of them will be turned away. Not much short of fifty percent of the veterans will not get in; for the simple reason there isn't room for them. 'Room' in a university of course means staff and equipment and classrooms and instruction. But to a veteran hoping to go to college, it merely turns the knife in the wound he got when he first came home. For 'room' also means a place to put your head, a place to make a home.

And of all the failures of the period we call by the grand name of 'post-war reconversion', the most miserable, and possibly the most ominous, is the failure to meet even the modest goals of the Federal Housing Administration that were set in the first year of peace. The National Housing Plan, made in Washington, figured it this way: to prevent an alarming drift into *slumdom*, between twelve and sixteen million new houses have to be built in the next ten years, which is twice as many houses every year as America has ever put up. Why twice as many? Well, we are beginning to reap the crummy harvest of our stupidity after the last war, when the price of a new home was also so inflated that many people, in buying a home they could barely afford, bought a home much smaller and jerry-built than they would have had in what we call normal times. These houses, millions of them that went up, were small, and fairly fragile, and cheap. When the boom came, many owners got out of them into something more pretentious. When the slump came, their rents went down like a lift. Poorer people took over. The houses went unpainted (I should point out that most houses in America, great and small, are wooden) and unmended. They were already slums.

Well, of the proposed twelve million new houses, the government reckoned to build 1.2 million by the end of 1946. To date 290,000 are finished – less than a quarter. The government also reckoned to put up 200,000 shelter homes, like the pathetic wartime makeshifts called Nissen huts in Britain, done over for uncomplaining civilians, we hope. Twenty-five thousand have been finished, or one-eighth.

We now face the appalling fact that of the eight million men demobilized since VJ Day, four million of them are having to live with relatives or friends. Do you wonder, then, that of the half-million who will get into college, many of them will work, are working, under conditions unlike those of any student's life that America has ever known? Many of them are married, and have children. And I'd better catch up quickly with that wrinkle in your brow and explain how they can think of going to college at all. The GI Bill of Rights is the answer; it was passed by Congress and signed by President Roosevelt in July 1944; it made some flat promises to veterans for their return to civilian life. It stipulated their unemployment allowance, pensions, their disability allowances and the like, their right to the job they left behind, and set up a scale of government loans to help them build houses, buy farms, or set themselves up in their old or new businesses.

But the best reward it offered for a fighting-man's life was the silver spoon – as it looked then – of a university education. The veteran was to have free tuition and fifty

A former Marine Lieutenant
and his wife and children
move in to one of the
first Quonset huts on
the Evanston campus of
Northwestern University.

dollars a month (the equal of twelve pounds ten) to live on. But this turned out to be merely the fruitiest of the Bill of Rights' promises that turned sour on its exposure to civilian life. There was an ambitious rush for enrollment. A pause to wink, in the mind's eye, at the high-paid job the sprightly college veteran would land at graduation. (Most of them, you might notice, spurned what are called liberal arts courses, and went after the background of a profitable technical or scientific or business career.) And then the freshman, alias veteran, turned up in the college town, alone or with a wife and child. He looked his fifty dollars a month in the face, and it laughed right back at him. If he could find an apartment or a house or a room and kitchenette, he would think of himself as blessed. But, alas, few towns anywhere make special rents for veterans. And his fifty dollars would be gone right away. The civilian society that he moved into – and there was the rub – didn't make way for him or do itself over; it was a civilian society, lush, heedless and slightly money-drunk – which was what he had to fit into. This society would expect him to live by its standards and its prices. He has watched in despair while prices rose, food vanished from the shelves, and the Office of Price Administration continued its brave but rather squinting prosecution of retailers – nothing radical like controlling distribution, just going after grocers and butchers – like giving an aspirin to keep down the fever of a man with tuberculosis.

So, today, a Pennsylvania college is housing some of its students in an orphanage.

At Kansas State College, twenty are in a gymnasium, sixty-four in a stadium, fifty in an old church, and seventy in an art museum. In Alabama, one hundred eighty-six men are in ninety tugboat cabins. At the University of Virginia, seven hundred of them are in a hospital. In Illinois, a skating rink. At Yale, a boathouse, and at Princeton, with its tradition of what the ads call 'gracious living', the Rhineland and Okinawa defenders of the faith will live in trailers, gymnasiums, garages, and stables. There is perhaps little solace for the self-righteousness of civilians in the fact that these men will take it better than most of us. For in spite of the grisly prospect we were warned against, of a returning army of cynics, emotional misfits and trained killers, the Veterans Administration has found from a national survey that eight out of ten of them have found jobs, that on the whole they work more sympathetically with their fellows than civilians, that their instability was a false alarm, and that as college students they get better marks. If, however, half of those with ambition can't get into college, and more than half of all veterans are living like paupers, it must mean that four million potentially better than average citizens are being tantalized into revolt.

For there's no denying the cynical appearance, in the cold light of peace, of the much-beloved GI Bill of Rights. I have mentioned the guarantee of a college education – if you can keep several bodies and bones together on the equivalent of three pounds a week, in this land of Black Market milk and inflated honey. The bill also guaranteed loans up to $2,000, at 4 percent interest, for a house or farm or business, and droves of veterans turned up at banks their first day out of uniform asking, 'Where's my two thousand?' Well, for the first two million veterans, there were just over ten thousand loans granted, practically all of them safe loans for homes. In some cities, as many as half the loans were refused, because, by the government's own guarantee, the veteran was a 'poor risk' in a time of inflation.

These four million men, who were led to expect too much, and wound up sharing a trailer with two other families or falling over disgruntled in-laws, are getting restless. In the last Great Depression there was a veterans' march on Washington, and the present General Douglas MacArthur found himself, as Chief of Staff, in the ugly predicament of having to order fire on men that he had once led. The new veterans, fit and skilled, and ambitious and desperate for privacy in this vast land, have a restless eye cocked on London and its squatters. In New York, the American Veterans Committee has warned that in a hard winter (and they can be hard indeed), veterans will not look kindly on the locked-up little beach houses and country estates of Long Island, or on the boarded-up mansions of Fifth Avenue. In the university towns these days, many a cloistered professor is embarrassed by the sound of a woman's voice floating quite legally into the midnight air from what was once a man's study, or embarrassed by baby clothes strung across a college lawn. Their embarrassment will be a high-pitched squeak in the roar of defiance that will go up in the cities of America this winter if the GI Bill of Rights is not improved, and if the GI's right to a room of his own is not honoured.

Harry S. Truman: A Study in Failure*

Guardian, 1 November 1948

There is often a heartless contradiction between American ideals and the general willingness to accept them in action. Mr Truman's biography is the stuff of which all Presidents are supposed to be made. It is made of the character and the career party campaign handbooks attribute to their chosen leader. It is on file in every Hollywood studio, heading the category of thoroughly reliable 'characters' whom not even the House Un-American Activities Committee would question. It is described in the schools as the very root and flower of what is best about the American way of life. Yet it appears uneasily in the White House and is remembered as the object of characteristic jokes. President Calvin Coolidge's memory is green in the popular recollection for his cracker-barrel cynicism and his opposition to sin. And now we are ready to recall 'to err is Truman' and 'Don't shoot the piano-player, he's doing his best.'

Yet the fame of the Truman Investigating Committee was justly earned: it wrote the most searching and sympathetic record of a war Administration's blunders and successes. Mr Truman's history in the Senate was that of an alert debater, a practical humanitarian, a courageous New Dealer from a state festering with political corruption that never tainted his personal history. Many a more pretentious statesman would have quietly forgotten his political machine connections when that machine was exposed and punished in the law courts. But to Harry Truman it was a simple courtesy to leave Washington and his new glory as Vice President and go home to Missouri to attend the funeral of the squalid Boss Tom Pendergast, who was let out of jail to die at home. Pendergast had picked Truman as his man for the Senate, and Mr Truman came from the sort of people who despise a man who forgets a favour. Truman had come up the 'folksy,' traditional way of the machine politician – a road overseer, farm-tax collector, a bridge-mender, a drainer of dirt roads after heavy rains, then a postmaster, a club organiser, then tedious nights learning enough law to justify his election as a county court judge. But he knows as well as most that it is also the hard way. At various times he had gone into debt and worked at all sorts of jobs because the convention of going bankrupt was odious to him. 'He ploughed the straightest line of corn in Jackson County,' his mother kept on telling reporters. To Harry Truman the moral implications of that compliment are as binding as the words of a Methodist hymnal. Being present at Pendergast's funeral was an obvious duty.

It is, I think, the acting out of such straightforward maxims in a great office that requires tact, timing, and a goodly gloss of two-facedness that has bewildered Mr Truman and made his administration in the end admittedly inept. When Secretary of the Navy Frank Knox made a pre-war speech in Boston and, with Roosevelt's private approval, came out for Atlantic convoys for British shipping, the grateful cries of Englishmen were as loud as the screams of protest over here. Questioned at a press conference, Mr Roosevelt said surely Mr Knox had a right to speak for himself. Truman would have told all, as he did over the misbegotten plan to woo Stalin with Chief Justice Fred Vinson. When he was a haberdasher he bought at boom prices and sold at depression prices. His shop failed, but he is not a despondent man, and one can admire the sigh and the plucky grin with which he has, throughout his life, tried to learn from his mistakes. Unfortunately it is too late to learn when you reach the White House, and Americans who admire the hard-luck story in their neighbour will not tolerate it when the that neighbour is raised to 'the elective kingship'.

The failure of President Truman cannot be called a failure of principle or even a betrayal of the programme he inherited. The things he has genuinely wanted to have done have been every bit as New Deal as Roosevelt. In one proposal, the uncompromising 'Fair Deal' for a federal fair employment code, he went headily beyond even

Like A.C. and other reporters the *Chicago Daily Tribune* jumped to an erroneous conclusion as early election returns came in.

Roosevelt's boldness. And of all campaigns his has made the most sense as merely the politics of survival. While his political rival Governor Thomas E. Dewey has promised in his presidential campaign 'a firm hand on the tiller' and 'a rudder to our ship'; Truman has been talking about the need for veterans' housing, about drastic enlargements of the Social Security and health insurance programmes, about federal ownership of transmission lines, about the Taft-Hartley (labour relations) Act, about inflation, about longer terms for the Atomic Energy Commission.

But there are over sixty million Americans at work. In this time of deceptive prosperity, Mr Truman's voice sounded somewhat hollow as he went on asking for the things that the country was ready to accept during a Depression. The recoil against Roosevelt's New Deal is too easily interpreted abroad as a positive reaction against liberal reform. There is enough evidence in the fight for Senate seats, and in the good showing of unrepentant New Dealers even in states where Dewey will be chosen over Truman, to show that if an impressive man is spouting the New Deal doctrine he will be heeded. But Mr Truman is by now worse than unimpressive. He has committed the unwritten, un-American crime of being outsmarted. When he took the oath of office he was helped along by the legendary assumption that, when all is said and done, homespun men are the shrewdest. His early press conferences gave pause to this comfortable notion. He made impulsive answers that had to be corrected later. The episode of Vice President Henry A. Wallace's dismissal as a candidate to retain his post, demanded by the secretary of state, was only the first of the rude disillusions.

It will not do to say that greatness is lacking. Very few Presidents have had any claim on it. But mediocre Presidents must depend on careful advice and preserve in public the appearance of authority. Mr Truman surrounded himself partly with sincere political hacks and made impressive military men substitute for the grand façade he lacked. This latter has been the most interesting and could be the most serious fault in his conception of the President's office. It has puzzled many who would expect so humble a man to be uncomfortable in the presence of so much big brass. It seems to be, however, a true character trait. As a small boy he was 'mercilessly ridiculed' in school for reading books from choice and, what is worse, taking piano lessons. He made up for the ridicule by boning up, in stealth, on military history. He amazed the town by applying for and winning a place at West Point. Then he was turned down on account of bad eyesight. It must have been a shocking blow. He has revealed throughout his administration a fearful respect for the judgment of military men. And, by the same mechanism of wistful envy, the Truman Doctrine was conceived the day he sat at Fulton, Missouri, in the immense shadow of Churchill.

This piece was published the day before the presidential election, in which Truman defeated Thomas E. Dewey by 303 electoral votes to 189.

Joe Louis: The Champion Retires

Letter No. 117, 20 March 1949

Joe Louis has just retired as the world's heavyweight champion. He is an unforgettable man whom we shall very likely never see again – shuffling with great grace up to some wheezing hulk of a man, to bait him with a long left and then to bring up the shattering awful thunderbolt of his right, and then to toddle considerately away and wait for the referee to call the roll on yet another ruined reputation.

But I doubt I should have thought to write about Joe Louis or ever been interested in him if I had not gone down to Baltimore in the spring of 1937. I was staying with a friend, a doctor at the Johns Hopkins Hospital, who had managed a half-day off from his grisly labours with stomach aches and corpses. We'd been out in the scarlet countryside. The short twilight fell. 'How about,' said my friend, 'we go down to Dark Town and catch some jazz?' There was a little vaudeville house deep in the coloured section of town where the best coloured bands play. It was the perfect end to a great day. So we packed ourselves in with about a thousand Negroes, who clapped and stomped in time and sweated like Christians at a Roman circus. It was possibly ninety degrees outside, and about 120 inside, but nobody cared. In the middle of the last number, though, something happened outside that rode above the rhythm of the band and the hallelujahs of the audience. From somewhere far off came a high wave of sound; the band played on. It came on nearer, a great sighing and cheering. Suddenly there was a sound of doors splintering and cops barking and women screaming and men going down grabbing their toes and snarling oaths. The band stopped and the lights went up. The black faces all around us bobbed and flashed. Women threw their heads back and howled great cries at the roof. Some people embraced each other, and others cut and swung at each other. This, it turns out, was the night that Joe Louis had won the heavyweight championship, and for one night in all the lurid dark towns of America, the black man was King.

The memory of this night has horrified and exhilarated me ever since. The phrase 'Arise, you have nothing to lose but your chains' must have a terrible appeal to the Negro; most Southerners know it, and it's why in some places they watch fearfully for every Negro flexing his muscles, and wonder if he's connected with the Communists. That immediate fear was not besetting America as it does today, but the lesson was

Joe Louis travelling with his equipment in 1946.

plain. One Negro had out-boxed all the living contenders no matter how white, and James Braddock was white, and he was a racial God.

It took several years and a run of inevitable victories and wide familiarity with Joe in the ring and in the newsreels for Americans to learn a strange respect for this quiet, beautiful, mannerly youth who never thought of himself as anybody's God, who never played his colour up or down, who never questioned a ruling, never flirted with the crowd, kept his mind on his work, stepped scrupulously away when an opponent stumbled, and who, when it was all over, said such embarrassing things over the radio microphones that the commentators would often whisk the mike away from him to the loser, who could be expected to say the proper sentimental clichés. They pushed the mike up to Joe in December 1947 when he'd been fought into a parody of his younger self by old Joe – Jersey Joe Walcott. A sharp little announcer said, 'Did he ever have you worried, Joe, at any time?' This is a question expecting the answer, 'Oh, no, I felt fine all the time.' Joe said, 'I was worried all the way through; yes sir, I ain't twenty-three any more.'

When you come to look at the life and career of Joe Louis, there is the special dilemma that he is a black man, and that even when you've done your best to judge him as you would other men, there's no way of denying that if he's not the best boxer that has ever lived, he is as near to it as we are ever likely to know.

He was born in 1914 on a sharecropper's cotton patch in Alabama, and was as poor as it's possible to be. It was a farm in theory – it had been rented to them as a cotton and vegetable farm, but the vegetables didn't feed the family, not by the time Joe, the seventh child, came along. His father broke down, as sharecroppers do, from the daily strain of working from dawn to sunset and often beyond, and not making enough in crops to feed his children, or to buy them all shoes. They had no money to send him to a hospital, so he went to a state institution and died there. A widower came to help out and soon married Joe's mother; his five children moved in with the eight of the Louises. Joe got a little more food and went to a one-room schoolhouse, and then the family moved to Detroit where the stepfather worked in a motor car factory. Joe went on to a trade school, and worked in the evenings delivering ice from an ice wagon. Then came the Depression, and the family went on relief. This, said Joe, made his mother feel bad. Years later he wrote out a check for the $269 that was the amount of the relief checks they'd had from the government. This, said Joe, made Mrs Brooks, as she now was, feel better. She seemed to have very definite ideas about debt.

When Joe was eighteen he came home late one night and found his stepfather blocking the door. 'Where have you been, Joe?' he asked. 'Over at the gym,' said Joe, 'working out.' 'I thought so,' said Mr Brooks, and lectured Joe about wasting his time with no-goods in gymnasiums. 'You go on fooling around with boxing, you're never going to amount to nothing.' Joe says this had him really worried. The next day he asked his mother about it. She said it was all right to be a boxer, if that's what you wanted to do, and that was, in a way, the end of Joe's wayward life. The rest was practice and learning, learning to be beaten to a pulp, and coming up again with a new trick or two.

Maybe you'll get from all this, the idea that Joe Louis is a simple soul with quiet manners, a good boy who never had a crafty thought. Of course he doesn't talk about his respect for his opponents, and his decency and casualness with the crowd, because these are fundamental, the characteristics that a man hardly knows about himself, or if he does, keeps quiet about them. But there is one remark he makes about his pride in money that should round out the picture. 'People ask me,' he says, ' 'Joe, what will you do when the big money from fighting stops coming in, won't you have to cut down on your way of living?' I tell 'em, I'm going to live good, retired or not retired. I've got investments and I've got ideas, I'll keep on living good; it's them who lived off me who won't be living so good.'

Well, there he is, the Brown Bomber no more; a memory of incredible speed, a slow shuffle, a solemn face, a gentleness, a shy acceptance of his greatness. All things considered, a credit to his race – so long as you add the necessary afterthought: the human race, that is.

A Lighter New Year's Eve, 1951

Letter No. 250, 4 January 1952

On New Year's Eve a year ago, we had a very quiet time in our house. I am sure it was due to a combination of various domestic things. But mainly, we didn't feel like going wild or staying up till all hours. 31 December 1950, was a very depressing time. We had only three friends in, and however much we chuckled and guffawed and beamed a toast at each other, we thought of the hopeless turn in Korea, the sudden and very real prospect, as it then seemed, of a war carried into the vast plains of China. Prime Minister Clement Attlee had come to Washington and gone again, and some of us wondered aloud if it were possible that a year from then we'd still be sitting in our warm house with our children and our friends. One of the closest of our friends, who lives a way up the Hudson Valley, confided to us without fuss but quite seriously that she had bought some camp beds or cots, and if the thing we all dreaded happened, we could get the family up there and stay with them for the duration.

As we were talking, and as the first bells of the New Year started to chime, and as a forlorn hooter sounded from some drunk down on the street below, another sound came up to us. It was a siren, over across the park, on the West Side, a moaning up and down. We all went to the window and threw it open and listened. Sirens had been prohibited months before then, and the police cars and fire trucks had taken to ringing inoffensive and very un-American little bells. Sirens were to be kept for the dreaded thing: an air raid. We laughed off this little siren, but only because nothing happened. And we figured that some jokers on the West Side had defied the ban and were announcing the New Year in their own grim little way. Then somebody said, 'What a terrific plot it would be if the Russians waited for midnight of New Year's Eve, and just when the hooters and the bells went off they sent over the first plane. Nobody would believe the sirens anyway.'

Well, it all seems a very long time ago, more than a year and several nightmares ago. Here we are, and we hear 1952 called again – as we've been calling it for three or four years – 'the year of decision', without feeling a slight chill of the flesh and a curdling of the blood.

Some of you may laugh and some of you may even sneer at this panic of a year ago. If we come through another year, or two or three, there seems a better than reasonable chance that another generation will live into a peace getting less uneasy every spring. A great many Europeans will then say, 'You see, there was nothing to fear after all.

Canadian officers read about the truce in Korea in
Stars and Stripes, August 1953.

You Americans are too jittery to live.' This kind of reasoning can never be answered, because no one ever knows for sure why the dreaded thing never happened. Americans were convinced, however, two years ago, that unless Europe re-armed with a will and all together, the invitation of an undefended Europe would be too much for the Russians to resist. This too cannot be proved. And which Americans, you may ask, felt like that? Such Americans as our panicky friend up the Hudson Valley? Well, yes, though I ought to add she is a very serene and rather serious woman. And two of the three New Year's Eve visitors who dashed to the window were Englishmen, and they felt the same way.

There was, however, one American who felt this way, and I think you will grant that his opinion is at the very least one to respect. He is General Dwight D. Eisenhower. Who shall say, now that we care to think the tide is turning, how much we owe to him, and the example of his leadership and his character. Certainly the very different feelings with which we let in the New Year this time are due in some part – in great part – to him.

Again a British prime minister is descending on Washington. But the whole mood and timing of the visit is very different from Mr Attlee's famous and grim little mission. It is the first understatement of the New Year to say that Americans are looking forward to Winston Churchill's visit. They are sitting back to enjoy it. They are waiting for the memorable cracks that are bound to come out of the Prime Minister's address to Congress. An old and very diehard and hard-headed Republican said to me the other night: 'You have to hand it to the old man, that line about "Nobody wanting to keep the British lion as a pet...." That line would have been worth a million votes to us if we'd thought of it first.'

The Churchill visit is the big political flutter in Washington, and naturally I am reporting to you for once from Washington. There are other things on American minds, pleasant things that flow, I think, from the change of heart, from the feeling that we are not just yet going to have to camp out in the storm cellars. For instance, the travel agencies report that this is the best year for winter vacations since the winter of 1945. Day after day the papers stream full-page advertisements for Caribbean cruises, holidays in the blinding sun of Arizona, on the beaches of Florida, or skiing in the crunching snows of New England and the Laurentians. A new twist has been given to this fond dream of every American who lives in the northern parts of the country, this wish to ditch the local freeze and local politics and send skittish postcards back from a beach in Florida. A New York resort hotel has fixed itself up so that you can ski and swim at the same time. All right, then, ski and swim the same day. I haven't been up there, it's only a hundred miles from New York, but like many another skeptic who's looked at the ads I've had a yen to try it. They show a couple of happy skiers, all togged up in ski pants and windbreakers, skis on their strapping shoulders, standing on one side of a vast pane of glass. Behind them ripples a hillside deep in snow and speckled with mad little skiers. On the other side of the glass is another couple, in bathing suits, and wearing dark glasses. They are dripping still because they have just emerged from a pool. They have towels over their arms and are stepping over the lazy brown thighs of other people lying down in the streaming sun. What sun? The sun coming through the palm trees, naturally. Which palm trees? The palm trees planted inside this great hothouse swimming pool, which is bathed in the ultraviolet light from great sun lamps sunk in the roof.

You can see that it's easy to light and heat an indoor swimming pool, even when it is surrounded and protected from the elements with walls of glass. But how about the snow outside? The snows don't come till the New Year in this part of New York State. How do they know people will have the snow to ski in? They know it because they provide the snow. When Nature fails, they switch on their snow-making machine and ice over a couple of hills as nonchalantly as you'd ice a couple of cakes – if you had the scarce sugar to make the icing.

This little bit of nonsense may be exercising poetic license in its advertisements, but it would be too risky to keep publishing this picture week after week. I think it's probably on the level, because while it is a universal thing to want to have the best of both worlds, it is a typical American thing to arrange it, preferably by electricity.

I am able to go off so jauntily on something as light as this because the general mood is far lighter than it has been for several New Years' now. I don't want you to think I'm being mystical in attributing this lift of the heart to one man. But I would be simply muffing my job as a reporter if I didn't tell you that 'the year of decision' has lost its original meaning of 'the year of the Russian decision' and has come to mean 'the year of Ike's decision.' Every day the tension tightens – you know that we can't get along without tension – and every week the question booms louder, in railway stations, cafeterias, homes and offices: is Ike going to run?

Part of the maddening but undeniable excitement of American politics, especially in a presidential election year, is that the excitement is deliberately contrived. The curiosity that frets us for a year before the election is quickly demolished by the simple rule in Britain that election campaigns will last no longer than three weeks. There is no limit here, and as long as two years before the event, prominent men who have idolatrous friends start going around trying to look like a dark horse. The typical trick of American electioneering is the management of timing: of knowing when to announce a candidacy and when to lie low. Europeans often notice that Americans are the slaves of fashion, in amusements, in books, ideas, clothes, foods, admirations, everything. Americans themselves don't say it, but they act on it. The election agents know in their bones that it isn't the virtue of their man that matters most. It is the ability to dangle that virtue just out of the voters' reach long enough to make the voters bay like famished wolves to have him. He may not be very juicy when they get him, but tell an American that this food he can taste but that he must lay off and he will organize a caucus or emergency squad to snaffle the forbidden fruit. Dwight David Eisenhower, the boy from the cow town of Abilene, Kansas, the toughest town of the not-so-Old West, quite simply looks like the original apple in the Garden of Eden. He will go on looking so as long as he goes about his great business and does not say he means to run. The day after he says he will run, then he becomes something people can take or leave alone. And inevitably, many Americans will start to look around for some other prohibited apple.

Until the General comes out and says 'yes' or 'no', it is going to be very hard not to talk about him, even in talks that are supposed to be nonpolitical. We all know about his directness, his tact, his great ability, his modesty, his roguish good looks, and the charm that people newly exposed to it all agree is 'incredible'. But less is known about the boy from Kansas who was born only fifteen years after Wild Bill Hickok stood in the main street of Abilene and tossed a hat into the air and perforated it with a perfect circle of bullets before it hit the ground. Mr Hickok did this to announce that he had come to Abilene as marshal to bring a little law and order into town. He had already killed forty-three men in this praiseworthy cause. And before he was himself shot in the back, he disposed of another fifty-seven in the civic interest.

It is surely a gorgeous joke we can all enjoy that the wise and ancient continent of Europe and the newer giant of America should be silencing their scholars and statesmen and nuclear physicists for the moment when 'Marshal' Eisenhower of Abilene, Kansas, shall toss his hat into the ring and riddle it with bullets, by way of announcing that having brought a little law and order into one continent, he means to run for marshal of the other.

A Year of No Lynchings

Guardian, 8 January 1953

This year has been a harrowing one in America in many ways, but in one respect it shook off at least an infamous if waning habit. It was the first year on record that there was no lynching in the United States. The good word was reported last night by the Tuskegee Institute, the Negro college established by the State of Alabama in 1881, which has kept records of all lynchings and race riots since the year after its founding.

In the intervening seventy years only the six states of New England have never lynched anybody. Thirty-seven states have at some time or another lynched a Negro. But in this century the annual incidence of lynching has declined steeply. In the last ten years of the nineteenth century the annual average was 154. From 1920 to 1930 it was thirty, and fifteen for the next ten years. In 1945, 1947, and 1951 there was only one American death by lynching.

The word, which has the strict meaning of illegal execution by a mob, has no proved origin. It has been variously derived from Lydford in England to the Lynches of South Carolina. The writer and lexicographer H. L. Mencken says that the likeliest claim is that of 'Captain Charles Lynch of Virginia, a primeval 100 percent American who devoted himself to harassing Loyalists before and during the Revolution.'

By any other name, the practice of lynching got off to a brisk start during the sittings of the popular tribunals that looked for and found disloyalty to the new Republic rampant throughout the victorious colonies. But lynching came to be thought of as a peculiar American institution during the period of westward expansion, when desperadoes of every sort preyed on the frail civil governments of the shifting Western frontier.

Yet it is not the righteous vigilantes of the West that come to mind when the word is mentioned: it is the Negro. And the record of lynchings since the late 1880s has been overwhelmingly the record of Negroes taken out of a local gaol and hanged or shot by a mob for proved or alleged rape or homicide. Three-quarters of the victims in the Tuskegee records have been Negroes. And since the numbers dwindled, more than 91 percent of them have been Negroes.

The Institute, however, tempers its pride in the new record by warning about 'other patterns of violence' that are replacing lynch law. The most marked since the last war is the practice of bombing private homes, especially 'where members of the race have

Members of the National Association of Colored Women picket
the White House in protest of lynching, 1946.

moved into what were considered white neighbourhoods.' Occasionally, the report
says, the victims are 'Negro leaders who were thought to be too active in improving
the status of their people.'

From the ghastly race riot in Detroit in 1943 to the bombing of a Negro's home in
Florida last year, it is plain that the most inflammable places are urban areas where Negroes have spilled over districts traditionally inhabited by poor whites. The poorer the
white the tighter is the social tension when Negroes rent houses nearby. The day after
the Detroit riot nine years ago I remember one shabby, raddled white man confessing
in a corner saloon: 'I may be low and poor but I ain't as low as a nigger – not yet.'

It is a text for sociologists and housing experts. And little good will be done unless
they discover some methods of easing the housing conditions of poor whites whose
only hold on dignity is their pale face.

President Eisenhower

Guardian, 20 January 1953

At thirty-five minutes after noon today in Washington, with grey winter skies rolling away before a warm winter sun, General of the Army Dwight D. Eisenhower was inaugurated as thirty-fourth President of the United States. He stood high on a rostrum before an encircling crowd on Capitol Hill, where the inauguration has always taken place since the burning of the Capitol by the British in 1812, which forced the ceremony out of doors. He stepped up with a solemn face to Chief Justice Fred Vinson, raised his right hand, kept his left hand on an open bible, and repeated the oath: 'I do solemnly swear that I, Dwight David Eisenhower, will faithfully execute the office of the President of the United States and will to the best of my ability preserve, protect, and defend the Constitution of the United States, so help me God.'

We have come a long way in public courtesy and public pomp since the first inauguration in Washington, 152 years ago, when John Adams refused to accompany his successor to the Capitol and left Jefferson to ride up the hill alone, tie his horse to a fence, walk through the mud, go indoors, take the oath and ride home again. This morning the General drove first to the White House escorted by Senator Styles Bridges and Mr Joseph Martin, the majority leaders of the Senate and the House, was received there by President Truman, bowed into the Presidential car, and the two of them relaxed in the back seat and smiled and quipped together with all memory of 'the master race' and the 'bumbling, stumbling' exchanges of the campaign forgotten.

But whereas Jefferson had the consolations of his privacy, President Eisenhower and Mr Truman, journeying to the hill after the invention of the cathode tube, could not hide a whisper or a grimace from the forty million families sitting as close as an oculist all the way from snowbound farms in Vermont to the beach-houses of Southern California.

Before the drive began General Eisenhower looked ruddy but glum and a little restless. Mr Truman grinned and chuckled and flashed his glasses. A shockingly uninformed stranger could have thought at first that the General was the defeated champ and that this was the inauguration of Harry Truman.

At eleven-fifty the cavalcade had swung up the noble avenue of Constitution Hill and arrived at the East Portico of the Capitol, where the inauguration has been per

Dwight D. Eisenhower takes the oath of office from Chief Justice
Fred Moore Vincent. Far left is Harry Truman outgoing President
and far right Richard Nixon, incoming Vice President.

formed since 1829. Behind the stand, the old and new dignitaries assembled and came
down two by two to take their places, the Diplomatic Corps conforming to a man with
the General's preference for a black Homburg – British ambassador Sir Roger Makins
at the end, as the junior member.

Then the new Cabinet; Mr John Foster Dulles, a quaintly old-fashioned figure in a
big wing collar, and a grinning Charles Wilson, the only man not yet confirmed by a
senatorial committee. After them the nine Justices of the Supreme Court in their bil-
lowing gowns, and then the dispossessed – the Truman Cabinet, led by an immaculate
and stoic Dean Acheson. The Secret Service detail closed in on the procession, ushered
the last stragglers to their seats, and the crowds coughed and settled down through a
crisp selection by the United States Marine Corps Band.

The Most Rev. Patrick O'Boyle, the Roman Catholic Archbishop of Washington,
invoked a blessing on the 'august office' of the Presidency, indicated 'the path of rec-
titude' for 'the framers of our laws,' and hoped that 'justice may be made manifest
in our judiciary'. Then a small coloured lady, the celebrated soprano Miss Dorothy
Maynor, sang the almost unsingable national anthem. Mr Richard Nixon moved forward to receive the oath as Vice President, which he did with an intense solemnity.

followed by a solo by a tenor from the Metropolitan Opera, a prayer by Rabbi Hillel Silver of Cleveland, and another bright burst by the Marine Band.

It was time now for the translation of the General into a President. All through these preceding ceremonies he had stood immediately behind the parsons and the singers, his generous mouth immobile, his eyes down, visibly protecting his deepest feelings against the appalling challenge of this modern office to a candid man's humility.

When the oath was taken, he gave his first smile, shook hands with the Chief Justice, crossed over to embrace his wife, shook hands with Vice President Nixon, moved to the microphone and raised his arms high in his giant variation of the V for Victory sign. There was a quick round of applause and then he began, asking first for 'the privilege' of a personal prayer. He flexed his shoulders and started on an inaugural speech as sombre as any since Franklin Roosevelt's first.

Only three times did applause break in, not because the huge audience was laggard but because it was intent. The first time was at the pledge to abhor appeasement, not to trade 'honour for security'. The last time was at the assertion that the United States looks on 'all continents and peoples with equal regard and honour'. The President stepped back at the end, an Episcopal bishop said the benediction, and the Marine Band piped and wheezed again at the national anthem.

The President turned to his right, quickly shook the hand of the beaming Truman and the ageing ex-President Herbert Hoover. Then everything relaxed. The President brought Mrs Eisenhower, blooming with orchids, to the microphone. The band struck up the President's private march, 'Hail to the Chief'. The clouds were skulking off to the horizon and the sun blazing. It was a mild Washington winter day, or a balmy summer's day at Old Trafford. The cathedral clock struck one. On to lunch, with tramping elephants and swishing soldiers and twinkling girls and lumbering floats. Tonight, at ten, there is not one inaugural ball but two, for one armoury could never contain the dancing legions of the Republicans incarnate.

Cancer and Smoking

Guardian, 20 February 1954

For thirty years or more, the scandal sheets have printed articles on 'The Tobacco Habit' as a mild variation on their standard high-voltage treatment of such shockers as prostitution, political graft, and the traffic in dope. Most of these pieces, furtively hinting at heart trouble and even tuberculosis, were about as medically convincing as the 'Methodist' credo that smoking stunts the growth. The tobacco companies paid only sidelong heed to them, with bold hints that, on the contrary, a cigarette was a relaxant, a soothing syrup, and a social grace. The manufacturers were not much better than the Puritans in their respect for the known scientific facts about tobacco, and have tended to meet every impromptu accusation with an equally flip defence. In the social history of our time, it may well be that the *Reader's Digest* will come to claim a decisive part in dating the fashion of cigarette smoking.

Although three separate reports were published here in 1949 suggesting a plausible relationship between smoking and cancer of the lung, they were folded away inside the pages of medical journals. But a year later the *Digest* ran an article with the resounding title, 'Cancer by the Carton'. This started a lot of talk in America and a noticeable adjustment of cigarette advertising to remind the customer that the tobacco companies keep a twenty-four-hour laboratory watch on every chemical intruder that might possibly sully his breath, tickle his throat, or otherwise impair his health and comfort. A few of the tobacco companies had in truth been financing quiet research, but it was concerned with heavier matters than a sore throat or an acrid taste. And, since Americans went on buying cigarettes by leaping billions, the manufacturers maintained their code of contemptuous silence, which is almost as rigid as the taboo at a Victorian dinner table on the mention of the female leg. Two years later the *British Medical Journal* published a weightier study, and it began to look as if the cigarette manufacturers would never be shut of the nuisance.

Last November their long golden age – twenty years of continuously soaring sales – exploded in a bombshell prepared by Dr Ernest Wynder of New York and Dr Evarts Graham of St Louis. They reported that they had produced skin cancer in

Movie stars often advertised cigarettes to help promote their latest movies, as Ronald Reagan is here in 1952.

I'M SENDING CHESTERFIELDS to all my friends. That's the merriest Christmas any smoker can have — Chesterfield mildness plus no unpleasant after-taste

Ronald Reagan

see RONALD REAGAN starring in "HONG KONG" a Pine-Thomas Paramount Production Color by Technicolor

CHESTERFIELD *Buy the beautiful "Christmas-card" carton*

44 percent of the mice they had painted with tobacco tar condensed from cigarette smoke. This study was hardly as comprehensive as the British study of nearly fifteen hundred human lung-cancer patients, but it was piquant. It sprouted the joke: 'It only goes to show, mice shouldn't smoke.' But the newspapers sat up and took notice in their heartless, disinterested way when the Institute of Industrial Medicine of this city, an incomparable branch of the New York-Bellevue Medical Center, examined all the tumours reported in the Wynder-Graham study and declared them to be malignant.

Last 9 December the papers carried the report of two speeches made by Dr Wynder and Dr Alton Ochsner, Chief of Surgery at Tulane University School of Medicine, before a meeting of New York dentists. Dr Wynder quoted thirteen American and foreign studies, to conclude that 'the prolonged and heavy use of cigarettes increases up to twenty times the risk of developing cancer of the lung.' Dr Ochsner was bolder still. He foresaw that the male population of the United States might be decimated within fifty years by this type of cancer if cigarette smoking increases at its present rate. Within an hour of the opening of the Stock Exchange that day, big blocks of tobacco stocks were up for sale. One stock, which opened at 65 ¾, dropped to 62. Others lost between two and three points. By the first of this year, the horrid truth was out that the sale of cigarettes in the first ten months of 1953 was off 2.1 percent. It seems a negligible fraction in the face of the triumphant record that in the past twenty years cigarette sales have gone up from 100,000 millions to over 400,000 millions. But nothing gets to feel so normal as unrelieved luxury, and a desperate tobacco executive reflected that if every American smoker used 'one cigarette less a day, our sales would drop by 5 percent', which is to say three million packs a day, or an annual loss of $255.5 millions.

The makers of filter-tip cigarettes made a virtue of adversity and came out celebrating the providential insight that had led them to manufacture a cigarette that 'filtered out' all those menacing and, by implication, cancerous tars and fumes. Filtered cigarettes sold as many in 1953 as they had sold in the preceding seven years. The dignified silence of the tobacco companies was broken. At last some of them reluctantly confessed that for several years they had been subsidising cancer research. Their advertising took on an almost testy tone of reassurance, but it was a reassurance about their concern for the health of the smoker, an apparent psychological blunder in that it insisted on the very context of disease from which they were consciously praying to be set free. The advertisers defend this reflection on interesting grounds. They say that their studies over many decades have shown a deep-seated public guilt about smoking, which has nothing to do with medical findings and everything to do with an old Puritan tradition, and which can best be allayed by a bedside manner, carefully sustained through what is already known to the trade as 'anxiety advertising.'

The way to restore the tobacco companies' phlegm and their prestige might be obvious to an Englishman: to combine in a huge donation for cancer research. It is not as easy in this country as in Britain. Whenever two manufacturers of the same product think to strengthen their case by joining forces, the shadow of the Sherman Antitrust Law falls across their best intentions. The tobacco companies are still wincing from the bruises of a famous antitrust suit of 1941, in which they were punished for an alleged conspiracy. However, they have appealed for help to the middlemen – the tobacco distributors – who have taken the risk of forming a Tobacco Industry Research Committee to finance an independent study of lung cancer.

Meanwhile the medical profession is going ahead on its own. The Institute of Industrial Medicine means to break down tobacco tars into their component parts and hopes to discover which fraction caused the skin cancer in mice. This ambition is evidently so beset with chemical and biological problems that it has taken almost a year to build and set up the necessary equipment.

Standing apart from all the interested parties who would seek to prejudice the truth by arraying the doctors against the manufacturers, there is one odd and important figure, a man possessed of a Voltairean disdain. He is Dr Cuyler Hammond, the American Cancer Society's chief medical statistician. He has deep doubts about all the studies reported so far. He suspects that the interviewers of lung-cancer patients probably induce an emotional bias in their victims, who will thereby be led to make suspicious confessionals of heavy smoking. He says that it is extremely difficult to find a control group with the matched characteristics of age, social standing, occupational habits, and regional location of any given sick group. He warns against the false premise that might be exposed to prove only that smokers produce earlier symptoms rather than more cancer. He suggests that even if there were no significant association between smoking and cancer in the general population, a telling one might be found in the hospital population. He is even sour about the claims of the filter-tipped cigarettes, remarking in his wry way that the carbon in tobacco smoke probably neutralises some toxic agents, and that if the filter removes those carbon particles, 'filter cigarettes would do more harm than good'.

Dr Hammond is an ominous figure in this whole controversy because he happens to be conducting, on behalf of the American Cancer Society, the most exhaustive study yet attempted. He began in January 1952, composing a staff of interviewers who will study the life histories of 204,000 healthy white men between the ages of fifty and sixty-nine, who together form a statistical sample of the American white male population. Their smoking habits in particular are being punched up on the bewildering file cards of the International Business Machines company. Whenever a man dies, his clinical history is recorded and any cancer history traced and studied. The study will not end until the whole two hundred thousand are dead, but Dr Hammond says he will have the first significant findings ready by the end of 1955. One leading cigarette company has already said that it will accept the results as unquestioned. What Sir Walter Raleigh began, Dr Cuyler Hammond may either end or set free for a new lease of life.

Revulsion Against McCarthy

Guardian, 12 June 1954

Senator Joseph McCarthy was all over the front pages again this morning, but the instinct that put him there was for once not his. It looked as if, finally, an impulse of moral revulsion had galvanised the country and braced the backbone of an incongruous variety of his victims. The Department of the Army, a middle-aged coloured woman, the spectators at a session of the Senate's permanent sub-committee on investigations, two Democratic Senators, and a suddenly blithe host of columnists and radio critics were moved to furious protest at the Senator's tactics and his stature.

The Army published a long report that documented in shocking detail the threats of the young Mr Roy Cohn, McCarthy's chief counsel, to 'wreck the Army' and break Secretary Robert Stevens if David Schine, a McCarthy investigator, was not given consistently preferential treatment after he had been drafted into the Army as a private.

The report told how Senator McCarthy had directly approached the Army's chief legal counsel to seek a commission for Private Schine; how the Army found him unqualified to receive one; how Senator McCarthy and Mr Cohn then demanded that Schine be assigned to New York in order to study 'evidence of pro-Communist leanings in West Point text-books', and how this request was also refused; how, when the Army told Mr Cohn that after Private Schine had finished his basic training the chances were nine to one that he would be sent overseas, which provoked in Mr Cohn the threat to wreck the Army and make sure that Mr Stevens would be 'through' as Secretary of the Army.

The Army insisted at one point that a policy of special treatment for any Army private was not in the national interest; whereupon Mr Cohn, who is all of twenty-seven, told the Army he would give it 'a little national interest' by showing it up in public 'in its worst light'.

The report listed the many occasions on which Private Schine was given special passes to come to New York, supposedly on the sub-committee's business. Last December the commanding general of his camp complained to the Army's legal counsel that Private Schine was 'becoming increasingly difficult because the soldier was leaving the spot nearly every night', and usually returning 'very late at night'. The day after this warning Senator McCarthy told the Army that he was no longer

Televised McCarthy–Army hearings held on 22nd April 1954
were essential viewing.

interested in having special treatment for Private Schine. But apparently Mr Cohn was furious and told the Army's counsel that he would show him 'what it meant to go over his head'. Six weeks later the battle to have Private Schine assigned to New York was still going on and Senator McCarthy warned the Army's counsel of the consequences of thwarting young Mr Cohn.

Two weeks later Senator McCarthy told an assistant to telephone the Army's counsel that he was very angry about the honourable discharge granted to a New York dentist who had claimed his privilege not to answer questions about past associations. Ten days after that, General Zwicker, the commanding officer of the dentist's former Army camp, was called to testify before the McCarthy sub-committee. And that, as all the world now knows, was the guerrilla episode that led to the famous 'memorandum of understanding', or as some say the terms of surrender, between the Army of the United States and Senator McCarthy.

Inevitably there was standing room only in Washington yesterday when the sub-committee called Mrs Annie Lee Moss, a middle-aged coloured woman, who was suspended by the Army Signal Corps after Senator McCarthy had described her as a 'code clerk' whose 'Communist record' was known to the Army. Mrs Moss was a cafeteria worker who quietly told the sub-committee yesterday that she had never been in a code room in her life. Mr Cohn tried to establish her personal connection with a staff member of the *Daily Worker*, but it turned out that the man she knew was a coloured man who happened to have the same name.

The audience was uncommonly ready with applause for Democratic committee members and Mrs Moss's lawyer whenever they protested at the tactics of Mr Cohn. At one point Senator Stuart Symington, Democrat of Missouri, asked if she knew who Karl Marx was. 'Who's that?' she gravely asked, and the crowd laughed itself silly. When she finished her testimony and stepped down from the stand Senator Symington leaned into his microphone and angrily cried: 'I may be sticking my neck out, but I think you are telling the truth. And if you're not taken back in your Army job, you come around and see me. I am going to see that you get a job.'

Senator McCarthy was mercifully absent from these rebellious proceedings because he was busy composing a broadcast reply to Adlai Stevenson's condemnation of him at Miami last Saturday, to the first outright attack made on him by a Republican Senator, Ralph Flanders of Vermont, and to a trenchant analysis of his methods televised to a national audience last Tuesday night by the celebrated American commentator Edward R. Murrow, and sponsored by the Aluminum Company of America.

Senator Flanders on Tuesday vindicated the honour of the Republican party on the floor of the Senate by suddenly putting the rhetorical question: 'What party does he belong to? One must conclude that his is a one-man party, and that its name is McCarthyism, a title which he has proudly accepted.' Senator Flanders then launched into the first open attack on McCarthy by a Republican in this session of Congress. He said that McCarthy was diverting the attention of the nation away from 'dangerous problems' abroad and that he was 'doing his best ... by intention or through ignorance to shatter the Republican party.' Next day President Eisenhower sent a letter of commendation to Senator Flanders and told his news conference that the Senator had done the country 'a service' by calling attention to 'the danger of us engaging in internecine warfare and magnifying certain items of procedure and right and personal aggrandizement.'

But it may be that the spark that has set off this fiery and so righteous explosion of popular indignation was laid, with deliberate courage, by Mr Murrow. He came to great fame in America during the war through his broadcasts from London. He is a tireless news reporter and, in his weekly television dramatisation of the news, a consummate showman. Last Tuesday night Mr Murrow gave over his whole half-hour to a pictorial analysis of 'McCarthyism' by projecting visual excerpts from the Senator's speeches and sessions of his sub-committee. It was McCarthy exposed by McCarthy, and Mr Murrow added only the sparest narrative comment. But at the end, after the huge audience for this programme had seen McCarthy merciless, McCarthy jocular, McCarthy cunning, McCarthy sentimental, Mr Murrow looked his audience in the eye and ended with these words:

'This is no time for men who oppose Senator McCarthy's methods to keep silent. Or for those who approve. We can deny our heritage and our history but we cannot escape responsibility for the result. There is no way for a citizen of the Republic to

The formidable Ed Murrow, host of *See It Now*.

abdicate his responsibilities. As a nation we have come into our full inheritance at an early age. We proclaim ourselves – as indeed we are – the defenders of the free world, or what's left of it. We cannot defend freedom abroad by deserting it at home.

'The actions of the junior Senator from Wisconsin have caused alarm and dismay among our allies abroad and given comfort to our enemies. And whose fault is that? Not really his. He didn't create the situation of fear, merely exploited it, and skillfully. Cassius was right: "The fault, dear Brutus, is not in our stars, but in ourselves."'

These words were spoken with the blessing of the Aluminum Company of America, which has obviously a lot to lose by taking this stand. The response, however, of televiewers across the country has been a stunning endorsement of Mr Murrow. So far the comments, by telephone, telegram and letter, are running about fifteen to one in his favour. Hence the surprising rally of candour in public men who have stayed astutely silent for three years. Hence President Eisenhower's relieved approval of Senator Flanders. Hence a morning chorus of suddenly uninhibited newspaper columnists praising Murrow for 'laying it on the line'. Hence the confident laughter of the big audience at yesterday's sub-committee hearing. Hence the delayed righteousness of Senator Symington, of Missouri. Mr Murrow may yet make bravery fashionable.

Bikini Island Detonation

Letter No. 358, 1 April 1954

With the promise of spring and the first warm wind from the West there came also, this last week, the shattering explosion from Bikini. It would be false and mischievous to say that the American people have responded in gloom or panic. I can't tell you what the American people feel, because I don't know how anybody, short of the Almighty, can be in touch with the feeling of a whole nation. But I ought to say that in my own observation frivolous people are still frivolous, optimistic people remain optimistic, and serious people are shaken. I think the situation is very much the way it was the morning after the first atomic bomb was dropped on Japan. It was surely not heartlessness that made people grateful for a sign that the end of the war was in sight rather than to be depressed by the horrible thought of the first atomic victims. It was much too early then to take in the human and political consequences of this first triumph of nuclear fission. People wanted to know how it worked, as they did after the first steam engine took to the tracks, or Lindbergh's airplane had crossed the Atlantic. And the papers were there to help them. Those were the days, you may recall, when for a month or two almost every paper and magazine that you picked up had little geometric diagrams of arrows shooting at what looked like Ping-Pong balls, and when the great cliché of our time was invented: the mushroom-shaped cloud. At the moment people are a little too dazed to attempt the feat of imagination required to picture an explosion seven hundred times as powerful as the one that devastated Hiroshima. It is breaking no confidences to say that the scientists and military men who were at Bikini on the first of March were themselves surprised to see and feel a detonation that was two or three times more powerful than anything they had expected.

The Atomic Energy Commission, which usually after these tests puts out a frank and concise report of what happened, was remarkably cryptic. It merely acknowledged, in an almost casual way, that some sort of weapon or device had been tested in its proving grounds in the South Pacific. It's clear enough now, I think, that all the people engaged in the test were sworn after it happened to even deeper secrecy and that nothing would have been published for a long time, until the President had been able to brief his advisers and probably have confidential contacts with the British Government. For it must have been clear, in the early days of last month, that we – meaning the human race – had come to a crisis in the history of war and peace. This conclusion is now available to all of us because of the bizarre accident – and apparently it was a really unhappy freak – that suddenly deposited a cloud of radioactive ash on the boat of those Japanese fishermen. I hope it doesn't sound too cruel to say that their misfortune brought out into the open a new and tremendous problem in human history. When I said that serious people were shaken by the new H-bomb, I didn't mean merely that they are aware, for the first time since we made an atom bomb, that perhaps we shall have to scrap all our accumulated skill in warfare and our entire understanding of what can constitute any sort of world society that can survive.

This is obviously a turning point in history that cannot be shrugged off or pacified with appeals to decent feeling. And it might seem at the moment that nothing is more useless than off-hand optimism. But I know people who are, to say the least, wise in the knowledge of atomic energy, who have had a good deal to do with its technical development and political management of it since the war, who are inclined to think that the Bikini H-bomb could be one of the best things that ever happened to us. They argue from such simple analogy that, say, for instance, there was no way to stop reckless motorists from injuring one another inside big cities until there were enough cars on the streets to force the invention of traffic lights. This simple invention managed to discipline the hopeless variety of human character in the stated cause of convenience but actually in the service of safety. Look around you next time your bus

The mushroom cloud from a 23 kiloton atomic bomb detonated
ninety feet underwater along the Bikini Atoll.

stops at a traffic light and look at the faces of the people driving trucks and cars who automatically consent to wait for twenty or thirty seconds. You see scatterbrained people, genial people, mean people, impatient and aggressive people. But after a quarter of a century, they all accept the dictates of a green light turning to red. And when that engineer in New Haven, Connecticut, first took his invention to the Patent Office shortly after the First World War, he was told by the best engineers and lawyers that although it was mechanically ingenious, it overlooked the incurable tendency of human beings to push weaker people to the wall. He was told it wouldn't work, and the poor man was forced, in the next five years, to become a crusader. He didn't die until 1939, by which time he was living high up on Riverside Drive in New York and had the satisfaction of looking down on swift streams of traffic running north and south on two sweeping levels of the riverbank. If he had ever cared to stop a few motorists and ask then if they thought traffic signals should be abolished, they obviously would have thought the man mad.

Well, I'm sure to some people this will all sound very trivial and foolish. But some of the most profound physical laws of our universe were discovered by equally humble moments of insight – the law of gravity, for instance, to say nothing of the first groping after atomic energy itself. Could it not be that we might all become compelled to obey a moral law by the discovery of a home-truth? What keeps showy and sadistic people from rushing through traffic lights is not the prospect of damaging somebody else's car or body, but the thought of damaging their own. And it may be that Bikini has proved beyond a doubt that the time interval between the extermination of the country attacked and the country attacking could be about two hours. We have had from the Kremlin, for the first time, an admission by a Soviet Premier that a third World War would be the end of everything. We don't have to take this as an agreeable and spontaneous change of heart in the power that has threatened and harassed the Western world for the last seven years at least. The Bikini bomb may have proved to the most ruthless governments that the new law of peace is safety first. In fact, the only profoundly gloomy note I have heard from a responsible man was the remark of a former atom scientist that 'the most depressing news of the century would be the discovery of a reliable defense against the H-bomb.'

The Untravelled Road: Montgomery, Alabama

Guardian, 7 June 1956

Twenty years ago the interest of anyone coming from England in the Southern 'back country' was with the music, the vernacular, and the general pathos of the Negro. On any blinding summer afternoon he could come on a fat coloured wench pausing from the chore of cotton-picking to throw her head high at the sun and whine 'Go down, Ol' Hannah, don't you rise no mo'. In the scruffy parts of towns he would sit deeply satisfied in dark corners of saloons while bent-over pianists beat out the immortal twelve-bars of the blues. If he was lucky, he could go down to Storyville, in New Orleans, at sundown, and hear half-naked slatterns reduce their lot to poetry by crooning, from behind the swinging door of their cribs: 'I ain't good lookin' and ma hair ain't curled, but my mother taught me somepin gonna carry me through this world.'

His interest was rarely political in those days, for the New Deal had conveniently shouldered the burden of the poor. There was the Civilian Conservation Corps for shiftless boys, the Works Progress Administration for idle hands of any colour, the Government's promise of the 'more abundant life' for all who were heavy-laden. When the poor had cried, Roosevelt had wept. It was a very satisfactory state of things for those who, having an English background, were artistic connoisseurs of someone else's tragedy. The New Deal was, if we had had the gumption to see it, a menace to this attractive view of the lowly. On his next visit to New Orleans he was apt to find the whores' cribs destroyed, the last transoms of the old sporting houses all pulled down, Basin Street itself turned into a housing project.

Today his motives would be quite different for seeking out Montgomery's darktown. Twenty years ago he accepted the 'white' and 'colored' signs everywhere as a natural distinction that even Roosevelt would not change. Today he would be here to see how it was with an embattled city whose whites, mobilised in a Citizen's Council 15,000 strong, were sworn to resist the Supreme Court's order to abolish these distinctions, to send children of any colour to school together, to allow a Negro to sit where he will on a bus or a train. The Negroes of Montgomery were now in the fifth month of their boycott of the city's buses. Useless for the bus company to heed a Circuit Court ruling in South Carolina and order its drivers to seat all passengers as equals. The city commission forbade the change, and the Negroes were enjoying their martyrdom too

much to accept a victory by compromise. Some of them walked to work, as to the Crusades. Most were picked up by car pools. When they were downhearted the militant faithful swarmed, so I heard, to the Mount Zion African Methodist Episcopal Church on Holt Street, to be fortified by the words of thirty-five coloured pastors, most of all by their leader, the Rev. Martin Luther King, Jr.

So I pushed open the doors of the railway station ('White Waiting Room') and hailed a cab and gave the address: '657 South Holt.' The driver dropped me off two blocks away ('Just so you won't be too conspicuous'), and when I turned into this frowzy street I heard the blues again. They were coming in spurts from the jukeboxes of small saloons and lunch counters. Then one of the screen-doors would slam back on its springs again and muffle the licentiousness within.

Even at the church the rhythm of it hung on the air, softened and slowed by religious ardour no doubt, yet the same minor chords and the same heaving melancholy. It came from five or six hundred people, blacker than the night around them, sitting forward with their hands bunched on their knees. They made little movement and were the best-dressed Methodist audience it has ever been my lot to see. But they were joined in God by memories of long ago, when they wore no clothes at all. Far off, under a brown-painted Gothic window, a sister was 'testifying', standing and improvising a prayer in many a King James sentence changed through the uvula in strangulated quarter tones. She went on as long as the spirit moved her, and then a man near me got up and cried, 'Oh, Lord, oh Lord, stay close at hand when my time is come.' Between each solo phrase and incantation the congregation surged in with a mass humming, of the four classic chords of the blues, the Devil's music.

This went on for over an hour before 'Old-Time Religion' was sung as a battle cry and there was a rustle of people at a side door, and the leaders came out. The Rev. Sims, the Rev. Hays, the Rev. Powell. The Rev. Sims appealed for steadiness 'in travelling this untravelled road.' To put it bluntly, they needed more drivers. The Rev. Powell counselled patience, for 'you can't hurry God.' There was many an obedient 'Yeah' at this, but when they were told that station-wagons had been bought from out of town and would soon be coming in they let out a salvo of applause, and when the Rev. King came forward it was like the Relief of Mafeking.

The leaders, he said with solemnity, had written a constitution for the cause, and he would now submit it to them. He took it in his hand and read it aloud. So far, the only English we had heard had come from the source and textbook of all their peace on earth: from the Bible itself, doubtless the only book that many of them had ever read. Now we were to hear from the Rev. King, an educated man.

This great movement had started, he said, 'without the external and internal attachments in terms of organisational structure.' They listened in awe. If they or their children came to be 'integrated' they too could get to write like this. The Rev. King was indeed a master of Pentagon, or Federal, prose, and the constitution was written

Martin Luther King, Jr. here speaks as Pastor of the Dexter Avenue
Baptist Church in Montgomery, Alabama, 20th March 1956.

almost wholly in it. It was 'implemented' with eight committees, staffed by the leaders, and was heady with executive boards, trustees, public relations committees, provisions for tenure of office, just like General Motors. Its first article was a declaration 'to ensure respect for the dignity of the individual with respect to transportation.' This document was heard in a marvelling silence. And when he had finished the Rev. King hardly paused for a 'moved' and a 'seconded' to declare the constitution received, approved, and adopted.

Though there had been some violence after the first of these rallies, and a couple of coloured homes burned, the whites now accept them like revival meetings. Before the first one, in December, Mr Bagley, the bus company's manager, was warned to dissuade his son, a war veteran, from opening up a gas station on the edge of darktown. Mr Bagley, on the contrary, cornered a coloured friend and suggested that the Rev. King might announce the new ownership in the middle of the rally. So he did, and the Negroes rolled off in droves afterward to christen the new pump. Eighty percent of young Bagley's business today is from coloured folk filling up their tanks to maintain the boycott of his father's buses. Such is the temper of the 'fight' between the resigned whites and the sassy Negroes of Montgomery, Alabama.

With a final prayer and a rolling hymn, this meeting broke up in ecstasy and good order. I was off down the street as the congregation rose, and a saloon door swung open and let out two Negroes. 'You goin' back home now, boy?' 'Why, sure,' shouted the other, walking fast, 'my old lady weighs two hunnerd and eighty pounds. Man, that's an awful lot of woman.' He cackled insanely, and the bad people went on dancing the blues inside the seedy saloons. And the good people came down the church steps and went home to bed, to strengthen themselves against an early rising, the smooth running of the car pools, the determination never to faint or yield in upholding the Rev. King, staying off the buses, and so giving glory to God.

Humphrey Bogart: 1900-1957

Guardian, 16 January 1957

Thirty years ago, toward the end of the first act of one of those footling country house comedies that passed in the 1920s for social satire, a juvenile in an ascot and a blue blazer loped through the French windows and tossed off the immortal invitation: 'Tennis anyone?' Possibly he did not coin the phrase, but he glorified the type, if wooden young men with brown eyes and no discoverable occupation can ever be said to go to glory, on stage or off.

This young man, whose performance the critic Alexander Woolcott said 'could be mercifully described as inadequate', yet seemed to be cast by fortune for the role of a Riviera fixture. He was the son of a prominent New York doctor. His mother was a portrait painter of socialite children. He himself dawdled awhile at one of the better private schools and was intended for Yale. Intended, but never ready.

Twenty years later he coined another phrase with which the small fry of the English-speaking world brought neighbourhood sneaks to heel: 'Drop the gun, Louie.' Could both these characters be Humphrey Bogart, the cryptic Hemingway tough, the man in the trench coat who singed the bad and beautiful with the smoke he exhaled from his nostrils? They could. Could any actor, no matter how lucky in his parts, how wild the gamut of his ambitions, swing so successfully between the poles of make-believe represented by 'Tennis, anyone?' and 'Drop the gun, Louie'? He could and did. He was always content to nestle in the camouflage of any fictional type, provided studios paid him and left him to himself, a very complex man, gentle at bottom and afraid to seem so.

It is fair to guess that far back in the era of dramatist Frederick Lonsdale, he was always his own man. He no doubt stood in the wings in his blazer chuckling acidly over the asininities onstage, just as he lately complained that he could not walk the streets of New York without having truck drivers and corner brats spring their forefingers and give him the 'Ah-ah-ah-ah-ah-ah' Tommy gun treatment. On Fifth Avenue two years ago, a wholesome young cop testing shop doors at two in the morning moved up on him from behind. 'Everything all right, Mr Bogart?' Everything was fine, and Bogie sighed after him: 'It does no good. I haven't played a gangster or a dick in nine years.'

The USA vs. the State of Arkansas

Guardian, 5 September 1957

The nine young Negroes of Little Rock, Arkansas, who tried yesterday to obey the orders of a federal court by attending a white high school picked for them by their own school board, were politely turned away by state militiamen carrying rifles, under the command of a full major-general. Today the National Association for the Advancement of Colored People advised them not to go back for awhile; and none of them turned up today to enjoy their right, under the Constitution, of being jeered and spat at by an early crowd of five hundred white cretins.

Overnight, the Governor of the state, the intrepid Orval Faubus, assured himself the safety of his rest by ringing his mansion with another detachment of militiamen. Nobody at all, according to the exasperated mayor of Little Rock, was endangering the life of the Governor, or even posing a threat to law and order sufficient to justify calling out the state guard in a situation that, he avowed around midnight, 'grows more explosive by the hour'. He had heard, correctly, earlier in the day that the federal judge who ordered the schools of Little Rock to 'integrate' white and coloured children had appealed to Attorney General Herbert Brownell for help, and that the prompt response was to send FBI agents to investigate the morning's uproar outside the school and to determine who was threatening whom. The governor suspected that the FBI men might decide that in calling out the militia to resist a federal court order the Governor might be guilty of contempt, a crime that provides, in the civil rights bill the President will sign today or tomorrow, for federal punishment through the new Civil Rights Division of the Department of Justice. The Governor was even alerted to the rumor that the FBI men were on their way to lasso and transport him to the nearest jail. Yet other fears besieged him. He confided to the President, in a midnight telegram that was at once given to the news services, that he had reason to believe the telephone lines to the governor's mansion were being tapped by the FBI men; a great waste of diligence, since wiretapped evidence is inadmissible in the federal courts.

However, a Southern governor instructed against his deepest instincts to betray the Southern way of life cannot be too careful. Last night, Governor Faubus called for the protection of his palace guard, and another detachment of the state militia, equipped with rifles, guns, and Jeeps, ringed the executive mansion to protect his uneasy rest.

African American students attending Little Rock Central High are escorted to a waiting army station wagon for their return home after classes.

The motion before the court is a teasing one. Indeed it has not before come up in this acute form during the three and a half years since the United States Supreme Court threw down its ultimatum to the South and provoked the Civil Rights War. The question is this: when is a sovereign state a sovereign state in a federal system, and on whose troops may it call to defend itself against the federal government?

In the foregoing paragraphs, the words 'militiamen' and 'state guard' may look, at first glance, like colourful euphemisms for the United States Army. They are, however, precisely used, and signify a body of troops the like of which is on reserve in all the forty-eight states, whose first allegiance is to their commander-in-chief, the governor. The situation grows murky, but necessarily so, when it is explained that the state guard of Arkansas is recruited from the National Guard, the state's reserve of volunteers on whom the federal government has first call. After a Pearl Harbor, the United States may mobilize the National Guard in all the states, and the men of Arkansas who so gallantly defended three hundred white citizens against the immobile force of nine Negroes would in a national crisis put on their federal caps. To protect law and order within their own state borders, they hurry, at the governor's discretion, to put on their state caps. They were acting, Governor Faubus contends, as the state guard, the duly constituted relics of the old colonial Minutemen, whose first duty was the defence of their homes and sacred honour against marauders from other states or fifth columnists.

But the Department of Justice may dispute the status of the Arkansas state guard. Its equipment is supplied by the federal government (to the tune, in the last fiscal year, of five and a half million dollars; a sum innocently contributed by taxpayers, in Massachusetts, California, and New York among other places, who hardly expected it would be used by Arkansas to defy the federal government). A Democratic Senator Richard Neuberger of Oregon has not hesitated to judge the Governor of Arkansas as a man using federal money and arms to equip his own state in a pitched battle against the federal courts. Senator Neuberger shot off a telegram to the Defense Department and publicly wondered 'if it is advisable from the standpoint of public policy, or within the law, for such contributions to continue if the Arkansas National Guard is to be an instrument used for avoidance of complying with an order of the federal district court.'

The Governor is within his rights, however, in saying that it's for him to define the nature of a threat to the peace. He admits that he instructed the troops to forbid the coloured children to go to the school the federal government had ordered them to attend. He is, no question, wholeheartedly against integration. But his legal stand is taken on his judgment that an attempt to enforce the federal order, on the first or second day of the school year, would have caused rioting and bloodshed. So, he says, he summoned the National Guard, or the state guard, whichever way you care to label it, to 'keep order'. That is his privilege under the law and the Constitution, which precisely says that the authority of the United States may move into a state to secure it 'against domestic violence' only when the state legislature asks for it, or if the lawmakers are in recess, when the governor himself appeals for it.

What has happened in Little Rock is that the governor has called on his own state guard to fulfill their legal function in a threat to law and order that is provoked by command of the federal government. If the federal government ordered the firstborn of Arkansas to be drowned in the Mississippi, the Governor would no doubt call on his state troops and their national equipment to resist the ruling. Who would then be the outlaw? The Founding Fathers in their wisdom actually anticipated such a Herodian aberration and supported the sovereign right of self-defence of any state so cruelly instructed. Unhappily, they did not foresee the day when the authority of the United States would be vested in nine coloured children on their way to school, and the resistance to it would come from the standing army of the state.

Castro in Control of Cuba

Guardian, 3 January 1959

All of Cuba today was under the precarious control of Fidel Castro, the thirty-one-year-old rebel whom the Batista Government pictured to its graceless end as a ragamuffin hiding in the scrub hills of Oriente Province.

Castro today chose his birthplace, Santiago de Cuba, as provisional capital until such time as he could safely install in the Presidential Palace at Havana the man he has proclaimed provisional President. He is Manuel Urrutia Lleo, a fifty-eight-year-old judge unknown to fame until, after thirty-one years on the bench, he faced last year 150 youths charged with inciting to revolt. He set them free on the brave principle that the Batista Government had left Cubans no other means to defend their constitutional rights.

He became a revolutionary hero and today he has his reward. His first act was to declare a general strike so as to curb the rioting and to demonstrate, through the patrols of the revolutionary militia, that Castro is indeed the Government in fact.

The Batista Government and most of its lackeys are already in the United States, or in one of several Caribbean havens. A plane load of ninety-two of them landed at New York's Idlewild airport last night, and a Cuban merchant ship sailed for the Dominican Republic, where Fulgencio Batista is safe in the embrace of his former ward and enemy, the dictator Rafael Trujillo.

The last act of Batista's abortive junta was to tell the government troops to lay down their arms. They appear to have done so, but Castro broadcast today an order to his forces everywhere to go armed and fire on sight at all looters, agitators, and pockets of resistance. Most Cubans, and certainly the onlooking dictators of Nicaragua, Paraguay, Haiti, and the Dominican Republic, find it hard to believe that Batista's domain could be conquered by an angry though wealthy young man whose first putsch against the island on 1 December 1956, left him with only twelve of the original force of ninety-three men.

Castro may doubt it too, but he is taking no chances. The mob, which yesterday tooted and rejoiced through the streets, betrayed him in an outbreak of pillage and rioting. This morning the streets of Havana were reported to be empty, except for the Castro patrols cruising in the cars that were chasing them only two days ago. But by

Fidel Castro acknowledges the cheering crowd upon his arrival in Havana after dictator Fulgencio Batista fled the island.

midday a radio dispatch said that the city was taking on again 'a dangerously lively air'. Units of rebel militia were ordered to the Manzana de Gomez block of buildings, where groups of followers of Senator Rolando Masferrer, a leading Batista supporter, were hiding. Fighting went on for two hours, watched by crowds of spectators.

Today in Ciudad Trujillo, Batista admitted the absurdity of his rout by an amateur, but said that the first men sent to wipe out the rebels were 'soldiers of the rural guard who were not prepared for guerrilla warfare. When the rebels extended their operations and met the army in open battle they were well armed and their weapons were superior to ours.' The last excuse is doubted by Latin American experts and businessmen who say that up to the end Batista was receiving planes and arms from Big Powers. What doomed him, they agree, was the treachery of his own leaders, widespread desertions in the Army, and the final dash for safety of men bound to him only by bribery.

Late this afternoon one of Castro's lieutenants took over the Havana remnants of this faithless army and passed the cue to Castro to begin his triumphal entry into the capital city. If he subdues it without much bloodshed he must quickly repair the heavy damage to the railroads, highways, and sugar farms in three provinces, set the economy flowing again, and keep the people quiet until he can arrange free elections. Then he must answer the question that confronts all resting heroes who have raised their flags in the capital and put the tyrants to flight: how free dare the elections be? Castro has advertised an elaborate and drastic Socialist programme. He proposes to nationalise all utilities; to give their working land to tenant farmers, who make up 85 percent of the farming population; to distribute to the employees of every business in Cuba 30 percent of the profits; to confiscate all the property of 'corrupt' (i.e. former) government officials; to modernise the island's industries and begin a huge rural housing and electrification project. In a country where Army officers on the winning side instantly inherit palaces, where there is little experience of parliamentary government, and where the idea of a loyal opposition is tantamount to treason, Castro may, like others before him, come to demand a rubber stamp and permit only token opposition.

At the moment, though, all is joy and glory. The liberals among the South Americans in the United Nations are toasting the great day and calculating the present arithmetic of tyranny in Latin America. The present score seems to be, as one man put it, 'four down and four to go.'

expects to lose another small fortune on the thriftless project of manufacturing about 400,000 forty-nine-star flags that will be obsolete by 1960.

He is possibly the second unhappiest man in the United States. The first is undoubtedly Representative W. R. Poage of Texas, who carried the ball for the South and for sanity till the last moment of defeat. It was bad enough for a Texan to suffer the admission of Alaska, a state more than twice the size of Texas. But now appeared an applicant with a higher per capita annual income than the oil barons can boast: moreover a state whose main industries, sugar cane and pineapples, are said by no less a segregationist than Senator James Eastland of Mississippi to be caught in 'the stranglehold' of the Communists, or at least of Harry Bridges' International Longshoremen's Union. It was hardly mentioned in the Congressional debate that the Hawaiians long ago solved their problem by the nightmare expedient used to frighten children in the South: by carefree intermarriage, so that today the islands flaunt a vigorously polyglot people whose strains include 37 percent Japanese, 17 percent Filipino, 24 percent Caucasian, 7 percent Chinese, and only 3 percent of the original pure Hawaiians. This frightful statistic was always in the front of the Southerners' minds and explains the fifteen opposing senators, and two-thirds of the eighty-nine 'nays' in the House.

The South indeed, is the political loser in more things than ideology or racial cant. Its grip on the Senate is increasingly flaccid. In the 'great days', which are almost any days before the Supreme Court's 1954 ruling, the twenty-two Southerners in ninety-six could always promise support for the conservatives in many fields in exchange for a vote against civil liberties. Next year there will be twenty-two Southerners in a hundred. Some of their own have broken with them for good on the crucial question. Men from the Southwest rally guiltily round Senator Lyndon Baines Johnson of Texas and, since the political fulcrum is moving to the West, hope to be mistaken for Westerners rather than Southerners. And now both the Alaskan senators, and probably the Hawaiians, will be Democrats actively allied with the Northern Liberals.

As the latest and last territory eligible for statehood, Hawaii has put the seal on its political and economic maturity in a way that Alaska could not claim. Hawaii already bears the costs of its public schools, has an excellent system of courts that needs only to change its inscriptions and its notepaper to become a state judicial system. Its annual income exceeds that of twenty-six states, and its per capita income is only two dollars less than the national average. Its shipping is thoroughly unionized (by the aforesaid International Longshoremen's Union) and its minimum wage is a dollar an hour. Today it was not bothering to advertise these healthy qualifications. The sirens, the bells, the Klaxons, and the hula dancers were letting off the headier steam of pride in their first-class citizenship, in the real power they can wield in Congress, in the luck of history that has made them, two thousand miles out in the Pacific, the first all-American ambassadors to suspicious Asians of the same breed and bone structure.

A Catholic As Presidential Candidate?

Guardian, 10 December 1959

After a rather harrowing autumn, spent wondering if our entertainment heroes are bribed, our cranberries are poisoned, and our meat weighed down by the butcher's thumb, we in the United States have now turned to comparatively academic subjects, like birth control for the Africans and Asians, or what will life be like in AD 2000 when there will be just enough room on the globe for one human being per square yard. The official United Nations calculation says per square *metre*, and this may be pure propaganda on the part of the UN to make Britain change, before it is too late, to the metric system, or forego those extra ten or eleven square inches of living space.

Birth control for Asia is about the unlikeliest slogan you can imagine for an American presidential election, but that is the way it came at us this week, producing a peremptory quarrel between the World Council of Protestant Churches and the Catholic bishops of America, causing the President to say as quickly as he could at his press conference that he could not imagine a subject less proper for political discussion, and putting Senator John F. Kennedy of Massachusetts on the firing line.

I can hear some people say: 'I haven't the foggiest idea what you're talking about, and will you start all over again and take it gently?' I will. May I say, too, that I am not going to upset anyone, I hope, by going into a debate about birth control. Not because, at this late date, we need to be squeamish about who believes in it and who does not, but because I should be a poor reporter if I got off on that tack. For the United States has not been debating birth control either, or even the wisdom of countries like India having increasingly more mouths than it is possible for them to feed with even a starvation diet. What Americans have been arguing about is Senator Kennedy, who is the first serious Roman Catholic candidate for the Presidency since 1928, when Al Smith, the Governor of New York, was actually nominated by the Democrats, was subjected to dreadful humiliations and hysterical abuse from the old Ku Klux Klan especially, and lost, disastrously, in the election that put Herbert Hoover in the White House. Ever since Senator Kennedy appeared on Stevenson presidential platforms, and on some of his own, in 1952, he impressed the country markedly, if not strongly, with the image of a coltish, fair-haired, all-American boy, modest in manner, conspicuously bright and well-informed, with the still visible halo of a heroic war record. He came close to panicking the 1956 Democratic Convention, for he almost snatched the vice presidency away from Estes Kefauver.

I should explain, in a hurried footnote, that Estes Kefauver is not the vice president of the United States, but, in the roar and tramp of a convention, everyone who is nominated is hailed and introduced as 'the next President', or 'the next Vice President', or whatever is the office. Kefauver got the nomination by a hair, and Kennedy, being then thirty-nine years of age, lived to fight another day, not this time for the vice presidency but for the supreme office itself. In the last three years Kennedy has become a considerable, if still boyish, figure in Washington: the most alert of prosecutors on the Senate committee that looked into the sins of the Teamsters and other Labour Unions, and yet the man who has remained Labour's idol, if it has such, in Washington. Last autumn he was returned to the Senate from Massachusetts with the hugest majority ever given a senator in that state, and his stock went as high as it is likely to go before the Democratic Convention next year – his stock, that is, with the pros. For nothing is more impressive to the politicians who have to choose the candidate than a smashing victory in an off-year election: that is to say, in an election year when there is no presidential contest.

For the last year Senator Kennedy has been pulling steadily ahead of all the newcomers in the Democratic Party; and though he has not actually come out and declared himself as a presidential candidate, that, in this country, is a pure courtesy that waits for the arrival of a man's fans in New Hampshire to put his name on the ballot there. New Hampshire, a small New England State, carries no weight and few votes in the election itself, but it has the distinction of staging the first primary election, at the beginning of March, when both parties put on the ballot the men they would like to have for President. Thus it is possible that there will be two or three Democrats running against each other in New Hampshire, and perhaps a couple of Republicans. New Hampshire's primary has been called a popularity vote or beauty contest, and its only power, like that of some other primaries in Wisconsin and Ohio, is the dreaded power, in politics, of killing off an ambitious man.

We won't get our blood pressure up too high just yet about the Ides of March, when the New Hampshire primary takes place. Certainly, however, we know that Senator Kennedy is going to have his name on the ballot there, and probably, also, in Wisconsin, Ohio, and Oregon. He is running as fast as any man ever has: as fast as Thomas Edmund Dewey did before he too was willing to pause around the bend and admit that he was in the race.

According to the polls, Kennedy has pulled ahead of Adlai Stevenson as the most popular choice for the Democratic nomination. And here again I must pause, because explaining American politics is often a sequence of bloodcurdling statements, followed at once by rather niggling apologies. Adlai Stevenson is not in the race. Positively, Mr Stevenson says, he is not going to run for President. He does not want it, and if any-

The Presidential candidate John F. Kennedy relaxes in his Boston apartment.

body puts his name on the Oregon ballot he is going to file the proper legal form to have it taken off again. Oregon is the only State where a man may be put on the ballot against his will. Stevenson has done this once before, and though I am sure that his motives are of an impeccable purity, the effect on the people who are for him, on the voter, is to deny him his favourite bride. The result of this is to make people go mad. There is nothing an American wants quite as much as something he is told he cannot have. So what happens is that the frustrated Stevenson fans ignore the regular ballot, I mean the actual printed form, and write in the name of their man. Stevenson got a tremendous write-in vote in one famous primary last time, and though he says that having lost twice he would not think of embarrassing the party again, there are still millions of Americans on their knees chanting: 'Say it ain't so, Adlai!'

I hope the relative positions of Kennedy and Stevenson are now clear. Kennedy is forty-two, the biggest vote-getter in his party, and he is absolutely running for President; and he is catching up with Adlai Stevenson, who is fifty-nine, the most disastrous Democratic loser in two generations, and not running at all. In other words, it must now be childishly plain that Stevenson, standing still, is just ahead of Kennedy, who is running like mad.

I still have not got around to birth control, and you must not put this down to coyness or any other embarrassment. The moment you begin to talk about any issue that touches on next year's presidential election, in no time at all Stevenson's name pops up, and we begin to talk about him as the man whose opinion and public appeal will have to be reckoned with, if not consulted. It is Stevenson's peculiar and to some people infuriating strength that the more thoroughly he takes himself out of the race and retreats into darkest obscurity, the more he looms up on the distant horizon as a blinding light. Stevenson had nothing at all to do with the birth control row, but I don't seem to be able to get away from it. Down, Adlai, down.

To begin at the beginning of this tantalizing theme we should have to go back to last winter and the report of a United Nations commission. It was a commission on population. It issued a report on the coming population explosion on our globe, introducing some pretty scary stuff: for instance, that the population of the United States would double in the next forty years, whereas it took us before that a hundred years, and before that two hundred years, to do the same thing. Oddly enough, nobody seems to be getting excited about birth control for the Americans. Maybe we are waiting for some disinterested African or Indian to put that one up.

The report gave us the basic figures on which we now gloomily calculate our hemmed-in future. In particular the report said that one of the most striking and ominous signs of our time was the dramatic decline in the death rates of Asia and Africa, while their birth rate stayed as high as ever. The consequence was, the report said, that unless something was done, these people would breed more and more people who would have to live on less and less food.

The World Council of Protestant Churches pondered this report and thought that maybe something should be done now about recommending birth control to countries that could use it. Ten days ago the Catholic bishops of America came out with a counterblast, saying that they were against birth control here, there, or anywhere, and that the only decent cure for groaning populations who were also starving was to increase the world's supply of food. The Episcopal bishops of America snapped back. And then a week ago Senator Kennedy's telephone rang one Friday evening, and on the other end was the familiar voice of Mr James Reston, the chief Washington correspondent of the *New York Times*, who (and not for the first time) brought a great but vague issue into sharp focus and discovered that in this country a political doctrine has its greatest pull in the force of a political personality. He asked Senator Kennedy how he felt about the Catholic bishops' statement. The Senator said that since this country had never laid down a birth control policy for the United States or Western Europe, it would be a psychological mistake for us to suggest that the black, brown, and yellow countries should begin to limit their populations. He also said if he were President and the government did lay down a policy of spreading birth control information as part of our foreign aid, he would have to use his best judgment at the time. Pressed still further, he said that if Congress passed such a law, then he would uphold it as the law of the land.

It is hard to think of a more astute or statesmanlike attitude for any man to take, but Senator Kennedy is a Roman Catholic, and what Mr Reston was asking him in effect was: Would there ever come a time, come a point, when his loyalty to the Church might clash with his presidential oath of loyalty to the Constitution?

If this seems a little unreal, even spiteful, across the Atlantic, let me say that Mr Reston's question touches the nerve of one of the great realities of American politics and history. The people who crossed the Atlantic to escape religious persecution set up here a government that contains a famous prohibition. The government says in the Constitution, the Congress shall make no law respecting an establishment of religion. Americans are told from the earliest days of their Constitution to never forget that Church and State must be forever separate. The fear that dogs the candidacy of Senator Kennedy is a fear that he, as a devout Catholic, might one day forget this unforgettable law.

1960–1969

THE 1960S WERE the crunch years, I think, for my father. His pieces for the *Guardian* seemed to me, and I think to him as well, unrelenting. During this especially eventful decade, the daily article often expanded to three or more. His weekly radio broadcast also carried the deadline gavel, but it was the dessert of his professional offering and he had a very big sweet tooth. Though in those days he generally didn't plan what he would talk about until he actually sat down at the typewriter, he relished the freedom and license that the *Letter from America* provided. Sometimes this was getting away from the politics he had been masticating all week, and sometimes it was the simple pleasure of savoring the more subtle nuances of a particular event or individual.

His pedal was to the metal at this time, his professional life still accelerating, his energy full, and his commitment to both the *Guardian* and BBC entrenched. It is worth repeating that he was not much of a celebrity during this particular decade in America, since *Omnibus* was over and *Masterpiece Theatre* was yet to begin. During this time he was 100 percent reporter, and there was much to report. Not a great fan of President Kennedy, he was, nevertheless, intrigued by America's fascination with the Camelot White House. Though he questioned on several occasions Kennedy's leadership, he appreciated the sophistication and cultural awakening he, and especially Mrs Kennedy, brought to Washington. He took to Lyndon Johnson, however, pretty much immediately. Whether this came, following Kennedy's assassination, from the kind of relief a drowning person feels on being thrown a lifeline or from a genuine appreciation of his apparent country-boy directness, he saw him from the first through rose-coloured glasses and remained loyal to him during his increasingly troubled presidency.

The social and political unrest of the 1960s was at first somewhat of a nagging irritant to my father. He was initially dismissive of the generation of young people who took to the streets in protest against the establishment's politics or social norms. At best he considered them naive and disrespectful, and at worst rude and dangerous. He disapproved of the methods, though clearly not the goals, of many of the leaders of the Civil Rights movement, Malcolm X and the Rev. Adam Clayton Powell in particular. He held decency in high regard and was impatient and dismayed by the hippie movement and what he considered its flagrant disregard for manners and authority.

With Robert Kennedy, Attorney General, speaking at a lunch
meeting of members of Congress in New York, February 1968.

The trouble was that I was part of the generation he was inclined to dismiss. In 1965 I went away to school in Vermont and was thus distanced from inner city protests, the Civil Rights and growing Anti-war movements that were championed by people my age and just slightly older. Not a political activist, I didn't take a bus to Selma to work in the South or endeavour in any way to cross the line of acceptable discourse. I have wondered why this was, why, given the fact that I attended a very liberal school, I wasn't the adamant activist many of my friends were. Only in retrospect, and somewhat sheepishly, do I see that having my father's view so articulately and constantly expressed influenced my thinking and behaviour. I was torn between an impassioned, radical, and, I suspected, just stance and an erudite, reasoned, and persuasive argument that I questioned. In the end it simply was more important to me at that time not to rock the boat at home.

Perhaps as protection against what threatened to divide us, Daddy and I made more of an effort to tread neutral ground together. We began our tradition of regularly sharing jokes and watching late-night thrillers on television. Whenever an event not linked to politics captured the news, we delighted in consuming its every detail. The exploration of space enthralled us both. When John Glenn became a friend of my father's through their work as editors of *The World Book Encyclopedia*, he relished sharing the titbits Glenn had imparted. Daddy was fascinated by science and technology, and both the space programme and medicine would prove lifelong interests, providing relief from constant political reporting.

S.C.K.

Mr Kennedy Takes Over

Guardian, 26 January 1961

Snow swirling from high winds and twelve degrees of frost, the worst inaugural weath-er in fifty-two years, did not ruffle the smooth succession of John Fitzgerald Kennedy to the Presidency today or prevent the American people thousands of miles from Wash-ington, millions of them in snowbound homes in the East, from seeing a Presidential Inauguration more intimately than all the dignitaries present.

Most of the Washington press corps were also either compelled by the overnight storm or persuaded by their memories of television's earlier conquests to stay in their homes and share the privilege of the ordinary American householder to switch a knob and hop around as a fly on the wall of history.

From the moment in mid-morning when we saw some of the rumply thirty-five White House staff members, who had been marooned in the White House overnight, join President Eisenhower at a coffee break in the Navy Mess, the cameras of three net-works kept up an unbroken scrutiny of every move of the Eisenhowers, the Nixons, the Lyndon Johnsons, the Kennedys leaving their house, the ride to the White House, the ride from the White House, the bland demeanour of the Diplomatic Corps exchanging compliments of each other's hats, the close-up of a saturnine Justice Felix Frankfurter and an expansive Justice William O. Douglas, the lifted eyebrows of Eisenhower and Mrs Kennedy as a rabbi burst into a Jewish prayer, the restrained alarm of the Marines and Senator John Sparkman (the Inauguration host) when the smoking breath of the principals grew dense and was seen to be a separate cloud issuing from a fire that had broken out in a heater under the lectern.

This momentary fright, and a mix-up in the seating, delayed the taking of the oath for a full half hour. But Kennedy was sitting on the left hand of Eisenhower, and Eisen-hower is a famous talker, and Ike regaled the new man with anecdotes and reflections and busy gestures for twenty minutes or more while we went through the traditional rituals of patriotic selections played, as always since 1801, by the band of the Marine Corps, while various rattled officials sniffed at the fire and argued with it.

The people could share, in fully amplified sound, the boredom of the famous as they listened to long prayers being intoned or rasped out by a Catholic cardinal, a Greek Orthodox archbishop, a Protestant clergyman, and a rabbi, who always prolong their finest hour by turning these supplications into their own variation of the inaugural address.

While the invocations and beseechings barked or droned on the winter air, the cameras put together a portrait gallery of the victors and the falling in action: Adlai Stevenson, the only member of the Executive branch in a felt hat instead of a topper, chewing the cud of his two defeats and talking to no one; Harry Truman, in unbelievable Christian fettle, chatting affably with the enemy Nixon; the features trenched with age of a little old lady nestled close to the peach bloom fuzz of Mrs Kennedy's pretty face; Chief Justice Earl Warren, sitting at the alert immediately behind Kennedy and preserving at all times the impassivity of a melon; and all the time Kennedy inclining over to the voluble Ike and listening without a fidget, his fine hands slightly clasped.

At last, old Speaker Sam Rayburn rose to administer the Vice Presidential oath to his fellow Texan, Lyndon Johnson, whom he had laboured so to install on the President's throne. Then there was a prayer, handsomely praising the earthly capacities of Mr Johnson, by a Texas clergyman.

Then old Robert Frost was summoned to read an old poem with a new introduction composed specially for this day. The sun flashed wounding reflections on his failing eyes, and he stumbled through the introduction, threw in a despairing aside ('I'm not in a good light ... I can't get through this thing'), abandoned his text, and spoke the poem loud and strong, but with his fingers kneading his palms in a secret fury and his white hair lapping in waves against his forehead. Kennedy was the first to tap his shoulder and reassure him with a grasp of the hand.

After that Chief Justice Warren stood to the right of the lectern. Kennedy put his left hand on a family Bible, raised his right, and repeated the immemorial oath to 'preserve, protect, and defend the Constitution of the United States, so help me God.'

Then with never a quaver he delivered the simple, rolling cadences of what is certainly one of the simplest and most eloquent of inaugural addresses. 'This is not a victory of party but a celebration of freedom ... let every nation know whether it wishes us well or ill that we are here to assure the survival and the success of liberty ... To those old allies we pledge the loyalty of faithful friends ... To those in huts and villages of half the globe we pledge our best efforts to help men help themselves ... If we cannot help the many who are poor, we cannot help the few who are rich ... This hemisphere intends to remain the master of its own house.'

At the end, when the cheers rose from the shivering crowd, Eisenhower gave two slaps, tweaked his nose, shook Kennedy's hand. And Kennedy walked out as cool – but alive to small courtesies and distant nods – as an admiral being piped aboard. That, in a way, is what was happening, for the Marine Band, which had been interspersing the oaths and prayers with homely but traditional ruffles and flourishes, now burst with new zest into the Presidential tune, 'Hail to the Chief!' The cameras roamed over a huge square packed with thousands of ordered dots. Beyond these frozen 'eye-witnesses' was Constitution Plaza and the Hill and Pennsylvania Avenue – a continuous ribbon of bare highway, the only naked street in Washington.

Beyond that were the houses slumped in snow banks and a frozen landscape for thousands of miles housing the warm, remote population that had seen Robert Frost's moment of misery, and Mrs Kennedy's smooth throat twitch for a second as the 'unbearable office' passed over from the oldest President to the youngest.

President Kennedy gives his inaugural speech which included the immortal line 'Ask not what your country can do for you — ask what you can do for your country.'

Fiasco in Cuba: The Bay of Pigs

Letter No. 675, 23 April 1961

On Wednesday evening last week, you could have seen a band of pickets marching and stamping in front of 'The Russians' House' on Park Avenue. They carried placards reading 'Cuba, si; Communism, no' and 'Hands Off Cuba'. A mile away, over by the East River, another band of pickets marched and stamped across from the United Nations Plaza. They too carried placards reading, 'Yanks Stay Home, Hands off Cuba.' At least one picket in each group had to be led away by the cops for passionate behaviour constituting a threat to the public safety.

It would be useful to know the names of these foaming partisans, because they mark the two extremes of the wild and wobbly gamut of views on Cuba, which have been exposed here by the UN General Assembly's political committee; in Washington by the Congress, the State Department, and the President; by the press of the Western hemisphere; and by pickets and newspapers in a score or more countries of Europe and the Middle East. Most people interested or aroused by the Cuban invasion, from United Nations' delegates to Ukrainian peasants, from sugar importers to British Labour leaders, seem to be convinced that they have got to the heart of the matter. At best, they allow the plausibility of one other argument and then reject it. But it strikes me that nobody has laid out the range of arguments (it becomes plainer with every new debate in the UN) that can and will be applied to practically every uprising anywhere in the world. Now if this sounds like a rhetorical phrase, tossed in to make the sentence end with a bang, let me quote the words spoken before the United Nations Assembly by the delegate from Saudi Arabia on Thursday. Mr Ahmad Shukairy challenged UN Ambassador Adlai Stevenson to deny that refugees from Castro's Cuba had been trained and armed in the United States. Mr Shukairy said he respected the right of any refugees to struggle for the freedom of their homeland, but he wondered whether the United States would be prepared to let refugees from Oman train in the United States against Great Britain, the power that occupied their homeland. The day before, Britain had been under much the same sort of fire from the Arabs, who introduced a protest in the political committee against British intervention in Oman. They said that

Picketing outside the White House, 'At least one picket in each group had to be led away by the cops for passionate behaviour.'

British soldiers and bases were in Oman not to protect the freedom of the people but to protect Britain's domination of the oil deposits. It has been an uncomfortable week both for the Mother of Parliaments and for the Land of the Free, or in the Russian translation, the colonial imperialists and the American monopolists.

Now back to our bewildering collection of views on Cuba. I cannot pretend to offer an orderly progression of arguments, but only a random collection of raw materials for an anthology of opinion that somebody ought to make. None of these views was delivered mockingly by the sources I shall quote. Some of them, we are bound to deduce, are held cynically or expediently. But most of them are the sincere conclusions of men who have looked at what they take to be the facts. Perhaps we should say at the beginning that the facts, even the most elementary events of the rebel invasion, are extremely hard to come by. Most American information about the rebellion comes from a combination of sources, none of which – until Friday when the American correspondents in Cuba were released – was in sight of the hostilities. The main dispatches about the fighting, where it took place, the numbers engaged, the actual identity of the rebels, came out of Miami, Florida, which during the winter has tried to house and feed refugees whose numbers are variously estimated at 30,000 or 75,000. It is hinted, but never positively states, that many of these people are ex-Castro soldiers, civilian patriots, malcontents who have volunteered at known recruiting stations to go back to Cuba and fight for their land. Miami, too, receives the broadcasts of powerful transmitters near Havana; but the most powerful broadcasts of all, which bombard southern Florida, the Bahamas, and the Caribbean, are English-language news broadcasts from Moscow. They are incessant and they are alert and, in their fashion, informative; and it may explain why the blood pressure of Floridians is always a little higher than that of most of us when the threat of Communism to Latin America is mentioned.

The other sources of our information are the statements of the Cuban Revolutionary Council and its president, Dr Jose Cardona, in New York; the statements of Secretary of State Dean Rusk, and of the President. Already you will see that I am lumping together sources of fact and one-sided interpreters of those facts. We had better confess now that none of us here, and none of you in Britain, neither your leader-writers nor ours, nor the pickets and demonstrators anywhere in the world, know for certain whether 50,000 men or 500 landed in Cuba. The Havana radio went off the air immediately after the invasion was announced and came back on, on Friday morning, to announce that the uprising was a failure and that Dr Fidel Castro was in fine shape and personally supervising mopping-up operations in or near Matanzas. The reassurance about Dr Castro's health was necessary because even the most serious Republican newspaper reported in its early-bird edition on Friday morning that Dr Castro was 'out of circulation' because of a 'mental or physical collapse', probably mental. This news came from something described as a private organization for inter-American affairs in Miami. The newspaper quietly deleted this story from its breakfast edition.

All we knew a week ago, and all we can be really sure of today is what Havana admitted: that three Cuban air bases were bombed, with the loss of seven people and twenty-four wounded; that there were two or three landings on Cuban soil last Monday at possibly three places, probably one in Oriente Province (which was Castro's landing place), another in Las Villas Province. We can say pretty certainly, what Mr Stevenson admitted on Thursday night as a 'melancholy fact', that the rebellion had fizzled. That same night, reams of lamentations came out of Washington regretting, quite correctly I believe, that the whole invasion had been ballooned beyond its reality by the Miami correspondents, by the anti-Castro groups here, by the first bulletins issued by Dr Cardona's Revolutionary Council.

On the frail basis of these rags and snatches of fact, what were the distinguished delegates in the United Nations saying about it all? Mr Stevenson at first repeated the President's assurance that no American forces would under any circumstances intervene in Cuba. (By Thursday the President himself had changed this to read 'any unilateral American intervention in the absence of an external attack upon ourselves or an ally would have been contrary to our traditions and to our international obligations … But let the record show that our restraint is not inexhaustible.') Mr Stevenson said the next day that the failure of the rebellion proved that it was not an American military operation, 'for how long do you think Cuba, a small almost defenseless island, could resist the military power of the United States?' Dr Roa, the Cuban Foreign Secretary, showed the Assembly photographs of Browning and Thompson machine guns, and said they had been captured in Cuba. Mr Stevenson showed the Assembly photographs of the bombers that escaped to Florida, and said the markings on the planes showed them to be Castro's own.

Then came the deluge of dialectic, unsupported accusations, evidence quoted but never ascribed to a common or an agreed source. The Russians, of course, and the Poles and Czechs and Bulgars and Romanians have had a field day. They have revelled in quotations from the *New York Times* of weeks ago, dispatches from Washington and Florida and Guatemala rather sadly warning the reader that anti-Castro Cubans were being trained by the American military in camps in Guatemala, in Florida, and in Louisiana. The Russians, echoed later by the Arabs, say that these people were mercenaries. Dr Roa says not a single Cuban was among them. Nobody gives proof of either opinion. And thickening the atmosphere outside the Assembly were the black headlines of the evening newspapers saying that 50,000 Cubans had been thrown into emergency concentration camps, that priests had been jailed, that two Americans and seven Cubans had been executed. Dr Roa jumped in just before lunch one day to announce that a young American, a Bostonian, had been captured in Cuba and his American airplane brought down. He gave the man's address and his Social Security number. That was the first and the last we heard of him. No confirmation of this came out of Havana or from any other documentary source the Communists or the Cubans cared to offer.

Meanwhile, back in their rocking-chairs, the Washington correspondents were speculating why President Kennedy had suddenly toughened his threat to see that

Cuba would not be abandoned to Communism. Some of these correspondents have access to the State Department and the Central Intelligence Agency, and it is a safer guess than most that the best of them were repeating fears felt in the State Department arguments being bandied about the White House. The most relevant of them, and one that any fair-minded Briton or American has to consider, is simply this: there is no doubt at all that the Russians and the Chinese have been sending into Cuba, all through the winter, technical commissions and military advisers. There is ample proof that thousands of bright high-school students are being shipped from Cuba to be educated in the Soviet Union; there has been no denial from the Russians that brigades of Cuban flyers are now in Czechoslovakia learning to fly MIGs. And that they soon will be back and hope to form the expert nucleus of a considerable Cuban Air Force. There is also no denial that the tanks Castro's armies used came from the Soviet Union and the machine guns from Czechoslovakia.

Who, then, is the interventionist? That is the question we have to answer. The Indians, the Arabs, some Africans, and the Mexicans do not hesitate to echo the Soviets and say, 'The United States'. We all know that the United States was arming the rebel side and the Communists the other side. Unfortunately, for the legal position of the United States, the other side was a government in being. The interventionist is the man who wants to upset any government in power, no matter how threatening in the long run that government may become to his own security. The non-interventionist is the man who builds up the threat, provided he is arming a government in power. This was the dilemma that faced President Kennedy. He realized that the Monroe Doctrine, which 140 years ago warned all foreign powers to stay out of this hemisphere, was written when foreign powers moved physically by sea. Now they move by subversion, by ideology, by educating the young, by exporting arms and importing aviators. The President took the risk of embarrassing the legal and moral position of the United States by backing a small rebellion in order to warn the Soviet Union that any big excursion out of Cuba into Latin-America, when the Cubans become powerfully armed and trained, will be met by American arms.

This I believe to be the gist of American policy. Unhappily the United States was the nearest place the refugees could flee to; and so this Kennedy doctrine was applied to a rebellion encouraged in the United States, and to an adventure so puny that when it fell it brought down with it the prestige of the United States as a keeper of international law, and her reputation as a powerful defender of the weak.

Gary Cooper: 1901–1961

Guardian, 18 May 1961

When the word got out that Gary Cooper (who died on Saturday, aged sixty) was mortally ill, a spontaneous process arose in high places not unlike the first moves to sanctify a remote peasant. The Queen of England dispatched a sympathetic cable. The President of the United States called him on the telephone. A Cardinal ordered public prayers. Messages came to his house in Beverly Hills from the unlikeliest fans, from foreign ministers and retired soldiers who never knew him, as also from Ernest Hemingway, his old Pygmalion who had kept him in mind, through at least two novels, as the archetype of the Hemingway hero; the self-sufficient male animal, the best kind of hunter, the silent infantryman padding dutifully forward to perform the soldier's most poignant ritual in 'the ultimate loneliness of contact'.

It did not happen to Ronald Colman, or Clark Gable, or – heaven knows – John Barrymore. Why, we may well ask, should it have happened to Frank James Cooper, the rather untypical American type of the son of a Bedfordshire lawyer, a boy brought up in the Rockies among horses and cattle to be sure, but only as they compose the unavoidable backdrop of life in those parts, a schoolboy in Dunstable, a college boy in Iowa, a middling student, then a failing cartoonist, failed salesman, an 'extra' in Hollywood who in time had his break and mooned in a lanky, handsome way through a score or more of 'horse operas'? Well, his friends most certainly mourn the gentle, shambling 'Coop', but what the world mourns is the death of Mr Longfellow Deeds, who resisted and defeated the corruption of the big city; the snuffing out of the sheriff in *High Noon* heading back to duty along the railroad tracks with that precise mince of the cowboy's tread and that rancher's squint that sniffs mischief in a creosote bush, sees through suns, and is never fooled. What the world mourns is its lost innocence, a favourite fantasy of it fleshed out in the most durable and heroic of American myths: that of the taut but merciful plainsman, who dispenses justice with a worried conscience, a single syllable, a blurred reflex action to the hip, and who must face death in the afternoon as regularly as the matador, but on main street and for no pay.

Mr Deeds Goes to Town marks the first gelling of this fame, and *The Plainsman* the best delineation of the character that fixed his legend. These two films retrieved Cooper from a run of agreeable and handsome parts, some of them (in the Lubitsch films

for instance) too chic and metropolitan for his own good. At the time of *Mr Deeds*, an English critic wrote that 'the conception of the wise underdog, the shrewd hick is probably too western, too American in its fusion of irony and sentimentality, to travel far.' He was as wrong as could be, for the film was a sensation in Poland, the Middle East, and other barbaric regions whose sense of what is elementary in human goodness is something we are just discovering, perhaps a little late.

It is easy to forget now, as always with artists who have matured a recognisable style, that for at least the first dozen years of his film career Gary Cooper was the lowbrow's comfort and the highbrow's butt. However he lasted long enough, as all great talents do, to weather the four stages of the highbrow treatment: first, he was derided, then ignored, then accepted, then discovered. We had seen this happen many times before; and looking back, one is always shocked to recognise the people it has happened to. Today the intellectual would deny, for instance, that Katharine Hepburn was ever anything but a lovely if haggard exotic, with a personal style that might enchant some people and grate on others, but at all times what we call a serious talent. This opinion was in fact a highly sophisticated second thought, one that took about a decade to ripen and squelch the memory of Dorothy Parker's little tribute to Miss Hepburn's first starring appearance on Broadway: 'Miss Hepburn ran the gamut of human emotions from A to B.'

At least until the mid-thirties there was no debate about Gary Cooper because he presented no issue. He belonged to the reveries of the middle-class woman. He reminded grieving mothers of the upright son shot down on the Somme; devoted sisters of the brother sheep-ranching in Australia; the New York divorcee of the handsome ranch hand with whom she is so often tempted to contract a ruinous second marriage in the process of dissolving her first. To the moviegoer, Cooper was the matinee idol toughened and tanned, in the era of the outdoors, into something at once glamorous and primitive. He was notoriously known as the actor who couldn't act. Only the directors who handled him had daily proof of the theory that the irresistible 'stars' are simply behaviourists who, by some nervous immunity to the basilisk glare and hiss of the camera, appear to be nobody but themselves. Very soon the box offices, from Tokyo to Carlisle, confirmed this theory in hard cash. Then the intellectuals sat up and took notice. Then the Cooper legend took over.

For the past quarter-century Cooper's worldwide image had grown so rounded, so heroically elongated rather, that only some very crass public behaviour could have smudged it. There was none. After a short separation he was happily reunited with his only wife. He spoke out, during the McCarthy obscenity, with resounding pointlessness and flourished the banner of 'Americanism' in a heated way. Most recently, there has been a low-pressure debate in progress in fan magazines and newspaper columns about whether his 'yup-nope' approach was his own or a press agent's inspiration, like the malapropisms of Sam Goldwyn, another happy device for blinding mockers

Gary Cooper, affectionately known as 'Coop', who represented 'everyman's best secret image of himself.'

to the knowledge that they were losing their shirts. This was decided a week or two ago by the *New York Post*, which concluded after a series of exclusive interviews with his friends, that Cooper's inarticulateness was natural when he was in the presence of gabby strangers, that gabbiness was his natural bent with close friends.

He could probably have transcended, or dimmed bigger scandals or more public foolishness than he was capable of, because he was of the company of Chaplin, Groucho Marx, W. C. Fields, Bogart, Louis Jouvet, two or three others, give or take personal favourites. He filled an empty niche in the world pantheon of essential gods. If no cowboy was ever like him, so much the worse for the cattle kingdom. He was Eisenhower's glowing, and glowingly false, picture of Wyatt Earp. He was one of Walt Whitman's troop of democratic knights, 'bright eyed as hawks with their swarthy complexions and their broad-brimmed hats, with loose arms slightly raised and swinging as they ride.' He represented every man's best secret image of himself: the honourable man slicing clean through the rolling world of morals and machines. He isolated and enlarged to six feet three an untainted strain of goodness in a very male specimen of the male of the species.

Glenn Home and Dry

Guardian, 22 February 1962

The morning of Colonel Glenn's eleventh date with an orbit dawned without clouds over Cape Canaveral and without high waves off Bermuda. And so at last the eighteen tracking stations around the globe, the recovery ships, the 1,500 expert watchers were alerted for a 'Go', the syllable the American people have been waiting to exhale since the middle of December.

A few miles away, on Cocoa Beach, 5,000 people, hundreds of whom had slept in their cars by the seashore, set up radio and antennae, focused telescopes, rocked babies, and faced the rocket and his escape tower and saw the Colonel wave and waddle aboard.

At nineteen minutes after eight, a batch bolt broke and was quickly replaced. Twenty-two minutes before the zero hour there was a failure in one of the loading valves that feed liquid oxygen from the ground tanks into the rocket itself. In a rare burst of tact, Mercury Control did not report the slip until it was within a minute of being repaired. At thirteen and a half minutes to go, the helicopters at Canaveral began to spin their blades against the extreme possibility of an instantaneous recovery if the flight was aborted right after the take-off.

At eight minutes, the last assurances squawked over the public address system: 'All Systems Go.' At six and a half minutes an electrical power failure in the computer system at Bermuda was reported as restored.

Two and a half minutes to go, the escape tower swung off. Twenty seconds from the word, the umbilical cord dropped away and Mercury Control intoned the countdown in seconds. There was the deep low-frequency rumble modulating to an enormous whoosh of sound and a vicious tongue of flame. Soon the Atlas rocket was a fiery keyhole, and then an acorn and then a snowflake.

Within a minute or so the army of workers at Canaveral and the five hundred-odd reporters had lost all visible connection with their personal project and were at one with the silent crowds on the Florida beaches, in railroad stations and airports from New York to Seattle: gaping in extraordinary silence at giant television screens and hearing the elated exchange between Glenn and Mercury Control: 'On trajectory ... booster engines off ... tower gone ... go, baby, go ... 5.8 cabin pressure holding.'

He was already five hundred miles down range, in contact with Bermuda, and off

decision had to be made to bring him down or let him go into the third orbit. They let him go, and the drama began to move to a tidy end as he spanned the Atlantic for a third time, and the North Atlantic Recovery Fleet disbanded. The curiosity now was all about the place of his landing, and while the tapes discussed nothing but the time to fire the three retro-rockets that would diminish his speed and bring him down, we were already hearing a cavernous cheer go up from the crew of USS *Randolph*, which had been plotted as the probable rescue ship.

Back in the capsule, Glenn was counting his chickens with jocular confidence. He told a groundling astronaut to 'get the cake ready', a 993 pound invitation to gastritis, exactly the dimensions of the capsule (9 ft x 6 ft) that had been baked for the 27 January attempt and been embalmed in an air conditioned truck ever since. Over Muchea again he delivered a solemn message: 'Hey, Gordon, get this to General Shoup, the Marine commandant: I have four hours required flight time. Request flight chit be prepared for me.' All fliers get a bonus for four hours flying time a month. Colonel Glenn undoubtedly will be rewarded at the usual rate of pay: three times round the globe equals $245.

There was only one other jolting moment before the smooth descent, the succession of parachutes, and the rescue by the destroyer *Noa*. Over the Pacific he was having trouble deploying the heat shield, which pushes away the 3,000 degrees of heat when the rockets fire. This agony lasted for about four minutes until he said over Hawaii that the switch had worked; it was the signal that was out. Then the rockets fired, no doubt about it: 'I felt it was going to send me clear back to Hawaii.'

The *Randolph* spotted the big parachutes through the clouds. The USS *Noa* was only six miles away. The helicopters went off like flying lobsters, and they saw him and the capsule in a rippling sea with a water temperature of 81 degrees. After that we switched to Washington to the well-tempered President, then to the ecstatic parents, and to Grand Central Station and the dissolving crowds and strong men blowing their noses. John Glenn inscribed his name after the Wright Brothers and Lindbergh: 'I am go.'

Marilyn Monroe: 1926–1962

Guardian, 6 August 1962

Marilyn Monroe was found dead in bed this morning in her home in Hollywood, only a physical mile or two but a social universe distant from the place where she was born thirty-six years ago as Norma Jean Baker. She died with a row of medicines and an empty bottle of barbiturates at her elbow.

These stony sentences, which read like the epitaph of a Raymond Chandler victim, will confirm for too many millions of movie fans the usual melodrama of a humble girl, cursed by physical beauty, to be dazed and doomed by the fame that was too much for her. For Americans, the last chapter was written on the weekend that a respectable national picture magazine printed for the delectation of her troubled fans a confessional piece called 'Marilyn Monroe Pours Out Her Soul'. The plot of her early life is as seedy as anything in the pulp magazines, and to go into the details now would be as tasteless as prying into the clinical file of any other pretty woman whose beauty has crumbled overnight. It is enough, for summoning the necessary compassion, to recall her miserable parents, her being shuttled like a nuisance from foster home to orphanage, the subsequent knockabout years in a war factory, her short independence as a sailor's wife, the unsuspected first rung of the ladder provided by a posing job for a nude calendar.

She talked easily about all this, when people had the gall to ask her, not as someone reconciled to a wretched childhood but as a wide-eyed outsider, an innocent as foreign to the subject under discussion as Chaplin is when he stands off and analyses the appeal of 'The Little Man'.

Then she wiggled briefly past the lecherous gaze of Louis Calhern in John Huston's *Asphalt Jungle*, and his appraising whinny echoed round the globe. Within two years she was the enthroned sexpot of the Western world. She completed the first phase of the American dream by marrying the immortal Joe DiMaggio, the loping hero of the New York Yankees; and the second phase by marrying Arthur Miller and so redeeming his suspect Americanism at the moment it was in question before a House committee.

To say that Marilyn Monroe was a charming, shrewd and pathetic woman of tragic integrity will sound as preposterous to the outsider as William Empson's Freudian analysis of *Alice in Wonderland*. It is nevertheless true. We restrict the word 'integrity'

Norma Jean Baker: 'cursed by physical beauty, to be dazed and doomed by the fame that was too much for her.'

to people either simple or complex, who have a strong sense of righteousness or, if they are public men, of self-righteousness. Yet it surely means no more than what it says: wholeness, being free to be spontaneous, without reck of consistency or moral appearances. It can be as true of forlorn and bewildered people as of the disciplined and the solemn.

In this sense, Marilyn Monroe was all of a piece. She was confused, pathologically shy, a straw on the ocean of her compulsions (to pout, to wisecrack, to love a stranger, to be six hours late, or lock herself in a room). She was a sweet and humorous person increasingly terrified by the huge stereotype of herself she saw plastered all around her. The exploitation of this pneumatic, mocking, liquid-lipped goddess gave the world a simple picture of the Lorelei. She was about as much of a Lorelei as Bridget the housemaid.

This orphan of the rootless City of the Angels at last could feel no other identity than the one she saw in the mirror; a baffled, honest girl forever haunted by the nightmare of herself, sixty feet tall and naked before a howling mob. She could never learn to acquire the lacquered shell of the prima donna or the armour of sophistication. So in the end she found the ultimate oblivion, of which her chronic latecomings and desperate retreats to her room were tokens.

Meredith Registered:
The High Price

Guardian, 1 October 1962

James Meredith was registered this morning as a student at the University of Mississippi in Oxford, Miss., the town that in the last week was honoured around the world as the hometown of Pulitzer Prize winner William Faulkner. So far the price of Meredith's admission is the death of a foreign newsman and an Oxford youth, fifty injured and wounded, ninety-three arrests, the destruction of seven army trucks and the damaging of twenty more; the bitter surrender of Governor Ross Barnett; the inflaming of the populace of Mississippi; and the calling out of 2,500 regular Army infantrymen and military police. Not to gloss over the incalculable political liabilities, one ought to mention the heavy reprisals the Democrats may suffer in next month's Congressional elections, and the forfeit of more Southern states in the Presidential election of 1964, which President Kennedy has calculated and which the Republicans cannot help but count on, though at present in a secret and guilty fashion.

Up to half past seven last evening, when the President was supposed to address the nation, Governor Ross Barnett had given no public sign that he would yield. Then it was announced that the President had postponed his broadcast till 10 o'clock, and it was rightly guessed that a settlement was brewing. This rumour crackled among the crowds that had been milling around the Oxford courthouse square and set them moving toward the university campus, which was being guarded by the state Highway Patrol. When it became known that Meredith had been safely installed in a university apartment on the campus, the troubles began. It was soon too much for the patrolmen, and they gave way to 350 federal marshals, who had set up a tent city out of town. Rocks and bottles and stink bombs were thrown at the university office building, and the gathering crowds of students, local citizens, and outlanders began to charge the marshals. By half past eight, the riots were getting so out of hand that the marshals put in a call to Memphis, an Army base, for help from a military police battalion or the Mississippi National Guard, which President Kennedy federalized shortly after midnight yesterday.

About 9 o'clock, Governor Barnett broadcast a statement, and many of the rioters heard it over transistor radios. The State of Mississippi, he declared, was now 'completely surrounded by armed forces, and we are physically overpowered.' He assured his fellow Mississippians that 'my courage and my convictions do not waver … but my calm judgment abhors the bloodshed that would follow.' He urged 'all Mississippians and every state officer under my command to do everything in their power to preserve peace and to avoid violence in any form.' After condemning the United States for converting the '10,000 good Mississippians in the National Guard' into federal troops who are 'now required to oppose me and their own people', he invoked the mercy of God on the federal government for 'tramping on the sovereignty of this great state and depriving it of every vestige of honour and respect.'

An hour later the President appeared on all the TV and radio networks with a quite different definition of the honour of Mississippi and the United States. He appealed to the people of Mississippi to uphold federal law, to accept a federal judgment that might be 'difficult' for them. He paid lyrical tribute to the courage and the learning of Mississippians, and their prowess in the Second World War and in Korea, and even on the football field. The courage of Mississippi would now be tested by its willingness 'to accept those laws with which you disagree … the eyes of the nation and all the world

James Meredith walking amid stares and jeers of fellow students on the University of Mississippi campus.

are upon you and upon all of us, and the honour of your university and state are in the balance.'

This healing talk, which made no capital or mention of Governor Barnett's surrender, reassured the listening millions; but Oxford responded with massive lunges at the embattled marshals, who now had one man severely wounded and several others out of action. By midnight several hundred people from out of town or out of state had joined the mob. Among them was former Major General Edwin Walker, the cashiered commander of the troops who integrated Little Rock. He urged the rioters to 'protest, protest, keep it up.' At one this morning, 200 military police at last came in from Memphis, and federal troops made their first intervention.

It was what the President, and the marshals, had dreaded. The campus and its buildings were clouded with tear gas, and a nine-hour battle was under way. It was not over until the Mississippi National Guard, including Negro soldiers who offered the rioters their most detested targets, had joined the MPs; and until the word got around that 2,500 regular Army police and infantrymen were converging on the city. By then, Paul Guihard of Agence France-Presse and one Ray Gunter of Abbeville, Mississippi, were dead, and the campus was a shambles.

Not until half past five this morning did President Kennedy hear that the worst of the night was over. He went to bed. At 6 a.m. the commanding officer of the federals reported that 'the campus was secure.' The Justice Department said today that it was possible that many of the ninety-three persons arrested might be charged with insurrection, which could entail twenty years in prison and a $20,000 fine for each conviction. A possible culprit, the Department admitted, might be Gen. Walker, whom Senator Wayne Morse, Democrat, castigated this morning on the Senate floor as 'a sick man who ought to be committed.'

There was no disposition today, either in the Justice Department or in the Memphis Army headquarters, to believe that this battle is the end of the war. Meredith was solemnly registered this morning. Tomorrow he will have to go to classes. The next day, and the next, he will need protection. The Army might have a unit stationed there for months. After that, as one sad commentator mused last night, he is not likely to lead 'a carefree life'.

Ultimatum to USSR

Letter No. 741, 28 October 1962

Today was, on this seaboard, another jewel of a day, one of those New York days that are almost as crystalline in January as they are in June or October. Like many millions of other people, I put the clock back last evening in order to justify staying up later than usual. A couple of friends came in, the man a member of the United Nations Secretariat, and between bouts of personal talk we tuned in the bulletins every half-hour in the hope (which seemed last midnight to be draining away) that the United States would not feel it essential to have to use force to destroy the Russian missile bases in Cuba. More photographs were coming in to the Pentagon and being rushed to the White House, and they showed that way down below, the Russian technicians and their Cuban help had been working overtime on Friday and Saturday to finish the bases and mount the missiles and confront the United States with a dreadful accomplished fact, which the President in the long, long week behind us had laboured to thwart.

The bulletins last night kept breaking into the rock-and-roll and the melancholy vibra-harps all through the night. But there comes a point when anxiety must have a stop. And the last two items we heard were that the President had turned down Mr Khrushchev's offer to trade his Cuban bases for our Turkish ones; more numbing still, that Mr Adlai Stevenson, US Ambassador to the United Nations, had told the delegates of thirteen nations (from NATO and Latin America mostly) that unless work on the missile bases was voluntarily stopped, the United States would take military action to eliminate them in exactly forty-eight hours.

It was interesting, to say the least, that this apparently ultimate warning, the very last step of brinkmanship, was given not by the President or the Secretary of State, or Secretary of Defense, but by Ambassador Stevenson, a man who, to paraphrase a famous complaint of Marshal Foch, is a man very well known but still Ambassador Stevenson: in other words, a courier or servant of Presidential policy, certainly not its maker – a fact that Mr Stevenson has sometimes found hard to accept, since only two years ago he seemed a grander figure than the Senator Kennedy who was about to become President.

I ought to point out that Mr Stevenson was the man who, in April of last year, went before the Security Council of the United Nations and defended with passionate sincerity the good faith of the United States; who honestly ridiculed the Soviet charge that the invasion of Cuba (which was then in its earliest stages) had been planned and assisted by the United States. He brought in photo exhibits of captured planes, whose markings showed that they were from Castro's Air Force. Unfortunately, it came out later that similar markings had been faked on planes used in the invasion. In a word, the Khrushchev Administration had faked the planes, and used Ambassador Stevenson as an honest dupe.

Mr Stevenson had a rough time of it, then and afterwards, from Mr Valerian Zorin, the Soviet chief delegate, and Mr Stevenson had no public way open to him to recover his self-respect. For he had made his honest defense of American motives before he was informed that the abortive invasion was in fact an American show. Mr Zorin brought this up, with relish, on Thursday evening, when once again Mr Stevenson brought easels and photographic blow-ups into the Security Council, and mounted them and described them, in order to force the answer to the question Mr Stevenson had hammered at Mr Zorin, and which Mr Zorin airily waved away. That question, in Mr Stevenson's words, was: 'Let me ask you one simple question. Do you, Ambassador Zorin, deny that the USSR has placed and is placing medium and intermediate range missiles and sites in Cuba? Yes or no?' Mr Stevenson is a man of great dignity and patience, but Mr Zorin's face began to crack, somewhere between a smirk and a sigh, and in that split second Mr Stevenson leaned forward and rasped out, 'Don't wait for the interpretation. Yes or no?' Mr Zorin replied that he was not in an American courtroom and had no wish to answer a prosecutor's question. 'You'll get your answer,' he said, without deigning to look at the now crouching figure of Stevenson, 'don't worry.' It was at that moment that Mr Stevenson leaned even further forward and said a sentence that will surely, if only from its repetition in film clips, pass into the lexicon of famous American phrases like 'Don't shoot till you see the whites of their eyes' and 'You may fire when ready, Mr Gridley.' 'I am prepared,' Mr Stevenson rasped out, 'to wait for an answer till hell freezes over, if that's your decision. And I'm also prepared to present the evidence in this room.' Which he promptly did.

Now in all the long and tortuous sequence of events since the President cancelled his Midwest campaign tour on account of that strategic cold-in-the-head, this seems to me, to coin a phrase, the moment of truth. It was the moment that lots of thoughtful people on both sides of the Atlantic were waiting for. It was the root question they wanted to pluck up and have answered. Mr Zorin refused to look at the photographs that everybody else was eyeing like eagles. If I'd been talking to you two days ago, I should have gone into the detail of those pictures and reported the reliable assurance of high altitude photographers, military and Air Force reconnaissance men, and not only Americans, that a trained and disinterested eye was bound to see in them, shot over Gandelaria and San Cristobal and Guanahai, unmistakable missile sites and missile equipment and accessories that can be used for no other known military purpose. Since, however, we are talking on Sunday evening there is no need to stress the point

President Kennedy meets with his cabinet officers and advisors in
October 1962 to discuss the Cuban Missile Crisis.

that the chances of these pictures being of cunning camouflage, or clever movie sets,
are about one in a thousand. The military say the chances are much less.

Mr Zorin, at the time, was simply obedient to his instructions. 'Falsity,' he shouted,
'is what the United States has in its hands, false evidence, forgeries.' Between then
and now, Mr Khrushchev himself has given the lie to Mr Zorin's lie; only this morning Mr Khrushchev said to the President: 'The weapons you describe as offensive are
grim weapons. You and I both know that they are.' It is almost a parrot echo of Mr
Stevenson's well-bred snort at the end of Thursday's crackling exchange in the Security
Council: 'I hope we can stop this sparring; we know the facts, and so do you, Sir.'

You may have gathered from this tremendous scene, which will never be forgotten
by those who saw it, that Mr Stevenson was the logical man to enunciate last night's
warning, since he is the man who has carried the American case in the United Nations,
the one place where the Soviet Union, the United States, and Cuba are meeting face
to face. It is logical, but it is not inevitable. All exchanges with foreign governments,
and even with Bertrand Russell, have been handled by the President. It was left to Mr

Stevenson to give yesterday's warning, to say that the first move would be an air strike, because it was essential for the credibility of the United States before the rest of the world to show that this time Stevenson was in on the most secret information, that he knew, that he believed, and that this time he spoke with both knowledge and good faith. When the history of this, the longest week, comes to be written, I think that the decision to entrust an ambassador (and this Ambassador) with the final warning will be seen to be a master-stroke of diplomacy and goodwill. Below the surface of even the most world-shaking political events, the actors remember old grudges. The role that Mr Stevenson was asked to play (or by default was allowed to play) in the Bay of Pigs disaster was humiliating to him and damaging to the honesty of the Kennedy Administration in its first showdown with Communism in this hemisphere. But in the second, the much more momentous showdown, since it was not between a giant and the other giant's puppet but between the Titans themselves, it was crucial that nobody should infer a clash of wills inside the Kennedy Cabinet.

When we went to bed last night, we had this small and honourable satisfaction to set against the immensity of the risk, the trembling of the fingers on the nuclear buttons. When we woke up this morning the glad tidings came pealing in, breaking into Mozart and Gilbert & Sullivan and solemn sermons and rollicking hymns up in Harlem: the news that Mr Khrushchev had accepted unconditionally every point of Mr Kennedy's demand for the dismantling of the Cuban missile bases under UN super-vision. We had to wait four more hours, by which time the Khrushchev text had been studied at the White House, before, not much more than an hour ago, the President came through with his warm welcome for this contribution to peace and his earnest hope that the governments of the world will turn now to the compelling necessity of ending the arms race.

This is not the time to review the last week, to mete out blame and recrimination or study the furious diplomacy of the last seven days as a possibly perilous precedent for a similar crisis over, say, Berlin. I can only say that if the conditions are met, President Kennedy will emerge in his own country incredibly strengthened as a president and leader.

An hour ago, a neighbour of mine, who is a hi-fi buff and mighty proud of an amplifier that practically fills the building, telephoned me and asked me to listen to the raging sound of his gramophone. He was playing, 'Oh, What a Beautiful Morning!' It was corny, but it was spontaneous and good, and I looked out over the riffling waves of the reservoir in Central Park; a bird rose from the water and was airborne and soared off to the ocean. I should like to say it was a dove. It was, however, a seagull whose clean swinging flight I shall remember till the day I die.

Questioning the President

Letter No. 781, 4 August 1963

On Thursday afternoon as I was sitting looking out across the reservoir in Central Park, fishing in my mind for some missing adjective, I saw the most curious thing. For days the sky had kept that cloudless, leaden, absolutely featureless quality of our sky when we are having great heat. Now, quite suddenly, and without any clouds moving in, the sky began to get some colour, as if some enormous dye were slowly seeping into it. It intensified to what we used to call a battleship grey, then to a deep lead. And by now, the pigeons and gulls in the park, which had been soaring lazily around, began to get panicky and wheel and squeal. It went darker still, and I was unable to read the few lines I'd written with my typewriter. I went and got a camera and threw open the window (the air outside is much hotter these days than any air inside, however suf-focating, so it's better at all times to keep the windows shut) and I focused on the high twin towers of an apartment building across the park. I'd clicked the shutter when a sort of shiver ran across the glassy surface of the reservoir. Then the trees in the park shuddered and waved madly, and without any other warning the rain came slamming so hard and so fast that I had a time getting the window down and locking it. Then I heard another noise, a gurgling sound, and there at my feet was a rising pool. The rain was rolling in across the vent between the top of the radiator and the outside sill. And so it was in two other rooms. I rushed off to a linen closet and picked up half a dozen bath towels and flung them on the floor beneath the three windows. It was all over in ten minutes, and the bath towels oozed; the sky broke up, and little clouds appeared, the first, it seemed, in weeks, and the thermometer nose-dived. And at last we were out of the soaking high nineties, and next morning the weather bureau was able to announce, with almost a croon, its usual summer forecast: 'Tomorrow fair and comfortable, seasonable temperatures, high about 84 degrees.' Next morning I drew the attention of a weatherman to a small headline in a London paper, air mail edition. It said, '75 degrees, another scorcher,' exclamation point. 'Well,' said the weatherman philosophically, 'only goes to prove, one man's scorcher is another man's comfort.'

Without wanting to squeeze a moral out of this line, I couldn't help thinking of it when someone interviewed a Negro who'd been lying down in the street day after day as part of the organized picketing of two housing projects and a hospital construction

A relaxed President Kennedy at a press conference,
'saved once again by his wry humour.'

site in New York. They're protesting against discrimination in the building trades. The reporter suggested, what I think must have occurred to a lot of people, that the Negroes who are demonstrating and picketing and sitting down and lying down, and in general running the risk of arrest and prison, not to mention getting their heads broken, that such people are a special breed of men and women, either specially brave or specially reckless. The coloured man was unimpressed by this suggestion. He replied in much the same vein as many a war hero: 'Well,' he said, 'at first you're scared witless, then the day comes when havin' a coupla cops pick you up and carry you off, gets to be kinda snug.'

Snug or not, thousands and thousands of Negroes who once used to say nothing and fume inwardly are now ready to march, and rally and risk their safety and that of their young to get what they were given on paper one hundred years ago.

You will have noticed how impossible it is, even if one tried, to write a *Letter From America* without bringing in the Negro. It would, in fact, be as odd as writing a letter from Noah's Ark without mentioning the wind and the waves. I've been looking back at the President's press conferences in the past six months. There has never been a time when he wasn't challenged, at least once, on some aspect of the racial question.

On Wednesday, it came up in a form so familiar to generations of blacks and whites that it was a marvel this particular point had never been made before, at least to the President. It was put by a lady who has been going to presidential press conferences since the early days of Roosevelt. Her name is Miss May Craig, and she writes for a paper in Portland, Maine. She never, to any President, asks soothing questions, or flattering questions. They are not exactly needling, but they usually bring up some knotty, awkward problem that is on everybody's mind. On the mind, anyway, of the average laconic New Englander, of the hardy, sceptical Yankee type that is still around in large numbers and that doesn't waste words.

Well, Miss Craig (she is really a widow, in her sixties, who's been a newspaper woman for over forty years, but she's Miss Craig to everybody) is a worthy daughter of this tight-lipped Yankee tradition. The fact, which I whisper, that she was born in South Carolina does not in any way detract from her standing as a professional Yankee. She has served the newspapers of Maine long and faithfully, and like most people who become identified as the symbol of a particular place, she came from somewhere else. Napoleon, remember, was not a Frenchman, nor was Hitler a German.

Well, Miss Craig stood up and put to President Kennedy this highly uncomfortable question: 'Mr President, in some twenty-four states there are, all over the country, there are miscegenation (intermarriage) laws in various forms. The California courts once found them unconstitutional under the 14th Amendment and said that marriage is a fundamental right of free men. Now, in your crusade against racial discrimination for all races, will you seek to abrogate these laws, and how would you go about it?'

This was a loaded question. Miss Craig was blithely asking what everybody thinks and nobody says aloud, namely the old chestnut – but one that cannot be airily dismissed by anybody. 'Would you like your sister to marry a Negro?' To give you the exact tone of the President's reply, I should have to be a consummate actor, because all that the transcript shows is that he was sufficiently thrown to be pretty inarticulate. But I'll try anyway. This is what the transcript shows: 'Well, I, the law would, if there was a marriage of the kind you described, I would assume that, and if any legal action was taken against the party then I, they would have a relief, it would seem to me, in the courts, and it would be carried, I presume, to the higher courts, depending on the judgment, so that the laws themselves would be affected by the ultimate decision of the Supreme Court.'

Not surprisingly, this didn't satisfy Miss Craig, for he was ducking his own opinion and saying, in effect, it would be up to the Supreme Court. Miss Craig stayed on her feet. She said, 'Can't the Department of Justice take some discrimination cases to the courts themselves?' The President paused again, and the auditorium was very quiet. 'I'm not sure,' he said, 'I'm not sure they could, as you describe it, because I'm not sure they would be a party in the case. It would probably be an order to have the case heard, and this is legal matter about which I'm not familiar with, and I speak with some – the valour of ignorance, as I'm not a lawyer … I would think there'd have to be a party at interest who would bring the suit … er.' Now he was looking up and down.

'Which party, who do you have in mind?' he seemed to be wondering. Then he pulled himself out of this flounder with a typical swift and cunning little stroke that released a great burst of laughter on the last few words. 'But this is a matter which I'd be glad to have the Attorney General or the Solicitor General speak to you personally about, Miss Craig.' Miss Craig flopped down in the ocean of laughter, and the President was saved once again by his very wry humor. Of course, it's no laughing matter. It is, in raw fact, the secret mainspring of, I should say, most middle-aged fear of the ultimate consequences of integration.

While we wrestle every day with this great rebellion, it is very humbling, or it may at least be very enlightening, to discover that the cast of characters in this national debate is by now so well understood by the Negro himself that he has developed a whole lexicon of slang to describe them. We are indebted, I hope, to *Time* magazine for having dug out this ruthless and fascinating index to the mind of the black man, whose troubles most of us, no matter what our point of view, pretend to understand. Well, when there are enough folk who feel deeply about something to spawn a slang phrase, there you have a genuine piece of folklore, and I believe this little dictionary of slang might give us all profitable pause about the purity, the intelligence, and the sophistication of our own motives.

We have all known for some time that the contemporary American Negro refers to the quiet, subservient Negro of the old tradition – and refers to him with contempt – as Uncle Tom. It is now applied to all these Negroes who warn against violence, either from their personal disposition or religious conviction or whatever. Mr Tom is a middle-class Tom, and a coloured woman who urges moderation is called Aunt Tomasina. Understandably, Negroes who are working toward the day of deliverance realize acutely that their cause is damaged by hoodlums or flashy types. They call them, 'butter heads'. They maintain a keen suspicion of Negroes who are acceptable to whites as negotiators. They are called 'clean, safe, and certified'. The Negroes who preach militancy but stop short of violence are dubbed 'upside-downers'. A demonstrator who has not enjoyed his baptism of fire by being jailed is called an 'untouchable'. And one who stands aside from the civil rights movement is 'a sleeping beauty'.

There is little point in retailing the rest of this astute and ruthless lingo; for the Negroes are alert to the instinct of bright white sympathizers who try and get hip to this argot by adopting it. With a mild sneer, one Negro says, 'When it's hip among whites, it's already square among Negroes.'

There really seems no place for us to go, does there? No place, at any rate, acceptable to the Negro as the decent, responsible place for an intelligent, humane, sympathetic white, who would like to see the Negro win and enjoy his constitutional rights. You know, in fact, what they call such people as you and I – white, sympathetic liberals? They call us – 'innocents'.

President Kennedy Assassinated

Guardian, 22 November 1963

President John Fitzgerald Kennedy, the thirty-fifth President of the United States, was shot during a motorcade drive through downtown Dallas this afternoon. He died in the emergency room of the Parkland Memorial Hospital thirty-two minutes after the attack. He was forty-six years old. He is the third President to be assassinated in office since Abraham Lincoln and the first since President McKinley in 1901.

In the late afternoon the Dallas police took into custody a former Marine, one Lee Harvey Oswald, aged twenty-four, who is alleged to have shot a policeman outside a theatre. He is said to have remarked only, 'It is all over now.' He is the chairman of a group called the 'Fair Play for Cuba Committee', and is married to a Russian girl. He is described at the moment as 'a prime suspect'.

The new President is the Vice President, Lyndon Baines Johnson, a fifty-five-year-old native Texan, who took the oath of office in Dallas at five minutes to four at the hands of a woman judge and later arrived in Washington with the body of the dead President.

This is being written in the numbed interval between the first shock and the harried attempt to reconstruct a sequence of fact from an hour of tumult. However, this is the first assassination of a world figure that took place in the age of television, and every network and station in the country took up the plotting of the appalling story. It begins to form a grisly pattern, contradicted by a grisly preface: the projection on television screens of a happy crowd and a grinning President only a few seconds before the gunshots.

The President was almost at the end of his two-day tour of Texas. He was to make a lunch speech in the Dallas Trade Mart building, and his motor procession had about another mile to go. He had had the warmest welcome of his trip from a great crowd at the airport. The cries and pleas for a personal touch were so engaging that Mrs Kennedy took the lead and walked from the ramp of the presidential plane to a fence that held the crowd in. She was followed quickly by the President, and they both seized hands and forearms and smiled gladly at the people.

The Secret Service and the police were relieved to get them into their car, where Mrs Kennedy sat between the President and John B. Connally, the Governor of Texas. The

President Kennedy and his wife and entourage at the start of the
fateful motorcade journey in Dallas, Texas, on 22 November 1963.

Dallas police had instituted the most stringent security precautions in the city's history:
they wanted no repetition of the small but disgraceful brawl that humiliated Adlai
Stevenson in their city when he attended a United Nations rally on 24 October.

The motorcade was going along slowly but smoothly. Three muffled shots, which
the crowd first mistook for fireworks, cracked through the cheers. One hit the shoulder blade and the wrist of Governor Connally, who was taken with the President to
the hospital, where his condition is serious. The other brought blood trickling from
the back of the sitting President's head. His right arm flopped from a high wave of
greeting, and he collapsed into the arms of Mrs Kennedy, who fell unharmed. She was
heard to cry, 'Oh, no,' and sat there all the way cradling his head in her lap. As some
people bayed and screamed and others fell to the ground and hid their faces, the Secret

The moment of the shooting as the presidential motorcade passed through Dealey Plaza on Elm Street in Dallas.

Service escort broke into two groups, one speeding the President's car to the hospital, and another joined a part of the heavy police escort in wheeling off in pursuit of a man fleeing across some railroad tracks. Nothing came of this lead.

The President was taken to the emergency room of the Parkland Hospital, and Governor Connally was taken into the surgery. Mrs Kennedy went in with the living President, and less than an hour later came out with the dead man in a bronze coffin, which arrived shortly after two priests had administered the Last Rites of the Roman Catholic Church. The body was escorted by Generals Clifton and McHugh, the President's chief military and Air Force aides, to the Dallas Airport and flown thence to Washington.

Within an hour of the President's death, the Secret Service had found a sniper's nest inside the building from which the first witnesses swore the bullets had been fired. It is a warehouse for a school textbook firm, known as the Texas School Depository, on the corner of Elm and Houston streets. In an upper room, whose open window commanded the route of the Presidential motorcade, the Servicemen found the remains of a fried chicken and a foreign-made rifle with a telescopic sight. Alongside it lay three empty cartridges.

The Assassination

Letter No. 794, 24 November 1963

By now it may well be impossible to add any sensible or proper words to all the millions that have been written and spoken about the life and cruel death of John F. Kennedy. Those of us who have ever sat down to write a letter of condolence to a close friend know what an aching task it is to say something that is pointed and that touches the right vein of sympathy. But I hope you will understand that there is no other thing to talk about – not here. At 3,000 miles it may be easier to speculate about policy, the new administration – not here. For I cannot remember a time, certainly in the last thirty years, when the people everywhere around you were so quiet, so tired-looking, and for all their variety of shape and colour and character so plainly the victims of a huge and bitter disappointment. That may sound a queer word to use, but grief is a general term that covers all kinds of sorrow, and I think that what sets off this death from that of other great Americans of our time is the sense that we have been cheated, in a moment, by a wild but devilishly accurate stroke of the promise of what we had begun to call the Age of Kennedy.

Let me remind you of a sentence in his inaugural address, when he took over the Presidency on that icy day of 20 January 1961. He said, 'Let the word go forth from this time and place to friend and foe alike that the torch has been passed to a new generation of Americans, born in this century, tempered by war, disciplined by a hard and bitter peace, proud of our ancient heritage and unwilling to witness or permit the slow undoing of those human rights to which this nation has always been committed … Let every nation know, whether it wishes us well or ill, that we shall pay any price, bear any burden, meet any hardship, support any friend, oppose any foe, to assure the survival and the success of liberty.'

This is, of course, the finest rhetoric, worthy of Lincoln, but what made it sound so brave and rousing on that first day was the clear statement that a young man was speaking for a new generation. It concentrated in one scornful sentence the reminder that the old men who had handled the uncertain peace and the Second World War had had their day and that there was at hand a band of young Americans ready not to ignore the wisdom of their forefathers but to fight for it.

It would be hard to say more exactly or more bravely that it was a fresh America that would have to be negotiated with, but that, as always, liberty itself was not negotiable.

Now, even in the moment of knowing that the promises of an inaugural address are bound to have a grandeur very hard to live up to the morning after, this remarkable speech, which the President had hammered out, sentence by sentence, with his closest aide and companion, Theodore Sorensen, did strike a note to which the American people and their allies everywhere responded with great good cheer. Of course we knew, older men and women have always known (what in their youth they blithely rattled off as a quotation from Shakespeare) that 'golden lads and girls all must, as chimney sweepers, come to dust.' But it is always stirring to see that young people don't believe it. We chuckled sympathetically then at the warning that Senator Lyndon Johnson had chanted all through the campaign: that the Presidency could not safely be put in the hands of a man 'who has not a touch of grey in his hair.' John Kennedy had turned the tables triumphantly on this argument by saying, in effect, that in a world shivering under the bomb it was the young who had the vigour and the single-mindedness to lead.

If we pause and run over the record of the very slow translation of these ideals into law – the hairbreadth defeat of the medical care for the aged plan, the shelving after a year of labour of the tax bill, the perilous reluctance of the Congress to tame the Negro revolution now with a civil rights law – we have to admit that the clear trumpet sound of the Kennedy inaugural has been sadly soured down three short years.

Any intelligent American family, sitting around a few weeks ago, would grant these deep disappointments; and many thoughtful men were beginning to wonder if the President's powers were not a mockery of his office, since he can be thwarted from getting any laws passed at all by the simple obstructionism of a dozen chairmen of Congressional committees, most of them, by the irony of a seniority system that gives more and more power to old men who keep getting re-elected by the same states, most of them from the South. But that same American family, sitting around this weekend, could live with these disappointments but not with the great one: the sense that the new generation, 'born in this century, tempered by war, disciplined by a hard and bitter peace, proud of our ancient heritage, unwilling to witness or permit ...' was struck down lifeless, unable to witness or permit, or not to permit, anything.

When it is possible to be reasonable we will all realize, calling on our everyday fatalism, that if John Kennedy was forty-six and his brother Robert only thirty-eight, most of the men around him were in their fifties and some in their sixties; and that therefore we fell, for a day or two in November 1963, into a sentimental fit. However, we are not yet reasonable; the self-protective fatalism, which tells most of us that what has been must be, has not yet restored us to the humdrum course of life.

I am not dwelling on this theme, the slashing down in a wanton moment of the flower of youth, because it's enjoyable or poetic to think about. It seems to me, looking over the faces of the people and hearing my friends, that the essence of the American mood this very dark weekend is this deep feeling that our youth has been mocked, and the vigour of America for the moment paralyzed.

Three-year-old John F. Kennedy Jr. salutes as the casket of his father
is carried from St Matthew's Cathedral in Washington DC.

It is, to be hardhearted about it, fascinating – when it is not also poignant – to see in how many ways people express the same emotion. Many of the memorial photographs in the shop windows have small replicas of the Presidential standard on one side, and a Navy flag on the other, recalling the incredible five days' gallantry on that Pacific island that Kennedy himself never recalled, except to the men who were with him and survived. A young socialite, whose life is a round of clothes and parties and music, bemoans the fact that the Kennedys will leave the White House and take with them 'the style, the grace, the fun they brought to it.' An American friend from Paris writes: 'I think his death will especially be felt by the young, for he had become for them a symbol of what was possible, with intelligence and will.' An old man, wise in the ups and downs of politics, says: 'I wonder if we knew what he might have grown to in the second term.' A child with wide eyes asks, 'Tell me, will the Peace Corps go on?'

There is another thing that strikes me, which is allied to the idea of a young lion shot down. It is best seen in the bewilderment of people who were against him, who felt he had temporized and betrayed the promise of the first days. One of them, a politically active woman, rang me up, and what she had to say dissolved in tears. Another, a veteran sailor, a close friend, and a lifelong Republican, said last night: 'I can't understand, I never felt so close to Kennedy as I do now.' This sudden discovery that he was more familiar than we knew is, I think, easier to explain. He was the first President of the television age, not as a matter of chronology but in the incessant use he made of this new medium. When he became President-elect, he asked a friend to prepare a memorandum on the history of Presidential press conferences. He wanted to know how much the succession of Presidents since Wilson had been able to mould the press conference and how much it had moulded *them*. What he received was a plea, disguised as a monograph, to abandon Eisenhower's innovation of saying everything on the record for quotation and letting the conference be televised. He looked it over, at his usual rate (of about a thousand words a minute), granted the arguments but said simply: 'Television is now the main personal link between the people and the White House. We can't go back.' He allowed his press conferences to be televised live. He also made another decision that ran counter to the wisdom of all incumbent Presidents. No man who is in power invites a debate with an opponent who is out of power and who can speak not of the things he's done but of the things the incumbent has done wrong. In spite of knowing well that next time he would be the man with his back against the wall, he had decided that the television debate was now an essential element of a Presidential campaign.

So for three years and more, we have seen him, at the end of our day, on all his tours – in Vienna, in Dublin, in Berlin, in Florida, Chicago, Palm Beach, in – alas – Dallas, in his own house talking affably with reporters, rumpling up the children, very rarely posing, always offhand and about his business, talking to foreign students in the White House garden, making sly, dry jokes at dinners, every other week fencing shrewdly and often brilliantly with two hundred reporters, and sometimes at formal rallies stabbing the air with his forefinger and bringing to life again, in his eyes and his chin and his soaring sentences, the old image of the young warrior who promised 'the energy, the faith, the devotion that will light America and all who serve her.'

The consequence of all this is that the family, the American family, has been robbed, violently and atrociously, of a member. When Roosevelt died, the unlikeliest people, the very young who thought of him as a perpetual President, and some of the very old who hated him, confessed that they felt they had lost a father. Today, millions of Americans are baffled by the feeling, which seems to have little to do with their political loyalties, that they have lost a brother, the bright young brother you are proud of, the one who went far and mingled with the great, and had no side, no pomp, and in the worst moments (the Bay of Pigs) took all the blame, and in the best (the Cuban crisis) had the best sort of courage, which is the courage to face the worst and take a quiet stand.

This charming, complicated, subtle, and greatly intelligent man, whom the Western world was proud to call its leader, appeared for a split second in the telescopic sight of a maniac's rifle. And he was snuffed out. In that moment, all the decent grief of a nation was taunted and outraged. So that along with the sorrow, there is a desperate and howling note over the land. We may pray on our knees, but when we get up from them, we cry with the poet:

'Do not go gentle into that good night.

Rage, rage against the dying of the light.'

L.B.J. the Thirty-Sixth President

Guardian, 28 November 1963

It is hard to describe the appearance and personality of President Lyndon Baines Johnson in any words that would mean the same thing to readers of different nationalities. To say that he is fifty-five, just over fourteen stone, 6 ft. 3 in., clean-shaven, has crinkly, quizzical eyes, and a blue-rimmed chin, is about as objective and blank a description as one could give. It only begins to acquire life through the lens of the observer's preconceptions.

Thus, in a French paper, he is an 'earthy yet dapper son of le Far-west'. In a score of Northern tabloids he is 'a rangy, back-slapping Texan'. To an English politician he is 'one of those ingratiating, shrewd Southern types the Senate seems to breed'. Because he decided ten years ago that 'segregation is doomed,' most Southern conservatives look on him darkly as the native son who betrayed the Southland. To Texans of liberal bent, and there are many, he is an easy combination of sentimental New Dealer and smooth operator in oil, ranching, natural gas and insurance. To the Congress, he is quite simply 'Lyndon', the supreme strategist of the Senate in their day, an alternately engaging and terrifying figure on Capitol Hill who, in the ironical progression of American politics, achieved the honour of the Vice Presidency and got lost in its tomb-like vacuum; although every succeeding President swears to transform the office into that of an active deputy commander, somehow the system can accommodate only one leader, and the Vice President becomes a powerless Pooh-Bah, a ceremonial courier, a certain attender of funerals in Addis Ababa.

It is from this hallowed void that, like seven other 'accidental' Presidents before him, Lyndon Johnson has now been plucked to assume the supreme command. He comes to it from a background about as far removed from that of John Fitzgerald Kennedy as Boston, the terminal for immigrant Irishmen, is from Stonewall, Texas, where, until very recently, the shooting of an unarmed man 'who made threats' was legally interpreted as justifiable self-defence. Both of them, however, were the grandsons of practising politicians, and the gap between the farmer's son and the second generation Ivy Leaguer was bridged when they came to Washington by the politician's code of teamsmanship and party loyalty. The contrast between a boy who taught in school to

Lyndon Baines Johnson, 'a doggedly untheoretical man.'

Mexicans and Negroes and a boy who had his own car in Palm Beach shrivelled before the same tough facts of political life; the means whereby campaign funds are raised, a city machine is disciplined, a winning coalition is forged at the expense of personal friendships. It was this bond that made them close and admiring allies in the Senate. It was the reason why Kennedy, surveying the disorder and dissension of the South in 1960, picked Johnson to save it by wheedling, cajoling, and bullying its leaders in the last weeks of the last campaign.

Johnson was born to a small farm and few comforts. At the age of nine, he was a shoeshine boy in a barber's shop, at fifteen he had left school for a road-building gang, and went from there to California by way of odd jobs in garages, lunch counters, and hotels. He came back to Texas having been convinced in his odd moments that formal education was not the sissy frill he had been led to think. He worked his way through the South-West State Teachers' College, at San Marcos, Texas, and three and a half years later took a B.Sc. degree. One endowment that simply required polishing was his gift of the gab; and it should be no surprise to anyone who has seen him woo and win an audience that in his early twenties he was a teacher of public speaking and debating.

In 1931 he decided to go into politics as a political secretary to a Texas congressman. In Washington the engaging young man with the dark eyes and the energy of a mustang came under the eye of Franklin Roosevelt, who became from then on, in Johnson's special phrase, 'a daddy to me'. In 1937 he scraped into the Congressional seat of a dead congressman, and the next year was elected to his own term. In 1948, the year of Harry Truman's miraculous reincarnation, he slipped into the Senate by eighty-seven votes. The rest of the story is his rise as Democratic Whip to the leadership of the party on the Senate floor. To those who had watched him calculate the possible and contrive the impossible, it was the inevitable mating of a round peg in a round hole.

At this moment of hasty recall, political reporters remember him most vividly as the Senate leader who kept a mental file on the men who balked him, who yet liquidated old enmities in an unflagging gift for compromise. They reflect that there are not many senators, even now, who are not beholden to him. And they hope that in some way, never yet discovered by a congressman translated to the White House, he will be able to mesmerize the legislative arm of government that was set up as his watchdog.

What is more plausible to anticipate is the strengthening of his instinct for compromise, for his whole professional life has been lived in the rooted belief that politics is 'one long accommodation of contesting forces'. This conviction has often made him contemptuous of the liberal Jeremiahs. What matters, he used to swear, is not the throbbing speech (though no one can throb in better iambic pentameters) but the bill that emerges; not the scarifying abuse of McCarthy but the contriving of his censure on the floor of the Senate; as what he honestly regards as the supreme American issue of the day – the civil rights of the Negro – not the sword but the guarantee that it shall not cleave the nation in two.

So, to look over the last chapter of his active record with a cold eye, he catered to the North by steering through the Senate, with considerable courage, the first Civil Rights Bill in a hundred years; and while he first tried to redeem himself in the horrified South by protecting its rights to filibuster, he saw, with the same delayed but irrevocable honesty, that the filibuster must soon go, and so he incensed his fellow-Southerners again by cautiously restricting the right of unlimited debate.

Until a few years ago, his glaring liability as a President for the 1960s seemed to be his vague, baffled view of foreign affairs. Indo-China he thought to be 'futile war'. Algeria was a remote nuisance, the contested islands of Quemoy and Matsu the proud ramparts we must watch, Africa and Asia were 'growing suburbs'. But nothing could be more unfair than to leave him with this air of a petulant provincial onlooker. In the last three years he sat in with President Kennedy through all the worst hours of the Bay of Pigs, Berlin, the missile crisis, South Vietnam, the McNamara-Pentagon feud, and the rest. 'The President,' he said a couple of years ago, 'carries heavier burdens than I ever envisioned. You feel goose pimples coming up on your back.' Because he is a doggedly untheoretical man, he has a capacity to digest unpleasant facts beyond his early experience. 'I hate this thing as much as you do,' he once shouted at a Senate colleague, 'but this is what is happening.'

What he has lately discovered 'is happening' is the enfranchisement of Africa, the revolt of Asia against the white man, the feudal upheaval of Latin America, the yearning of democratic Europe for self-reliance. Luckily, in ceremonial line of duty, he has visited most of the Allies as also Scandinavia and the Middle East, and is personally acquainted with some of the African leaders. He has declared himself most pungently on three great issues:

On civil rights – 'The words of the Declaration of Independence do not need to be further interpreted. They need to be implemented for all Americans.'

On the United Nations – 'It is very necessary. We would be at war without it.'

On peace – 'Reciprocity is the key. If the Soviets want America's cooperation, they can earn it. If the Soviets want America's hostility, they can certainly provoke it.'

In the melancholy waiting interval between the requiem and the inauguration, there are few certainties about the Johnson Administration. One of them is that he will take hold. And though the high style of the Kennedy regime is gone forever, as the White House reverts to the folksier manner of the county courthouse square, it will not surprise the friends of Lyndon Johnson if he emerges as a second Harry Truman, who arrived blinking in the White House one day, a failed haberdasher needing all our prayers, and the next, sprang fully armed as a brave, irascible all-American legionnaire, and more astonishing still, a twentieth-century statesman.

Coming Through

Letter No. 799, 29 December 1963

The carols, wrote an old New York writer, have not drowned out the requiem. I guess that puts it about as simply and truly as it can be said. But they made a brave try, once the mournful thirty days was over and the flags were hoisted to the top of their masts.

On the last day, last Saturday, I went across the Potomac River, which separates Washington from the state of Virginia, and went up the hill into Arlington National Cemetery. It is surely one of the most beautiful of cemeteries, planted on one of the noblest sites. Its four hundred acres describe a crescent-shaped plateau that slopes down across lawns and flower beds to the Potomac. From any of its ten gates, the road leads uphill to the top of a hill and the Doric columns and portico of a mansion once lived in by General Robert E. Lee. The cemetery was first laid out for the dead of the Union armies. As often happens with well-laid plans, the first man to be buried there was a Southerner, a Confederate soldier. He was only the first of many, and all the Confederates now lie on high ground to the west in a meadow known as Jackson Circle.

All the leaves had gone from the trees last Saturday, and it was possible to stand almost anywhere on the sloping ground and look around the crescent from the north and the west to the south and see the rows of simple white slabs running over the little hills as rhythmically as vines: these are the dead, the known and always one unknown, from all the wars since the Civil War. You look down to the river and Memorial Bridge, and beyond that are the weaving line of trees on the riverbank and, on the Washington side, the very white saucer dome and the supporting columns of the Jefferson Memorial, and just above it the pinkish white marble of the Lincoln Memorial, and to its right, towering over everything, the huge five hundred fifty-foot masonry shaft of the Washington Monument in the centre of its park and mall. On the rim of the horizon was the dome of the Capitol.

It was a brilliant winter day, cloudless and fogless, but as the sun burned out over the snowfields the temperature was down to a piercing twelve degrees: twenty degrees of frost. Crossing the Memorial Bridge going away from Washington and toward the cemetery, what you see straight ahead of you is the hill and main slope down to the river and the single, commanding Custis-Lee Mansion. But on Saturday, on a little plateau below it you could see a white square, and in the middle of it a curious point

President Kennedy's grave at Arlington National Cemetery.

of orange light. I suppose that from now on, as long as anyone can foresee, all the motorists who cross the bridge, either to go south or to go to work in the Pentagon, or to take an aeroplane at either of the Washington airports, will see this white rectangle and the light inside it. For this is the gravesite of John F. Kennedy. That, of course, was where I was bound.

I am not, myself, much disposed to lingering over these mournful rituals, and I must say I have always approved of the dispatch with which Americans bury their dead, usually within two days of the death. But one of the curious things about this event was its magnetic attraction for the young people. My son, in his early twenties and just graduated from college, is still living in the college town of Cambridge, Massachusetts, and on the Monday of the funeral he came into New York looking like a ghost. He came to tell me about his trip to Washington. He had flown down there from Cambridge the evening before and arrived outside the Capitol at about seven-thirty in the evening. He lined up with the longest and quietest queue anyone could remember, about a quarter million people who waited to go into the Capitol and see their President lying in state under the great Rotunda. My son, as I say, got there at half past seven in the evening. He stood, in biting cold, and got in at six in the morning, into the warmth of the Rotunda and the overpowering scent of flowers. He walked around the bier and came out and went to the airport and flew to New York and slept through the afternoon. Like many of his generation, he is not overly sentimental. He said, though, that he felt he just had to do it, and that what he would never forget was the way the crowds stood and talked, and there was only the smallest grumbling if someone jumped his place. 'I'd guess,' he said, 'that half, maybe three-quarters, of the people in line were students or kids of college age.'

Well, I don't know whether I inferred from this a rebuke that certainly was not intended. But finding myself in Washington last weekend, and knowing that Sunday was the last day of mourning, and seeing the hundreds of flags drooping at half-mast (for Washington, a city built as a political capital and nothing else, has more government buildings in one place than you will see anywhere), I thought I had better go and see the place where he was put to rest. As I walked down from the Lee mansion, down a hillside planted with wide, stone steps, the white rectangle revealed itself as a white picket fence; and already it was possible to feel that some small corner of New England had been planted there. A hundred, maybe two hundred people were lined up in single file along a narrow path that was covered with matting against the frost and snow. While I was there, and afterwards, and as long as the last of the sun allowed you to look back and see them, there were always the same number, moving and halting in a snake line. They stood there, again very many young people, freezing in blue jeans or shivering in corduroys and burying their heads in short jackets. The main problem for everyone was holding on to his ears, for after five or ten minutes the sensation was of having lost both your ears and your feet. We stamped and crouched against the knifing wind, and went up the hill and came nearer to the white rectangle and its guard of soldiers. Now you could see on the left a flat standing stone inscribed with the name of the lost baby of the midsummer. On the right was a small cross bearing the inscription, 'Baby Girl Kennedy', this one never came alive. In the middle was the mound with no stone or slab but at its head only a circle of flowers, with the seal of the United States described in purple flowers, and around the circle the words, 'President of the United States'. There was nothing but the mound of evergreen fronds and pine leaves and a few wreaths leaning up against it, and in the centre, a guttering flame, and around that the caps of the Army, Navy, Air Force and Marine Corps.

Considering that Washington is a monumental city, with avenues as wide as Paris, laid out as it was by a Frenchman at the end of the eighteenth century, you would naturally expect something austere and very grand. With all respect, indeed with a curious kind of respect you never would have anticipated, this looked like the hasty grave of, say, the town clerk or selectman of a small New England village who had died in the night. The picket fence is irregular, because the ground below it buckles and tilts: there had been no time to straighten it out or, I imagine, to hew and carve a tombstone. So there it was, the earthly remains of the thirty-fifth President beneath a tumble of leaves and fronds and pine cones and a few caps thrown on top, and no name. It had a sort of rural pathos about it, as if all our pretensions to riches and a career and power had been swept aside in the impromptu energy of some poor village gardener wanting to do his best, by way of tribute, before the nightfall.

The snake line of people paused on the hill side of the rectangle, and some people froze a stance and snapped pictures, and some just sauntered by, and a soldier or a Marine would pull himself straight and salute, and people lifted their necks out of their collars and looked awhile, or lifted up their small children and put them down and mooched on.

Then we drove back into Washington, dizzy with the cold, and got warm again and got ready for the evening. All kinds of random, and no doubt some bold and guilty thoughts came to me after this curious visit. But the one thing that stayed, and stays, with me, was the accidental humbleness of the grave, for though there was time to arrange a great funeral, and the great of many nations emphasized the loftiness and the solemnity and the splendor of the avenues all the way from the Capitol to the cathedral, and then down and across the Memorial Bridge, and all the way to Arlington, when you got there you saw this pile of leaves, and a straggly uneven fence around it. And John Kennedy might just as well have been the promising son of an Irish forbear who, like many another immigrant in Boston, was plucked untimely – by some swift epidemic – and buried in a bit of ground.

Then the Sunday came in, and then the Monday morning with a whirling snow-storm, and the flags, which, after all, are as neutral as clocks, flew high and angrily from the top of their staffs. This snowstorm, which blew in from, of all places, the Gulf of Mexico, chilled the usually warm Southland and tore across the Ozarks and the Plains, and blotted out the Eastern Seaboard and upstate New York and New England and blew itself out to sea.

So I think Tuesday was the dawn that we had been waiting for: a typical shining

Police force a rioter into a police car during the
second night of rioting in Los Angeles.

warned California to expect trouble from the Negroes in the Los Angeles suburbs. Just about the safest bet you could make today, except in the rural Midwest and in Vermont, which has practically no Negroes, is that you can expect violence almost any day, any month, in any Northern city you care to put your finger on.

'Northern' was not a slip of the tongue. We are just beginning to realize that the chances of open violence are greater where the Negro has more legal and social equality but still does not have the money or the jobs or the housing he would like. A sociologist at the University of Pennsylvania puts his finger on the irony that hurts. Dr Seymour Levantman says: 'The history of revolution shows that when conditions get better, people become more openly dissatisfied. The disparity between their lot and that of others becomes more evident. It is not accidental that rioting is occurring after the civil rights legislation, not before.'

This, naturally enough, is the puzzling part to most people, and the wounding part to President Johnson, and the civil rights leaders, and the young crusading students who go south to join the marchers, and to the former Attorney General, Robert Kennedy, and his successor Nicholas Katzenbach, who did so much to start the historic landslide of civil rights legislation that thundered through the Congress this year. Of course, every Negro is not going to get the vote this year or next, or share a white schoolteacher, good or bad, or have brand-new housing, or be given a white-collar job. Vast numbers of whites, by the way, are not going to get these things either. The simplest but most excruciating mistake that runs like wildfire through much testy criticism of the United States is to believe that the Negro is, if not in chains, everywhere subjected to a special and shameful code of legal humiliations not shared by white people at the same level of society. In the South, until lately, this has been true. Now, in the South, the energy and determination of the Federal Government, sending registrars and marshals and FBI agents and many brave, anonymous clerks into the last ditches of segregation, is something to see.

So, while the Negroes of the South are acquiring the common but vital privileges of citizenship – the ballot, the right to sit on juries, the right to a friend at court – the North, which has had most of these things for generations, explodes in an ecstasy of protest, against what? – against law, property, civil order, and its guardians. It happened, and it was much the same story last week in Los Angeles, in Chicago, in Springfield, Massachusetts. But the Los Angeles rioters, unlike the mobs in the seven rioting cities of last summer, took their protest a stage beyond the first great orgy of looting, which to people rattling around in the same smelly rooms, with the same jobless friends, must seem like an intoxicating whiff of freedom. The Los Angeles riot by the third night gave us sure warning of the next stage in the disintegration or protest of the cities. It turned into a race riot, a hard thing to define and something the Department of Justice very usefully pointed out last year did not describe the riots in those seven cities. It should be said that these things always seem to start the same way. A white policeman arrests a Negro, and having looked into several thousand pages of the records I dare to fly in the face of advanced opinion and say 'usually arrested for just cause.' The Los Angeles rioters, having taken their fill of liquor and television sets and groceries and furniture and cameras and cash registers and automobiles, turned then to the people of whom these luxuries are the symbols – the owner (not literally the owners, though I believe there was plenty of resentment and plenty of damage against absentee landlords); I mean the property owner's surrogate – the white man. They roamed after white men, and beat up light-skinned Negroes by mistake, and the fact that they also maimed and beat white people who were as poor or shiftless as themselves is not an accident but an inevitable incident of what had become a symbolic act of rage against the white man.

Let us be fairly clear about the kind of people we are talking about. We, as distinct from *Pravda* and the African radio, and I regret to say quite a few otherwise intelligent liberals, are not talking about decent Negroes hungry for a decent house and a place in society. We are not talking about people who want a vote or a seat on a jury, but people who want a television set, a case of bourbon, a girl, a snazzy car, and a wad of folding money. There are living in Watts the rather appalling number of over 500 criminals out on parole; and it would be a relief to tie up this discussion with the clincher that they started and led the riots. I am sure they were in there, and they must at all times form a ghastly elite corps for the young unemployed (twice the white rate), the bastards (one in four), the artful dodgers by the thousand who thus have 500 Fagins to instruct them in everything from petty thievery to drug addiction to the manufacture of Molotov cocktails.

But we have to remember that something very like the Watts explosion happened in Rochester, New York, last year, and in Springfield, Mass., last week, to the bewilderment of its sober citizens. I believe that the seed of these upheavals, the seed if you like of anarchy, is in the poor Negro's envy – not of the white man's vote or his education, but of the white man's fancied wealth and the baubles it buys. Whatever Watts lacks, it does not lack television aerials; I suppose if you sit in a mean room all through the day with a litter of listless children and a worn-down mother (the chances of there being a father in residence are only three in four), and you keep seeing the svelte girls in the automobile ads, and the young white Apollos, and the glowing families and the house in the pines secured by a mortgage from the silvery-haired saint in the friendly bank, I suppose you come to believe that this is the way the whites live. They have everything – not only the vote and the clean jobs and the mathematics, if you are interested – but all the goodies, and the money, and the golden girls. It is a kind of idiot version of the persistent European belief that all Americans are rich. (I saw a poor young student a few months ago trying to cross Germany on about ten dollars, and pretty empty-bellied most of the time. In one place a woman suggested he take a ferry up the Rhine. He mentioned he could not afford it. She almost fell down in a faint. She went off instead in a huff: 'Imagine,' she said, 'an American without money.')

Last year, I saw some of the looting in Harlem, and the signs were unmistakable in Watts, and Chicago, and Springfield. The envy satisfied in the moment of seizing sometimes useless luxuries, but luxuries that are the shortcut to the good life, which is not coming soon, a truth that all the trumpets about civil rights only mock.

I said earlier we could list forever reasons why this should not have happened in Watts. The sociologists and psychologists and police and politicians have rushed in with all the reasons why it should happen: the Negro birthrate is half again as high as the white; illegitimacy four times; unemployment twice as bad; school drop-outs three times; therefore, two or three times as many people to a room; therefore, crime rate four or five times that of the most comparable white neighbourhood: a steadily growing population of young, idle, and corrupt Negroes, already beyond the reach of appeals to citizenship and beyond much interest in liberty or education but only in the more dazzling fruits of education.

I do not know if it will help much to have isolated this tragic strain of envy, a twisted form of ambition. Or to have mentioned the pimping role of television with its tantalizing exposure of the white man's dainties for sale – perhaps for looting – at your nearest grocer or department store. But these things do not get mentioned by the city fathers, who either moan about morals or say the rioters of Watts must be given a new high school, or more federal funds. What they need at the moment is a full-time birth-control programme, the safe return of some of those parolees to jail, a couple of churches, a public-works project, six playing-fields, and an army of coloured men in the police force.

Walt Disney: 1901–1966

Guardian, 15 December 1966

Walt Disney, the Pied Piper of Hollywood, who made a mountain of money out of a mouse, died today in Burbank, California, at the age of sixty-five.

There was very little in the early life of Walter Elias Disney to show that he would emerge by his twenty-fifth birthday as the most revolutionary motion-picture talent after Chaplin. The vital statistics, padded out from newspaper files, suggest a boyhood as corny as Kansas in August.

A Midwestern upbringing, the son of a carpenter who tried his hand at farming (so as to introduce the young Walt to a menagerie of adorable animals), a full stretch of grade school, an incomplete spell in high school, a boy of little scholarship and a lively appetite for games who picked up pin-money in winter as a newspaper delivery boy, and in summer as a candy butcher (sweets salesman) on the Kansas City-Chicago train. It is the standard biography of many another American folk hero.

But there are, as always, details that mar the stereotype. His father had a burning passion for Socialism and a worship of its embattled hero, Eugene Victor Debs. Old man Disney voted for fifty years without picking a Presidential winner. He also took in an inflammatory weekly called *The Appeal to Reason*. Its appeal to the young Disney was a regular front-page cartoon always showing, in opposition, two other stereotypes: a fat capitalist and an honest working man.

The boy had their likenesses down cold after several issues and was admired in the family as an up-and-coming artist. He was so regarded by the local barber, who encouraged him to exchange a cartoon for a free haircut. In the country, he sketched away at animals and flowers, and after 'a course in photography' quit high school for good and, at sixteen, enlisted in the First World War as an ambulance driver.

His first job when the war was over was as a commercial artist with an advertising company. He went from there to a cartoonist's job on a film weekly and began to experiment on his own with cartoon slides. He soon wanted to see them in motion and drew a series of Kansas City doings for local theatres. They bore the awful name of Laugh-o-Grams.

That was in 1922. The next year, the pioneer's legend takes up again with his flight to Hollywood – with a borrowed capital of forty dollars and the sketches of a film that

would set a living girl against a cartoon background. At last, in 1926, he was signed by a genuine, licensed studio, Universal no less, to draw and direct its *Oswald the Lucky Rabbit* cartoons. At the end of two years, there was a violent artistic quarrel over the next stage of the Rabbit's career, and Disney went out on his own and brooded over a mouse he had drawn on his railroad runs.

After two efforts that were scrapped as amateur, he came through with *Steamboat Willie*, which had the luck to make shrewd use of the new device of sound. Disney never had any further need to borrow money.

Within the next three years, and throughout the next ten, the English-speaking world cheered Mickey Mouse, the Japanese clucked over Miki Kuchi, Spain and Latin America saluted Miguel Ratonocito.

In no time he was the first cartoon millionaire of the film industry, and for the next decade there poured out of his studio (an original staff of three soared to 700) skeleton dances and 'Silly Symphonies' and the noisy adventures of Pluto, Donald Duck, and the rest of the irascible family.

So long as he cherished his outrageous ducks and mice and wolves, he was the darling of the intelligentsia. But *Snow White and the Seven Dwarfs* (with their sweetness, cuteness, and light) doomed him as a highbrow renegade. But it also doomed him to a world gross of eight million dollars.

Luckily for most of the world's moviegoers, Disney was a rollicking and uncomplicated soul, who never felt that his ardent sentimentality was at odds with the Marx Brothers anarchy of Donald Duck. He went ahead with his *Pinocchio*, *Fantasia*, *Bambi*, *Peter and the Wolf*, and all the other 18-carat whimsies of the pre-Beat children's world.

Just when he had found a golden formula and an unflagging world market, he returned to his first passion: the delineation, in colour and sound, of the natural world. The critics have not forgiven him for upsetting his well-taped reputation by producing the glowing *Beaver Valley* and *Nature's Half-acre* and then invading television with brilliantly stylised documentaries of the life of the desert and the ocean bottom.

For this prodigal output, he was rewarded with more than 120 foreign and domestic decorations and honorary degrees. His epitaph must be not unlike that bestowed by Chesterton on Dickens: 'The critics blushed but the people wept and cheered.'

Walt Disney, 'the first cartoon millionaire of the film industry.'

Muhammad Ali's Challenge

Guardian, 4 May 1967

The pugnacity of Muhammad Ali (Cassius Clay) has moved out of the ring into the courts and now onto the leader pages of the American press.

He may be a source of mixed emotions to the Black Muslim cult that is subsidised so heavily by his earnings. He may be merely a celebrated nuisance to the Army in which he refused to serve. But he is an idol to the militant young Negroes, a useful cat's-paw to the liberal critics of Vietnam, a fine scapegoat for the racialists, and an awkward challenge to the constitutional doctrine of freedom of conscience.

'In a somewhat blurred but discernible form,' wrote the *New York Times* last week, 'he poses to the nation the issue of selective conscientious objection to military service.'

'Selective conscientious objection' is known to the young of all shades of pigment and opinion as 'picking the war that's worth fighting'. Other objectors have been fined for tearing up draft cards or refusing to fight in Vietnam after getting into uniform. But Ali is the first famous man to rationalise his deep distaste for the Army by combining in a legal plea all the arguments that are being used by saints and sinners against the system of compulsory military service.

He claimed exemption on four main counts. That while he is not against war on principle, he cannot fight a war unsanctioned by the will of Allah. That he is entitled to deferment as a practising minister of religion. That he cannot submit to a system that denies to Negroes a fair representation on the draft boards. That, as a coloured man, he cannot fight in a war waged against the dark skins of Asia.

The first two claims were disposed of by the federal courts for the obvious reason that the judges did not believe that Muhammad Ali is by profession a full-time minister of the Lost-Found Nation of Islam (commonly known as the Black Muslims), who picks up a little money on the side as a part-time boxer, commonly known as Cassius Clay.

Though this pretence is thought to be the least plausible of Clay's arguments, it will be brought up in the subsequent appeal, as the denial of a citizen's right to belong to a minor religion. The tradition is, of course, as well established in this country as anywhere else that a regular practitioner of religion who renounces all war can be classified without fuss as a conscientious objector. In the past, several odd religions, like the Sons of Heaven and the Jehovah's Witnesses, have had trouble convincing the

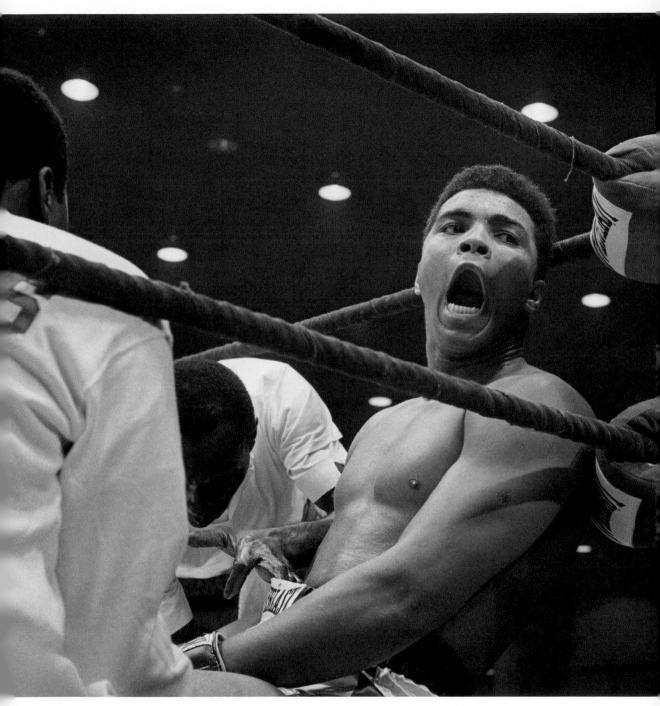

Muhammad Ali at a moment of victory having defeated Sonny Liston
for the heavyweight championship of the world in 1964.

Army, not to mention the neighbours, that they were a legitimate and dedicated cult. Out of Ali's protest on this ground has arisen the debating cry: 'Why excuse only the Quakers?' The last two objections (those of a Negro against the war in Vietnam) are part of the new and general thesis that says a citizen has a constitutional right to express his liberty of conscience by refusing to serve in a particular war.

It is generally assumed that Ali's delaying tactics will simply put off his commitment to a maximum five years in jail and a $10,000 fine. But by the time his case comes to the Supreme Court, it might appear to contain hard nuggets of debatable law that could challenge the whole democratic theory that the dissenting citizen must bow to the majority of assenting citizens.

The editorial argument is being put forward that the majority decision about Vietnam has been made by the President of the United States and the Congress. No doubt Congress would declare war if the President asked it to; but so far Congress has forgone its exclusive constitutional privilege to make a declaration of war. Over a century ago, a vice president of the United States, and the Southern leader of the 'War Hawks' (so called at the time), advanced his theory of the 'concurrent majority', the idea that a federal law should not be binding on a dissenting state. Muhammad Ali has now extended to the dissenting citizen the theory of John C. Calhoun, and probably he will get no further with it than Calhoun did.

But he has behind him the most courageous as well as the most irresponsible voices of the young rebels. They could, in a legal upset, make mincemeat of the general assumption that if a citizen has the right to tear up his draft card, the state has the following right to put him in jail.

The Permissive Society

Guardian, 26 October 1967

If the 'permissive society', as the phrase is now used, has a manifesto, John Dewey's *The School and Society*, published in 1899, is it. And the Teachers College of Columbia University was its seedbed.

Naturally, there had been rebels against traditional education before Dewey, notably Horace Mann, who died in 1859, the year Dewey was born. But the turn of the century heard the first piping cries of 'progressive education', so called, and its midwife was Dewey. By the late 1930s, the word 'permissive' had come into American English bearing a special meaning. It was pronounced in a low, proud tone by Dalton and other progressive teachers. It was an invocation that banished slavery from education and promised enlightenment, spontaneity, the 'identification' of the child with his studies in a new and passionate way. It implied that the three Rs, parrot teaching, learning dates, getting poetry by rote, boning up on Euclid, or the Battle of Austerlitz, had been exposed as the symptoms of an authoritarian system. God said, 'Let Dewey be!' and there was light.

From then on, happy pupils would bound like kangaroos to schools where 'expression' (expressed with astounding and illiterate verbosity) was encouraged; where handicraft gave way to rubbing the soul in 'textures', and the study of historical periods was supplanted by trips into the Fenimore Cooper country to bring home to the budding New Yorker the very touch and smell of the life of the Algonquin Indians. To be truthful, I have known such children who really did leave school with a vivid and accurate knowledge of the way the earliest inhabitants of Manhattan lived and ordered society, even if they had never heard of the Bill of Rights, a dangling participle, or the Thirty Years' War. Of course, it is easy now to mock the later absurdities of progressive education, which came under brutal attack in the early 1950s, so much so that rednecks from Louisiana to Southern California, egged on by the late Senator Joseph McCarthy, howled for a return to the rod and the little red schoolhouse. But progressive education had already done its duty, or its mischief, and not in the private school either. Its reforming course had so changed the elementary schools that many a McCarthyite, screaming for the blood of the progressives, was unaware that his own strong belief in unit teaching, school projects, individual attention, and compulsory

courses in a life science and civics had come from nowhere but Columbia and nobody but Dewey. The Progressive Education Association, founded as a standard bearer in 1915, had done its work so well that it was dissolved in 1955.

This stress on the origins of permissive learning and teaching is worth making because, outside the United States certainly, so many bewildered parents, conservatives, and reactionaries talk as if the permissive society had sprung up spontaneously on a signal out of Millbrook, New York, from Dr Timothy Leary under the influence.

I am not, on the contrary, saying that it all goes back in an orderly and sinister fashion to John Dewey, or to Marx, or Freud, though much of what now passes for individual expression, freedom, and constitutional rights derives from a mass misinterpretation of all three. But the actual vehemence and universality of the beatnik, hippy, teeny-bopper, acid-head revolution is harder to explain. It cannot be said to be a revolt against authority, for authority has been crumbling in all Western societies, as it has been stiffening in Communist countries, since the First World War.

But it is, I take it, the freewheeling young we are talking about. Who are the hippies? Lamentably little scientific work has been done on their genes and their social history, though a limited New York psychiatric study asserts that as many as 60 percent are seriously sick, mostly with schizophrenia. But we do know that they tend to come from better rather than worse educated families, that their parents are rarely impoverished but have a high incidence either of divorce or of rigid morality. We know also that the children of Catholics and religious Jews are very much in the minority among the new rebels. And – a saving statistic – that hippies and their vagabond variations account for less than 10 percent of the young.

Drug addiction, however, widely overlaps the 'squares'. Nor are hippiedom, sexual licence, the flower phenomenon merely indigenous to metropolises that have always tolerated a Bohemian quarter. Of course, they flourish there in most conspicuous anonymity. The provincial strictness of the Old South and the farming Midwest covers up, for the time being, the more outlandish forms of hippiedom. But their children too are off to the cities; and cities across the whole continent have their proportionate quota. The draft card burners know no geographical limits. The mystery, which no mere perambulating journalist should try to solve, is how it comes about that the rebel young appear, in East Berlin and East St Louis, in the same international uniform, that they profess the same half-baked 'philosophies' and rustle as indistinguishable as cockroaches over three or four continents.

The mass media take the blame for everything these days. And until a better theory comes along, it will have to do to wonder why the children of Nigeria have forgotten their native songs and echo the Beatles; why a sit-down in the London School of Economics is inspired by the same types as organised the shenanigans at Berkeley. We can be sure of only one thing: that he who runs no longer has to read. He can simply see a Californian smoking pot on the telly, rush out into a Wimbledon backyard, grab a handful of the stuff, and do the same.

A summer solstice celebration at Golden Gate Park in
San Francisco, June 1967.

Harvesting the Grapes of Wrath

Guardian, 4 January 1968

Ronald Reagan, who went at a bound from a television serial star, General Electric promotion man, and Goldwater helper to the Governorship of California, has been sitting in Sacramento, amid the cypresses and gingko trees, under the great white dome of the State Capitol, for over a year now. In the contrived intervals of a working schedule as tight as an invasion plan, he is off and around the country at rallies, college debates, and banquets, raising packets for the Republican campaign fund, a service that is either done in an orgy of altruism or on the off-chance, about which he is not quite able to convey the incredulity he mimics, that he might hold the trumping ace over the next Republican Convention, and panic it into nominating him for President.

For the time being, there's no doubt that he has his homegrown troubles. His handling of them is more significant than it would be in Vermont or, for that matter, in Ohio, because in twenty-five years California has developed from a lush fruit bowl, film studio, and sunny haven for retired farmers and playboys into the First State of the Union in more things than numbers. All the chronic social, industrial, and rural problems of America today are here in acute form. A man who can administer California with imagination and good order is one who, unlike anyone else, except perhaps a mayor of New York City, would hold powerful credentials to preside over the United States.

Once you have boasted about the power, the population, and the resources of the First State of the Union, you have to do something about the jungle growth of the cities; the turmoil on the campuses; the conflict about compulsory unionism between organized labour and the freewheeling labour force; the unceasing inflow of 1,200 new settlers a day, loading the relief rolls and straining the welfare budget; not to mention the bewildering mobility of hundreds of thousands of part-time workers, deadbeats, runaway hippies, 'suitcase' farmers, and the shuttling agents of the Mafia.

All this is producing ruinous invasions of the treasury and subjecting a governor who campaigned on economy to the embarrassment of a record five-billion-dollar budget, which by state law he is bound to balance. 'In the last eight years,' he says, 'the budget has had a 12 percent annual increase. Last year it was 16 percent.' He puts

Governor Reagan stands by a mosaic of the California State Seal in the state capital, Sacramento.

this down partly, of course, to the openhanded fiscal extravagance of his predecessor, the Democrat 'Pat' Brown. But after a few months of a new administration the voters are indifferent to the sins of the absent: they ask the immemorial question of the incumbent, 'What are you doing for me right now?'

Committed to a show of economy, he maintains that inflation and the state's growth would justify an annual budget increase of just over 7 percent. He has doggedly instituted a study of the tax system to try to achieve this miracle. But the demands of welfare, Medi-Cal, and free higher education for everybody 'are increasing at a rate so fantastic that to satisfy them we'd have to have a state tax increase every two years. Illinois, for instance, has reduced the number of people on welfare by 8 percent. Ours goes up by 54.6 percent a year! And Medi-Cal by something between 30 and 60 percent.' Medi-Cal is California's name for the state medical care programme which the Federal Medicare law allows each state to adopt. Reagan believes that in this, as in other forms of bounty, the theory of social welfare has gone way beyond the capacity of the state to afford.

'Look at this,' he snaps as he slides open a drawer and seizes a handbill, a promotion item for a free state convalescent hospital: 'fully carpeted rooms, modern automated beds, the best of modern treatment, television, three succulent entrées on every menu; the atmosphere of a resort hotel.' 'This,' he says, 'is a delusion – that you can give everybody free the same level of care as the richest man can afford. The medically indigent are something else – and they should come first. But we've given a credit card to 1,300,000 people.'

In his big hassle with the Regents of the University of California about 'the traditional right of free education,' he tried, and failed, to institute a small tuition fee. He believes that somebody, the Federal Government or the State, is going to have to charge a fifty-cent fee for a doctor's visit, something for drugs, and some check on the general assumption 'that you can dash off to a brain surgeon with a headache.' 'I think you will find,' he says without producing the documents, 'that in the countries where they've introduced a national health service, they have underestimated their health budget by as much as five times.' California, at any rate, seems to be having its own grim experience of subsidising hypochondria on a mammoth scale.

What about the cities? He heaves a sigh and pops a cough tablet in his mouth against what he grinningly describes as 'a slight case of instant pneumonia'. He has deep doubts about the President's Commission study, or about encouraging the surplus farm population to come into the cities. 'My God, the O.E.E. [Office of Emergency Employment] brought the Indians in. It was a disaster – they learned to be delinquent, or alcoholic. I think we have to take a new look at the whole idea of great cities. I doubt that stacking them higher and higher is the answer; we should explore decentralisation, and I don't mean the fringe suburb. If the jobs stay in the city the suburbanites are chained to the old cities, and the traffic and maintenance programmes will become unbearable. I'm talking about settling new towns in the open spaces. We might see how far the people would move if the job moved with them.'

This is the long run. How about the short and frightful run of riots and racism, burn, baby, burn? He is suddenly quite calm. 'Once we have violence, we've got to have enforcement – prompt and certain. We've been lacking in enforcement. The criminal must know he'll be punished at once.' He is so clear and unspeculative about this that we don't pursue the toughening procedures of the Oakland police or the questionable threats of Mayor Yorty of Los Angeles to crack down with force on all malefactors or apparent malefactors when the trouble starts.

And supposing he had to declare himself on the election issues for 1968? 'Vietnam may not be there, but if it is it'll be issue number one. Either way the great issue is an umbrella issue, what I call the Morality Gap: crime, obscenity, delinquency, the abandonment of law. Demonstrations must be within the limits of civil disobedience. Labour and student disputes should start with negotiations, not, my God, with a strike. Now, they all take to the streets at once.'

You leave him having gained an impression of an engaging kind of energy. He is precise and thoughtful on finance and the mechanics of welfare, quietly dogmatic about the social ferment. He talks no jargon, which is a rare relief. He chants few slogans. He does not preach or intone. He sounds like a decent, deadly serious, baffled, middle-class professional man. This, as an executive geared for social rebellion and reform, may be his weakness. But it is his strength among the voters that, in a country with a huge middle class, he so faithfully reflects their bewilderment at the collapse of the old, middle-class standards, protections, and, perhaps, shibboleths.

The Cost of the Vietnam War

Letter No. 1000, 24 March 1968

I wish that this thousandth *Letter From America* could be about the Spring or American children, or any one of the many amiable things we've talked about down the years. But it must be about the thing that bewilders the American people like nothing else in all these thousand weeks. For last week, the Administration was brought to the bar of a standing committee of Congress and nothing, either in a parliamentary or a federal system, can offer such an inquisition as a Congressional inquiry, which is the nerve system of what Americans like to call 'the democratic process'. And nowhere is it seen to more impressive effect than in the cross-examination of a Secretary of State by the Senate Foreign Relations Committee, which, among other things, has the power to reject ambassadors and treaties proposed by the President.

So now the committee was anxious to recall the President to his constitutional duty to seek the advice and consent of the Senate on a war that had got away from both of them. The undeclared war in Vietnam. Here was the Secretary of State called as the President's understudy and subjected to the third degree by the representatives of the people. And if that sounds a little lurid or sentimental let me remind you of the cast of characters that sat like a court of judges the other day and challenged Secretary Dean Rusk from ten in the morning to six-thirty one day and from nine to two the next. There was a farmer from Vermont, a mining engineer from Montana, a Rhodes scholar from Arkansas, the schoolteacher son of a hardware merchant from South Dakota, an electric products manufacturer from Missouri, a stockman from Kansas, a professor of Far Eastern history, a former Secretary of the Air Force, six lawyers – not too many to reflect the preponderance of lawyers who sit in Congress and who do, after all, make the laws. None of these men had been in the Senate for less than twelve years, and the farmer had been there twenty-eight years and two others for twenty-four years.

Secretary Rusk had resisted this call for two years, but then there was a well-substantiated rumour that General William Westmoreland wanted another 200,000 troops, and suddenly the world expressed its distrust of American policy by losing its confidence in the dollar. For two days Secretary Rusk was questioned and quizzed and lectured to and pleaded with by a committee whose old ratio of hawks to doves was

Wounded First Cavalry men wait to be evacuated from
a hilltop during their advance on Khe Sahn.

significantly shrinking. The role of Chairman William Fulbright as a scold and ironist
could now be presumed. So could the ringing patriotism of Senator Karl Mundt of
South Dakota and the troubled curiosity of young Senator Frank Church of Idaho, and
the holy wrath of Senator Wayne Morse of Oregon, God's favourite maverick.

But last week only Fulbright and Morse stayed with the usual script; the others
were sufficiently disturbed to think aloud with more honesty and eloquence than they
had shown before, and all of them maintained a gravity and courtesy such as men
do when they're scared, when they're losing an attitude and acquiring an anxiety.
Nothing was more startling than Senator Mundt's suspicion that elections in South
Vietnam were not alone worth ensnaring half a million Americans into the continental
bog of Southeast Asia. And a bugle sounding the retreat is not more ominous than
the confession of Senator Stuart Symington, a resolute hawk, that he was now a prey
to misgiving. Senator Symington had been saying for years that the war had better
be won or written off, since the day was coming when the United States would have
to weigh the cost of it in gold that wasn't there. He's always been indulged by his
colleagues and friends as a man riding a comical hobbyhorse. Last week he had the sad
satisfaction of being taken seriously.

And, at last, the American casualties in Vietnam surpassed those of Korea, a turn
that I suggested a year ago would be the hardest test of the people's tolerance of the

war. So we were starting all over again with the fundamental questions. How had it come about? Was it indeed a crusade or a vast miscalculation? Would Asia crumble to Communism if South Vietnam fell? Was it the wrong war in the wrong place or the right war in the wrong place? Was the United States the only man in the boat rowing in time?

A hundred books and a thousand editorial writers have recited and disputed the political origins of the war and enlarged on the human tragedy of its conduct. What matters or will come to matter to most people, I think, is not any new balance we can strike in the old argument but the realisation that America, which has never lost a war, is not invincible; and the very late discovery that an elephant can trumpet and shake the earth but not the self-possession of the ants who hold it. So when I say how did it come about I'm not thinking of splitting the hair between the Southeast Asia Treaty's pledge to resist aggression and the American protocol that stipulated Communist aggression. I mean how did the American people move from their early indifference or complacency to the recognition of a nightmare?

Well, the war crept up on us with no more menace than a zephyr. South Vietnam was only one of many strange place names that joined the noble roll call of countries that America, in the early glow of its world power, swore to protect and defend. If Russia, that atomic dinosaur, could be scared off Iran and Greece and Turkey and foiled in Western Europe, it never crossed our minds that we couldn't intimidate Asian Communists who fought with sticks and stones. Certainly it would have been churlish to deny these brave little countries the handful of American technicians they needed to train their armies.

Lyndon Johnson came in, and for a year or more, the shadow of Vietnam failed to darken the bright procession of legislation he drove through the 89th Congress. It dawned on us very slowly that the American technicians were turning into American soldiers. Then we admitted that the men were off to the rice paddies and not to desks behind the lines. The draft felt the chill, and the college boys and the Vietniks were born. It was not with most of them a conscientious objection to war itself. Most, I think, would have admitted that Hitler had to be stopped and that Korea, the first United Nations war, was a good war. But they were baffled by the morality of this war that killed more civilians than soldiers and devastated the land we were sworn to protect, a war in which there were no attacks at dawn, no discernible lines, and few human restraints, either of rules or weapons. 'Napalm' and 'fragmentation bombs' entered the language and sickened us, though our own strategic bombing of Dresden in the Second World War had been worse than Hiroshima, and millions of women and children had been routed from their homes in Europe too. War, the administration could only remind us, was hell. So we piled up the forces and piled on the force and dropped more bombs than all the bombs dropped in Europe and Africa in the Second War.

These and many other doubts and disasters were aired and tossed before Dean Rusk. The administration's position had something of the straightforward grandeur of Johann Sebastian Bach. If only Bach were the tune that's called for. The theme was that the war in Asia was a continuation of the European struggle, first against Hitler, then against the Russians. The United States was pledged to resist aggression against free nations; if one pledge was betrayed then the other wards and dependants would panic and succumb to Communism. The countries of Southeast Asia are a stack of dominoes, and if one falls, so will they all.

It seems to me that anybody who ridicules this theory is obliged to say how and why it's wrong and to suggest some better way of, as Dean Rusk puts it, organising the peace, either through the United Nations or through some other alliance that can guarantee preponderant power. Preponderant power – that has always been the true deterrent – in spite of the Christian rhetoric that breathed so piously through the pre-amble to the Treaty of Westphalia (1648) and through the preamble to the Charter of the United Nations (1945). All these favourable balances of power have expressed that power through their willingness to use their ultimate weapon. Today, it seems to me, the United States is the world's greatest power, but only through its nuclear power. And what is never acknowledged – the universal taboo against the use of this power – dis-arms America at a blow and leaves it a large and rich but far from omnipotent power capable of fighting one or two unconventional wars with conventional weapons.

This, it seems to me, is the real American position in the world today and the rea-son why its best aims are frustrated. The United States has 132 military bases abroad and solemn treaty commitments to come to the aid of forty-three nations if they're attacked or, what is more likely these days, disrupted from within. The earnest and gentle Senator Church put his finger on this Achilles heel by asking the Secretary if the great conflict was not between commitment and capacity. In other words, America may be right but is she able?

How did it come about that this country, led successively by a soldier, then an alert foreign affairs student, and then by the shrewdest of politicians, committed itself to play St George to forty-three dragons? We must go back to what I called the early glow of American world power in the early 1950s. That is when the pledges were given and when the cost of them was never counted. The Communists, not to mention the nationalists, and the millions of Asians who simply want to see the white man leave their continent for good, had not attempted a test of American power. As late as the day of Kennedy's inauguration, the United States was still flexing and rippling its muscles for lack of exercise. And on that day the President delivered himself of a sentence magnificent as rhetoric, appalling as policy. Secretary Rusk, very much moved, recited it the other day to the Committee as the touchstone of America's resolve: 'Let every nation know, whether it wishes us well or ill, that we shall pay any price, bear any burden, meet any hardship, support any friend, oppose any foe, to assure the survival and the success of liberty.' This, I suggest, is fine to read but fatal to act on. It may be the wish of a strong nation to do this, but in reality it will not support any friend or fight any foe or bear any hardship or support the burden, say, of a civil war in its own land, in order to rush to the aid of forty-three friends and fight forty-three foes. Vietnam, I fear, is the price of the Kennedy inaugural.

The Death of Martin Luther King, Jr.

Letter No. 1002, 7 April 1968

This is certainly a bad time for the lighter side of American life. I had meant to report President Johnson's astonishing notice of withdrawal from running again given last Sunday night. For a day and a night, a very rare mood of benevolence and hope settled on the American people. The old, the unloved L.B.J. was dead. On the second day, he was sanctified. But the third day saw the resurrection of Foxy Grandpa. We had bombed well over two hundred miles inside North Vietnam, and a great gust of disillusion swept over the land, only to be dispersed again by the word from Hanoi that it was ready to meet and talk, if only about what a bombing pause really meant.

It was on this almost elated note that most of us went out on Thursday evening, waiting for Vice President Hubert Humphrey to put himself in the race, chattering about Vietnam, wondering all over again if L.B.J. might not after all, be making a sincere, and succeeding, attempt to leave an honoured name. Few of us were thinking, for once, about the troubles of the cities, the troubles past or the violence to come. I walked into an apartment house just before 8 o'clock that evening to spend, as always, a genial evening with my droll old friend, Donnelly. After six years in London and one in New York, he is going back to live in California and bring to that stimulating but distracted state the balm of his irony and humour. He was neither an ironical nor a humorous man, and when he opened the door I knew it at once. He looked like a man who had just suffered some shattering private loss. 'Have you heard?' he said. And then I did.

We stayed for the whole evening and part of the night with the television, as most of us do these days in despairing times. And if you think that the night of the riot in Detroit was a bad time, it was nothing like last Thursday. 'The last prince of nonviolence,' as one violent Negro leader called Dr King, was dead and gone. We had heard, we had been warned, for a year or two now, by the Black Power boys and the more militant Negroes, that Dr King was a sop to the white conscience, a failing Kerensky whose very patience and moderation guaranteed the revolution. 'Old Uncle Tom King', the more malign people of his race called him.

But in quieter moments they hoped, and in all our moments we prayed, that he could remain the flywheel, the one sane and stabilizing influence on the Negro rebel-

On the balcony of the Lorraine Motel immediately after
the assassination of Dr Martin Luther King, Jr.

lion. He was a thoughtful and serene man. But he was essentially a simple man also,
preaching nothing but the precepts of the New Testament. I think we all felt guilty
about his patience and enormous courage, as he walked into the valley of death so
many times. He was in this sense the white man's stand-in, and braver than any of us.
Because he acted out what we only thought and hoped, we feel very guilty about his
murder. Guilt, as we all know, breeds anxiety, and there's no doubt that everywhere
people look with bated breath toward the immediate retaliations of this early warm
spring and to the possible inferno of the hot summer.

There is no sensible point in going into the details of Dr King's last journey to Memphis. This is yet another American town, by the way, that echoed pleasantly through
the American memory – until one ugly night. When you think of all these towns that
have stained their name with a single night of violence: Oxford, Mississippi, which
once we thought of as the home and the seedbed of the genius of William Faulkner;
Little Rock, Arkansas, passed into the lighter folklore of the country with the help of
the gargoyle charm of Miss Carol Channing, the 'little girl from Little Rock' who gave
to the wisdom of the race the idea that 'diamonds are a girl's best friend'; Birmingham,
Alabama, used to be the home of Bessemer Steel. Rochester, New York, was where the
Kodak came from. Detroit was the proud inventor of the assembly line, and it was a
compulsory stop in the old days for tourists who wanted to see with their own eyes the
marvel of motorcars forming on a belt like sausages. And now Memphis.

Over and over, the television commentators kept saying that the dangerous core
of the city was around Beale Street. And I remembered my first visit there, long ago,
a very young white man strolling on a hot August morning, safe as the wind, along a

street that to me was as magical as the Acropolis to a classical scholar. Two Negroes were bent over a tire they were fixing. And one of them was tapping the rim and setting the beat for the blues they were singing together in low harmony. I thought the other night of the lyrics of the *Beale Street Blues*:

'Well, if Beale Street could talk,
If Beale Street could talk,
Married men would have to take their beds and walk,
Except one or two, who never sing those blues,
And the blind man on the corner who sings his Beale Street Blues,
Well I'd rather be there than any place I know,
Because New York may be all right,
But Beale Street's paved with gold.'

Well, on Thursday night, it was paved with blood. And it will be from now on like the Dallas Blues, one song that no party will care to play or sing with any taste or tact. 'Don't ever ask me again,' said Donnelly's wife, 'where I come from.' She was born in Memphis.

Bobby Kennedy stood on Thursday night before a crowd of Negroes in Indianapolis. It was dark, and it was cold, and he stood hunched up against the glare of a harsh spotlight. 'I have some very bad news for you all,' he said, and he told them. 'Those of you,' he went on, 'who are black can be filled with bitterness, with hatred, and a desire for revenge. We can move in that direction as a country, or we can make an effort, as Martin Luther King did, to understand and to replace that violence with compassion and with love. I can feel in my heart,' he said, 'what many of you must be feeling.' He paused. He had never said in public what he said next. 'I had a member of my family killed, and he was killed by a white man.' I think he is the one white man in the United States on Thursday evening who could have walked safely anywhere through the Negro slums.

But now, what? All the advice of our leaders, no matter how nobly written or spoken, cannot supply another stand-in for the white man who had hoped, against all the mounting violence, that enough could be done for the Negro to settle the cities and give the country a sense, which it has lacked since that other Black Friday in Dallas, that it was meeting its problems and moving ahead of them. One thing you have to say if you have travelled much outside this country. We are not complacent or apathetic about the actual social problems of 1968. I myself have marvelled in other countries and in other vast and stinking ghettoes that the people seemed so resigned, and their leaders so smug. You get back here, and you sigh for a while, and then you talk to mayors and social workers and Negroes and governors and officials big and small; and you have to recognize that an awful lot of people in power are bending what energies they have to perform the Herculean labors that the poor, and the Negroes most of all, demand of them.

The Swedish economist and sociologist Gunnar Myrdal wrote a book twenty-some years ago, called *The American Dilemma*. It was a huge study of the sore thumb in the American landscape. I'm talking about the position of the Negro. I read Myrdal again some months ago. I'm afraid he called the turn exactly, but not – it should be said crisply – in his 1,482 pages. The gist of his conclusions were two: that after the Second World War (the book was published in 1944) the Negro would begin a new and radical move toward securing his paper rights in the flesh; and that the more his condition improved, the worse things would be for everybody.

It's odd that we never guessed this in the early and rousing stages of the Negro revolution, after the Supreme Court integration decision of 1954, after the first civil rights bill of 1958, after the succeeding, and more emancipating bills. As the Negro got the vote, and went onto juries, and sat in lunchrooms and trains alongside white men, and mixed in theatres; and increasingly as Negroes have moved up (and they are moving up) from field labour and unskilled factory jobs into offices and telephone switchboards and white collar management; as this has happened, and even more if a Negro has found a decent low-rent house, he is not to our amazement overcome with gratitude. He is furious. He sees what he's been denied all these generations. His friends now envy him, and he envies what he might have been.

This is the essence, I think, of what is happening now. And what is going to go on happening. We used to say, with a silly sense of injured fair play, that the Negroes, having had a distant glimpse of the Promised Land, wanted the millennium by Monday morning. Well, there are still footloose, vicious Negroes who think and act like that. But what is in a way more threatening for a stable country is the new recognition in the solid mass of poor Negroes of what life might be like, and what it might have been. They always knew they were poor. Now they feel poor. It can convert placid people into dynamos.

Yet the pace at which any government – federal, state, city – can move with the best will in the world is not miraculous, not miraculous enough perhaps for the aroused slum populations. Again I'd like to say, as I did some months ago, that the idea abroad of Americans living in unimaginable slums is nonsense. Watts, for a glaring example, would not be a slum in almost any other country. But God knows we have them, and I'm not going to start the shabby business of comparing one slum with another. I'll only say that one American in ten lives below what the government calls subsistence level. That is, earns less than the equivalent of 1,300 pounds a year. The slums are awful, but so are they in many cities I know and you know. Yet here, the people rise because they have had dinned into them the gorgeous promises of the Declaration of Independence and the Constitution and the mumble-jumble of the American way of life. We talk too much. And promise too much. We are victims of our own advertising. We whites hoped the Negroes would follow Dr King in forgetting the advertising and the gaudy promises and in living by deeper, older values to counsel patience and embrace martyrdom. He had his Martyrdom.

A Mule Cortège for the Apostle of the Poor

Guardian, 9 April 1968

Once before, the ninth of April was a memorial day throughout the South. One hundred and three years ago today, Robert E. Lee tendered his sword to General Ulysses S. Grant and was granted in return the release of his 'men and their mules to assist in the spring ploughing.' Today, on a flaming spring day, with the magnolias blooming and the white dogwood and the red sprinkling the land, they brought a farm wagon and its mules to stand outside the church on the street where Martin Luther King was born and, after the funeral service, to carry his body four miles to his college and lay it to rest. The 'mule train' is the oldest and still most dependable form of transport of the rural poor in the Southland. And somebody had the graceful idea that a mule train would be the aptest cortège for the man who was the apostle of the poor.

From the warm dawn into the blazing noon, the black bodies, wearing more suits and ties than they would put on for a coronation, moved through the Negro sections of the town toward the street of comfortable, two-storey frame houses where the coloured business and professional men live and where, across from Cox's Funeral Home, the Rev. Martin Luther King, Jr., lived and preached, in the Ebenezer Baptist Church, a red-bricked nondescript tabernacle.

Thousands of college students had volunteered to act as marshals to hold the crowds; but though there was a tremendous push and jostle of people before the service began, there were enough police on hand to stem the crush and hand the visiting celebrities through like very pregnant women.

The bell tolled out the tune of 'We Shall Overcome' and big cars slid up to the entrance, and out of them climbed Attorney General Ramsey Clark, and Mrs John F. Kennedy, and Richard Nixon, and Senator Eugene McCarthy, Governor and Mrs George Romney of Michigan, and Governor Nelson Rockefeller and Mayor John Lindsay of New York, the new Roman Catholic Archbishop Terence Cooke, Sidney Poitier, the Metropolitan Opera's Leontyne Price, Eartha Kitt, Sammy Davis, Jr., Bobby and Ethel Kennedy and brother Edward, and Ralph Bunche, U Thant's man and Dr King's friend.

Over the breaking waves of street noise and the tolling bell, the strong baritone of the Rev. Ralph Abernathy, Dr King's heir, chanted from time to time: 'We will please be

The mule cortège carrying the casket of Dr Martin Luther King, Jr.
en route to the memorial service.

orderly now … let us have dignity … please … there are no more seats in the church.'
Somebody lifted a squalling baby and passed it out over the tossing heads to safety.

It is a small church, and shortly after 10:30 the last cars and the last mourners
were slotted in their places. First, Mrs King and her four children and the dead man's
brother, and Harry Belafonte. Then at last an alert squad of aides and Secret Service
men surrounding Vice President Hubert Humphrey. The conspicuous absentee was
Lester Maddox, the Governor of Georgia, a segregationist whose presence could upset
a coloured funeral any place North or South.

The inside of the church impressively belies its outside. It is a pleasantly modern
room with a single oriel window above a white cross over the choir and the pulpit. The
flanking walls have two simple Gothic windows decorated alike with a single shield
bearing a cross and surmounted with the crown of Christ. Tiny spotlights embedded in
the ceiling threw little pools of light on the famous and the obscure equally. The warm
shadows these shafts encouraged gave an extraordinary chiaroscuro to the congregation, making Bobby Kennedy at one point look like the captain of Rembrandt's *Night
Watch* amidst his lieutenants slumbering in the shade.

It was a normal Baptist service, with Southern overtones of gospel singing and
solos by black girls in white surplices of Dr King's favourite hymns, sung with impassioned locking of the hands and closed eyes. Through it all, Mrs King sat back at a

sideways angle with the carved, sad fixity of an African idol. Dr King's brother covered his face with a handkerchief once, and others dabbed at their eyes; and the youngest King daughter sagged over in a deep sleep like a rag doll. But Mrs King was as impassive as Buddha behind her thin veil while the prayers were given, the hymns, the eulogy by a New York dean as white as Siegfried, who had taught theology to Dr King. Once there was a suspicion of a glitter in her eyes when Rev. Abernathy told of the last meal he had with Dr King, an anecdote as simple as a parable.

'On that Thursday noon in the Lorraine Motel, in Memphis, Tennessee, the maid served up only one salad, and Martin took a small portion of it and left the rest. Then someone reminded the girl that she had brought up one order of fish instead of two. And Martin said, "Don't worry about it, Ralph and I can eat from the same plate," and I ate my last meal that Thursday noon. And I will not eat bread or meat or anything until I am thoroughly satisfied that I am ready for the task at hand.'

There was one innovation that was nearly forgotten at the end. Both the casket and the family were ready to go, but there was a quick whisper in Rev. Abernathy's ear and he announced that Mrs King had requested a playback of one of Dr King's last sermons. It was that premonitory vision of his inevitable end, and his voice resounded through the hushed church:

'I think about my own death, and I think about my own funeral ... and every now and then I ask myself what it is that I would want said, and I leave the word to this morning ... I don't want a long funeral, and if you get somebody to deliver the eulogy, tell him not to talk too long ... tell him not to mention that I have a Nobel Peace Prize – that isn't important. Tell him not to mention that I have 300 or 400 other awards – that's not important ... I'd like somebody to mention that day that Martin Luther King tried to give his life serving others. I want you to say that day that I tried to be right and to walk with them. I want you to be able to say that day that I did try to feed the hungry. I want you to be able to say that day that I did try in my life to clothe the naked ... I want you to say that I tried to love and serve humanity.'

Then the doors were opened, and the family went out with all the parsons, and the mule team bore its flowered casket and moved toward the many, many thousands that had gone on before to Morehouse College.

Coretta Scott King with her youngest daughter Bernice during the funeral service in the Ebenezer Baptist Church.

At the Ambassador Hotel

Guardian, 13 June 1968

Early last Tuesday afternoon, I flew into Los Angeles. I had seen a score of these elec-tion-night entertainments – they are amiable but blowzy affairs – but to give me a fresh view of a ceremony that had staled by familiarity and also to make some compensation to a hostess who had offered me a bed, I had asked her if she would like to mooch around the town with me and see what we could see. She was agog with anticipation, for just as a foreign correspondent thinks a movie actress must have a fascinating life, so a movie actress thought a correspondent's life must be glamorous in the extreme. So, high in the Santa Monica hills, amid the scent of the eucalypti and the splendid California cypresses, we sat for a while in the evening after the polls closed and waited for a sign of the outcome. You do not have to wait long in these computer days; the Oregon result was predicted exactly by the Big Brain, twelve minutes after the polls closed, when the returns already in were under 1 percent. Somehow, the Brain in New York was having trouble with California; there the party politics are, for various historical reasons, very loosely organized, and the northern end of the state tends to contradict the verdict of the south. So the computers were silent, but the writing was on the wall, and, just before 11 o'clock, we took off for Senator Eugene McCarthy's campaign hotel.

There was no doubt when we got there that the college students and the mini-skirted girls and the wandering poets and the 'chin up' McCarthy staff were whistling in a graveyard. There was a rock band that whooped it up all the louder, to drown the inevitable news. They would pause awhile, and another ominous statistic would be flashed, and an MC would shout, 'Are we downhearted?' and the ballroom crowd would roar its defiance of the obvious.

The Ambassador, a venerable hotel miles away on Wilshire Boulevard, was Senator Robert Kennedy's headquarters, and that was the place to be. We took off and, in the long driveway, lined up behind hundreds of cars containing all those sensible people who love a winner. At last, we got into the hotel lobbies and into a tumult of singing, dancing, music, and cheering. Guards and cops blocked the entrance to the ballroom,

Above, Senator Robert Kennedy addressing the packed ballroom crowd, moments before he was shot, and below, he lies wounded clutching his rosary beads, his wife Ethel lower left.

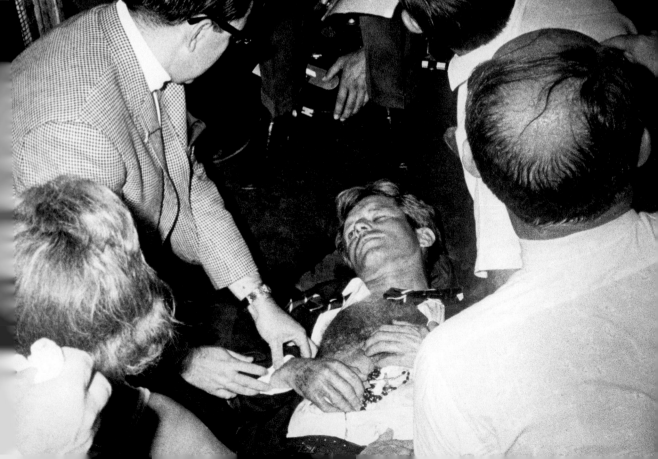

and passport and birth certificate and, I believe, a personal recommendation from Senator Kennedy, could not have got you in. My own general press credentials were quite useless, and, screaming at each other through the din of all these happy people, my companion and I decided the whole safari had been a mistake and we would go home.

We turned and started down the corridor. On our left, about forty or fifty feet along, was another door and a pack of people trying and failing to get through it. There was a guard, and a young Kennedy staff man turning down everybody. The Kennedy man suddenly shouted over the bobbing heads: 'Mr Cooke, come on, you can get in here.' So we were sandwiched or folded in through the mob and emerged as from a chute into an open place: a cool, almost empty room, a small private dining-room of the hotel. It was fitted up as a small extra press-room, and there were about half a dozen women telegraph-operators, two newsmen I knew, and half a dozen others: a radio man untangling cables, and a photographer, and one or two middle-aged women, a fat girl in a Kennedy straw hat, and a young reporter in a beard and, I suppose, his girl. It was a perfect way through to the ballroom, for, in between, was a serving pantry that led through a passage right into the ballroom. 'You don't want to get in there,' a friend of mine said. 'It's murder in there, and when Bobby gets through his speech, Pierre Salinger has promised us, he'll come through into this room and talk with us.' It was an unbelievable break, so we sat down and had a drink and heard the telegraph girls tapping out copy and tried to hear the television set in a corner that was turned up to an unbearable decibel level. A few minutes later the TV commentators gave way to the ballroom scene, and Bobby was up there with his ecstatic wife, and he was thanking everybody and saying things must change, and, so, on to Chicago. It was about eighteen minutes after midnight. A few of us strolled over to the swinging doors that gave onto the pantry; they had no glass peepholes, but we soon heard the pleasant bustle of him coming through. There was suddenly a banging repetition of a sound that I do not know how to describe: not at all like shots, like somebody dropping a rack of trays.

Half a dozen of us were startled enough to charge through the door, and it had just happened. It was a narrow lane he had to come through, for there were two long steam tables and somebody had stacked up against them those trellis fences with artificial leaves stuck on them that they use to fence the dance band off from the floor. The only light was the blue light of three fluorescent tubes slotted in the ceiling. But it was a howling jungle of cries and obscenities and flying limbs and two enormous men – Roosevelt Grier, the football player, and Rafer Johnson, the Olympic champion, piling on to a pair of blue jeans.

There was a head on the floor, streaming blood, and somebody put a Kennedy boater under it, and the blood trickled down like chocolate sauce on an iced cake. There were flashlights by now, and the button eyes of Ethel Kennedy turned into cinders. She was slapping a young man, and he was saying, 'Listen, lady, I'm hurt, too.' And down on the greasy floor was a huddle of clothes, and staring out of it the face of Bobby Kennedy, like the stone face of a child, lying on a cathedral tomb.

I had and have no idea of the time of all this, or even of the event itself, for when

I pattered back into the creamy green, genteel dining room, I heard somebody cry, 'Kennedy – shot,' and heard a girl moan, 'No, no, not again', and my companion was fingering a cigarette package like a paralytic. A dark woman suddenly bounded to a table and beat it, and howled like a wolf, 'Stinking country, no, no, no, no' at the placid television commentators who had not yet got the news. And then a minute maybe, or an hour later, or a day, the cops and the burly Johnson shot through the swinging doors with their bundle of the black curly head and the jeans, and I recall the tight, small behind and the limp head and face totally dazed.

Well, the next morning when I saw and heard the Pope in his gentle, faltering English, I still could not believe that he was talking about this squalid, appalling scene in a hotel pantry that I had been a part of and would always be a part of. I have no doubt that this experience is a trauma, and because of it, no doubt, several days later, I still cannot rise to the general lamentations about a sick society.

I for one do not feel like an accessory to a crime, and I reject almost as a frivolous obscenity the sophistry of collective guilt, the idea that I or the American people killed John Fitzgerald Kennedy and Martin Luther King and Robert Francis Kennedy. I do not believe either that *you* conceived Hitler and that, in some deep unfathomable sense, all Europe was responsible for the extermination of six million Jews. With Edmund Burke, I do not know how you can indict a whole nation. To me, this now roaringly fashionable theme is a great folly. It is difficult to resist, because it deflects an attack at one's own conscience to some big corporate culprit. It sounds wise and deep, but really is a way of opting out of the human situation.

I said as much as this to a younger friend, and he replied: 'Yes, and I, too, I don't feel implicated in the murder of John or Bobby Kennedy, but when Martin Luther King is killed, the only people who know that you and I are not like the killer are you and I.' It is a tremendous sentence and exposes, I think, the present danger to America: the more people talk about collective guilt the more they will feel it, and after 300 years of subjection and prejudice, any poor Negro or desperate outcast is likely to act as if it were true that the American people, and not their derelicts, are the villains.

President-elect Nixon Hits the Television Networks

Letter No. 1038, 15 December 1968

Last Wednesday night, we saw a remarkable performance on television that, if it becomes a regular thing, may get to be known as 'The Dick Nixon Show'. The itch to present our politicians as, above all, lovable creatures is now so irresistible that their advisers are turning more and more into TV producers, using the medium that above all others establishes public entertainers as favourite members of our private family. I take it this is the aim of President-elect Nixon, and it is nothing revolutionary, only an extension, a bolder extension into the world of entertainment, of Franklin Roosevelt's really revolutionary decision to go on the radio and set up what he called his 'fireside chats'. He saw sooner than anybody that the microphone is not simply, as all politicians before him and many after have thought of it, a means of amplifying a public speech, but a private medium of conversation with two or three people in a room. It's weird today to think back to those chats as anything revolutionary. But radio was well along before any President of the United States regarded it without suspicion.

The first time radio was ever used by a President was in Glendale, California, which was – in the middle 1920s and beyond – the railroad terminal for Hollywood. President Calvin Coolidge had been on some sort of political swing through the West, and everything he had to say was put out over the wire services for the newspapers. However, when he took the train at Glendale to go East and home again, the radio boys were agog at the idea that they might get him to say a few parting words to the nation. His train was giving off its warm-up puffs and snorts, the Presidential party advanced along the platform, and at last the little dried-up man appeared, and a trembling announcer stationed himself by the steps of the Presidential carriage. President Coolidge came to a stop and waited to be introduced. The announcer, in that soaring theatrical tenor that all announcers used in that time, carolled, 'And now, for the first time in history, the American people are to hear, by the magic of radio, the voice of the President of the United States. Mr President, sir, what message do you have to give the people as you go aboard your train at the end of this historic trip?' There was a crackle and a pause. Coolidge leaned quickly into the microphone. 'Goodbye', he said, and jumped aboard. There were commentators at the time who approved of this less than beautiful gesture as a becoming rebuke to an upstart medium. Today, I should imagine, it would lose him millions of votes.

Richard Nixon is interviewed for the TV programme *60 Minutes*, 1968.

Well, we have come a very long way since then. The last campaign so accustomed us to the idea of regular television appearances by the candidates that nobody is shocked any more at the idea of seeing their President or President-to-be in full pancake make-up. I am still slightly thrown by the difference, for instance, between President Johnson in life and in those appearances where he is caught, so to speak, on the hop, and President Johnson in full battle paint in the White House studio. The first time we saw it, it was not to be believed. His hair was darker, brushed straight back, the wrinkles and canyons of his face were flattened and powdered out; he was barbered up like a circus ringmaster; he was so be-dazed and bedazzled with theatrical lighting that even his glasses looked like very delicate pince-nez. The effect was, and has been since, to make him look like a Hollywood actor impersonating Franklin Roosevelt. Another bizarre note is the fact that he looks like this only at moments of crisis, or when he's going to make some historic announcement – a moon shot, or the decision not to run again – so that at the most realistic moments of the national life, he looks like a fantasy, a substitute President.

In the campaign, it was noticed that the hair of Vice President Hubert Humphrey and the hair of Mr Nixon had suddenly gone from grey to black. Am I suggesting that Mr Humphrey and Mr Nixon dyed their hair for the campaign? I am suggesting nothing. I speak only that which I do see. I remember, seven, eight years ago Mr Humphrey had a dusting of iron grey around the ears. Mr Nixon six years ago had streaks that were then considered marks of distinction. There was a fellow in a whisky ad – way back in the fifties and early sixties – who was presented as the all-American 'man-of-distinction', so-called. He looked like the British actor C. Aubrey Smith in his prime presiding over the Empire. He had stiff graying moustaches, glittering grey hair with tufts of white sprouting from his temples. This stereotype has been abandoned. I sat in a theatre at an opening once last winter and looked around before the curtain went up and realised that only I and one other man, some insensitive fogy in his seventies, had white hair. I saw men I knew who looked as if they were sitting incognito in blue-black wigs, till I noticed the telltale touches of reddish brown, or a fringe of dark green hair at the ears. They had been using, as we say, 'the bottle'. Whether or not the Messrs Humphrey and Nixon have been secretly using the bottle – the hair-tinting bottle – I wouldn't know or dream of hinting at. They both have fine heads of hair, or half heads of hair, that are black and glossy. And the implication, first dropped I believe by the *Wall Street Journal*, that they had gone the whole hog on a dye job is one that has not been refuted, with or without high dudgeon. There were times when Mr Humphrey was so carpeted with pancake that he looked like an aged doll, or a stockbroker with a drastic facelift. I ought to repeat that nobody shows the slightest shock. Nobody except me.

Well, Mr Nixon looked fine on Wednesday evening, certainly about ten years younger than he looked on that first television debate with John Kennedy more than eight years ago, when a lot of people believe he lost the election. Kennedy, that fatal night, was wearing no make-up. There was nothing prudish in this decision. He was told, and luckily believed, that he looked fine without it. Mr Nixon, his advisers swore, was given the wrong make-up and not enough powder around his impressive jowls. The result was that he looked remarkably like the standard caricature of him used by Herblock, the cartoonist of the *Washington Post*, something not far removed from the senior witch in *Macbeth*, or a back-alley assassin with a three-day growth. Kennedy, on the contrary, looked like an adorable choirboy, a choirboy who had just taken a double first at Harvard and was astonishingly well up on the crises and knotty problems of the day. It was the first time that even political scientists were given pause and made to reflect whether a good-looking profile isn't more of an asset to a Presidential candidate than a grasp of the national destiny.

When Mr Nixon strode the other night with his wife through an admiring crowd in the Shoreham Hotel ballroom in Washington, he looked like a very masterly master-of-ceremonies on an evening talk show. The five o'clock shadow is something that's been banished for good. He looks now as if he'd been shaved for the rest of his life. His cheeks were smooth and lightly tanned. His hair curled and glistened. He had no crow's-feet. He was in the pink, though if you are a Democrat you can fiddle with the TV knob and turn his complexion yellow and his eyeballs purple. Such are the resources of the present American two-colour system.

He came not to make a statement, an appeal, a proclamation. For the first time, a President was going to announce his whole Cabinet at one time, and he was doing it in a planned ceremony over all the networks at one time. It was done with dignity and urgent good humour, and as Mr Nixon called off each name, the camera cut to a placid and modest face, and an adoring or interested wife, and we heard (most of the men were totally unknown to us all) that this man, like the one before and the one to come, was not only a rare expert in his field – agriculture, banking, defence, foreign policy – but he had been chosen because he had 'an extra dimension' of judgment, maturity, tolerance, perspective. It was, in fact, an extended commercial, and the way it was done was not unlike the unveiling of a new line of groceries or automobiles by the president of the company before a convention of national salesmen. Afterward, people didn't so much discuss whether the appointments were impressive; they commented on it as a show, approved the resolute good looks of Mr William P. Rodgers, the new Secretary of State, wondered why they hadn't heard more of these rare Americans with the 'extra dimension'. But on the whole judged it to be a 'good show and a justified novelty'.

Change in the White House?

Letter No. 1044, 26 January 1969

It's obviously going to take a little time to be able to judge the political style of the new President, but in the meantime there are striking changes of a sort that, I believe, are more likely to fascinate many more people than those who are interested in political programmes. I mean quite simply the way a man lives. What he does with his day, the gadgets and objects he likes to have around him, the sort of food he chooses to steal from the ice-box for a midnight snack.

The trouble with political writers is that on the whole they are solemn men; they spend so much time thinking heavy thoughts and weighing international trends that they overlook the men behind the policies. Yet I've noticed that when politicians get together in the evening and sit and reminisce, they don't recall Clause Nine of an old housing bill; they remark that the big housing administrator himself couldn't replace an electric light bulb.

There used to be an old parlour game called 'If I had a million', and long ago Hollywood made an engaging episodic movie about what happened to a cowboy, a gangster, a prostitute, a humble clerk when suddenly they were handed a million dollars. The humble clerk, by the way, was Charles Laughton, and I vividly remember how he fulfilled a lifetime's ambition. Most other people in the movie were baffled by the problem of how to use the actual money. Charles Laughton knew exactly what a million dollars would do to him and his dignity. He opened the envelope, read the miraculous news, put it neatly in his pocket, gazed at his desk for a moment, lifted his great bulk, and shuffled slowly but with a single purpose out of his office and along several corridors. He looked sad beyond telling. He was a cowed hulk of a man, a big bag of dandruff, and his rounded shoulders spoke for all the office slaves that ever lived out a dingy, clockwork life. He padded on and on, and at last he came to a door with a frosted panel of glass on which was inscribed the mighty name and title of the president of this great firm. He knocked respectfully. The basso profundo of the boss, the big tycoon, bade him enter. He did so, lifted his dropsical eyes, adjusted his lips as if he were about to play a trumpet and let forth what in that long ago was known either as a raspberry or a Bronx cheer. That was all.

Well I tell you, I think that uncounted millions of people this week must have enjoyed in secret another fantasy. What is it like to move into the White House? What would you do if the impossible office ever came your way? A few of us were mulling over this the other evening, but alas, we were mostly men and therefore one-track, ponderous creatures, and in no time we were arguing such trivialities as whether Nixon was truly a confident man or whether Mr Finch would make a good Secretary of Health, Education and Welfare. There were two women present, and they quietly retreated into a private bout of gossip about babies, but I rescued one of them and said, 'If you suddenly found yourself the First Lady, what's the first thing you'd do in or to the White House?' She knew at once. 'I'd get rid of,' she said with some heat, 'those damn Remingtons.'

Frederick Remington was an American painter and sculptor of the Old West, born the first year of the Civil War, just at the right time to see the last upsurge of life on the Plains. If he had been born out West, no doubt he would have taken for granted the old corral, and the trail herd, and the branding, and the buffalo runs, and the occasional Indian massacre. But he was born in New York State, and following the rule that no true believer is so bigoted as a convert, he did more than 2,700 paintings and drawings of horses, cattle, cowboys, Indians, soldiers, and horses horses horses. They were all done with almost depressing realism; every hoof and muscle and lariat and nostril was painted exactly as a photograph would have shown it. I have never heard it said by any competent judge that he was an artist at all, but he prompted in strong, simple men the glow of recognition that comes to yachtsmen when they see a painting that reflects the sunset light on ballooning sails, the gasp of wonder that comes over us all when we leave a portrait and find that the eyes are following us wherever we go. Yet, like many another indifferent painter (I can think of an appalling one who concentrated for about twenty years on painting every stagecoach in England), his pictures now bring incredible prices. Two of them were loaned, at the insistence of President Johnson, to the White House and were hung in a room outside the President's big office. It was absolutely routine, if you were a visitor to Johnson's White House, to be led out of the office and stopped in front of these huge bucking broncos and urged to admire them. The President would look at them as other men look at a Botticelli or a Rubens, or an Arnold Palmer, and a tear would form in the corner of one eye. He would sniff and brush it away with the back of his great hand, and he would smile and say, 'Mighty good to see you, and come back.'

Now if one thing is more certain than another in the transfer of power from Johnson to Nixon, it is that the whole style and flavour of White House family-life would change. It always does, of course, though some new occupants – Mrs Truman was one – are so modest and undemonstrative that they hesitate to change anything for a while, feeling rather that they have inherited something as sacred and unchangeable as the British Museum. Mrs Truman was served cold, hard rolls of a kind surely very familiar to most English-speaking people at dinner every night for six weeks, and nibbled at them so as not to hurt the chef. But she had been brought up in Missouri and inherited the Southern taste for hot, crumbly rolls. What's more, she was a whiz at making

them. It was only on the command of President Truman, who was – you may recall – less of a shrinking violet than his wife, that her recipe was passed on to the chef, and the Trumans reverted to breaking the bread of their fathers.

Well, I don't suppose if any of us had been challenged we would have known what to say about the changes the Nixons might make. In spite of the painstaking work done on the Nixon image by advertising men and other plastic surgeons, we really know very little about his tastes and personal prejudices. He was so anxious for so long to be all things to all men that we got the idea he had no preferences whatsoever in, for instance, food. On his campaign trips, his enthusiasm was carefully banked for the regional food that came his way. In Idaho, he simply had to have a baked potato. In Maryland, he drooled to get at the crabs (and he is not to be blamed). In the state of Washington, he couldn't get enough apple and boysenberry pie, and down South he confessed a lifelong passion for chicken creole gumbo. In California, his native state, which has an alarming variety of foods, to each of which some part of the state owes its livelihood, he had to be pretty spry. Praise an orange in Merced County and you're likely to lose the votes of all the Armenians who pack apricots or bottle sweet wine. He used to settle for hamburgers everywhere, and make a big thing of wolfing chilli con carne in the Mexican districts.

But now, he's there and he can do what comes naturally. Well, the first thing he did was to throw out those Remingtons, or rather, sent them back politely to the museum that had lent them. Within twenty-four hours, he made some other changes that wiped out at a blow the more theatrical mementos of the Johnson era. First of all, he announced that he's not comfortable working in a big, pretentious office. The President's office is a large and beautiful oval room. It has two or three superb portraits of the Johnson forerunners, some very elegant eighteenth-century furniture, a great sofa, and in front of it a white console. It looked like a miniature organ or a private computer with many winking lights, signifying all the people who were trying to phone the President, who gazed at it fondly, as a Roman emperor might have gazed at a roaring crowd begging to have him lift his thumb. A way off and facing the sofa were three television sets, each tuned to one of the three networks, for if ever there was a man who wanted to know what the world was saying about him on three circuits, that man was Lyndon Johnson. Well, the console has gone and so have the television sets. 'I am not,' Mr Nixon hastened to comment, 'against television.' The oval office will be used only for ceremonial occasions. Anyway, he has taken over a small room no bigger than your office or mine in the executive wing of the House. The East Room, which saw such things as swearing-in ceremonies and formal press conferences, has practically been stripped. Gone is the enormous Presidential podium, and a technological erection of TV lights, and a blue canvas backdrop that covered the gold curtains. Mr Nixon stands at a small podium against the normal curtains. The East Room is a room again, no longer the number one television studio of the emperor of the world.

President Richard Nixon in the Oval Office on his first
day in office with a conspicuously uncluttered desk.

This, most people agree, is good and surprising. Nixon is a small-town boy who, in spite of the trappings of power that surrounded him since he came to the Vice Presidency sixteen years ago, likes small surroundings and homely things. There is an anxiety among some old courtiers from Camelot that the Nixons will return other fine paintings and reduce to suburban parlours the great rooms that Mrs Kennedy did over so splendidly in the old Federal Style. There is no sign of this, at the moment. But a President has considerable say in how he wants the House to look while he's in it. Theodore Roosevelt, another New Yorker converted to the manly life of the Wild West, converted several rooms into menageries of moose and buffalo heads; and his successor couldn't wait to ship them away. Harry Truman liked to sit in his rocker on a porch, so, after a long squabble with Congress and the architects, he had a high porch built under the back portico. Franklin Roosevelt was not much concerned with decoration; everything had to be as comfortable and stuffed as his house up the Hudson. By the way, the only ceremonial he insisted his guests should attend was his nightly mixing of the martinis, of which he was extremely proud. During the following hour, anxious aides noticed in Churchill's visits, the Prime Minister retired frequently to deposit in the bathtub the drink he loathed.

How about the Vice President? Spiro Agnew is the name. In spite of the usual promise that he will be given wholly new, vast, and sovereign powers, he is tucked away in a tiny office he has commandeered from a female secretary. He thus gives substance to H. L. Mencken's old definition of a Vice President: 'He is a man who sits in the outer office of the White House hoping to hear the President sneeze.'

Shooting for the Moon

Letter No. 1067, 20 July 1969

For days and nights, we have been reading the most inflated prose that even Americans can write. One of my favourite American columnists, a man notable for intellect, balance and restraint started his last column: 'There has never been a moment in human history so massively and carefully prepared, so intensely watched by the whole sweep of the earth's population.' Well, I know of one small sweeping of the earth's population who was not watching at all. He is a coloured cabdriver I had the other night, probably as good a man as any other with his own kind, but in the present moment of American history a man committed, as lots of his race understandably are, to hating the sight and sound of a white man. There is no technique of dealing with such people. You say little and stay as polite as possible. New York was like a furnace that night – it had been in the middle nineties – an oven of a city, and I said something about its being an awful day to drive a cab. Nothing, no response. I shut up until I got home, and handed him a dollar bill, and I hope I didn't expect a sweeping bow for a twenty-five cent tip. A 'thank you' perhaps, a grunt of recognition. Nothing, but I could almost feel his seething calm, the intensity of his sullenness. He pocketed the bill and threw his meter flag. And then he muttered, with a long sneer: 'Moon shot, big shot ... ' and a four-letter word that even now, prude that I am, I cannot bring myself to spit at you on a public programme.

The same thought was expressed a little more elaborately by another favourite columnist of mine, Harriet Van Horne, a tiny lady who writes like an angel but with all the guilt of a fallen angel. 'After today's glorious moon shot, what? Well, eventually, the National Aeronautical and Space Administration see the moon as a way station to Mars, and beyond ... (and) despite the inhospitable atmosphere of the moon, astronomers expect it will be a fine place for robots to work. By the late 1970s, assuming Congress continues to stop its ears to the cries of the poor while writing billion-dollar checks for the space programme, we'll have a lunar laboratory to probe the long night of infinity ... Before the end of this century we shall know for sure whether or not we are the only living creatures in the solar system.' (Arthur C. Clarke, by the way, the space fiction and fact man, has predicted that the discovery of other living beings on other planetary systems could act on us all as a fatal trauma, presenting – as he puts it

Union would be sending up joint crews and pooling their researches into outer space. But some of the most double-domed commentators have been wrestling with the psychological problem of why the Russians should have invited Borman there just before their own Luna 15 was to be shot up on an undisclosed mission; why, if they are as far ahead as they claim, should they suggest a truce or an alliance in outer space? Every word written in *Tass* and *Pravda* was read here on some television programme or other – the announcement of the Apollo 11 flight, an admiring cable sent from a Russian correspondent in New York, and above all the Russian description of the three Americans as 'courageous people'. Nothing very original about that. But they haven't done it before. They have either ignored our flights altogether, or reported the bare bones of the facts afterward.

American-Soviet relations, which many people here believe are the key to the only guarantee of a stable peace, are also highly suspect by many other people. The feeling is divided in this country, and only the pollster Dr George Gallup could tell us how evenly, between those who believe the Russians have seen the folly of world conquest and feel their only safe future is tied up with a strong America; and the people who feel that every new gesture of friendship is a trick masking the unchanging Soviet design to provoke and lead the world Communist revolution. There are excellent, thoughtful, and benign people on both sides. You certainly don't need to be a paranoid personality to harbour continual doubts. All our foxiest guesses about what the Russians are really up to, in any political or scientific move, are dogged by the knowledge that the Russians are easily the world's masters at chess; and that to a merely good chess player the moves of a superlative chess player are either incomprehensible or strangely naive, until the moment when he clobbers you.

Well, as I say, most people are, this weekend, enjoying the luxury of not probing beyond the adventure itself. On Wednesday morning a reporter for the New York *Daily News* was nauseated by a radio commercial that came on just before the blast-off. It presupposed that a man had just landed on the moon, and the mimic controller warned him that his first words would be historic. He replied, 'Yeah, and this underwear too is historic.' Can vulgarization go no further, the reporter howled. I guess it can. This little episode illustrates in miniature what to me is the false equation between the money for the moon and the money for the poor complainers. It reminds me of a famous crusading doctor who used to say, 'If Americans would stop drinking alcohol and smoking cigarettes, the money could provide an indoor toilet, an annual medical check-up, and a sanitary home for every American.' So it could, but human beings being what they are, the equation is just not on. No nation, except under an extreme crisis of survival, gives up this for that. Unless and until the poor rise like a mighty army, I see no sign that we shall not be going on voting billions for space and millions for relief. We are – on this planet anyway – naturally ornery folk.

Buzz Aldrin stands beside the Stars and Stripes at
Tranquillity Base on the surface of the moon.

Chappaquiddick

Letter No. 1068, 27 July 1969

While we were all getting set to gape at those inflated and gallant little figures gallop-ing in slow motion across the surface of the moon, a motorcar fell off a bridge on a tiny island off the coast of Massachusetts, and a girl was drowned; and we were sud-denly confronted with the most damaging aspersion on a public character since Justice Abe Fortas resigned from the Supreme Court, the first Supreme Court judge to quit under fire in the history of the Republic.

It's impossible for me to know how much confusion has crept into or been forcibly injected into the accounts of the accident you have read. And so that we shall all be talk-ing about the same thing, I'd better tell the bare story as simply and truly as it can so far be told. I say 'so far' because my own suspicion is that since Senator Edward Kennedy's first account and his later televised confession, some troublesome gaps are left.

Well, briefly then, Senator Kennedy, the last male heir of the Kennedy fortune and the Kennedy political line, sailed south from his summer home on Cape Cod last Fri-day to the small island of Martha's Vineyard, where he was off for a day of sailing and after that a party for some of his closest political friends. It was to be a reunion of the small inner circle of men and women who had slaved night and day for the Presidential campaign of the dead brother Robert. There were six women, all of them still working in or close to politics, and this was to be the fourth such reunion since Robert Kennedy was killed.

When he landed on Martha's Vineyard, the Senator checked into a suite of rooms in a hotel in the main village of Edgartown. It had been reserved for him and his male companions in the races. The girls were to stay the night at a motel on the other side of the island. The races were held. The Senator came in ninth, and another race he was entered in was washed out by the rain. But this didn't dampen anybody's spirits. They all dolled up for the evening party, which was to be held in a small rented cottage on an even smaller island to the east known as Chappaquiddick – like so many such odd, rollicking names in the Northeast, an Indian name. To get from the Vineyard to Chap-paquiddick you have to take a ferry. It carries only two cars at a time. So they went

Senator Edward Kennedy returning to the Senate for the first time since the Chappaquiddick car crash.

their ways, and around seven in the evening they met in the cottage, which was about a mile and a quarter from the ferry.

The first drinks were served, according to the only girl present who has talked, and about 8 o'clock the steaks were put on the outdoor grill and the cook-out (as we now call the venerable barbecue) began. There were six men present and six women. The party went on through the evening, and there was much boisterous singing and laughing, so much so that one or two of the neighbours wished they would quiet down. The last ferry for the Vineyard left at midnight, and by the time the merrymaking was wearing itself out, the ferry – they figured – must have left. So they bedded down, in the two small bedrooms or on the living room floor or on sofas.

By this time, however, there were only ten people in the cottage. At some point, which is still vague, a twenty-eight-year-old woman, Mary Jo Kopechne, mentioned to somebody that she wanted to go back to her motel. Senator Kennedy went out with her, they got in his car, and they drove off on the moonless night to the ferry. He says this was about 11:15. There is a hardtop road that turns left to the ferry, and a dirt road to the right. The Senator took the dirt road and came up suddenly on a narrow, high pitched bridge, and his car overturned and fell in . He says he found himself in the car underwater, thought at one point he was done for, but managed to get out of a window and surface. He says he repeatedly dived down to look for the girl, didn't find her, and staggered back to the bank and walked drenched and in shock the mile and a quarter back to the cottage.

First of all, in no state can you leave an accident with impunity without calling in the police as soon as possible. Well, the fact is the police heard nothing about it till eight in the morning when two young fishermen spotted the car, went to a nearby housewife, who called the police. About two hours later, not till just before ten, did Senator Kennedy walk from his hotel in Edgartown into the police station and tell the local chief about it.

Of course, the first big question that everybody asked, and many are still asking, is precisely what was the Senator doing between his arrival back at the cottage and his appearance at the police station about nine hours later? The girl who talked said he never appeared at the party again. He first said he fell into a parked car and forgot everything, that somebody took him across the channel, and he came to in his hotel room, brooded awhile, and went to the police. In his television confessional, given to the people of Massachusetts on Friday night but watched and heard by a good many of the other hundred and ninety million Americans, he said he had gone to the cottage, attracted two of his close friends, both lawyers, and they had gone back to the scene and tried and failed to rescue Miss Kopechne. Then, rather amazingly, he plunged into the waters and swam across to Edgartown and nearly drowned again.

We can only surmise what was the attitude of the two close friends, watching a man do this who was recently in shock. It was first thought that they too were negligent under the law, but the police chief says there's no such thing as an accessory to a misdemeanour, and their first duty was not to speak without their client's permission.

So no charges were brought against them. This little account telescopes a lot of detail. But it also combines the Senator's first statement to the police and his quite different account over television. The story did not come to us that way. There were six days of silence from the Senator, and as with Justice Fortas before him it is the implication of that long silence that could damage him most. At first he said he would challenge any prosecution. The police chief had already made it plain that no criminal charge was anticipated. The police and medical reports absolutely ruled that out. The charge would be leaving the scene of an accident and failing for so long to report it. Then, surrounded by his family, friends, political advisers, a former assistant attorney general, several old Kennedy staff people, and former Secretary of Defence Robert McNamara, he recanted, pleaded guilty, and was given the usual suspended sentence. Then he went off to compose, with all these sophisticated helpers, his television address. The best they could come up with was a still sketchy account of the mysterious nine hours, very little at all about the two vital helpers – the lawyer friends – the weird incident of the swim ashore, and the admission that his conduct was 'indefensible' and was due to 'a jumble of emotions, grief, fear, doubt, exhaustion, panic, confusion, and shock'. We can well believe it. Here is a man of public responsibility, who has had to shoulder the immense private responsibility of his own and his brother's eleven children and Jack Kennedy's two. He is also, true to his clan, a man of driving political ambition. We cannot possibly doubt that the Presidency is, or has been, his aim.

So all he could do, and most people seem to think he did it with great candour and sincerity, was to throw himself on the people of Massachusetts and ask them, Am I worthy to represent you? On their verdict, he said, he would decide whether or not to resign from the Senate. Well, the Democrats in Congress have closed behind him. And there appears now little doubt that the verdict of Massachusetts will be a resounding endorsement. The name of Kennedy in Massachusetts is as politically magical as the name of Churchill in Essex. The Kennedys were the tribe of immigrant Irish who clobbered the bluebloods, the Saltonstalls and the Cabots and the Lodges, and there are many more mementoes of Ireland in Massachusetts than relics of the Mayflower. So the guess at the moment is that his own people will back him and he will be vindicated, perhaps by a thumping majority if he runs for the Senate next year.

But this thing goes beyond Massachusetts. The final verdict is with the country. And by appealing for a national judgment on his conduct, many people feel that a fuller investigation is called for.

Maybe time and compassion will work on his side. There are people who say he is headed for national political oblivion. I recall, though, a press conference in Los Angeles in 1962 when the defeated candidate for the California governorship drooled and ranted like a hysterical child in front of a shocked press corps. He was, we were absolutely convinced, out of politics forever. His name was Richard Nixon. Ever since then, I have taken a sceptical view of the permanence of political oblivion.

1970–1979

IN THE EARLY 1970s my father came to a crossroads. His professional success had opened new opportunities while at the same time rendering his daily and weekly routine somewhat burdensome. As he contemplated the making of the *America* series, the idea of stopping the daily piece for the *Guardian* lifted his spirits. Simply to be relieved of the constant pressure gave him new life, and he looked forward to a bit more freedom. Both *America* and *Masterpiece Theatre* afforded an outlet for his love of the arts. His old fascination with photography and the landscape of the United States found full expression as he travelled across the country during the filming of the *America* series. For the twenty-two years he would host *Masterpiece Theatre*, the necessary exposure to literature and drama provided a welcome balance to his continuing political reporting. It is worth mentioning that although ending the *Guardian* routine was a relief, the idea of quitting the *Letter* never crossed his mind.

Though he travelled a great deal during the filming of *America*, when he was at home the routine in the apartment settled into a pattern that would be broken only days before he died. As my mother spent her days painting in her studio, he worked at home. But no matter what was going on in the world or the family, come 6 p.m., work stopped. Until his arthritis prevented him from doing so at about the age of ninety-one, he went into the living room and practised the piano for half and hour. This, even more than the scotch that followed, let him unwind and forget the news, the phone, the demands on his time, as it transported him to an entirely different world. Then he filled the ice bucket and joined my mother for the nightly news and a drink. Sitting down with pad and pen, he studiously took notes during the broadcast, collecting fodder for the *Letter* and any article or speech for which he might be preparing.

As the protests against the war in Vietnam escalated, my father found himself in a difficult situation. Ever inclined to defer to authority, especially in times of war, his patience with the protesters' impatience grew thin. Ironically, even though he had been one of the first television personalities, he tended to blame the protesters' righteous outrage in part on the media, on the simple fact that the people at home saw the war every night on television. He was ever intrigued by the power of television to affect public opinion and policy.

Never was this more evident than during the Watergate hearings; in a nation glued to the television, my father was as stuck as everyone else. He relished the proceedings and, keenly observant of the slightest alterations in body language, delighted in being able to see the key people on the screen.

Included in this section is a report on Patty Hearst's kidnapping. In this piece he uncharacteristically and indirectly refers to an especially difficult time for our family, when both my sister and I fell prey to a predatory religious cult. It was never his inclination to air his dirty laundry in public, but the rush to judgment against Ms Hearst and what he perceived to be a general misunderstanding of the term 'brainwashing' left him no option. Though the event to which he referred happened nearly a decade earlier, it was still fresh in his mind. Perhaps he also felt safe in talking about it because by then I was married and the mother of two little boys and thus, he felt quite rightly, I was settled and secure.

The 1970s were a time of great accomplishment and satisfaction for my father. His professional life was well rounded, his health good, and his addiction to golf in full swing. In this stretch of fair weather the sun shone especially bright one day in September of 1974. His address to a joint session of Congress in celebration of the 200th anniversary of the first Continental Congress, in Philadelphia, was certainly one of the great moments of his life. Winston Churchill and Lafayette were the only other people not born in America who had been so honoured.

In looking back on it, I try to pinpoint why it was so noteworthy and moving. It was noteworthy because he was clearly nervous; rarely did he seem especially agitated before speaking engagements. In this instance, however, we just tried to stay out of his way. It was not noteworthy because he did an excellent job; most of the time he did. For all who attended, the air was charged, the moment extraordinary, the well of the chamber commanding.

The reason it was so moving for me was that looking down on him from our seats in the balcony, I saw not the distinguished, articulate, and respected man he was, but a young man in love whose best girl has just said, 'Yes.' He had been in love with America since he was a small boy; he had made a living and a life getting to know her whims and fancies, her history and hopes. He both admired and forgave her. In his being invited to speak before the most prestigious body in America, I felt him kick his heels in delight, shiver in anxiety, and shed a tear in deep-felt thanks and humility.

S.C.K.

Louis Armstrong: 1901-1971

Letter No. 1169, 10 July 1971

A few years ago, maybe ten, twenty (I refuse to believe it was forty!) – anyway, it was in the summer of 1931 – I ordered a record from the local gramophone shop, and it took an awfully long time to arrive. When at last it did, I hustled it on to the turntable. My mother was intrigued by its title, which she thought odd, not to say gruesome. It was called, 'The St James Infirmary'. It began with a shattering chord and a trumpet taking off like a supersonic jet. Long before it was over, I took it off the machine because I saw that my mother was sitting there in tears.

She was not moved by the beauty of the piece, or the artistry of the mad trumpeter. She was frightened by it and aghast that her son could listen to this jungle band without a blush. To her, in those remote days, it was as if today a mother had seen her son nonchalantly take out a needle and give himself a shot of heroin.

I suppose there is no generation left now that hates jazz simply as such. Even the 'flappers' of the 1920s who doted on the new fad of jazz are now in their seventies. In my youth, it was the normal thing for people over fifty to be either frightened of jazz or contemptuous of it. Old soldiers, doctors and other establishment figures made a point of equating the word 'jazz' with the adjectives 'Negroid' and 'decadent'. English magistrates rarely missed an opportunity to ascribe petty thievery and illegitimate births to the fearful influence of the saxophone. My mother was too simple, too unpretentious a person to be contemptuous of jazz. It simply scared the wits out of her. Well, I was young and callow but also, I like to think, responsive to all sorts of music, from Mozart to Sullivan (both Sir Arthur and Joe). And I was frankly exhilarated by this record and mesmerized by its solo trumpet. I took the record back to college and never again bootlegged it into our house.

Even so, I should never have expected then that when that solo trumpeter died, the *New York Times* would bow to him as 'an authentic American folk hero, a legend in his time' or that the austere *Guardian* of Manchester (which is now, as you know, the *Guardian* of all England) would salute him as 'a great and noble artist who served the world and his people well.'

Louis Armstrong died last Tuesday. On Friday they buried him, and among the pallbearers were the Governor of New York State Nelson Rockefeller, New York

Mayor John Lindsay, Bing Crosby, Ella Fitzgerald, Duke Ellington, Count Basie, Bobby Hackett, Pearl Bailey, and Frank Sinatra. The President of the United States released a tribute that noted 'the sorrow of millions of Americans at the death of … one of the architects of an American art form, whose great talents and magnificent spirit added richness and pleasure to all our lives.'

There's no point in trying now to solve the insoluble problem of taste and fashion, though it is a problem that faces every generation and every true artist and every fake. After all, Stravinsky's 'Rite of Spring' produced a riot in Paris. And at one time the musical world was torn apart by the question of whether Wagner was a genius or a barbarian. Forty years ago, the death of Louis Armstrong would have received about the same notice in the daily press as, in that year of 1931, the death of Bix Beiderbecke received – which is to say, no mention at all. Yet Beiderbecke was the first white jazz musician whom Armstrong – a man of well-developed ego – embraced as a brother genius. It seems incredible now that anyone whose taste in music takes in, say, Ravel and Delius, should not recognize in the lovely melancholy cornet of Beiderbecke one of the unique and enduring sounds in jazz. I have collected Armstrong since he did a series of improvisations, in I think 1927, with the father of jazz piano, Earl Hines, who happily still lives and is still the master. But when I got the news of Armstrong's death, maybe it was the memory of that rare first compliment to a white jazzman that moved me to get out an old Paul Whiteman record, one of the precious batch recorded over a single winter and spring that redeemed band leader Whiteman's lush commercialism by giving rein to the sad, firm arrangements of Bill Challis and a marvelous strutting trio of true jazzmen: Beiderbecke, Trumbauer and Bill Rank. And I played Bix's lovely solo of 'Lonely Melody' and somehow felt that Beiderbecke had transcended and re-fined Armstrong's original inventions.

But Armstrong was more than a music man. He was an American folk original, and he epitomizes and files away once and for all a kind of a black man's life that will not happen again. One of the fine things about him is that unlike many a poor and shifty boy, he neither glossed over his squalid origins nor – which is harder – did he in the years of his success boast about them. He was born to a father who stoked furnaces in a turpentine factory and who left his wife when Armstrong was an infant. From the age of six on, Armstrong lived with his mother in a ratty coloured section of New Orleans given over to gamblers, pimps and prostitutes' cribs. 'Whether,' Armstrong once said, 'my mother did any hustling, I can't say. If she did, she kept it out of sight.' But he did recall that 'until she got religion and gave up men in 1915, I couldn't keep track of the step-daddies.' Young Louis was out on the streets by day delivering coal to prostitutes' cribs, picking up his meals from garbage cans, and by night hanging around the early honky-tonks. He used to say that the 'greatest thing that ever happened to me' was being arrested and sent off to a waifs' home on New Year's Day, 1914. He had celebrated the New Year by stealing a .38 caliber pistol from one of the step-daddies and running out on the street and firing it.

In the waifs' home there was a poor teacher, a coloured man, who taught him to

Louis Armstrong: 'more than a music man, he was an American folk original.'

play a bugle and a cornet. He got to play with the home's band at funerals.

He came out and sold some more coal to make money to lose by night in the gambling houses. 'In two hours, man' he said, 'I was a broke cat, broker than the Ten Commandments.' He tried pimping for a while, got a stab wound in the shoulder, and when he was eighteen married a prostitute. 'It didn't last,' he explained a couple of years ago, 'for a simple reason: she wouldn't give up her line of work.' A year later, he joined a ragtime band and then graduated to a riverboat band, and he began to blast himself to fame among the early musicians. So that he was sent for by the great King Oliver, went to Chicago, and the rest is history. The rest being the simple, crucial fact that he moved in on a kind of music that was improvised ensemble work, and he cut through it like a knife through butter by creating the jazz soloist in his own person. For the next forty-five years, jazz developed and waned and grew again, simple and complicated, but always along the path that Armstrong blazed with his remarkable lungs and his even more remarkable musical imagination.

Lately, as with all black men of any sort of talent, Armstrong came to be judged not so much by his music as by his social attitude as a successful Negro: a fierce moral test to which, by the way, we don't equally subject successful whites. Was he or was he not an Uncle Tom? Well, in his early film appearances, he was a standard variation of Uncle Tom – Cousin Tom, if you like – the stereotype of the jolly, roguish Negro, as Steppin Fetchit was the more disreputable stereotype of the shiftless, witless, country black.

I don't know whether Armstrong fretted over this. He was, I suspect, much too independent, too blithe to change his character at age sixty-five. He knew he'd been lucky, he was adored by all but the most politically conscious blacks and whites. He could have moved to any of the expensive enclaves in Harlem, or, like many a black basketball or baseball player of late, bought some acres in a very leafy suburbia and built a mansion. But through all his fame and wealth he stayed in the comfortable, humdrum house in a lower middle-class section of a New York borough, and he died there. In 1965, though, he recoiled in public from the police beatings in Selma, Alabama. He summed up his attitude quite crisply: 'They'd beat Jesus if he was black and marched. I'm not in the front line, but I support them with my donations. My life is my music. They would beat me on the mouth if I marched, and without my mouth I wouldn't be able to blow my horn.'

He certainly was never blind to the strict mores of his hometown, New Orleans, which today wallows in its true reputation as the cradle of jazz but does not, in the publicity, mention how very lately Negroes have played in public there. The blacks brewed jazz in the whorehouses on sour pianos; and when jazz broke loose from its smelly origins, the boys with talent broke out of the South and wound up in the glory days in Chicago and New York. Armstrong refused ever to play in New Orleans until the Civil Rights Act was passed. In 1965, he went back and led an integrated band in the new Jazz Museum down there. It was a wry touch that this hallowed hall, which today tourists visit as they might patter into the Louvre, was built around the crumbling timber of a wretched shack in which Armstrong was born.

Even the Soviets changed their mind about him. When he made the first of several triumphant tours of Africa, Moscow officially dubbed him a lackey helping in 'a capital-ist distraction.' He had a reply for that: 'I'm African-descended down to the bone, from my grandmammy on my mammy's side and from my grandpappy on my pappy's side.'

Last Wednesday, Moscow gave us permission to think of Armstrong as an okay figure: 'a symbol' said Isvestia, 'of the best traditions of Negro classical jazz … the huge talent of this musician, his love of work, and loyalty to his people enabled him to penetrate the impregnable barrier of racism in the U.S.A. and to achieve worldwide recognition.'

So now it's official.

Anti-Hijacking Plans

Letter No. 1180, 24 September 1971

I should like to pause and say, 'spare a sympathetic sigh for the airlines.' We read their full-page advertisements in the papers (when we have papers) and we drool in anticipation of the enormous range of luxuries they offer us. In the early days of civil aviation, forty years ago, it was startling even just to read that you no longer had to spend eighteen hours on a train getting from New York to Chicago. You could fly there in something like six hours. Astounding. Way back then, there was no mention of silent, dreamy flights, of beguiling stewardesses, of meals fit for a Greek ship-owner. Even ten years or so ago, the airlines' ads were content to make the astonishing boast that with the new jets you could balance a cup of coffee on the armrest and it would not wobble or spill. They were right. What next? Well, next, as always with a new product, in what we used to call the Western world (which now decidedly includes such prosperous Western nations as Japan), the advertising men really went to work polishing up their adjectives and burnishing that special prose that is the folk poetry of the affluent society. 'Pillow-soft' was the way one airline described its flights on a plane known as a 'whisper jet'. Ordinary, nice-looking girls turned into 'your adorable pampering nurse, waitress and protector'. One airline even annexed the upper atmosphere and begged you to fly its 'friendly skies', which provoked a cartoon in *The New Yorker* showing a middle-aged couple crashing around in a high altitude storm and the man saying to his wife: 'Thank God we're not in the unfriendly skies.'

Well, this lush, lulling prose still goes on, and the airlines still offer painless luxury at cut-rate prices in ads that still cover whole pages of the *New York Times*. Few of us stop to consider that the advertising contracts of these airlines were signed before they hit the appalling air pocket of the recession and plummeted down into a depression in which they seem to be stuck.

So, it's now news that they are all in deep trouble. They have cut their domestic services drastically. But the ones that fly overseas are in cutthroat competition with the Japanese and the Indians and the British and the Australians and the Germans and the Swiss, and so on. For many years, the international trade association of airline companies had an agreement that standardized the fares, so that it didn't matter which line you flew, the first class and economy flights cost the same. Now the Germans,

I believe, have announced they will not be bound by any general agreement and will begin flying the Atlantic at fares way below the old minimum. Several other lines are rushing to improvise their own bargains. So a price war is on. And I don't think it bodes much good for the lines or, in the long run, for us.

While the airlines are losing money, they are more or less obliged to subject their passengers to a new and tedious routine on embarking that makes some people swear that (a) they will switch to another line or (b) they will never fly again. This routine was introduced with a bang about a year ago; the week after that plane was hijacked by Arab irregulars and the terrified passengers found themselves imprisoned, if that is the word, in the desert.

And what is this fearful routine? Simply that when you leave the United States to fly to Europe, or for that matter when you leave Chicago or Atlanta or Minneapolis to fly south, to Texas or Florida say, the company has to consider the possibility that your next stop may be in Havana. That used to be the chronic fear till Castro apparently got tough with the hijackers – since when straightforward, non-political maniacs may hijack you to anywhere they have a mind to.

So, a year ago, Mr John Volpe, the Secretary of Transportation, announced that the government would join the industry in trying to stop the hijacker from getting on the plane. Most of the airports now have electronic devices – a beam you pass through on your way into the plane that detects any metal you might be harboring in your hand-held luggage or on your person. Obviously this involves slight delays, though a determined hijacker is not going to carry a gun at the level of the detection device. Asking him if he is carrying a firearm is obviously about as useful as those loyalty oaths demanded of government and state employees in the 1950s: 'Are you now or have you ever been a member of the Communist party?' Naturally, no thoroughgoing Communist is going to say yes. And I seriously doubt that even the old-fashioned, simpleminded type of English criminal, once memorably parodied in a newspaper piece by the late Westbrook Pegler, is going to say: 'Yes, I am carrying a .35 automatic, and I am sorry for what I done.'

Well the metal-detection gadget is by no means all. Safety razors, cigarette cases, and the like can show up as suspicious objects. And if we had to dump all our hand luggage on a table before we took the shortest flight, it would – would it not? – sort of detract from the prospect of the pillow-soft flight and the attentions of those adorable nurses, waitresses and protectors.

So now, when you leave New York for Europe as I did recently, when your plane is announced and you are shepherded to the proper gate, you find three or four pluckily smiling officials of the airline who send the males behind one screen to be frisked, searched, and patted by a male, and the females behind another screen to enjoy the same treatment at the hands of a female. (So far, Women's Lib has not protested this segregated practice.) All this takes time, but most people submit to it, for they realize it's being done for their own safety. And the friskers themselves are more delicate and tactful than a Miss America inspector taking what we call your vital measurements.

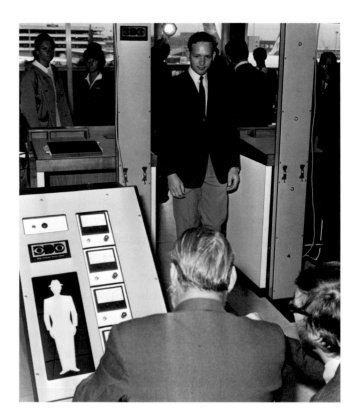

New anti-hijacking
security detectors on the
first day of operation
at Heathrow Airport,
September 1970.

But in spite of the warmth and friendliness and tact, you know what? It isn't work-ing. The airlines now admit in understandable desperation that really to check out a fully clothed human for a hidden gun requires a United States Marshal, who could hardly be summoned in less than fifteen minutes. The men who go aboard the planes on behalf of the government are armed and are known as Sky Guards. The airlines say there are nothing like enough of them. Planes are still being hijacked. I talked to an official of the airline that frisked me, and while he was apologizing for having de-tected on my person a nail file, a key chain, and one English-type golf ball (1.62 inches in diameter, and don't ask me what that was doing there), he said to me, 'You know, we simply can't keep up this routine all the time. Lots of people complain, and they'll desert to an airline that's more easygoing about the whole thing. But every time we suspend the routine, something happens. Or we have to hold up the plane on the run-way because we find there really is somebody aboard with a gun.' The really staggering thing he told me was that since they instituted this stand and search, while there'd been no hijackings on his line, they had in the last year taken over two hundred guns from intending passengers. I asked him – and I must have looked as if I didn't believe him – what sort of people? 'Mainly stupid,' he said. This is so puzzling as to defy further analysis, and I think we'll leave it there.

Anyway, the airlines are now in the position of having to promise, in their ads, im-possible amenities and luxuries while they are losing money and while they are forced to make the business of taking a plane actually arduous, if not painful.

State and the Secretary of Defense. And the Administration, it was painfully clear, had its back reared against the wall. What we had all been told years ago, and what lately we had come to believe, was that the American involvement would relax in direct proportion to the ability of the South Vietnamese to defend themselves. It seemed to be working out. The policy of turning the war over to the South Vietnamese bears the rather horrid name of 'Vietnamization'. Mr Melvin Laird, the Secretary of Defense, was bluntly challenged to say whether or not 'Vietnamization' was failing. Not at all, he said, it was succeeding. What, asked Senator Fulbright, is the aim of Vietnamization? The answer, in the simplest words, is to help the Vietnamese defend themselves. Mr Laird said, 'It is to give them an in-country security capability.' That's federal prose for fighting your own war. 'In-country security capability.'

I often wonder, and it is no doubt a blasphemous thought, whether men who regularly use such language are capable of thinking out the strategic problems of the war, what indeed it is all about. Tactics they know about. Weapons and arms, what we now call hardware, is a particular specialty of Secretary Laird. But what you fight with is not what the American people want to know just now so much as why they are fighting and to what end. The Administration is on wobbly ground when it tries to answer this question. It tends to oscillate between the threat of Communism to the whole of Asia and America's obligations under the South East Asian Treaty Organization. It's interesting to remark that the excuse of SEATO was not used until President Johnson and his Secretary of State were getting deeper and deeper into the war. In fact, way back in the middle 1950s, when France was on the verge of defeat in what they then called Indo-China, Eisenhower's Secretary of State John Foster Dulles said that the Vietnamese war was not started by open aggression but was a civil war fomented from within on the long-range advice and help of Communist China. 'It cannot be met,' said Mr Dulles, 'by unilateral armed intervention.' Incidentally, the SEATO Treaty itself forbids any intervention unless there is a unanimous vote of the members (Australia, France, New Zealand, Pakistan, the Philippines, Thailand, the United Kingdom and the United States), which most surely never happened, was never taken. But now the Administration has gone back to claiming a solemn duty under SEATO, and Secretary Laird says that so long as the North Vietnamese go on invading – since they are being successful, they're hardly likely to stop – so long will the United States feel free to bomb any part of North Vietnam and will 'not rule out the possibility' of blockading the harbour of Haiphong.

There are two reasons for doing this. The explicit one is to protect withdrawing American troops (though nobody suggests they're going to withdraw through the enemy's main port). The implicit reason, which Mr Laird all but proclaimed, is to 'emphasize' to North Vietnam and the Soviet Union 'the need for restraint.' This, I imagine, really means, 'please stop invading, or please wind down the war on your side.' It seems they are as unlikely to do it as we were to call off the invasion of Europe once we'd got a secure foothold in Normandy and a continuous supply line across the English Channel.

American B52 dropping payload of bombs onto the Vietcong, 1968.

So we are back to the old arguments, reinforced by frustration. And as the B-52s poured more bombs than ever down on North Vietnam, a couple of hundred Harvard students smashed up the University's Center for International Affairs, and the long lull in student rioting was broken. It is, we should remember, a new generation of students (four years is the lifetime of a university class). If they heat up again across the land, as the heat of war intensifies, we could well be back again in the black year of 1968. At any rate, the ordeal of face-saving that defeated President Johnson could, at the very least, make Mr Nixon a beatable man in November.

Army Chief Master Sergeant Max Bielke was the last US
serviceman to leave Vietnam on 29 March 1973.

armoured trucks ready for delivery to the poor and the housewives. Two Adminis-
trations have warned us, perhaps not loud enough, that most of that money will be
swallowed up in rising costs of production in the missile industry, and in the much
bigger wages that are going to have to be paid out to an all-volunteer army. To most
people, I should guess, this truth will come as a surprise and a letdown.

And while Mr Nixon rides high, as the man who finally did triumphantly keep his
word about getting all the men out, there is another and a worse peril looming ahead.
The last man off the prisoner-of-war planes on Thursday said simply that when the
Americans were all gone, 'There is going to be a blow-up.' Nobody can know it better
than the President. The cease-fire is a very shaky stage, probably only an interlude.
For, as the Washington commentator Stewart Alsop put it this week: 'True peace is
impossible when both sides are armed, when neither side is defeated, when one side is
still determined to defeat the other, and when there are many thousands of people who
hate each other's guts living within a rifle shot of each other.' You don't have to believe
or disbelieve the charges that the South Vietnamese were reinforced with vast supplies
of American arms before the cease-fire was signed, or that the North Vietnamese are
now systematically building up their forces and their supplies in the South. You could
discount these very plausible reports and still have good cause to fear that sooner than
later the North Vietnamese will begin their campaign to do what Senator McGovern
offered to let them do: to conquer the South and obliterate its government. If this campaign begins soon, President Nixon is sworn to bring back the bombers over North
Vietnam, and he has them on hand. Maybe the Russians, those beautiful chess players,
will stay North Vietnam's hand, pointing out that an enemy must always be allowed

a dignified escape hatch, and that in a year or more the American people will be far more philosophical about a Communist takeover than they would be now. Even so, the President must have some restless nights figuring out how much of a token retaliation – 'clobbering' is the word in vogue – he would mount that would at once save face and yet not give America the impression that their wretched war was on again. It has been said 'modest clobberings don't work.' So you see, we are not at the end of the war, we are at a face-saving stage of it. The initiative for what happens to Indo-China, and for that matter what happens to Mr Nixon, is now with Hanoi.

Mr Nixon is also going to have to face Congress on an issue he was always able to defy or smother so long as American troops were in Vietnam. This has to do with the constitutional power of the Congress, and only the Congress, to declare war. Well, the surprising truth is that the last declaration of war ever made by Congress was on, I believe, the ninth of December, 1941, against Italy. Since then, five Presidents have mobilized forces and dispatched them abroad and claimed that they were acting in an emergency in their constitutional office as the Commander in Chief, and that such war powers were 'inherent' in the Presidency. The enormous hassle between the President and the Congress, about the war-making power in Vietnam, was settled in the summer of 1964 when the North Vietnamese attacked two American destroyers in the Gulf of Tonkin. The Congress, in a fit of outrage, couldn't wait to pass a joint resolution of both Houses giving the President unlimited authority to 'take necessary measures' of his own choice anywhere in Southeast Asia to protect American forces or help any SEATO nation asking for it. There was, of course, no time limit, but when Congress began to growl and then howl over the bypassing of its constitutional power, LBJ said if you don't like the Gulf of Tonkin resolution, withdraw it, or renew it. Congress grumbled and renewed it. But then in December 1971, Congress repealed it, and President Nixon signed the repeal a month later.

So now, his right to run a war depends entirely on helping a signatory nation of the South East Asia Treaty Organization. Well, Cambodia is not a signatory, and American bombers from bases in Thailand are destroying the Cambodian countryside.

This contradiction, discrepancy, outrage – whatever you want to call it – is plain to this Congress, which is plainly determined not to get into another Vietnam and not to let any President claim the right to do so. At the moment, the President is claiming, in practise, the right to use the Air Force as his private punitive arm, to use whenever and wherever a friend of the White House screams for help. It is a very frail right to set against the right of the Congress, in the Constitution, not only to declare war but 'to raise and support armies' and a Navy and 'to make rules for the government of the land and naval forces.' Naturally, the Founding Fathers couldn't anticipate Air Forces. Mr Nixon has them there!

Sixty years ago, in a flight of rhetoric, English author Hilaire Belloc said that the President of the United States was the last absolute monarch left. If the Congress acts on its present mood, he will once more be returned to the status of a constitutional monarch. At any rate, he had better enjoy, while he has it, his finest hour.

fund shortly before the government announced a change in policy and permitted a rise in the price of milk supports. The man already convicted of running the secret White House investigating team known as 'the plumbers', by such illegal tactics as spying, bugging, and burglary, is to be sentenced this month, and it's already known that he's ready to talk. He knows a great deal, as does the President's main accuser, John Dean, who's also about to be sentenced. Somewhere along the line of these judicial processes, it may well be that we shall hear the sound that has for such a puzzling long time not been heard. It is the sound of the squealer. For whatever you may think or suspect about the President, the plain legal fact is that in all the long cast of shabby characters none of them has come forward and corroborated the damning accusations of John Dean that the President knew all about Watergate from the beginning. The continuing mystery of Watergate is how so many people involved in a plot could stay silent. It's possible when two or three men conspire together that they can all tell the same story, whether it's a true story or a bluff. But it is against all the habits of human nature for twenty or thirty men caught more or less in the act to keep their traps shut.

So, at the moment we are still bewildered, though in a quieter, chronic way. We still don't have the answer to the first fundamental question. And nobody has said it better than Senator Barry Goldwater, the right-wing Republican who for so long was loyal to Nixon and believed the best about him. Senator Goldwater was interviewed on television last week. Whatever he's saying it's always a rare pleasure to hear a United States Senator talk plain English without the elaborate garnish of federal jargon that suffocates and disguises the meaning of what he might be trying to say. Goldwater was asked if Watergate had been fatal to Nixon's continuing capacity to govern the country. And he replied: 'I don't think it's Watergate, frankly, as much as it's a question in people's minds of just how honest is this man? I hate to think of the old adage, "Would you buy a used car from Dick Nixon?" but that's what the people are asking around the country.'

To see that somehow or other the question gets answered, the Congress did something that six months ago would have been inconceivable, when the President, with the considerable backing of constitutional lawyers, was quoting Jefferson and other great men to say that Congress could never, under the Constitution, force a President to yield the records of his private conversations. His lawyers had done a deal of homework on the famous case of Jefferson versus the Supreme Court in a vaguely similar case; and without anybody noticing it, the President started using Jefferson's own phrase that the Supreme Court was a 'coordinate, coeval' branch of the government and could never be superior to the President under the law. (Jefferson, by the way, in old age was almost gaga with the obsession that the Supreme Court had grown into a tyrant that would throttle the nation.)

Well, Congress has just passed a law that explicitly gives the courts the right to subpoena all the White House tapes and Presidential documents it wants. The courts alone are to decide which tapes concern national security, say, and should be kept secret from an investigating committee. Now the President could have vetoed the bill.

But he didn't. And the White House made the limp comment: 'He knew a veto would be misunderstood.' So saying he would never yield, he yielded. I don't imagine he ever dreamed what would happen next day. The Senate Watergate Committee issued subpoenas for nearly five hundred tapes and documents. Surely, somewhere in there somebody talked, somebody, in what was meant to be a highly secret record of White House dialogues, somebody must have dropped a hint, or boasted, or otherwise congratulated a colleague on the cover-up. If not, then the President would emerge as one of the most maligned and misunderstood Presidents in history. There are people who stubbornly believe so. But so far none of us knows.

Well, so much for the unflagging public concern about the President's honesty: his 'sincerity according to truth'.

The problem of public honesty impinged on another of those three words this week. The word 'energy'. The man in charge of conserving energy, who's doing his damnedest just now to prove Mr Nixon's point that the crisis is not critical enough to require petrol or oil rationing, put out another statement – a hope, rather – that people, you and me, would use no more than ten gallons a week – of petrol, that is. The distributors and oil companies have together agreed to sell no more than ten gallons to a customer. But this doesn't prevent a man driving another few miles and stocking up on another ten. It is plainly unworkable. Moreover, there are many reports that petrol stations are hiking up the price of petrol as high as the traffic bears. There is a government-fixed price for petrol, but it's being ignored wherever the wind blows cold or the trains don't run. And over a continent that once had a railroad grid as dense as a spider's web, you'd be surprised at the thousands of places – across many hundreds of miles – where no trains run at all because, since the highways took over the national shipment of freight, the railroads have gone bankrupt. Clearly, I should think, in a country also where ninety million cars are on the road at every hour of the day and night, the car-owner's decision to use no more than ten gallons a week would constitute one of the most sublime acts of voluntary restraint in the history of human nature. There was a sign or two that the people most aware of this absurdity are the owners of petrol stations themselves. First of all, there are small towns through the Midwest and across the prairie that consist of two or three big motels, a supermarket, and no railroad station. They are quickly being cut off from, you might say, American life. And out West, the word has come in that petrol station owners, driven mad by obvious violators who own big cars, and therefore capacious petrol tanks, have actually started burning up, literally setting fire to, the same big cars.

Looking to the long run, and when things go bad most of us retire into mass cures, people are ready to believe that the great age of cheap fuel, of all the energy we need for our new-found comforts, is over. And they then say: the answer in the long run is a massive improvement in public transportation. And that means, to most people, a vast outpouring of money into rehabilitating the railroads. That and, as Washington and San Francisco are doing, building their first underground tube system. It sounds sensible enough at first glance. But unfortunately, it is sensible only if you glance at the America of 1910 or 1950, and not at the America of 1973. It would apply to an America where the railroads ran most places people need to travel. And, even more, to an America where the word 'commuter' means a man, a worker, who lives in a suburb and commutes to the city to work. But, a government statistic just out gives a startlingly new definition to the species known as the 'commuter'.

In the ten biggest cities in America, saving only New York, how many people do you suppose live in a suburb and commute to the city? 70 percent? 80 percent? No. 18 percent, only. More than half of the working population of this country live in one suburb and commute to work in another suburb. Henry Ford, the grandson of the man who started it all, put it tartly: 'Subways, tubes, are fine for getting downtown and back. But most people don't travel downtown and back any more. They travel all over the place. And you can't build subways all over the place.' Or start, at this late date, building railroad tracks over hundreds of thousands of miles of empty land.

So Detroit, which has just laid off 290,000 automobile workers, looks to the long run. And the long run means contracts for nothing but buses.

That gloomy figure of the appalling, sudden unemployment in Detroit points to the third word: the economy. That is another story all in itself. We had better brace ourselves to go into it at another time.

Kidnapping of Patricia Hearst

Letter No. 1306, 22 February 1974

San Francisco, in one week, has become the laboratory of an experiment in terrorism that alarmed first the city, then very many wealthy and famous people, then whole governments with the threat of a new technique it may be impossible to overcome.

We should have been warned a year ago, when an official of the Ford Motor Company was kidnapped in Argentina. The kidnappers asked as ransom a million dollars in medical equipment, and they got it. At the moment, another Ford executive is being held for more than twice the price.

The San Francisco horror began two weeks ago when Patricia Hearst, the nineteen-year-old daughter of one of the heirs to the Hearst newspaper empire, one night opened the door of her apartment across the bay in Berkeley and faced a young white woman who said she was having trouble with her car, and could she telephone? Before Miss Hearst could respond, or shut the door, two black men with guns rushed in, seized Miss Hearst, beat up her fiancé, and carried her off in a car. It seemed, but not for long, like it was an old-fashioned kidnapping, nonetheless bloodcurdling for being that of a nineteen-year-old girl instead of, say, the Lindbergh baby. There was a day or two of silence on the part of the kidnappers, and of terrible anxiety on the part of the parents, who live down the Peninsula from here in a large and hitherto unmolested mansion.

Then a tape recording came in the mail to a radio station here with orders from the kidnappers that it was to be played in full over the air, and the whole text of it published by the newspapers. So, to begin with, we had the strange, defeated feeling of seeing the mass media meekly submit to the kidnappers. After the usual half-hour programmes the three networks devote in the early evening to national and international news, we had to sit through a whole hour of a programme, unbought, unsponsored and played for free at the dictate of an unknown gang of kidnappers. The gang, if that is the word, turned out to be a radical underground – no bigger probably than the one that started the American Revolution nearly two hundred years ago – calling itself the SLA: the Symbionese Liberation Army. At first hearing, Symbionese sounds like a Middle Eastern ethnic group we ought to know about, or one of the later admissions to the United Nations. However, 'Symbionese' is, as such things go, rather a scholarly title. It is taken from symbiosis, a Greek word meaning, roughly, the capacity of two or

Patricia Hearst with a machine gun, standing in front
of the emblem of the Symbionese Liberation Army.

more organisms or bodies to exist compatibly together. More symbolically, it signifies a radical group that aims to unite many sorts of people of all races in the struggle to destroy capitalism, or what the SLA calls, picking up the cant word of most extreme leftists, the Fascists.

The tape recording we heard was a very chilling sound. It was a long appeal from Patricia Hearst to her parents, telling them she was safe and getting food and medical attention, and begging them to understand that the SLA was a very serious organization and knew what it was doing. So indeed, it appeared. Her voice was followed by that of a so-called 'Field Marshal' who certainly was well-spoken and deadly calm and precise. The SLA was holding Miss Hearst as a prisoner of war, according to international convention. She would be 'executed' if any attempt was made to set her free by force. The blockbuster fell with the statement of the SLA's terms for her release. The Hearst family must personally subsidize the distribution of seventy dollars' worth of free food to every poor person, every old and needy person, every convict on parole, army veteran, social security applicant, in the entire state of California (which, may I remind you, is not Los Angeles with a fringe of mountains but a terrain that stretches from Edinburgh to Naples, nearly nine hundred miles long, inhabited by some twenty million people). The cost of this benefaction was figured first at something like 170 million dollars, and later at 400 million. The SLA precisely specified where the food should be distributed, and named several other radical groups (all of them nonviolent) that should supervise the procedure. The Hearst family has been wealthy for three generations, but none of them can put his or her hands on that sort of money.

Well, first of all Miss Hearst's father admitted that the cost of this incredible gesture was beyond him, but he promised to do everything he could to come up with a workable alternative. Mr Hearst's submissiveness may startle some people and appall others. But hearing that listless voice, and then seeing the forlorn faces of the parents on television, we could not yet begin to muster a judicial opinion. We were hearing a girl zombie apparently drained of all feeling except that of a beggar; and we were identifying, in a helpless way, with the sleepless anxiety of a mother and father at the end of their rope.

Then a few days later, another tape came through on which, the family said, she sounded more like herself. 'She didn't,' said her father, 'sound sedated.' Their initial popular theory to explain the tonelessness of her first appeal was that she'd been drugged. It then came to light that Miss Hearst is no country club doll but a young woman sympathetic to some social rebels (her fiancé is rumoured to have been an old member of the Students for a Democratic Society), but she's not necessarily an enthusiast for the Symbionese Liberation Army. Anyway, on the second tape, she lit a flicker of hope by saying that the Army 'wasn't trying to present an unreasonable request. It was never intended that you feed the whole state. So whatever you come up with basically is okay. And just do it as fast as you can and everything will be fine.' Well, Mr Hearst could raise two millions and started organizing the food supplies it would pay for, but the SLA said it was not enough – the family must raise another four million.

In response to that, the Hearst Corporation (which is not owned by Mr Hearst) says, all right, it will put up two million the moment Miss Hearst is released, and another two million in January 1975. That seems to be the final offer. Miss Hearst had said the first time, and said it again, that it would be fatal to have the FBI or the police try to track down the SLA's hideaway and burst in and shoot it out. But now, on a third tape, the so-called Field Marshal threatened the girl's execution if anything happened to two SLA members who are being held in the penitentiary on a charge of murder. That's where it stood Friday night.

Which brings us to the necessary, cold-blooded question: what do you do? What do the Hearsts do? What do the parents of the next victim do? How can our sort of society cope with this new kind of terrorism that appears rational, ideological, deadly serious; and while it may be practised by a tiny minority, can yet force the vast majority on the outside to take its prodigious demands seriously?

The first reaction of many otherwise compassionate people was to say, sooner or later such demands must be rejected and the victim sacrificed. Then we naturally turned to the existing institutions that are there to enforce the laws. For, remember, kidnapping is a federal crime, and so is a threat to overthrow the government of the United States by force. The Attorney General of the United States responded promptly by saying that the police would be guilty of dereliction of duty if they came to know where the SLA was holding the girl and did not 'go in to get her', a remark that Miss Hearst's father angrily called 'damn near irresponsible', and which the Attorney General later recanted in the rather flurried assurance that of course he hadn't meant to imply that the girl's safety was not the prime consideration.

Well, nevertheless, the FBI has sent in here 125 agents whose specialty is kidnapping. The FBI is a past master at infiltrating radical groups (it came out the other day that the Black Panthers' chief security officer, no less, was an FBI undercover agent). But apparently nobody, including the FBI, has an accurate notion whether the Symbionese Liberation Army consists of twenty members or twenty thousand, though the best guess is that it is a very, very small outfit.

But there is not much consolation there. The FBI, the police, the security forces of many countries, not to mention social scientists and psychiatrists, foresee a new wave of international terrorism and, if the SLA is the winner in this escapade, a rash of kidnappings by tiny, clever radical groups. On Wednesday night the editor of an Atlanta paper was kidnapped, and again a taped recording recited a ransom demand. Most of the legal and sociological experts – even when they are self-anointed – agree that the answer is to make kidnapping at once so unprofitable and so punishable as to deter the kidnappers. How? The answers so far are almost as wordy and jargon-ridden as the manifestos of the SLA itself. One needling point was made by a psychiatrist in Dallas who is the director of a clinic for behaviour problems. 'We need,' he says, 'a way to keep terrorists from taking over the media. The denial of publicity and reward would stop such groups as the SLA.'

It brings us back to Munich, and the Rome airport, and the Palestine terrorists, and the fears of wealthy Jews, and the universal demon we don't seem able to exorcise: which is the fact that somebody thinks up a new technique of terrorism in San Francisco or Athens one day, it is on the tube that same night, and it is imitated tomorrow in Beirut or London or Atlanta or Vienna.

Over the entrance lobby of the BBC in London is the legend: 'Nation Shall Speak Peace Unto Nation.' We might also inscribe up there the reminder that, thanks to the magic of the box, 'Nation Shall Flash Evil Unto Nation' in the twinkling of an eye.

Alistair Cooke returned to this theme in his *Letter No. 1314* broadcast on 19 April 1974

Because of what happened last week, I think we have to remind ourselves of what was known about Patty Hearst's character. For once she was captured, there started a weird sequence of exchanges between the kidnappers and the girl's parents that is, so far as we know, unique in the history of kidnapping. No warning letters written in clumsy capitals. No demands for ransom money to be delivered at a crossroads at midnight. But tape recordings mailed to a radio station; tape recordings of Patricia Hearst's voice in which she talked directly to her parents. In the first one, she appealed to her father to do what her captors demanded: to distribute millions of dollars' worth of food to the poor, indeed to anyone who lined up at specified places. You'll remember the first distribution was marred by mob scenes and people simply pillaging the supplies. Then the SLA demanded more money and more food, and the subsequent scenes were more orderly. Meanwhile, another tape had been received and played on the air, far and wide. Miss Hearst, who in the first tape sounded toneless and on the verge of stupor, was now, if not lively, more testy, blaming her parents for being laggard in doing everything the SLA demanded. Also, Miss Hearst proclaimed that the SLA knew very well what they were about, and she more than hinted that they were dedicated, as we say, idealists. Both times, the parents and old friends agreed, it was the voice of nobody but Patricia, though opinions varied about her mental state, whether or not she'd been drugged, whether or not she was speaking for herself or speaking, either literally or figuratively, with a gun at her back. Obviously, whatever her emotional state, she wasn't saying anything the SLA didn't approve of. There was then, you may remember, a couple of weeks or so when nothing more was heard, and people began to say they wouldn't give a nickel for her life. Since the SLA didn't appear to be satisfied with the charitable efforts of the Hearsts, maybe they had, as they had threatened, done away with her.

And then came the third tape: a real shocker. Without any question it was, once again, the voice of Patricia Hearst, but now angry, in a whining sort of way, carping, condemning the ineffectiveness of the food effort, despising her father as a liar, and for the first time incorporating some of the dreary, parrot-like jargon of the movement: the evils of the corporate state, the identification of anybody not of a like mind as a fascist and so on. The first thing to notice about this tape was that it was tied to no date or recent event. The previous tapes had mentioned something that had happened no more than a day before the recording, evidently to demonstrate that what we were hearing was not the voice of a dead woman. But the third tape, the scolding one, was timeless. It was followed by a triumphant proclamation from the leader of the group, who calls himself a field marshal, that Patricia had been told she was free to go but had been converted to the SLA faith and chose to stay with the movement and cut all ties with her 'fascist' parents, the 'corporate' state, etc., etc. A photograph was circulated showing Patricia in a sort of uniform, the modern guerrilla's belted jacket, the machine gun, the beret, the genuine get-up popularized originally, I believe, by the female followers of the Argentinian revolutionary Che Guevara. Indeed, Patricia, we were now told, had taken the name 'Tania' as her revolutionary moniker – Tania being the name of a woman who died with Che Guevara's guerrillas in Bolivia. To make things more certain, or more baffling, Patricia herself, in the last brutal tape, identified herself as Tania, the new, proud convert to the SLA cause.

Then, last Monday, there was a bank robbery in San Francisco, and not only was it committed by the SLA, not only were three of the robbers women armed with automatic guns on shoulder slings, but one of them was Patricia Hearst. When we first heard of this, it sounded highly suspicious as a fact – the sort of blob of melodrama that the headline writers of evening newspapers desperately reach for around noon, their first deadline. It was at first suspected she was there. Then it was alleged. Then she was plainly filmed by hidden security cameras. The first reports said her right hand was hunched and possibly tied up. However it was hunched because that's what you do with your right arm when it's cradling an automatic. Another early rumour said that during the raid one or two of the other women kept a gun trained on Patricia, the clear implication being that she might run amok or suddenly announce she was a captive being fraudulently put on display.

But on Thursday morning, all the previous plausible theories had to be abandoned. And let's just remind ourselves that there were, by that time, three. 1. That she had been drugged from the start or otherwise terrified into saying what the SLA wanted her to say. 2. That she had been forced to declare her conversion to the cause and her decision to stay with the group to cover up the fact of her death (this was the timeless tape). And 3. The last theory, that she was more or less on parade at the robbery but under the watchful muzzles of the robbers' guns, had to go when several bank employees and other witnesses were very positive in saying that Miss Hearst was a free and active member of the gang, that she had control of her own gun and was plainly ready to use it. The bank security guard and the manager watched the whole thing through a peephole window in the manager's office. The guard said Miss Hearst threatened, in her words, 'the first son of a bitch who moves' and then 'spat out obscenities' at random.

Her parents, Mr and Mrs Randolph Hearst, who have been existing in an unenviable daze through the last ten weeks, have almost given up trying to find one explanation more sophisticated than another. They seem to stay with their conviction that while the voice of the girl on the tapes is their girl, the character is not anyone they knew. The fiancé, the philosophy student, made the comment: 'She's sick. She's exhausted. She is being humiliated at the hands of people determined she is not going to get out of this alive. These people are staking all on the propaganda victory of Patty's conversion.'

The blanket word that covers a lot of doubt is 'brainwashed', by which a lot of people seem to mean that she has been either drugged or tortured into an insensibility in which she'll say anything that's spoon-fed to her. Or that she's acting out the tough guerrilla recruit under threat of having her sister kidnapped or her family murdered.

There is, however, one other definition of the word 'brainwashed', and I incline to it, maybe because of an old, painful experience with a group, not political but pseudo-religious, skilled at recruiting impressionable young people, able to tap the dynamite of their unconscious but not to guide it, so that, say, a daughter you knew deeply could explode into an unrecognizable monster giving her all – money, devotion, total belief – to the movement and, incidentally, renounce and despise the parents in a voice and in a language that had its own alien and brutal and wholly unfamiliar tone. It is, in such a case, what you might call malign conversion, a dreadful experience to be an onlooking parent. For the loved child has been brainwashed into a genuine conversion. And is, for the time being, lost. At worst, is lost forever.

Nixon Resigns

Letter No. 1331, 16 August 1974

It's hard not to begin this talk with one of the most expressive of human sounds: a long, happy sigh, followed by two cheers for Gerald Ford. Not three, just yet. All incoming Presidents get two cheers for the honeymoon. The third is reserved for a little later on, for that marriage between the President and the Congress that President Ford yearned for in his address to both Houses. I don't want to crab things at the start, but it might be as well to say now, as later, that the third cheer is never heard because, unlike a parliamentary system, the makers of the federal system arranged that the President and the Congress should be natural enemies. After what the old Colonials had been through with the executive power of a King, they were almost morbidly concerned to create a regular watchdog over the President, much more wary than the House of Commons is ever expected to be with a Prime Minister. And on four days

Reading the headlines at Washington National Airport, August 1974.

– what we can now see as four fateful days in the spring of 1787 – they discussed what you do with a President who takes to himself dangerous, or criminal, power. If they'd had tapes of that four-day debate, they would be wonderful to hear just now.

Anyway, the writers of the Constitution devised, to their satisfaction, a recipe for removing a President. And, after 187 years of all sorts of Presidents and every sort of turmoil, including a civil war, the provision was used. It took two years from a short report in the papers about some comic burglary in Washington to the blinding headlines: 'Nixon Resigns'. Two years for the vast and alarming literature of Watergate to reach a single recording of a few quick telephone conversations between President Nixon and his closest advisor, H. R. Haldeman, in which he expressed his alarm that the FBI was already on to the Watergate burglary and might trace it to the White House; in which he heard and cursed the rumour that his Attorney General, John Mitchell, had known about Watergate and perhaps ordered it; in which he thereupon, in tough gangster language, ordered Haldeman to get hold of the head of the CIA and tell him to get the FBI to call off its investigation. The charge of dynamite in this conversation was the simple fact that it took place on 23 June,1972, only six days after the burglary had taken place. Why did Nixon release this tape? Because he had to. Because he had kept it from his lawyer. And when the Supreme Court ordered the President to give it up, the lawyer heard it, was stunned, and threatened to resign. If he had done that, and was called later either in the impeachment proceedings or in the Watergate cover-up trial, he would have had to say what he knew or run the risk himself of a criminal charge. So the President had to release the tape, along with a pathetic hope that the House and the Senate would see it, as he put it, 'in perspective'. They were able to do that, as all of us were, right away. Because suddenly the only perspective that mattered was the perspective of the two years between June of 1972 and August of 1974, during which, it was now as plain as a red rag to a bull, the President had lied in every public statement about Watergate, every press conference, every speech. The conservative Republicans in the Senate, who had manned the last barricade on Nixon's side, who had doggedly insisted they wanted positive 'direct' evidence that the President knew about Watergate before March 1973 – well, now they had it, and knew it. And the Republican leader in the House said, 'from now on, it's all downhill.' The Republican leader in the Senate said the President was through. And the word was taken to this cornered man that it would be impossible for him to raise more than a dozen votes among the hundred Senators in his favour, when the thing came to trial in the Senate. Some people had guessed all along that the President would sense his doom if it were clear that he couldn't raise thirty-four votes in the Senate. And that's what happened. And others said that the only convincing proof the President would ever take would be the word of his old right-wing supporters in the Senate that he would have to go.

Well, both things happened. And now that the man was down and almost out, the first gesture of compassion came from the only black man in the Senate. Republican Senator Edward Brooke of Massachusetts, on the morning the President was to make his last speech from the White House, said he would offer a resolution, presumably to be followed by a similar resolution in the House, promising that Congress would grant the President immunity from all further prosecution. Senator Brooke knew enough not to propose a law: the Congress cannot do that. It would be bypassing or violating the authority of the courts. But there is nothing technically against a joint resolution expressing 'the sense' of Congress. Unfortunately, Senator Brooke did not check with the party leaders on both sides of the aisle. They and their counterparts in the House were quick to say, before the speech, that it was beyond the power of Congress even to suggest to the courts that they would be generous not to act. Senator Brooke recovered from this apparent gaffe by saying that his offer was predicated on the assumption that the departing President's speech would be contrite, full of penitence and apology, and would ask the forgiveness and the prayers of the American people he had betrayed.

With this in mind, we were all the more curious to know if Mr Nixon, such a master of rhetoric and piety and moral zeal, would so drastically change his spots and beg for mercy and charity. But I don't think that anyone, except those who have known and watched him in his Washington life for the past twenty-eight years, could guess at the extraordinary sermon we were to hear. Full of ringing declarations of bravery and quotations from Theodore Roosevelt about spending oneself in a worthy cause, and ending with a pledge to go on 'daring greatly' and to work for the 'great causes he had dedicated himself to, so long as he had breath of life in his body.'

When it was over, one can only say in all charity that the network commentators were stunned, or for the moment bemused, by the tune they'd heard so often from men who had fought noble causes and lost them. He sounded, somebody said, 'like Adlai Stevenson on the night he conceded his defeat by Eisenhower': the gallant loser in a great cause. Senators came on, and Nixon's opponent in the 1968 campaign, Hubert Humphrey, the aging Democratic liberal, said incredibly that it was 'a noble speech on the highest level of statesmanship.'

Well, there was one voice, and so far as I heard one voice only, that spoke for, I am convinced, millions of Americans aghast after a speech of breathtaking gall. I ought to mention his name. He is Roger Mudd, of the Columbia Broadcasting System. He is a blue-eyed, virile looking man with shortish hair and a look of agreeable surprise. After the Nixon speech was over, he had a look of total bafflement and incredulity. Not only could he not believe what he'd heard from the President, he couldn't believe the soft, indulgent things that were being said by his colleagues. What had Nixon said about Watergate? Nothing but the hint that he had made a mistake of judgment – not that he had plotted, conspired, obstructed justice, lied, was aware of bribes and hush money, that he had used the two chief intelligence agencies of the government to cover up a plot he publicly pretended to abhor. And why had he been forced out? There was not even a hint that he had been. He had mentioned only that he had 'lost' his 'political base' in Congress. Most Presidents, especially after the off-year congressional election, lose that. But Mr Nixon made it seem, as Roger Mudd put it, that for some obscure

Richard Nixon on the steps of Marine One leaving the
White House after his resignation.

reason he wouldn't go into, 'a bunch of craven politicians in the House' had deserted him. Too bad, after all that dedication to splendid causes.

There are, it seems to me, two explanations of Mr Nixon's extraordinary final speech. Either he is, and has been all along, a man without a conscience who genuinely believes that what he does, however dark and devious, is done for a worthy end. Or, he was deliberately doing what he had advised former Vice President Spiro Agnew to do in his dark hour: never give in, never admit you're down.

If this was it, then it's possible that once again Mr Nixon has been too smart for his own good. If he could have shown at the last a truly contrite heart, a humble air, it might have given pause to the courts, to special prosecutor Mr Leon Jaworski in particular, who is still charged with tracking down the wrongdoers. And to Judge John J. Sirica, who is to preside over the coming Watergate cover-up trial. That is supposed to start next month, and some of the defendants have already asked for a stay because of the new evidence uncovered by the tapes that incriminated Mr Nixon. There are thirty-five men indicted or already convicted of crimes connected with the cover-up. To them, the main fact about the transfer of power from Nixon to Ford is that President Nixon is now Mr Nixon, and therefore an ordinary citizen who, according to the Constitution, is quite liable to prosecution for crimes in the ordinary way. Mr Jaworski would be well within his rights in summoning a grand jury and, on the basis of the new and damning tapes, asking them to indict the man who could not be indicted as President. Quite apart from the move to see Mr Nixon come to trial, which by the way had strong backing at the American Bar Association's annual convention, there is the question of the feelings, and the probable strategy, of some of the main defendants in the coming trial. Haldeman is one, Mitchell another. Dare a jury send them to jail for conspiring to obstruct justice when it can be shown that they were the pawns controlled by the King himself? It seems inevitable, very likely anyway, that these men, who did what they did on the orders of the President, would want to have Mr Nixon called as a witness in their defence.

We're only within earshot of what could turn out to be a legal blockbuster. It's muffled from us now in the breaking waves of applause for President Ford, and for the knowledge, after the most grilling investigation ever done on one man by the FBI (it was done when Mr Nixon nominated him as Vice President after Agnew had to quit), the knowledge that whatever else he is, he is a plain, forthright, decent, and blamelessly honest man. The impulse to cheer prompts among many people the complementary impulse to forgive and forget, to say that Nixon and his wife and children have suffered the supreme humiliation and should be left alone. If he were alone in his crimes, so indeed he should. But there is, for instance, John Dean, in prison, who (it now appears) spoke the truth from the start. There are those thirty-five others. They too have wives and children, and jobs gone forever. They may not all be overcome by the milk of human kindness when they think of Mr Nixon, secure in his mansion at San Clemente, with the taxpayers' blessing of $156,000 a year for life.

President Ford

Letter No. 1332, 23 August 1974

Whenever a man runs for the Presidency, or thinks about it, and if there is a realistic chance he might possibly make it, he usually finds some boyhood friend who has gone into journalism to come along and produce a staple form of American literature known as 'the campaign biography'. I once knew a man of slightly cynical bent who collected campaign biographies. He maintained you could learn more about America from them than from all the history books, very much on a perverse principle held by the late Erwin Panofsky, a great art historian who came here as a refugee from Hitler in, I believe, the late 1930s. Though he began at once to plunge into American art galleries, he then came to the conclusion that the true key to American life lay not in any framed painting but in the background details that commercial artists put into advertisements.

The lesson these men were suggesting is that both the advertising artist and the journalist who runs up a quickie biography of a potential president are not so much concerned with life as it is but life as it ought to be. Not with the strangeness and unpredictability of a man's character but with the qualities his biographer believes a man ought to have to appeal to a majority of the American voters. And it's a peculiar thing that down through, I should think, nearly a century, and through all the violent history of that time and the overwhelming technological revolution, these campaign biographies strike an almost pastoral note, like to imagine the new national saviour as a simple, rural, all-American farm boy and football player, shrewd perhaps but no city-slicker, as honest and simple as a ripe apple. There are obviously some Presidents who are a little difficult to fit into this formula. Theodore Roosevelt was one, a comparative patrician as Presidents go, a wealthy man from an old, social Dutch family. So they stressed his muscular Christianity and the fact he used to like to rough it in the canyons of the West, and shoot tigers in India. Franklin Roosevelt was even more of a problem. He was a handsome, superior, young New York City dude, with a family mansion on the Hudson. He was never a whiz at football. He was the adored pet of a regal mother. He was never known to have churned milk or kissed a horse. So they had to stress his passion for fishing. Later on the news photographers felt like miners striking gold when they could show him serving hot dogs outdoors to the King and Queen of England.

But in spite of such oddities, it's surprising how many Presidents in the past fifty years or so could be easily made to conform – in their campaign biographies – to the Horatio Alger prototype of the humble boy born on a farm, or near a farm, who played on the local high school football team, swam in the ole swimmin' hole, married his boyhood sweetheart, and was astounded at about the age of fifteen to hear some local toothless gaffer say, 'You mark my words, that young fella'll be Praise-i-dent of the You-Nited States some day.'

With only minor variations in the given plot and in the local colour, it was possible to write more or less standard biographies along these lines of Calvin Coolidge, Herbert Hoover, Harry Truman, Lyndon Johnson and Richard Nixon. And as each of them achieved the White House, the newspapers got hold of their forgotten campaign biographies and began to instruct their readers in the folksy virtues of the regions that cradled them: Coolidge's Vermont, Truman's Jackson County, Missouri, the rough goat country of Lyndon Johnson's part of Texas, the simple Quaker values of Nixon's Whittier, California, a town actually named after the Quaker poet John Greenleaf Whittier.

We are all praying just now that Gerald Ford is safe and secure in his health and his security, because if anything happened to him it would be more than usually difficult to fit Vice President Nelson Rockefeller into the folksy mould. As a rueful Senator said the other day, a man who is on one of the two congressional committees that are now examining the sources of Rockefeller's worldly goods, 'We don't know if his net worth is five hundred million dollars or five billions. It could take a year just to go through the books of all the corporations and the family's international holdings.'

But in the meantime, the newspapers are having a field day letting us know something they didn't know themselves till about ten days ago: namely, what manner of man is the King in the White House. We learned for the first time that he was christened Leslie King, Jr., after his father, but when he was two, his mother divorced her husband (a new note, that) and married the president of a paint and varnish company (a prosperous business in Grand Rapids, Michigan, which is a famous furniture manufacturing town). The stepfather's name was Gerald Ford, and he adopted the boy and gave him his own name.

From there on, the story reverts almost dreamily to the standard romance. In high school, he asked for, and got, a double lunch hour, so he could pick up some pin money by washing dishes for an hour in a small Greek restaurant. The young Ford was no bent-backed bookish type (that's always a reassuring item). His passion was football, and his biographer can truthfully say that he was a very good footballer – he was the best. First he made his high school team, then his state football team, then when he went to the University of Michigan he became its star centre. In 1934 he was named the most valuable university player. He had offers from the Green Bay Packers, which is to say the equivalent of Manchester United and Liverpool, but he was now at the age, twenty-one, when it is not only allowed for a small-town football hero to break the all-American boy mould, it is, curiously, expected of him. I mean, it's now all right for him to decide on a profession and take to the books. He turned down the football

Gerald R. Ford takes his oath as the 38th President in a ceremony
in the East Room of the White House, 9 August 1974.

offers, but was so mad for the game that he stayed on for part of the year at the University of Michigan to be football coach. During alternate semesters he went off to Yale and entered the law school. One of his teachers was the then young and brilliant Professor Eugene Rostow (the brother of Walt, Lyndon Johnson's Henry Kissinger, and himself subsequently Under-Secretary of State). His old teacher says of him now: 'He was a "B" student, a very solid, straightforward, decent sort of bird of moderate ability. He worked hard and he did reasonably well.' Under-Secretary of State Rostow renewed his acquaintance in Washington with the man who was now the Republican leader of the House, and his comment on the political Ford is, 'He was sensible, very sensible, and he held his own and was well liked.'

Ford graduated from Yale Law School after six years. Those alternate stretches of football coaching naturally expanded his time as a law student, and he set up a law practice back in Grand Rapids. But not for long. It was 1941, and after Pearl Harbor he enlisted in the Navy. He served just four years, for nearly half that time on an aircraft carrier. He went in as an ensign and came out as a lieutenant commander. And then he went back to Grand Rapids and took up his fledgling law practice. He probably never would have thought of politics if he hadn't got to know Michigan's famous Senator Arthur Vandenburg, a man who made something of an international name during the founding of the United Nations by turning, at Franklin Roosevelt's persuasion, from a noisy isolationist and America-Firster into just the internationalist Roosevelt needed to get the Republicans to vote for the United Nations Charter. Vandenburg convinced Ford that America had a decisive part to play in restoring devastated Europe. And the young man beat an isolationist veteran for a seat in Congress.

That was in 1949, so he's been in and around Congress for twenty-five years, long enough for a sensible man who holds his own to know his way through the corridors of power. Apart from his internationalism, he has been a solid, undeviating feather in the conservative wing of the party. His voting record on such things as social welfare bills, minimum wages, forced busing of school children, softening civil rights legislation, and his unrepentant hawkishness on Vietnam is enough to give his liberal adversaries a steady attack of the creeps. But following the party line as a Congressman, and dictating it as a President are two different careers. And he has already pained the conservative Veterans of Foreign Wars by telling them that the time has come to give amnesty to the dodgers, deserters, and conscientious objectors of the Vietnam war, provided they earn their way, by some public work, back into respectable citizenship. And the other day, a powerful, and highly liberal black Congresswoman, who distinguished herself by her erudition in the recent impeachment hearings of the House Judiciary Committee, noted that the Black Caucus in the Congress had begged President Nixon for a private meeting for two years with no luck. But that one week after Ford was in office, he brought them all together on his own initiative. He undoubtedly knows, as well as Kennedy and Nixon came to know, that once you are President, your constituency is not the party but the whole Congress as a microcosm of the people they represent: namely, the people of the United States. There'll be more surprises ahead.

We shall have to wait to fill in the colour and personal detail of the Midwestern type that is now being so royally celebrated. He comes from a region, and therefore originally from a constituency, that has its minorities of Italians, Russians, Latvians, Czechs, and about 12 percent of blacks. But the solid core of the town he grew up in are the 100,000 people of Dutch extraction, the downright Calvinists of the Dutch Reformed Church. Not surprisingly, the name of the President's campaign biographer, and now his press secretary, is terHorst. Yes, the 't' is small and the middle 'H' is capital. A shirt-sleeved old resident, a man named Oudersluys, was asked what was Ford's best qualification for the Presidency. Without pausing to breathe, he rolled his cigar over in his mouth and snapped: 'His trust in God.' On a secular note, we might remark that when there were disastrous floods in Holland, Congressman Ford got a fifty-thousand dollar appropriation out of Congress to help the homeless relatives of his constituents. Congressmen are bred to think of such things. But he undoubtedly knows that once you are President, your constituency is not the hometown or the party, but the people of the United States of America.

Fall of Saigon

Letter No. 1365, 11 April 1975

Throughout the nineteenth century and on into our own time, military disasters were reported to the home front as, at worst, military setbacks. Thanks, I suppose, to strict censorship at the front and the unquestioned existence of official secrets acts and such, which concealed the unvarnished truth for so many years that by the time it was open for inspection, the people at home had other things on their minds. It was left to the historians to analyse and thrash over the ashes of once-burning issues.

I think of the ill-fated expedition to Dakar in the Second World War, and the ill-conceived British landings in Norway. True, they caused a rumpus in the House of Commons, since the brave invaders quickly came home again. But there were no nightly pictures on the television to show, for instance, our men landing in Norway without skis, on the assumption of generals bred in a temperate climate that the men were going off to fight a rifle-to-rifle battle in Surrey or on the fields of northern France.

The enormous catastrophe of the Dardanelles Campaign in the First World War was, I well remember, reported to us as a difficult but heroic undertaking. And when it failed, the tiptoe evacuation of our forces was glowingly represented as a triumphant success. In those days, they did not publish the human cost. Only the schoolboys of a later generation learned to be dazed by the news that Gallipoli cost each side a quarter of a million casualties. And those of you old enough to remember Dunkirk will recall how the relief at the evacuation of so many men from beaches under aerial bombing was turned by the government of the day, by the newsreels, and then by Hollywood, into a glorious thing. Until Mr Churchill brought us to our senses with a speech in the House of Commons in which he bluntly declared, 'It is a colossal military disaster … wars are not won by evacuations.' But there can never have been a time like that of the mid-nineteenth century, not in Britain anyway, when the romantic legend of our brave chaps out there was so deliberately separated from the reality. The dreadful idiocy of the Battle of Balaclava was celebrated – by the Poet Laureate no less – as an act of epic valour: 'Theirs not to reason why/ Theirs but to do and die.'

Well, the United States has just suffered the most unmitigated defeat in its history, and we know it. The cost, in casualties, and money, and pride is being counted now. And everybody is arguing 'the reason why'. What Kennedy started with the quiet infiltration of 'military technicians' is about to end, fourteen years later. It would no doubt have ended much sooner if the United States hadn't believed in the beginning that it had a duty to stem the advance of Communism in Asia and, what turned out to be more fateful, believed it had the capacity to do it. The most unrepentant hawks will maintain on their deathbeds that the United States did have the capacity, by a general invasion of North Vietnam or by the use of tactical atomic weapons. But none of the four Presidents who bore the burden, and the curse, of the Vietnam War was ready to do that. All of them knew that if America could keep its treaty commitments only by means of even a limited nuclear bombardment, America would be a monster's name everywhere on earth.

So the country is just now in a stew of recrimination. No doubt in time the arguments will straighten themselves out and people will come to take up one of two positions, which won't necessarily be closer to the truth because they've been over-simplified.

The most striking thing to me about this turmoil of public opinion is the way, while the Right is holding its ground, the Left is shifting its ground. The leftist and liberal commentators who have been against the American presence in Indochina more or less since the beginning have always tended to stress the corruption of the South Vietnamese government and the brutality of its treatment of prisoners and political dissidents, but have always turned a blind-eye toward – or refused to credit – the Hanoi government's brutal treatment of prisoners and political dissidents (if any were ever known to speak up). The Left has always said that if the United States got out, and if South Vietnam capitulated, then the people of South Vietnam would receive their conquerors with relief and, after thirty years of nothing but war, would settle down peaceably to be ruled by them.

But now that we've seen thousands of bedraggled and wounded civilians fleeing from their homes and jamming every escape route to the south, the Left is saying how shocking that we didn't evacuate these people sooner instead of leaving them to the mercies of the oncoming armies. This shock implies a belief in something that the leftists and the liberals have never been willing to concede: that vast numbers of the population of South Vietnam have been and still are terrified of the Communists and want to get out.

In other words, since the United States is no longer there as a military force, it has got to be blamed for something. And it is now being blamed for deserting the South Vietnamese in their hour of need. Some reporters, especially foreign correspondents, who throughout the war have been privileged to enjoy the luxury of neutral high-mindedness, have written dispatches burning with indignation at the thought of President Ford playing golf while babies were being bundled into planes and flown to camps in the United States (and – something I've not seen in an American paper – to homes in Britain and Australia).

Well, it was maybe a tactless time for the President to be practising his backswing,

South Vietnamese flee Saigon in April 1975 with the help of the US military.

but the inference of these angry men is that President Ford and his advisers callously refused to send in planes, and the old Marines, to arrange a mass evacuation when the Central Highlands were about to be overrun. But neither the President nor the Pentagon, nor an American military mission on the spot, seems to have been given much notice of President Thieu's independent decision to abandon the Central Highlands. The White House and the Pentagon seethed with their own sort of indignation when it happened, and had to improvise a makeshift Dunkirk operation. Naturally, they said hard words about President Thieu. And their anger gave him a God-sent excuse to declare that the United States had betrayed its ally.

In turn, the conservatives here who have gone on thinking of President Thieu as the poor man's Chiang Kai-shek were only too eager to pick up his accusation and turn it, not so much against President Ford, whom they've come to consider a well-meaning drifter, as against the Democrats' majority in Congress. Certainly, if the retreat of the South Vietnamese could have been held up by more millions of dollars from Congress, then those Democrats in power are to blame. At this point, the country is heard from. Over 70 percent of the American people are convinced that South Vietnam and Cambodia would be lost, sooner rather than later, no matter how much money the Congress voted.

Meanwhile, less positive people – middle of the roaders, weary newspaper students of the long war – are going back to see where the rot set in. Who was to blame? President Johnson blamed the doubters for having little faith. President Nixon called his opponents traitors. President Ford is going back to Kennedy's line – a rather forlorn battle cry so late in the day: that the United States has 'solemn commitments' and must honour them. He blames Congress. And he's helped by Henry Kissinger who sees, in the congressional echo of public sentiment, a dreadful determination 'to destroy our allies'. Others again, looking pluckily on the bright side, say that the administration is making a fundamental error in confusing the collapse of Indochina with America's real interests. They say that to let Vietnam go is no proof that the United States would let Japan go, or Israel, or Europe.

However, it is possible to recognize a pall forming over all this dissension in the reports that are coming in from Thailand, and Malaysia and Israel and other places whose governments – rightly or wrongly – are beginning to wonder whether the United States is an ally you can depend on. Hardly reported at all are the fears of the Australians, to whom what we call the Far East is the Near North, against which they had better prepare their own defences.

And through this bedlam of charge and counter charge, a still small voice rises, from people who were once dogmatic, and from people who are merely puzzled: what if, after all, the domino theory is correct?

President Carter

Letter No. 1461, 11 February 1977

The brutal winter eased up suddenly this week, though the forecast for the next two months suggests it is only a lull in the Arctic campaign. Still, the buried towns made the most of their present blessing. Chicago this week had its first day or night since December of above freezing temperatures, and people went out in the streets smiling and waving at each other in celebration, like a population of reformed Scrooges.

It was possible for the first time this year to emerge from the blizzard of concern for such purely personal but important things as staying warm and well. It was possible to sit back and look at, well, not so much the state of the nation (that's something only some demigod looking down on us from Mars could do) as the state of the Carter Presidency. He's been there now for all of three weeks and is well launched on the third and last act of what you might call the Presidential performance. In the past six months, I've more than hinted that for a successful Presidential candidate, the performance runs to three acts. Or, if you like, a trilogy of plays. The first is the election campaign and could be called, 'Promises, Promises'. The second play begins the day the man is elected, lasts till he is inaugurated, and could be called, 'The Honeymoon'. The third play, which is going to go on for the next four years, begins on the twentieth of January, and my title for it is, 'The Facts of Life'.

I hasten to say that these are not cynical labels to be stuck, in retrospect, on the Carter presidency but on all presidencies. Presidential campaigns, everybody agrees, are too long and exhausting, but the appalling size of the country has much to do with it. What happens (because the man can't stop long enough in big and little places to elaborate thoughtfully on everything he'd like to do), what always happens in these frantic one-hour safaris into mountains and deserts and cities and seaboards is that the man simplifies his policies, his promises, to the point of melodrama or high romance. Facing an audience of old folks in Florida living on scanty pensions, the best he can do is tell them that he'll see they get more money. Off, say, in Detroit, he has to promise the automobile workers that their wages will keep step with the cost of living. Out in drought-ridden California, he must say he's grieved to see their blighted crops and sagging cattle and will see that they get a price subsidy. Before a regiment of women, he's going to see to it there are more women in government. Before an audience of blacks, he'll never cease to look for the best blacks he can find to recruit for his administration, if only they will vote him in. And so on, and so on. Meanwhile, the other fellow is doing the same, and first they bicker, and then they deny. Then they are shocked at the way one of them misrepresented the position of the other. And at long last, on the first Tuesday in November, it's all over, and one of them is elected on this Hallelujah Chorus of promises, half of which cannot possibly be kept, many of which are downright contradictory.

But a new President does always suggest the prospect of change and movement. And in the second act, when he's in but not yet in the White house, he is allowed a honeymoon. We have no grounds yet to criticize him for what he hasn't done; he is powerless but very popular. We develop a lively interest in him and his family, getting to know his style in such things as manner, clothes, eating habits, sense of drama, and sense of humour, if any. It wasn't really till Mr Carter began to bring his family into the picture that we realized what an astonishing American story his rise to power had been. A man who a year ago precious few Americans had ever heard of – standing on street corners here, there, and everywhere, holding out a hand and saying to passersby, 'I'm Jimmy Carter. I'm running for President, and I'd like for you to vote for me.' Talking to any body of people that would listen, to church groups, YMCAs, women's clubs, a ring of farmers, starting so far behind that when the Democrats had nine candidates in the running, the one name even the most knowing of us kept forgetting was this farmer from a minute town in Georgia.

And now, there he is. And between November and Inauguration Day, any American who runs and reads could be forgiven for thinking he was reading a regular comic strip called 'The Carters'. Just look over the cast of characters. It would certainly be as bizarre and engaging as 'Li'l Abner'. First, there is Father Carter, peanut farmer and nuclear submarine commander – an artful combination for any comic strip hero, because you meld science fiction and an appeal to rural America. He has a pretty wife, Rosalynn, with eyelashes like bee's wings. They have an uninhibited daughter, Amy, with large round glasses and a habit of making faces at cameras. Also, Father Carter has a brother, a beefy, jolly owner of a petrol station who is a natural joker and is always shown carrying a six-pack of beer cans. Father Carter has his private troubles and has surmounted them manfully. He has a son who was busted from the Navy – quite rightly, the son says – on a marijuana charge. There's also a nephew in jail in Georgia, whose pleasure in seeing his uncle elected President is based in the hope that he'll get out of the Georgia jail into a nicer one in another state. Then there's Father Carter's mother, a splendid, spontaneous old lady of absolutely unflappable poise, with the typical Southern nickname of Miss Lillian. Father Carter has a sister, an evangelist, a female Billy Graham, who is not to be put off by her brother's rise to glory to abandon her soul-saving mission. In the White House, suddenly, there is not just one Carter family, as there was one Roosevelt family, one Kennedy family, one Ford family. Even the grown boys have moved in, with their children. There are three families living there. Finally, as our sheet anchor in American folklore, there is the Carters'

President Carter and his extended family.

little dog. And what is he called? He is called triumphantly by the name of that dish, a porridge of coarsely ground maize, which is nectar to all Southerners and anathema to everybody else. The little dog's name is 'Grits'.

I enumerate the characters in this folk epic with all respect. To me, it is a triumphant achievement and shows that, as Will Rogers used to say, any boy in America can get to be President (he added, 'in South America, every boy has got to be president.'). Certainly, I can't think of another country, another democratic country, where the choice of a President could be so completely open, so unpredictable. But as I say, if somebody had sat down two years ago and made up this family and suggested it to a newspaper syndicate as the cast of characters for a newspaper comic strip, it would have been rejected out of hand as too much of an all-American fantasy. Yet, here is that family – not in the papers but in the flesh – in the White House.

And now, the President has had three weeks of the third play, 'The Facts of Life'. First of all, he turned the thermostats down, and people put their topcoats on at their desks, and Mrs Carter, he said, was close to tears from the cold. If he let a literal breeze into the White House, he has already sent a fresh breeze blowing through many fixed traditions. Mr Nixon yearned for a little more pomp, and dressed up a White House honour guard in white uniforms, like courtiers in *The Prisoner of Zenda*. Mr Carter scorns all such folderol and is acutely aware that after what has come to be known as the Imperial Presidency, it was necessary not just to forget it but to replace it with something visibly more humble. He has abolished the custom of having a Marine Band play 'Hail to the Chief' wherever the President goes. He has abolished official White House limousines for his aides and advisers. He gave his first fireside chat the other evening and appeared in a cardigan. Only the widow of the late Ernest Hemingway protested to the *New York Times* that she is not used to receiving a gentleman in her living room after dinner without a jacket.

Beyond these small but significant gestures, he has done something not one President in a trainload has done, not in my time. Asked at his first press conference if he hadn't given Congress cause for complaint in not consulting his party leaders on appointments, he didn't prevaricate. He didn't, as the regular custom goes, chuckle and try to explain why you didn't understand the delicacy of his job. He simply said, with a chuckle, yes, he'd given cause. 'We've made some mistakes. I've learned in my first two and a half weeks why Abraham Lincoln and some of the older Presidents almost went home when they first got to the White House … we are here to learn.' It's refreshing to see how this simple acknowledgment of frailty gave the press actually more confidence in him than if he had done what Presidents always do: deny, carp, waffle.

That press conference (he will give one every fortnight) showed that he already had at his command a vast range of digested information and shrewd judgment. More than anything, he showed that, more than any previous President, he not only knows very much more about the intricacies of nuclear weapons but that he holds to his belief in a drastic reduction of nuclear weapons as a better guarantee of security, of survival, than the present race between America and the Soviet Union to outstrip each other in nuclear technology. He's in for his first big conflict here with the old Vietnam hawks and what has been called the new 'military-intellectual complex'. So far, then, he's a man of considerable simple dignity, surprising flashes of humour, and a tough mind. So far, very good.

New York 'Blackouts'

Letter No. 1483, 15 July 1977

On an evening in November, 1965, I was sitting in a hotel room in Chicago, placidly watching the telly, when the programme was interrupted by an announcer begging us to stand by for a news flash. In the vocabulary of the reporter, a 'flash' bears about the same relation to a 'bulletin' as an earthquake to a rainstorm. And to television executives, the word 'flash' coming over the tickers in the newsroom is about as painful an assault on their bankbook as a notice of bankruptcy. Especially if it comes in mid-evening, a word you will never hear from the mouths of television managers or advertising men.

From eight to ten p.m. is known to them as 'prime time'. It is the most expensive television time to buy, since it assures the largest possible watching audience to brainwash with your hard or soft sell of the wax that converts plain deal into antique walnut, the pill that cures a headache, whether – it is implied – it comes from a hangover or a brain tumour, the detergent that washes things whiter than white. All these enticing appeals to our stupidity may be a joke to some of us, but when they're interrupted or cancelled, they're no joke to the men who pay as much as one hundred thousand dollars for a one-minute commercial in prime time. Or to the network executive who has to decide in a flash that a 'flash' – so-called on the news tickers – warrants breaking into and breaking up a programme and its accompanying commercials. It was a flash that came at us just before six p.m. on the radio on the 12th of April, 1945, to announce that Franklin Roosevelt had dropped dead in Georgia. It was a flash that obliterated the early afternoon television programmes on the 22nd of November, 1963, and announced the shooting of President Kennedy. And both times, no regular programmes at all were shown until the dead Presidents were buried.

Naturally, the networks have to make compensation for the moneys paid into them. It is of course tasteless to mention this at the time of such a national disaster, but the thought does cross the minds of the men in charge.

Well, on that November evening eleven and a half years ago, the flash, coming over the line in Chicago, was one that concerned the whole country only at intervals in the regular television programming. It was the word of the sudden failure in a key power station in upstate New York, close to the Canadian border, that overloaded

and blacked-out the entire electrical system throughout New York State, neighbouring Connecticut, and some of New Jersey. Very soon after the flash came in, we were able to see the New York blackout televised for the benefit of comfortable viewers in other parts of the country, and I've wondered ever since how they managed, first to get the pictures, and second how they transmitted them over dead wires. But they did, and friends in Chicago were calling up and saying, 'Ooh, ah, have you seen those great pictures of New York?' There was, as I recall, a moon that night, which any camera-man will tell you is never bright enough to give you a picture of moonlight – not a motion picture, anyway. In the movies, romantic scenes, and even unromantic scenes by moonlight are always shot at high noon, through heavy filters that make the full sun look like the full moon. In Hollywood, they found out long ago that intimate romantic scenes where the sound track carries nothing heavier than a tender whisper, are better shot indoors, in soundproof studios, against backdrops of artificial skylines with an artificial moon the size of an approaching planet.

Well, this time the power failed, I was even further away from New York than Chicago, on a flying visit to London, England, no less, and I read and heard about it as you did, in the newspapers, and in foggy television pictures shot by the light of torches or motorcar headlights. Two impressions, I gather, came over that over-whelmed all others. One was the looting of shops and stores; the other was the sight of young men in jeans and T-shirts turning themselves into impromptu traffic cops, and helping people get out of the city. From telephoning friends in New York, I picked up a refreshingly comic note that I haven't seen reported in the papers. Manhattan is, as you know, an island, bounded on the east by, logically, the East River, and on the west by the Hudson. As you look across the Hudson from New York's West Side, you can see, reflected in the river, the lights of buildings on the New Jersey side. And on last Wednesday night, after 9:30 when the grid failed again, the people who were at their steering wheels, groping their way through the black streets, many of them heard that New Jersey was untouched by the blackout, so they headed there. There was a consequent rush, or dense crawl, of cars toward the George Washington Bridge, and of course, not by any means exclusively of people who lived across the Hudson. New Jersey was a haven, a sanctuary, a beacon beckoning the doomed away from the black night, the crashing shop windows, the screaming police sirens of New York. So what happened was that thousands of people who lived not only in New York but were in town from Connecticut, across Long Island Sound, drove farther and farther away from their homes, and the motels of New Jersey did a roaring business. This, it struck me, was exactly the opposite of the terrified traffic that drove out of New Jersey into New York, New England, anywhere, on the notorious dreadful night – was it in 1938? – when Orson Welles put on the radio his mock-documentary account of the invasion, along the New Jersey coast, of the men from Mars. The programme had started with a brief announcement that what followed was a fictional guess at what might happen

During the massive power failure a young looter shows the spoils taken from a store in the Bushwick section of Brooklyn.

Three Mile Island

Letter No. 1573, 6 April 1979

Who would want to be a politician, a President, or a Prime Minister? No sooner does Mr Carter get a very much-needed boost in the opinion polls by his triumph in the Middle East than the nuclear reactor in Pennsylvania develops a hydrogen bubble, the temperature inside the container goes out of sight, and the federal government begins to think of evacuating a million people, including the population of Harrisburg, which is the capital of Pennsylvania. I hasten to say two things.

First, the situation seems to be safe, if not yet under absolute control. By the time some listeners hear this, the reactor may have cooled and threatens no harm to anybody ever again. The chief of the government's Nuclear Regulatory Commission says all is going well, but he cannot say the emergency is over till the high temperatures have fallen off.

The second thing is that I know no more than any of you about the significance of hydrogen bubbles in nuclear reactors. This past weekend, all of us have become instant experts in a field in which there are no instant experts. So I don't want anybody to feel that I'm more qualified than the next man to assess the dangers of radiation or the efficiency or inefficiency of this nuclear reactor design.

What I can do is to feel and report the pulse of popular prejudice one way and the other. And to pass on some well-grounded facts about what is likely to happen now to the standing of nuclear energy in the United States.

I notice that whether qualified or not, simply everybody has an opinion about the accident at Three Mile Island. The very name, which none of us had ever heard before, will pass into the public memory along with such other names as Little Rock, Dallas, and Chappaquiddick.

There have been some very good programs on television, of two sorts. First, NBC put on an hour's show last Saturday about the structure of nuclear reactors, how they work, and how this particular one appeared to have gone wrong. Then there have been many televised discussions between experts who disagree: mainly the government nuclear people and the company managers versus groups like the association of so-called 'Concerned Scientists'. Unfortunately, for you and me, these debates or discussions got better and better the more complicated they became. It is, in a word, an immensely complex subject, and the ordinary doctor, or physicist for that matter, is no better equipped to give a judgment than the ordinary grocer or farmer.

But as I say, this fact doesn't stop lawyers, farmers, journalists, actresses and jockeys from airing strong and dogmatic opinions. And I've noticed – from my hearing and reading – that practically nobody switches sides. In other words, the people who are against nuclear reactors on principle, or I suppose I should say on instinct, feel that their fears have been justified. The scientists who are for it go on saying that nuclear power has to be, but we have to go back to square one, learn more about the behaviour of nuclear reactors and then devise stricter safety standards.

The government is shaken; I mean the government nuclear experts. They admit that they had never anticipated this sort of accident, that it was for a time out of control, and extremely dangerous if the container walls had given way and spewed radioactive matter into the atmosphere. And the last word we had before this broadcast was that the power plant would have to be decontaminated and overhauled before it could be put to work again, and that this process will take at least two years and maybe four.

When the first scare was reported, anti-nuclear demonstrators, especially people who lived near other nuclear plants in other parts of the country, began parades urging the closing down of the neighbouring plant. Protestors in northern California kept it up for a couple of days and nights till Mr Edmund 'Jerry' Brown, the Governor of California, ordered one plant of the same design as that at Three Mile Island to be closed. The Governors have the power to do that.

What is not arguable is that the whole nuclear power industry in the United States has suffered a shattering setback. The government simply arrested all plans for new construction, if only because the government recognizes the enormous force of public opinion. And, of course, so do the architects, the corporation presidents, the nuclear researchers, everybody who is in the business of building nuclear power plants and operating them. The company that designed the plant at Three Mile Island has several more of them around the country. And in those places, as you can imagine, the public pressure to close them down now is very great, whether or not there has ever been the faintest breath of a suspicion that they weren't thoroughly safe. When all of the technical instruction that television and the newspapers have been feeding us has been forgotten, the public will remember that at Three Mile Island the radioactivity behind the four-foot thick walls of the concrete container was measured at a hundred times the lethal dose! The reflex attitude of Americans (and maybe non-Americans in other countries), the reflex attitude of people who live close by a nuclear power plant is: if it didn't happen at Three Mile Island, it could happen to us.

And we now know, of course, they're right. The chances may be a hundred to one against its happening, or a thousand to one. They were such in Pennsylvania. But as long as there's a remote possibility, the power industry will be regarded not as an aid but a threat to life.

Of course, the industry goes on, though there are lots of people who say it shouldn't. Suppose, though, that all the nuclear generating facilities in this country were to be danger are possible.' Or as a simple soul, a lady in a small town in Pennsylvania put it, 'I don't know about that stuff, that nuclear. Seems to me so powerful, man can't tame it right.'

That puts in a nutshell the attitude of the anti-nuke people and the fear of the experts. And I should think it's a universal attitude. Well, maybe not quite universal. The one calm, complacent voice is heard from – wouldn't you guess it? – Moscow. I don't know how thoroughly the Pennsylvania accident has been reported in the Soviet Union. I'd be surprised to hear that it had been extensive, for the Soviets are always the first to guess the likely effects of frightening publicity on a national audience. They have not made a point of reporting to their own people several known accidents to their astronauts. A few years ago, they had an earthquake that was about two points higher on the Richter scale than the one that destroyed San Francisco in 1906. We heard about this only from Western astrophysicists.

Well, they have spoken out about Three Mile Island. The Deputy Minister of Electricity was interviewed by the national paper called *Truth*. The truth is, he said, that such accidents were likely to happen because of the slipshod attitude that exists where – as in this case – private interests are of paramount importance. All the same, I'll bet the nuclear inspectors are off on their secret rounds with new orders.

Why Iran Took the Hostages

Letter No. 1606, 23 November 1979

One of the two most influential American news magazines came out this week with a picture on its cover of the American bald eagle – the symbol of American power – with his feathers dropping off him like autumn leaves. Printed boldly on one wing was the title of the cover story: 'Has America Lost Its Clout?' The definition of 'clout' that the *Oxford Dictionary* has recently added says, 'noun, (colloquial), influence, power of effective action, especially in politics.'

So, *Newsweek* puts the resounding question, 'Has America Lost Its Clout?' The feature piece is a historical survey that laments how, in recent years, the United States has suffered a series of blows to its 'power of effective action'; how we 'have seen Soviet and Cuban forces marching unhindered across large parts of Africa', 'staunch, if unsavoury, friends' falling 'from power in places like Nicaragua and Iran ... have watched oil sheiks raising their prices recklessly' to make us realize in pain that 'for the first time in American history, the United States is dependent on foreigners for a vital resource ... ' Americans, it goes on, 'have seen their dollar plummet in value and their standard of living drop below that of countries as diverse as Sweden and Kuwait. And they have seen their armed forces, which once held a nuclear monopoly, struggle to maintain something called parity.'

Such a piece could have been written at any time in the past year or two that the magazine's editors were short of a rousing editorial. But I don't think it would have appeared now, or the question be put with quite such urgency, if it had not been for the uniquely frustrating crisis in Iran: the seizure and holding, by the Ayatollah Khomeini, of the American Embassy hostages in reprisal for letting the deposed Shah come to New York for medical treatment.

A recent comment by an American who was for a long time an expert in wielding the power of effective action takes on a special poignancy as we look at the paradox of what somebody has called 'the power of the impotent Ayatollah, and the impotence of the powerful United States.' Dr Henry Kissinger, who has been much in the news after the publication of a huge volume of memoirs, sighed almost a year ago: 'If we think back to the Cuban missile crisis of 1962, which all the policymakers of the time were viewing with a consciousness of approaching Armageddon, one is almost seized anywhere, any time.' All you have to do to defeat this wisdom is to go ahead and strike anyway, which is what the Boston police did. But Coolidge called out the state guard, and the police bowed. Today, they probably would stay out, till the state government got tired of trying to police a big city with improvised soldiery.

So, President Carter – not only he but the International Court of Justice – might declare that the action of the Ayatollah Khomeini is totally outside the bounds of international law and diplomatic tradition. But the Ayatollah simply says – in no doubt holy language – 'So, forget it.'

What has come out in the past week is some evidence, from documents captured by the students in the American Embassy and from the deep digging of a *New York Times* reporter, showing that the whole situation is by no means as simple as we'd thought. Let's very briefly say what that situation is, as most of us had understood it till this week. In October, the United States allowed the exiled Shah to come from his temporary home in Mexico and enter a New York hospital, after an American doctor, sent to Mexico, had gone into the Shah's history of lymph cancer and other afflictions and had decided that he needed an expert diagnostic opinion that he could only get in New York. So President Carter, having assured the Iranian government (meaning the official government of Prime Minister Bazargan) that the Shah was not being granted political asylum, he was coming in for emergency medical treatment and would be asked to leave the United States as soon as he was convalescent. Then on the fourth of November, without warning, the Ayatollah, or his student guerrillas (by the way, apart from the Ayatollah and a handful of advisers, the entire population of Iran seems to be students), the students marched on the Embassy and seized and bound its inmates.

Well, it now comes out that the President and his Secretary of State, Mr Cyrus Vance, had spent eight months resisting the appeals of many powerful American friends of the Shah to let him come in as a permanent exile. Through those eight months, the White House and the State Department were in constant touch with a Mr Laingen, the acting American ambassador in Tehran. Some of that diplomatic correspondence was captured by the students, and they were in no mood to split hairs. They probably cannot even honestly distinguish between the authority of Mr Carter and the influence, if any, of a Rockefeller who happens to be a banker. After all, it is standard Marxist (and maybe by now Islamic) doctrine that the United States is really run by the Rockefellers.

Apparently, Ambassador Laingen, through these months of private appeals to the President – one of them from Dr Kissinger – got the idea that, in time, when the Ayatollah and his regime cooled down and backed into the shafts, the Shah would come here without fuss. There's pretty certain evidence that Mr Carter may have toyed with the idea but saw long ago that it wouldn't do, in spite of Dr Kissinger's disgusted complaint that the Administration was treating the Shah 'like a flying Dutchman'.

Well, by October, the American doctor had made his clinical finding and the President told Ambassador Laingen that the United States intended to fetch the Shah to New York for medical treatment only. Ambassador Laingen told the Bazargan government. They were appalled. They said the Iranian people would never accept the medical story. They warned that the Embassy might be occupied, but they believed they could protect it. Mr Laingen reported back to Washington. Again, the White House said the Shah would arrive quietly in New York. Again the Bazargan government warned it wouldn't work. It didn't work for the Bazargan government; in fact, it fell precisely because the Shah did arrive in the New York hospital. After them, the deluge. The Embassy guard was caught napping, or rather it was a light guard, having accepted the word of Mr Bazargan that there would be no heavy raid.

In retrospect, it's now clear that the Carter administration hoped to let the Shah in, sometime in the future. At the same time, it resisted the urgent appeals of the Rockefellers and Kissingers and others to let him in now. The medical reason was not a pretext to rush the invitation. It was a genuine compassionate cause. And Mr Carter thought it would be seen and respected as such.

Even so, Mr Carter was dubious all along. At one staff meeting, at least a month before we ever heard of the Shah's illness, the President said to one of his aides, 'And when the Iranians take our people in Tehran hostage, what will you advise me then?'

The silence of the presidential candidates now on the stump is explained by the fact that once a candidate you are privy to such presidential secrets. They knew about the pressure to fetch the Shah here. Some of them were all for it. Now, they must wake up at night and shudder at Mr Carter's forlorn question, and go back to sleep thanking the Lord that they are not yet in the White House they so long to inhabit.

a turning of the tide. Surely the failure of the film projects disappointed him, but he took it remarkably well, casting his eyes to the future and forgetting what was past. What he could not ignore was his failing knee; it caused him considerable pain and hampered his ability to do the things he loved most, like play golf.

What wore at his spirit, however, was the death of so many of his dear friends. Not only were they gone, but he was expected to, and did, deliver their eulogies. As a minister I know the toll this can take; one must revisit and love all that has been lost, and each eulogy is a clenched fist around the heart. For the first time I was keenly aware that he was depressed. Finally, after a chain of funerals, my mother and I sat him down in his study and simply laid down the law, 'No more eulogies. Period.'

He sat in his red leather chair, raised his eyebrows, turned his palms up in resignation – a bit of the 'What's a man to do?' attitude – and said with a marked sigh of relief, 'OK.'

Another petal that floated to the ground was his increasingly stubborn stance on all matters that even hinted of being politically correct, 'PC.' He loathed the term, society's inclination to police thought and the suggestion that he was, on more than one occasion, on the wrong side of the fence. That may not be entirely true; I think he actually relished his counter-culture stance and delighted in taking on the establishment. In the eighties and nineties as the United States struggled with becoming more tolerant of diversity of all kinds, he took a public position that brought him some heat. He was a champion of the English First movement, whose goals were to 'Make English America's official language,' and 'Eliminate costly and ineffective multilingual policies.' He tended to overlook the implications of this last goal in favour of championing one of his great loves: the English language.

Of all social, political, and cultural changes that occurred in America in his lifetime, he was most out of sync with feminism. Religious and racial inequities were clearly wrong and unjust, but the business between men and women was deliciously more complicated; he relished its complexity and confounding allure. Let me say straight out that he adored women; he wanted to love them, joke with them, admire them, tease them, and play with them. But because of his generation and background, it was more difficult for him to accept immediately their intellectual and educated equality. Nevertheless, he had countless professional relationships with women whom he greatly admired, respected, and on whom he depended. But this was secretly just a bit of a delightful surprise to him, and, feeling he had discovered these gems, he became their greatest fan.

His growing dependency on the women around him was both touching and exasperating. If my mother did not return from a movie date or a luncheon when he thought she should, he worked himself into a lather of worry, pacing the apartment, a hair away from summoning the police. There was an occasion much later on in his life when one summer our daughter Eliza, who was in her twenties at the time, lived with him in the apartment while she worked in Manhattan and my mother was at Nassau Point. She was late getting home one night, and Daddy called me in a frantic state after

A.C. at work in his study with his favourite view before him:
Central Park and the reservoir.

midnight to report that she was missing. I assured him that she would be home soon and tried to soothe his panic. He would not be talked down from his worry or implied reprove. He put on his overcoat, plopped his hat on his head and went down into the lobby to wait for her. When she walked in at 1 a.m., he was sitting next to the door-man, his head in his hands, looking terrible.

Increasingly he gained comfort from predictability and constancy, certainly not an uncommon trait of advancing years. His growing appreciation for routine and security was, however, a change from his previously fast-paced and often spontaneous approach to both work and play, and it took some getting used to for all around him.

S.C.K.

The second thought is one with which Mr Carter must have been thoroughly familiar: the evidence of a reliable national poll that showed that 55 percent of the American people were in favour of a military action against Iran, and never mind 'a humanitarian mission not directed at Iran or the Iranian people.' Whether one or both of these considerations were on his mind, he decided to take the gamble. It is bad for him that it failed. It could be worse for him in a nation that prides itself on its technological know-how, and on its Air Force's scrupulous respect for flying by the book, that it was doomed because of 'equipment failure,' and then because of human error in maneuvering two lonely planes in the desert.

I am talking in the aftershock of the misadventure, and while the Soviet response could have been written beforehand, there is no telling just yet what the considered response will be of the three or four factions in Iran that seem to be jostling for power. What we can do is to speculate about the effect this disaster is likely to have on the Presidential campaign in general, and on the Carter Presidency in particular. I see no sign at the moment that the President is going to reap the peculiar gain in prestige that came so surprisingly to President Kennedy after his abortive defiance of Fidel Castro. For one thing, President Kennedy was in his first six months in the White House. President Carter is there in an election year.

If you can indulge your patience for a while, let me take you back to last Wednesday morning, a day that must seem to the President like an age away. Imagine him getting up on that morning, taking his early breakfast, listening – as is his wont – to a little Mozart, with which to rinse out his mind. It is natural to infer that he leapt with a whoop on the good news from Pennsylvania, which showed him in a dead heat with Senator Edward Kennedy for the precious haul of Democratic Party delegates that this fourth-most populous state has to offer. The promised thrashing from Senator Kennedy had not taken place.

The good news for the rest of us, imagine, only a day or two ago, was that the President could now relax in the knowledge that he was about two-thirds of the way toward a certain nomination by his party, that Senator Kennedy, in order to challenge him, was going to have to win 70 percent or more of the delegates available in the remaining primaries, and that these are to be held in country, mostly South and West, that for Senator Kennedy is unfriendly country. So, we innocently assumed the President could forget his campaigning obsession and attend to the perils of his foreign policy here and now.

There was, however, and now more than ever there is, another threat to his re-election that begins to wax as the omen of Senator Kennedy begins to wane. This threat is the name and presence of the white-thatched, owlish, little liberal Republican from Illinois: Representative John Anderson. After the last few Republican primaries, it became painfully clear to Mr Anderson that he had no hope of battling California Governor Ronald Reagan or anybody else for the Republican nomination. His appeal has been to Democrats disillusioned with Carter; to students inflamed by a new McGovern, a liberal ideologue; to independents who are thinking of voting for nobody; and to moderate Republicans who see in Reagan a right-wing leader on a white charger with a sword in one hand and a nuclear bomb in the other.

These disenchanted ones make up a considerable body of the voters – the independents alone claim to be just less than one third of all the eligible voters, and if they all saw in Mr Anderson the answer to a maiden's prayer, he might indeed stop both Carter and Reagan in their tracks. But under which party banner? He has decided – under none. I stress this, because I keep reading in European papers, and hearing (I regret to say on the BBC) that Mr Anderson is going to run as a third-party candidate. He is not. The history of third-party crusades in Presidential politics is a record of broken ideals. A third-party candidate, even one so popular and powerful as Theodore Roosevelt, emerges not as a realistic choice for President, but as a spoiler who manages to take enough votes away from his old party's regular nominee to throw the election to the opposition, which was what Roosevelt managed to do for Woodrow Wilson. So Mr Anderson is not, like Robert M. La Follette or Henry Wallace, starting a Progressive Party, or an American Party, or a Conservative Party. He will run as an independent. It is very late for him to get on the ballot in some states, too late in others. As a maverick, outside of a registered party, he is not eligible for federal campaign funds. He will have to hope for a legion of admirers, ready to put down the maximum allowed contribution of one thousand dollars each.

He has considered all this and appears to have yielded to the tempting prospect of taking so many votes from Reagan and Carter that neither of them would have a majority of *electoral* votes to win. The tally of popular votes, the totals of all the people who vote, is not in question. It *is* possible – it happened with Wilson and Truman. They each got less than a majority of the popular vote, but each of them got their majorities in states that had, altogether, a majority of electoral votes. So they went into the White House as what are known as 'minority Presidents'.

Suppose, then, that Mr Anderson succeeded – and the Iranian rescue disaster quickens the possibility – in leaving neither Carter nor Reagan (or whoever the Democratic and Republican nominees are to be) with enough electoral votes to establish a clear majority. What happens then? Under the Constitution, the election would then be decided in a vote of the House of Representatives. This *has* happened – once. In 1824 there were four runners. None of them got anything like a majority of the electoral votes, and the House voted to choose John Quincy Adams, who in the election actually had won less than one-third of the electoral votes.

Mr Anderson had better start hoping that there will be one or two other attractive men to run on other tickets, or like him, to run on no party ticket at all. A day or two ago, I would have confidently said that Mr Anderson's candidacy was doomed at the start. After the disaster in the Iranian desert, I, and a lot of other sceptics, are not so sure.

American Extremes

Letter No. 1655, 31 October 1980

A month or two after this country had gone into the Second World War, I was given what turned out to be the most rewarding assignment of my life in journalism. It was to roam around the whole country, driving alone on re-tread tires, at the prescribed speed limit of 35 miles an hour, to see and say what the war was doing to every part of the country and every sort of American. It was a surprising education in many things, not least in the obvious truth (though it's obvious only when you come on it) that every state and city believed it was playing a crucial part in the war effort. Not only that, but in every specialty, from a manufacturer of parachutes made from long staple cotton in Arizona to a raddled little tattooist in San Diego, California, everyone was eager to explain that the war might turn on his trade. Without parachutes, there might be no invasion of Europe. Without the ever-present reminder on the chest or the forearm of Mum or the girlfriend, the morale of the Pacific Fleet might slump. One night in New Orleans – where I had been looking at shipyards and sugar cane and the welding of five-ply paper into airplane wings – I fell in with some young people in a bar. The men were either in uniform or about to be drafted. Their girlfriends were working in war factories. All that I remember of the evening now was that two of the men, the sons of immigrants, jeered at some of the advisers President Roosevelt had recruited from the universities as 'professors'; and all of them, talking about an election for the Senate that was then impending, dismissed the three competing candidates as all equally corrupt. This was a shock to me then, and I recall writing that 'if the American immigrant comes to lose his traditional respect for the educated man or woman, and if the young of America came to be cynical about government, then America will be in deep trouble.' I think 'deep trouble' was just coming in as a vogue word, what we now call a buzz word, and I used it sparingly ever afterward.

Well, it has been established in the past ten years or so, through innumerable surveys and polls, and it can be attested by the evidence of one's senses, that there is today across America a deep distrust of government and the governors, from the Presidency and the Congress down to such collateral branches of the Establishment as soldiers, doctors, lawyers, and all city politicians. This distrust, resentment almost, goes beyond the knowledge of actual corruption in government, though there is an interesting shift in the general tolerance of it. There are a handful of Congressmen who have been either indicted or convicted for various crimes: bribery, homosexual solicitation, this and that, and only one of these men has resigned his office. The rest are running for re-election, and some of them are likely to make it, on the grounds, which polls have revealed, that many people feel a candidate is more human when he confesses to a human failing.

About the distrust of government itself (of the whole barrel and not simply the rotten apples), this surely is a frightening trait in a democracy. Maybe it's been there longer than we've known. One of the unpleasant but salutary things about the growth of scientific opinion-testing is to force us to abandon, in the light of the published facts, many a myth and prejudice and superstition with which our fathers and grandfathers could warm their toes.

As a matter of conjecture, if you try to look grandly at the structure of the American democracy, you might marvel how the system has worked, even imperfectly, for so long. This is a continental democracy, the only one, three thousand miles wide and four thousand miles long; with fifty state governments having powers that would amaze, say, the counties of England, not to mention the united kingdoms of Wales and Scotland. They have not quite absolute powers over such things as education, banking, divorce, highways, housing and liquor, but every state has its own written Constitution, including its own criminal code. Louisiana has a system of criminal law based on the Napoleonic Code. California and other states of the Southwest cling to their Spanish heritage in its provision, in divorce settlements, of a community property law, whereby anybody getting a divorce can claim one half of the mate's real property. (Several other states have adopted this as a matter of equity.)

Yet, forgetting now the political structure of the country, and just looking at what happens day in and day out, here and there across this vast nation, I find myself after all these years constantly amazed at the extent of corruption and the extent of people's goodness. You consider, and shudder when you do, that the ports of the Eastern Seaboard, from Boston to New Orleans, appear for all practical purposes to be owned by organized crime, so that it is difficult to unload grain or metals or bananas without kicking back to the lords of the waterfront. And then, bang up against such a revelation, in a special television news segment you see and realize the innumerable, modest, hard-working families – people in New England, in the Midwest, the desert, the rural South – who have gladly adopted two or three Vietnamese refugee children to add to the struggle with their own families. You look at such extremes and you can see either a nation bowed down by vice, or buoyed up by generosity; sapped by cunning crooks, or uplifted by unflagging civic feeling. I wonder in how many other countries are hospitals kept going by the Community Chest, by taking the hat round from door to door. What other country – I am asking not putting a rhetorical question – what other country maintains a national television network that carries no commercial advertisements because millions of people voluntarily subscribe fifteen or thirty or fifty or a hundred dollars a year?

President Carter and his Republican challenger, Ronald Reagan, before their debate on stage in Cleveland, Ohio.

I look at these conflicts and extremes, which are everywhere, and when I find myself despairing about the fate of this noble experiment in actually inventing a nation, then – once every four years for the past forty or more – I have heard myself saying, and yet, and yet, they manage in the Presidential election years to put up two remarkable men. Let me remind you of some of these choices.

Franklin Roosevelt ran, the first time, against a man whom the economist John Maynard Keynes had called (at the Versailles Peace Conference) 'the only man who imported into the councils of Paris precisely that atmosphere of reality, knowledge, magnanimity, and disinterestedness which, if they had been found in other quarters, would have given us the Good Peace.' He was Herbert Hoover, but since he was in the White House when Wall Street crashed, he was thrown out. Against Roosevelt the next time was the Governor of Kansas, a hardy, self-reliant man of the prairie, Alfred Landon, who now, in his nineties, has turned into a self-reliant radical. Then we had the choice of Roosevelt or Wendell Willkie, another Midwesterner of great charm and driving eloquence. And the fourth time, Roosevelt faced a lawyer able enough, and honourable enough, to become in his thirties New York's Special Prosecutor of Rackets, Thomas Dewey, a man who broke, for the time being anyway, the organized traffic in drugs, prostitution, and the so-called protection rackets. He went on to become a first-rate administrator as Governor of New York. But he wasn't good enough, at the polls, to defeat Roosevelt once he had established his imperial image as the Great War Leader and close colleague of Winston Churchill. Nor was Governor Dewey able to survive the 1948 election against the famous failed haberdasher who turned into the decisive and spunky Harry Truman. After him came the hero of the Second World War, General Dwight D. Eisenhower – the man whom Adlai Stevenson, his humane and civilized opponent, called 'George Washington on a white horse'. And then we had John F. Kennedy against certainly one of the most intelligent senators of our time, who turned into the complicated riddle known as Richard M. Nixon. And after Nixon's first failure, we had Lyndon Johnson, a manipulator larger than life, who managed within three months of Kennedy's death to get through Congress over ninety bills that had lain shelved or ignored. Gerald Ford, as we all know, was an accident, the first appointed Vice President after the shame of Spiro Agnew's resignation, and therefore, you might say, the first appointed President. And then, in 1976, I remember vividly watching this unknown man from Georgia accept the nomination for the Democratic Party in a speech of great simplicity and seeming honesty, which I thought had surely put an end once and for all to the usual performance: the manic grin, the spread-eagled arms, the thundering promise of the millennium in our time.

Well, that simple, honest man has turned into Jimmy Carter, the extremely complicated man we know, or what is a shock to realize after three and a half years, the man we don't know. He seemed, way back then, like a miniature, blonde Lincoln. What he is now, I cannot tell you. Some people say he is above all a technician, who absorbs the facts and arguments not of two sides to every question, but sixteen sides. He then wiggles an antenna here to take care of one fact, and another there to take care of another. And in the end looks like a centipede, all the legs in motion but the whole body not moving at all. And against him, we have Ronald Reagan, an affable young granddaddy, who says he stripped California, the seventh largest economic nation on earth, of big government, lowered taxes, and gave the government back to the people. It is, however, in the record that he imposed three enormous tax rises and gave California its most thumping deficit in history. It's all a question of how you shuffle the figures.

These two, as all the world knows, stood on the same platform for the first time and debated last Tuesday. Well, they didn't exactly debate. They strung together scores of campaign scripts. I doubt there was a spontaneous sentence in the whole ninety minutes. What, however, this performance did do was to reveal that, on a serious occasion and dressed in their Sunday suits, Mr Carter is not the tongue-lashing meanie he's appeared in the campaign, and Mr Reagan is not, as Mr Carter has made out, Attila the Hun. From the way things are turning in the nine big states with the most electoral votes, it seems to me that these comforting revelations may, this coming Tuesday, do more for Reagan than for Carter.

John Lennon and Handgun Laws

Letter No. 1661, 12 December 1980

Last Monday night, just before we went to bed, the television networks interrupted or suspended their regular programs as they haven't done, to my recollection, since the assassination of President Kennedy. And for the rest of the night, and on Tuesday and Wednesday throughout most of the nightly news programmes – Poland and the prime rate and the new recession were either forgotten or tacked on to the end of the overwhelming news story – the cameras roamed over silent crowds around an apartment building on Central Park West, and then on more crowds around the Lincoln Memorial in Washington, and out in Hawaii, and in London and Amsterdam and San Francisco and Tokyo. John Lennon was dead.

Since I do not belong to that generation that spent so much of its energy and idealism crying 'make love not war' and tramping in protest marches against the tragedy of Vietnam, I cannot pretend to understand the phenomenon of a singer whose death has produced, as it undoubtedly has, a worldwide outpouring of grief, a grief of identity with the lost cause of peace and brotherhood through the simple chanting of 'peace and brotherhood'. But John Lennon's murder came on the heels of an equally senseless and casual murder, that of Dr Michael Halberstam, a distinguished doctor and writer, who one night last week walked into his home in Washington, tangled with a burglar, and was shot on the spot.

President-elect Reagan was in New York the day after Lennon was shot and was stopped long enough for a reporter to ask him if gun control wasn't the answer. He said, 'No. If somebody commits a crime and carries a gun when he's doing it, add five to fifteen years to the prison sentence.' It may be a way out. At any rate, I don't think there's any doubt now that one of the first bills that somebody will put up to the new Congress will be yet another proposal for a federal gun control law. It has happened, and always in the first shock of a spectacular murder – John Kennedy, Martin Luther King, Bobby Kennedy – that Congress is momentarily outraged. A strong bill is drafted; it is weakened in committee; it is feverishly debated on the floors of both Houses; it is as vigorously opposed as it is advocated; and in the end it is shelved.

Since the United States is the most lax of all the Western nations in controlling the possession of guns, of handguns especially, you may wonder at the strength or the rationale of the opposition to a federal law. Well, first, throughout at least two-thirds of this country, everywhere in the South and the Southwest and all across the West, shooting (or hunting, as it is called here) is an immensely popular sport among all classes. There is by now a huge and profitable gun industry, and the National Rifle Association is one of the most powerful lobbies in Washington. Its slogan, or text, is taken from the Second Amendment to the Constitution, which says, 'the right of the people to keep and bear arms shall not be infringed.' Many a good American parrots that line with a kind of wry fatalism, as if to say, 'I don't know why it's there, but it *is* there and we should respect it.' What these patriots never point out, and rarely seem to know, is that that quotation is only the second part of the sentence. The first part gives the reason. In full, it says, 'A well-regulated militia, being necessary to the security of a free State, the right of the people to keep and bear arms shall not be infringed.' This prescription was written for a nation that did not yet have a standing army. It relied on a citizens' militia, to be made up of every male householder who could snatch the gun by his fireside whenever the call to duty came. The Founding Fathers thought only of that threat to 'the security of a free State.' They were not thinking of individuals or of any 'right' to shoot a pheasant or defend yourself against a burglar or mugger, let alone to go out and shoot a popular idol, whether a President or a singer.

However, while there are otherwise intelligent citizens who like to hunt and who in

Following John Lennon's death a group of protestors demonstrate outside the headquarters of the National Rifle Association.

passing mumble about a constitutional right, they strongly support the National Rifle Association and its concern with rifles and their use in sport, but it is handguns that cause something over 10 percent of the homicides in the United States. And it is the control of handguns that has been the issue in the many fractious debates in and out of Congress since the assassination of John Kennedy. Congress acted, for the first time in thirty years, within a year of the assassination of Bobby Kennedy. At the urging of President Johnson, it passed a Crime Control and Safe Streets Act. It banned the mail-order sale of guns across state lines. It forbade the sale of rifles or shotguns to anyone under eighteen. It forbade also the sale of guns to out-of-state residents. But it fell far short of Lyndon Johnson's appeal for the national registration of all guns, and the national licensing of all owners.

It was, and is, still deadly easy to buy a handgun if you want it. And any criminal, any disturbed person, anybody, can still in many states buy one of the so-called 'Saturday Night Specials' on the most offhand showing of a driver's license. The laxness of the federal law moved various states and cities during the 1970s to pass their own harsher laws. In Kansas and Maine, a prison sentence is compulsory for anyone committing a crime with a gun, irrespective of the damage done. Mississippi denies parole to people convicted of using guns. In Utah, the penalty for any use of a handgun is entirely at the judge's say so. Among the city remedies, two are worth mentioning, since they have proved a striking decline in shootings. The city of Cleveland, after a police battle with an irregular Muslim sect, passed a bill banning the sale, under any circumstances, of cheap handguns, and required the registration of all others. Baltimore, Maryland, I think, can claim the most effective law, one that banned the private possession of handguns. The police department paid fifty dollars for every gun turned in, once the law was passed, and a hundred dollars for information leading to the arrest of possessors. I question whether one's own safety as an informer is worth only a hundred dollars. But as for the other provision, seven thousand handguns were turned in the first week. Baltimore maintains that there has been a dramatic drop in gun-related crimes.

But the laws vary greatly in toughness and in enforcement. It is probably true that anybody who wants a gun hard enough can get one. And across the whole country, there is a vast silent opposition to gun control from householders who believe their first duty is to protect their families. Like it or not, great numbers of Americans are closet vigilantes. Until this uncomfortable fact is recognized and exposed as a form of fear breeding fear, I don't think there is likely to be a national gun control law.

President Reagan

Letter No. 1667, 23 January 1981

The party's over now, and the fortieth President of the United States puts on a working suit, leaves his bedroom every morning, and goes downstairs to work in the Oval Office, just as he did when he went to work in his father's grocery store, which was underneath his bedroom. He could look back on the best produced, the most word-perfect, the most elegant Inaugural any of us can remember. And one which, to time the taking of the Presidential oath with the hostages' planes taking off from Tehran, produced a dramatic coincidence beyond the most ingenious dreams of a Hollywood scriptwriter.

The last person we should forget, amid the splendour of the scene, the ruffles and flourishes of the Marine Band, and the explosion of champagne corks, is Jimmy Carter, who, after fourteen months of a daily grind of frustration and, at the end, forty-eight hours without sleep, was denied the supreme satisfaction of announcing the hostages' flight to freedom. He was robbed of it by only twenty-five minutes, a waiting interval contrived either by ill-luck or by a final malicious stroke of the Iranians. Nothing became his Presidency like the leaving of it.

In the sad, galling twilight of his Administration, one newspaperman, a man from the Deep South who had put up for four years with unceasing cracks about peanuts and hillbillies, said: 'Well, you-all may have had a wonderful time kidding us about Dogpatch North, but ah think you'll come to look back on it as preferable to Holly-wood East.' This was said in response to the mention that the Reagan Inaugural – the big pre-inaugural concert, the fireworks display, the parties and balls – was going to cost eight million dollars, though it was hastily added that the money had been privately subscribed.

It is true that many of us feared a riot of show-biz ostentation, beginning with the Inauguration itself and going on to doing-over the White House. And unrepentant Democrats, anticipating the worst in the coming months, were sniggering about an old MGM production of *The Last Supper on the Titanic*. I have to confess that I myself was caught in this shameful fear. I found myself, the night before the Inauguration, looking up an old film review by the Dorothy Parker of film critics, one Cecilia Ager, an old lady now but once the cinema's recording angel. Forty years or more ago, she wrote a review of Constance Bennett as the star of a Hollywood version of Somerset Maugham's *Our Betters*. And she had this to say: 'Constance Bennett flings herself into the hoity-toity, snobsy-wobsy elegance of *Our Betters* like the prodigal hot-footing it home. *Our Betters* is terribly smart, violently upper class. Insistently it shrieks toniness, graduation from Hollywood aristocracy. Its houses have not only drawing rooms and boudoirs, they have libraries, with books in them too. Some of its rooms are Empire, some Georgian, it even has a Directoire foyer. Positively nothing is modernistic, that's how swell it is. Constance Bennett is presented at Court and tops anybody Their Majesties have ever seen, that's how utterly ornamental she is … Every detail is so painstakingly indisputable, it sets up a positive nostalgia for the other side of the railroad tracks.'

After reading this again, and cringing before the coming blare of money and Hollywood high style, I was quite ready to write: 'My nostalgia takes the form of thinking back to the Inauguration of Thomas Jefferson, who scorned the dress uniforms and the military outriders of George Washington's precedent, thinking them as 'tending toward the luxury of monarchies' and away from the republican simplicity. Feeling strongly about this, Jefferson dispensed with all processions, rode his horse up to the Capitol, tied it to a post himself, went in and gave his Inaugural Address, came out, mounted his horse, rode back to his boardinghouse, and finding the other residents

President Ronald Reagan takes the oath of office during the inauguration ceremony in Washington, DC on 20 January 1981.

already in the best places, sat at the lower end of the table and ate his supper.

Well, the opportunity to express this self-righteousness was strikingly denied. The Inaugural didn't turn out that way at all. First, somebody had had the inspiration to stage the ceremony, for the first time, on the West Portico of the Capitol. It has always been done on the East, which looks out on long lines of streets relieved by a couple of leafy squares. But standing on the handsome stage constructed for the event, President Reagan looked down on the most beautiful and moving panorama in Washington: toward the vast green lawn of the Mall to the piercing monolith of the Washington Monument, and on beyond the Reflecting Pool to the white columns of the Lincoln Memorial, and off to one side the white saucer-dome of the Jefferson Memorial, and then the Potomac River, and up on the rising hill above the river the thousands of white markers of the Arlington National Cemetery, and the flicker of John Kennedy's perpetual flame, and on the horizon, where the sun was beginning to fall, the mansion that Robert E. Lee was compelled to leave to become the General of the Southern armies that fought the Union. I doubt that any country can offer in one unbroken view such a visual memoir of its greatest days and its saddest.

The Inaugural ceremony itself was as short as they ever come, a virtue rarely practiced in political ceremonies in this country, whether it's a nominating convention or a fund-raising breakfast. Everybody appeared on cue, the weather was blessedly mild and bright – after the ice age we've just come through. The Chief Justice administered the oath to the new Vice President, and then the no-nonsense 'put your right hand on the Bible' for the new President. And he repeated the traditional oath, the only oath there has ever been.

We then moved from one foot to the other and settled in for the usual forty-five minutes of soaring or shouting or droning eloquence. Not at all. Mr Reagan took eighteen minutes. And unlike any President before him, talked in a conversational voice, but with all the stresses right and forceful. Some of the newsmen, the television commentators who have been brought up on bellowing rhetoric, thought it was unimpressive as Presidential oratory. That's because they think of a Presidential Inaugural as the one time when every new President, however grand, however humble, must attempt a stage performance in the hectoring, booming Victorian tradition. Mr Reagan, it should not be forgotten, made – how many is it? – over seventy films. He is a film actor, that is to say a behaviourist. He was talking to the television audience, to two people sitting at home. And because he knows, as few Senators and Congressmen do, that a microphone is an electronic instrument for amplifying the smallest sound, his every syllable, his every phrase was clear and telling.

The only jarring note to me was a wry discrepancy between the substance of it and the first theme of the parson's prayer of invocation. President Reagan told Americans yet again that they are a great and unique people, destined to lead the free world. But the Reverend Moomaw, the pastor of Mr Reagan's church in Los Angeles, started in at once with an apocalyptic warning. 'Gracious God,' he began, 'we need you today perhaps more than we have ever needed you before. We have failed in our personal and our national lives. We have seen our world from our own selfish, parochial point of view. We have acted as though everything depended on us. We confess our sin and seek your forgiveness.' At that moment, I didn't notice a wince on the faces of any of the new Cabinet officers, and it must have been a relief to their consciences that the Reverend Moomaw's brave and gutty prayer was not printed next day in any paper they were likely to put their hands on.

Apart from President Reagan's opening vow to attack the economic ills he had promised to cure throughout the campaign, the main theme, which he appears to believe with his heart and soul, is that America can control its destiny. The belief was put in a nutshell years ago by Adlai Stevenson, who once said, 'America is a country that can gag on a gnat but swallow tigers whole.' Reagan passionately believes: 'It is time for us to realize,' he said, 'that we are too great a nation to limit ourselves to small dreams. We're not, as some would have us believe, doomed to an inevitable decline. I do not believe in a fate that will fall on us no matter what we do. I do believe in a fate that will fall on us if we do nothing.'

It is vague and stirring stuff, as inaugural addresses usually are. But he could speak it with confident force in the knowledge of his landslide. It is, no doubt about it, what most Americans want to believe.

By Tuesday evening, most Americans, I should guess, were buoyed up by the splendid spectacle and in an understandable emotional ecstasy over the release of the hostages. The unmixed joy of all this was short-lived. Next day came the ugly news of the brutal mistreatment of many of the hostages, and Mr Carter's hoarse and angry condemnation of it. The very moving scenes we had watched on television of the families talking to their sons or husbands were soured by even more moving scenes of them racked with anxiety over the fear that the men coming home to them would be bruised in body and twisted in mind.

This revelation had an instant and ominous effect on the general mood of benevolence in which most people had heard of the financial terms of the deal. There was talk, responsible talk, of the new Administration's looking into the provisions of the War Powers Act and seeing if it mightn't be invoked to justify reneging on the deal itself. There was keen debate in the corridors of Capitol Hill about whether or not the United States was honour-bound to sanction an agreement made, it now appears, with a nation that had treated diplomatic hostages like the inmates of a concentration camp. But former Vice President Walter Mondale maintained that the deal was equitable and 'served the best interests of the United States. A bargain,' he said. 'Sure,' said the cab driver who brought me to the studio, 'human life is always a bargain.'

Attempted Assassination of President Reagan

Letter No. 1677, 3 April 1981

Our plane was coming in from San Francisco, nosing in through endless layers of cotton wool, with the rain streaming against the windows and no land in sight, till we suddenly spun out of a ground mist and hit the runway. As the brakes roared on and the plane slowed to make the long taxi to the terminal, the captain came on the public address system. He said there was something he wanted to tell us, 'not by way of sensationalism,' but about something that had happened in mid-afternoon. I assumed there'd been some trouble with the plane, and he had sensibly waited to tell us about it till we were safe and sound. He was mumbling very low into his microphone. I think he didn't want to sound 'sensational,' but unfortunately he could hardly be heard. It was something about the President and a secretary. Then he said a little more clearly that two-and-a-half hours ago an assassination attempt had been made on the President, and he was now in surgery in a Washington hospital. It was something he thought we ought to know.

At Kennedy (which used to be Idlewild Airport before the assassination of that President), people waited for their baggage, and I don't think the most imaginative or hyped-up reporter could have seen anything different in the behavior of the people that day from any other day. Maybe there was less jocular small talk. Most people looked tired and patient. Perhaps by now we are resigned to atrocity, as infantrymen get used to seeing dead bodies.

We happened to get possibly the only Chinese cab driver at the airport, who spoke little English and had no radio. So it was nearly an hour before we were home and turning on the television and seeing – almost like a cruel replay of Dallas, 1963 – startled Secret Service men, people falling to the ground, and a sudden scrum of men huddled over a young man.

Fortunately, for the country, the anxious hours were blessedly few. The first authoritative spokesman, the man who conducted an evening press conference at the hospital, was one Dr Dennis O'Leary, the dean of clinical affairs at George Washington University Hospital. By great good luck, he was one doctor in a thousand, in that he had an immediate air of candour and authority; he sensed in a flash what sort of language would enlighten people without alarming them. He had humour, when it was

President Reagan enjoying a giant get well card while recuperating at George Washington University Hospital following the assassination attempt.

appropriate to have it; he was responsive to intelligent questions and courteously non-committal to idiotic questions. And he was able, as doctors very rarely are, to translate the abominable jargon of his trade into sensible and even subtle English that any of us could understand. Of course, the fates were with him. The President had been jaunty about his wound; he had the luck of what Dr O'Leary called 'fine physiological health … a very young seventy-year-old', and the bullet had stayed inches away from a fatal point of entry. Still, looking back on it, I think we all owe an enormous debt to Dr O'Leary. He is young enough to have come to take for granted what actually scandalized an older generation: the expectation that the press would want to know all the medical details and had a right to have them. (I digress here, but I hope, to the point.) This tradition is very new. I remember the shock of the ordinary people of New York when a tabloid daily came out with a headline, twenty-odd years ago, 'Dulles Has Inoperable Cancer' referring to former Secretary of State John Foster Dulles. That was the positive end to the old tradition of reticence, which allowed a man, however distinguished, to face the end with his family in privacy and in dignity. We were already inured to this historical shift in journalistic practice when President Eisenhower had his heart attack. Day after day, in Denver, his doctor came before the media, and described everything in great detail, down to the consistency of the President's bowel movements. Ever since then, a public man hides from the press the symptoms of any affliction, however mild, at his peril. Obviously, it has become harder and harder for a doctor to instruct the layman in the facts without leaving little loopholes through which the dumber sort of journalist will fish out lurid inferences. We have come a long way indeed from the day, not a hundred years ago, when the President of the United States, Grover Cleveland, could be taken out to sea on a yacht, operated on for cancer of the throat, and returned to the White House, to convalesce there and recover. And nobody knew a thing about it until, years later, he was dead.)

So, what Dr O'Leary did, on the evening of the wounding of the President, was to restore the morale of the country in a decent and authoritative way. He was helped, of course, by being able to report the heartening fact that the President had shown an almost puckish bravery of spirit. Dr O'Leary deserves the Medal of Freedom.

Especially because the scene in the White House, where you would properly expect authority to take hold, was a muddled, and for a time, a faintly alarming one. I'm afraid the culprit here was former General Alexander Haig, the Secretary of State. It is quite true that he was, very shortly after the shooting, the senior member of the Cabinet who happened to be on hand. He at once decided that since the Vice President was flying back from Texas, he – Mr Haig – was now in charge of the government. Of course, he wasn't. President Reagan was, until either the President declared himself disabled to continue in office, or the Vice President and a majority of the Cabinet informed in writing the pro tem President of the Senate and the Speaker of the House that the President was unable to discharge his duties. Then, and then only, the Vice President becomes Acting President. This is all set forth quite precisely in the Twenty-fifth Amendment to the Constitution. And suppose that the President dies, and after him – or with him – the Vice President, the succession then goes to the Speaker of the House. *He* is third in line. But Mr Haig, when all about him might have been losing their heads, rushed on to television with darting eyes and a sweaty forehead. He was nervous and he was dogmatic. He was, he said, 'in control'. He could have been in control in a purely practical sense at the moment, but his fatal remark came when he was asked why. He mentioned the Constitution and repeated the gaffe that the Secretary of State succeeds after the President and the Vice President, thus showing, as one commentator put it, 'an incredible lack of understanding of Constitutional succession.'

There is another line of succession, which has to do with the command structure of the military, the Pentagon. When Mr Haig got away from his unfortunate performance on television, he went back to what is known in the White House as the Situation Room, the place where crucial military decisions are made, invariably in the presence of the President, who, remember, is the Commander-in-Chief of all the armed forces. There, the Secretary of Defense, Mr Caspar Weinberger, felt it his duty to tell Mr Haig that he was not in charge of that structure either. The command passes from the President to the Vice President and then to the Secretary of Defense – nobody but Mr Weinberger. Altogether, an acutely unhappy time for Secretary Haig. But he, and the people, were put right at once by the chief Washington correspondents of two networks.

One of the more stupid, but I suppose inevitable, questions put to Dr O'Leary, of all political neutrals, was whether or not there was evidence of a conspiracy. He wouldn't think of commenting on that. And from what we know, and we know a great deal about the life and character of the pathetic John Hinckley, he was no more of a conspirator than the equally pathetic eighteen-year-old bartender who fired twice on Constitution Hill at the very young Queen Victoria and missed. Edward Oxford (his name) did not have a repeater. Unlike John Hinckley, he did not have the means to spray half a dozen shots in two seconds at several targets. Hinckley, at this time anyway, appears to be a sick (and lovesick) young man acting out a fantasy with a girl he had never met, and meaning, more than anything, to make himself important by a violent act.

Inevitably, old arguments have been brought up and old morals have been drawn. The campaign for stricter control of handguns (Washington, DC, by the way, has one of the strictest laws, as strict as anything that might be written into a federal law) takes on new strength through indignation after every murder or attempted murder of a prominent person. It raged after John Kennedy's death, then waned; raged again after the assassination of Martin Luther King, Jr., the paralyzing of Alabama Governor George Wallace, the death of Bobby Kennedy, the shooting of John Lennon. In fact, it seems only yesterday, and almost was, that I gave my talk over to the various state laws about handgun control and the general yearning for a ban on so-called Saturday Night Specials. But these crusades always fade away not, as many angry people charge, because the rifle lobby is very powerful in Washington – which it is. But because millions of Americans are scared enough of violence on the streets and against their homes to feel that a law to ban handguns would render the citizen helpless against the criminal, who will always get a gun somehow. At any rate, there is not likely to be much success in the next crusade, since President Reagan himself is strongly against gun control. His solution was, as Governor of California, and still is, a compulsory sentence of from five to fifteen years in jail for anyone committing a crime while in possession of a gun.

I leave the grave and undoubtedly sincere moralizing about the sickness of this country, indeed of our time, to others. If violence is a special sickness of our age, it is universal, and nobody so far has come up with a cure.

But I will end by reminding you that such characters as John Hinckley seem to be around at all times, especially in a country that offers to a fugitive the escape-hatch of a continent. The proper comparison between violence in America is not with any one country but with the whole of Europe. On any given day, the Protective Research Section of the United States Secret Service has on file the names of not less than 50,000 persons who have written threatening or obscene letters to the incumbent President. 1,500 new letters are added every month. Repeaters are tracked down simply from their letters, and the Secret Service claims an average of 98 percent of such people are apprehended, many of them tried and put away. John Hinckley, it appears now, was one of the 2 percent who slipped through the net.

Clear and Present Danger

Letter No. 1684, 22 May 1981

I was going to begin by asking a question: Is it ten or twenty years ago that people started hijacking planes, and then I realized that there must be young people about to leave school, maybe already in college, who have never seen an airport that did not have its two familiar security devices: the doorway frame without a door, through which you pass across a beam that identifies any metal you may be carrying. And the scanner machine built over a moving belt on which all passengers must put their brief-cases, handbags, and parcels.

When this system was introduced, shortly after the first American plane was forced on to Cuba at gunpoint, there was much bellyaching by regular air passengers. And I seem to recall some now-forgotten patriot threatening to bring suit against the airlines for violating the First Amendment to the Constitution. The grounds of his complaint was to be that these security devices, because they set up an arbitrary point beyond which friends and other non-travelling well-wishers were forbidden to go, infringed the First Amendment's guarantee of the right of 'freedom of assembly'.

Nothing came of it, because I presume his lawyer told him about the case of Schenck v. United States, 1919, in which a man named Schenck had been prosecuted for dis-tributing pamphlets during the First World War that urged young men to resist the Draft (or conscription) Act. The Court's opinion was written by the majestic Yankee Mr Justice Oliver Wendell Holmes, who invoked the power of the government to sus-pend laws, even the right of free speech, whenever there is 'a clear and present danger' to the country. This danger had been cited to justify the wartime Espionage Act, and Justice Holmes said it applied in that case.

Well, the offended airplane passenger was persuaded that he'd have a hard time convincing any court that the prospect of being blown to bits on an airplane by a man carrying a bomb, or threatening the pilot with a gun, did not constitute a 'clear and present danger' to the passengers. I don't believe anybody has ever sued an airline on this or a related ground.

By now, we not only accept the security check as an obligation of air travel as automatic as showing your ticket, but by an odd paradox, the checking procedure guarantees the passenger a place and period of calm before he takes off. It used to be

that the areas surrounding the embarkation gates were choked with friends and relations and, in New York and other polyglot cities, with whole families down to the
third generation come to cheer or weep as some favourite son or Mum went off to visit
grandma or the new baby a thousand miles away. Nowadays, these passionate pals
wave goodbye as their beloved goes through the doorless door. On the other side is a
long, empty corridor leading to the spacious calm of the gate area.

Unlike some of my friends, who complain about the bustle and the boredom of
airports, I enjoy them. I enjoy going anywhere rather than arriving, and I seize any
plausible pretext for meeting a friend. I went out to Kennedy the other day to meet a
friend coming in from London. A droll fellow who once said he'd come to the time of
life when all he looked forward to was 'to retire and go shopping.' Well, I'd just finished a book I'd been working on all winter. I'd cleared out ten years of accumulated
mail and newspaper cuttings and transformed my bedroom from a garbage dump into
a neat and friendly study. To complete this process, I had done something I never do except on holiday. I had gone shopping. And now I was happy to give over half a day to
meeting a friend at an airport. Pope John Paul II seemed definitely out of danger from
an assassination attempt, which has been a daily anxiety, and I was in fine spirits.

My fine spirits lasted as long as the ride. As we came into the terminal of this
particular airline, we were waved down by two cops with guns in their back pockets.
It was almost like entering Ulster. They peered at my face, wanted to see the driver's
licence, asked our business, and told us to ignore all the terminal entrances except
one, half a mile away. 'That,' they said, 'is the only way you can get in.' As we passed
a whole long wall of entrances, I noticed that they had been pasted over with signs
marked with arrows pointing to the one door you could get in. This led to the lounge
adjoining the baggage claim station, which had two other cops at the door. There were
no more than twenty or thirty of us strolling around and waiting under the scrutiny
of a covey of roving police. When at last my friend came through the baggage door,
looking rather dazed, and we got off and drove again into the brilliant sunlight, it was
a great relief. This had been the terminal where a bomb had gone off and killed a man
the day before. In fact, the entire Kennedy Airport, which handles more daily human
traffic than all but three other airports in the world, had been closed down and planes
diverted for five hours, all on account of an anonymous telephoned bomb threat.

Next day, there were more telephone calls, and the whole working staffs were
evacuated from such monster skyscrapers as the Chrysler Building, and the World
Trade Center, which is the tallest building on earth. By nightfall, many other buildings, including the Manhattan Criminal Court building and two department stores
had been evacuated. This outrage involves notifying and evacuating, in all, about a
hundred thousand office workers and visitors. It was to no avail. I should say, 'happily'
to no avail, since there were no bombs. The following day, by four in the afternoon,
the police had had eighty-three separate bomb threats, making a total of 268 in three
days. They had gone out to office buildings, to the Long Island Railroad, to the three
city airports, to Pennsylvania and Grand Central railroad stations, and to six foreign

consulates or United Nations missions. They all want extra police protection, but obviously the strain on the police force of buildings housing about one hundred thousand people is preposterous.

New York City has a special anti-terrorist task force of fifty members, made up of police and the FBI (the FBI, being federal, can only intervene in crimes whose suspects may have crossed a state border). This force, after a scary spring, had just about come to the conclusion that it had cracked and crushed the most active terrorist movement in the United States, which is a Puerto Rican group that almost always announces responsibility for its acts. But this blitz of bomb threats, which is unprecedented in the city's history, is a mystery. The Puerto Rican terrorists claimed responsibility for the first, but afterward stayed mum. Some officials think that all these calls could have come in from no more than two or three persons. And the bitter truth is that if that's so, as the Police Commissioner said on Wednesday, 'a small cell is the most difficult to break. You have to get a lead, and get lucky.' The deputy head of the New York office of the FBI was even more glum: 'We don't know,' he said, 'this could be one guy, it may be five hundred.'

All this may make a lot of you feel thankful that you are not in New York, just as those of us who live outside Belfast cannot believe that people live and work there, get married, have babies, and go out and take a walk. But from the police point of view in matters like this, the curse of a big city is its bigness. I am looking out on a tranquil scene in Central Park. Sunbathers are lying on towels in the meadows. The squeals of children can be heard from the playground, which is blanketed just now by the flowering horse chestnuts. You could walk forty or fifty blocks and see only strollers and bustlers and shoppers and traffic and no desperate evacuees, and hear no bombs.

If there had been no bombs, we could all bite our nails and wait a while and relax. But two unexploded bombs were recovered at Kennedy last weekend and four more since. A loud ticking clock was picked up in a washroom a telephone call had identified. And the police switchboards are swamped with agitated calls from well-meaning people who think they saw, think they heard, heard tell of, could swear an empty bag, a suitcase standing in a washroom, and so on and so on.

There are officials who believe that an assassination attempt on a world-famous person triggers a dangerous alert through terrorist groups and sends a shock wave through jails, psychiatric hospitals, and the population of the unhinged.

It's a dreadful thought that the attempt on the life of President Reagan may have, by a sort of contagion, suggested the outrage of an attack on the Pope. What sort of contagion? Well, there is a lady who thinks she knows. She is the police department's commissioner for public information. And she says that the telephone calls are 'being precipitated by all the attention that the media are paying to the calls.' By the media, of course, she means the papers, and the radio news round the clock, and most of all, television. We've all heard, and some of us have said over and over again, that it is impossible to exaggerate the effect of television reporting on most people alive: it's where they pick up their views of what's going on, their attitudes to other countries, and especially, their judgment of what is important and what is not. And that is decided by what television chooses to show. Six weeks ago, our TV news started every night with horrid scenes of the slaughter, from the left and the right, in El Salvador. It was given this prominence, I suppose, because Secretary of State Alexander Haig was saying just then that El Salvador was the first country on the Soviet Union's 'hit list' for dominating Central America. Then a couple of weeks ago, imprisoned IRA leader Bobby Sands led the news with a hunger strike. Well, this morning you have to look on page 11 of the *New York Times* to read that the third IRA hunger-striker has just died. And, on another inside page, there is a piece reminding us that there is in El Salvador, as the headline puts it, 'Still No Escape From the Horrors of War'.

Yesterday, the New York Police Department recorded 160 telephone bomb threats, all of which had to be investigated by police cars. But, after a week of it, even this news has retreated to an inside page. Will this idiotic and criminal fashion simply wane? Or shall we come to expect that once we've gone up to the thirty-second floor and settled in our offices, we may expect to be evacuated to the street as a routine of daily life? Nobody knows the answer, or a solution to this 'clear and present danger.'

Ronald Reagan vs. Darth Vader

Letter No. 1781, 1 April 1983

Well, first it was a nuclear 'freeze' as against the 'zero option'. And now it's an alternative: the limited deployment of intermediate-range warheads. If the new proposal has no other virtue, it's impossible to jazz it up into an acronym or a catchword to set us all marching behind banners with scary devices.

But I want to talk about another alternative, or rather an alternative role the President keeps playing with baffling frequency. One day he's the screaming eagle, the next he's a purring dove. These quick-change roles can best be illustrated by two speeches the President made in the past week or two, which express a puzzling or maybe two puzzling sides of his character.

First, let me say that whatever else he is, Mr Reagan is not a sinister character, nothing remotely as shivery and calculating as he appears in the puppet shows and horrendous caricatures paraded by the unilateralists and others who claim a monopoly on sincerity and peace-mongering. Mr Reagan, even in the Congress, which amounts to 535 humans of every known character and ideological flavour, has no enemies. I can't remember a President, in my time or before, that you could say that about. He is so amiable, so personally genial and thoughtful, that there are Democrats who've resolved not to accept social invitations to the White House for fear of being infected and debauched by the President's sunny and beguiling manner.

I said just now that he is not a calculating man. That's one of his troubles. Even his closest aides, his kitchen cabinet in the White House, wish he were more calculating. But between one day and the next, between a happy morning meeting in the White House and an evening speech somewhere off in the country, Mr Reagan, having given everybody the idea that he's going to play it cool on this policy or that, then appears in Florida or Texas or wherever and starts to exhale fire and brimstone or worse, to come out hot against sin.

The 'Star Wars' speech and the 'Darth Vader' speech are rather frightening examples of this Jekyll and Hyde impersonation. Darth Vader, as any toddler who happens to be lying about the house will tell you, was the leader of the Empire in the movie *Star Wars*. So, the Darth Vader speech – and that's what, for convenient filing, the White House calls it – was the one the President gave before that throbbing audience of evangelicals in Florida, in which he called the Soviet Union 'the evil empire run by Godless men.' After he'd left Florida, with the applause still tingling in his ears, Mr Reagan was astonished to read and hear that the speech, and most of all the characterization of the Soviet Union, was deplored of course abroad, but all around the United States as well.

Then whether by accident or design, but I'd guess by the natural trend of his character to make impulsive amends, he made what they call his 'Star Wars' speech. That was the one in which he foresaw, and even proposed, a one billion dollar a year development program to ditch the present Soviet-American system of deterrence by massive retaliation and go to an anti-ballistic system that would have laser beams pinpointing and exploding, way up in the sky, any missiles the enemy cared to launch. There's no doubt, I think, that the President thought of this as a friendly suggestion. A day or two later, he went so far as to say that once the thing was perfected, he'd be happy to share it with the Soviets, provided, I imagine, they are prepared to wait so long. The President says it may take till the end of the century, or beyond, before we've got this trick in perfect shape. By the way, no responsible scientist who's been heard from will guarantee that it will ever be perfected.

The Russians – Mr General Secretary Yuri Andropov, that is to say – responded to both speeches, the nasty one and the nice one, in one breath, which is not surprising. Call a man the leader of an evil empire, of a country also described as 'the focus of evil' in the world, and you shouldn't be surprised if he comes back and calls you a liar and a lunatic. Just for the record, I also can't recall any Russian leader at any time calling any American President a liar, let alone a lunatic. Then, having vented his proper spleen, Mr Andropov got down to the substance of the Star Wars proposal. He said it violated the 1972 Soviet-American Anti-Ballistic Missile Treaty. Mr Reagan had anticipated this move. Not so, he said. The United States was not testing or manufacturing such things yet. You may wonder, as I did, whether this treaty is distinct and separate from the first SALT (Strategic Arms Limitation) Treaty of the same year. No matter. I finally dug out the text, or rather the fifth article, of that first SALT treaty, and this is what it says: 'Each party undertakes not to develop, test, or deploy anti-ballistic missile systems or components, which are sea-based, air-based, space-based, or mobile land-based.' Well, Mr Reagan is offering to develop, at least, an anti-ballistic missile system, assuming a laser is a missile that is space-based. Clearly, wouldn't you say Mr Andropov is correct? A conclusion we shouldn't be hesitant about, even if Mr Andropov *is* Darth Vader.

Faced with what I should think was an unanswerable fact, there are people, even defence experts, who say, yes but you can't trust the Russians to abide by anything. If that's so, then there's surely no point in signing any treaties with them or holding any talks. The American people, so far as I can read the entrails, are divided on how to respond to both the Darth Vader and the Star Wars speech. I don't mean divided into two opposing blocs. I mean divided within themselves. From every source of tapping public opinion, it appears that most Americans do believe that the Russians have not

President Ronald Reagan addressing the National Association of Evangelicals in Florida. In his speech he called the Soviet Union an evil empire.

changed their old aim of world domination. Or, as the conservative columnist William F. Buckley puts it: 'Mr Reagan does well to remind us that we are dealing with men explicitly bound to the proposition that the morality of advancing world revolution superordinates (overrides) any other morality.'

Again, I believe most Americans would go along with this – did go along with it in the war against Hitler – if they did not believe and fear that any conceivable war with the Russians would in fact not prevent the nation from perishing but would hasten its doom. So, my guess, based not on a hunch but on all the available surveys, is that the Americans (and they are surely not alone) do believe that the Soviets want to dominate the world, do believe that the Russian people don't want a war to prove it, do believe that at the end of such a war most of us would be dead, and the rest would be neither dead nor red. So, even though the Russian leaders may be very wicked, most Americans want to go on talking with them. In fairness to Mr Reagan, I have to quote something he said that was assuredly not quoted in *Tass* or, I'd bet, in any other Soviet publication. 'Our nation, too,' he said, 'has a legacy of evil with which it must deal.'

I hope he meant by this what the Pope meant when he inaugurated, a week ago, the Holy Year of Redemption, and knelt at the threshold of the Holy Door at St Peter's to signify that he too is a sinner. But I fear that Mr Reagan was still thinking about Communism, though its presence in the United States must be minuscule. For, between the

Darth Vader speech and the Star Wars speech, the President issued an extraordinary comment on the budget proposals that the Democrats have handed down and which most notably cut the rate of growth of the President's defence budget. Mr Reagan called this Democratic document, 'a dagger aimed at the heart ... of the nation ... and a joy to the Kremlin.' (To go on piling up the record of astonishing firsts, I'd better say, too, that I don't remember any President ever accusing the whole opposing party of being a joy to the Kremlin. 'What's gotten into him?' was the despairing mutter in the House corridors. House Speaker Tip O'Neill retaliated by saying that the President was reverting to the tactics of the late Senator McCarthy.)

This is not pleasant to talk about, especially at a time when so many allies, Germany, Australia, and others, have just had elections and when Britain is girding up for one. When, in effect, important friends are shuffling into position and would be immensely relieved to feel that they knew, fairly precisely, where the United States stood in its foreign policy. It is no consolation to them to be told that there was much head-shaking in the State Department after the Florida (the Darth Vader) speech and complaints that it had not been cleared there. The fact is that the President does not compose his speeches by checking with government departments beforehand. He relies – after talking things over with three or four old advisers – on two young men, one thirty-nine, the other thirty-four. The thirty-nine-year-old is the temperate one, useful to calm any fears that might be generated by the prose of the thirty-four-year-old, Mr Tony Dolan, an ideological whizz-kid who falls just short of adoration of his boss. He was the one who drafted the Darth Vader speech, which we can only thank God even the President found too hot and heavy and himself toned it down. If 'the empire of evil' is an example of toning down, Heaven knows what we, and Mr Andropov, were saved from.

Mr Reagan's biographer, a journalist who has known him for sixteen years and who has written an engrossing and singularly detached book, wrote about him that when he became Governor of California, he was also very ignorant of State issues and State politics at the start, and also given to great soaring flights of rhetoric, based on what the writer calls his 'basic, optimistic simplicity,' which was (at the beginning of his presidency too) the source of his appeal, and that would also prove the source of his administration's most glaring inadequacies. In California, Mr Reagan learned a lot and developed what his biographer calls 'a proclivity for doing what is necessary at the expense of his rhetoric.'

For the rest of his term, I am sure that millions of people who want the United States to be a responsible and benevolent leader of the West – the Europeans especially – will hope and pray that sooner than later, the President will trust to that 'proclivity for doing what is necessary at the expense of his rhetoric.'

Chicago

Letter No. 1783, 15 April 1983

It occurs to me that it's been a long time since I had the idea of talking about Chicago. It is an idea whose time has come. Not, surely, simply because of a local election out there? Well, yes, because of last Tuesday's election; because Chicago has a new mayor. Because he is a black man; need I say, the first black mayor of Chicago. Because he has severely wounded the political machine that has had the city in its grip, or its pocket, for fifty-two years. But mainly because Chicago is *the* second city of the United States and is, in some ways, the most vibrant and fascinating of all American cities. And what happens there can affect many other cities around the country.

I have no doubt that even though I've been talking for only one minute, you must have in your mind a picture of Chicago. We all have at the back of our minds simple, vivid pictures of a thousand places on earth. They have to be simple, because if they weren't we'd go around in a continual daze, admitting that the world was complicated enough to drive us mad. Hence, the great boon – to our serenity and our self-respect – of the cliché, the firm preconception we usually pick up in childhood and file away for easy reference later.

Say 'Holland,' to millions of people, and they see at once windmills and tulips, a landscape enlivened possibly by a man with his thumb in a dike. Say 'Los Angeles,' and the world still pictures a suntanned girl in a bikini, either on a beach or on a movie set. Say 'London' to a million Americans, and I'm afraid the travel pamphlets have successfully done their work of imprinting on our minds the Tower of London, the Household Cavalry, Big Ben, and two old gaffers clanking mugs of ale in a country pub with a thatched roof.

And how about 'Chicago'? I'm not sure I can even guess at the present stereotype that most of us refer to. I know very well what the picture was to English men and women fifty-odd years ago, when Chicago had its last Republican mayor. His name was William Hale Thompson, known as Big Bill the Builder, because he swore he would pave Illinois with hard-surfaced roads, and did. His great and rambunctious popularity was due to a sound, if jingoistic, instinct. Chicago in the twenties was bursting at the seams, with more immigrants from a dozen countries and with a new influx of Negroes. Big Bill Thompson decided that to hold them together, to stem any more race riots (there was an appalling one in 1919), he must find a common scapegoat for everybody to blame and hate. He found it in, of all blameless candidates, King George the Fifth. The British, said Bill Thompson, had seduced America into entering a European war. The British and the traditions they had passed on to the United States were the enemies of a big, surging, polyglot, industrial city.

We in England knew nothing of this at the time. But Big Bill Thompson achieved immortality with a single sentence, which made headlines in the press of Britain and Europe. 'If,' Big Bill said, 'King George of England ever comes over here, I will publicly bust him in the snoot.' Well, King George never took him up on it. But we all remembered Big Bill Thompson. He was all we knew about Chicago, until by the middle twenties, the arrival of prohibition – the national act forbidding the manufacture, sale, or consumption of alcoholic liquors – had spawned an underground bootleg industry and competing armies of gangsters. So, throughout the late twenties and well into 1930s, if you said 'Chicago,' the penny dropped and you saw Al Capone and his mobsters wheeling round corners on two wheels of a screeching automobile and gunning down their rivals.

Chicago has suffered so long from the stigma of gangsterism that I doubt the picture is even now erased. I'd better say something about what Chicago is and has been to most of the country.

Of all American cities, Chicago is *the* phenomenon of mushroom growth. In 1833, it was a squatter settlement of two hundred people. In that year a canal was cut through a sandbar to the Chicago River, and Chicago had a harbour. There arrived a hustling mayor, a native of upstate New York, who poured money and energy into hundreds of bridges, sewage plants, water systems, and parks. He seized on a newfangled type of house construction known as 'balloon frame' – the first pre-fabricated house (this was in 1835) – and Mayor Ogden built them by the thousand. The bumper crops from the prairie poured in, and within only nine years of that settlement of two hundred souls, Chicago was the largest grain market in the world. In no time, it was also the largest railroad junction. And so on and on, its population doubling every ten years, till it also became the cow slaughterer and meat packer for America and Europe.

Chicago, first of all, has a splendid lakefront boulevard, with green parks in front of it, and beyond them the encircling horizon of Lake Michigan, which to the onlooker might just as well be an ocean, since it is just under half the size of England. Chicago has one of the three or four top universities of America, renowned especially for its work in economics, Biblical history, linguistics, and a pioneer department of sociology. It has an Art Institute that is a treasure house of, especially, French painting. It has today, by common consent, the first symphony orchestra of the world. It had the first skyscraper. It is the city of Frank Lloyd Wright. And also of Carl Sandburg, and more gifted writers than, I think, can be claimed by any other American city. For it is the city of Frank Norris and Theodore Dreiser, of Harriet Monroe and her *Poetry* magazine;

Harold Washington is sworn in and becomes the first
black mayor of Chicago, 29 April 1983.

of Vachel Lindsay and Sherwood Anderson and James T. Farrell and Nelson Algren and Thorstein Veblen and Saul Bellow. And a whole generation of gifted and racy news papermen, a clutch of whom moved to Hollywood and gave what we can now see as a brief but crackling vitality to the best American movie comedies of the 1930s.

But, behind the sparkling lakefront façade, the auditoriums and the Art Institute and the splendid Science and Industry Museum and the parks, there lie miles of, as you move west and north, increasingly dingy neighborhoods and flimsy slums. In no other American city has the immigrant's pot so noticeably failed to melt. In other big cities, in New York and San Francisco particularly, there are what we used to call 'quarters' – the Chinese quarter, the Italian quarter. But the other immigrant groups have long ago spilled and intermingled. Black America everywhere still packs into the poorest parts of any town.

But in Chicago, the successive waves of immigrants poured into the city, found their own breeding pond, and stayed there. Chicago has been said to be not so much a melting pot as a checkerboard – a chessboard. It is more like a closed maze, where access from one lane to another is not worth the effort. So, if you look at an ethnic map of Chicago, you are also looking at a political map, for each election district is a small nation, and its district leader is invariably of the same national origin as the first immigrants who settled there. So, if you look down on this maze from an airplane, you could call off the separate plots and see a German Chicago, a Polish Chicago, and a Swedish, Italian, Jewish, Lithuanian, Czech, Greek, Chinese, Russian, Irish Chicago. And, the largest of the plots: a Black Chicago.

For the past fifty years, the Democratic party has been quicker than the Republicans in serving the humblest needs of the immigrants and the poor, getting a job, a cast-off suit, paying a court fine, a street peddling license, hiring a nurse. During that half-century, the Democrats recruited their heelers and captains from each and every section and kept them there to minister to their own kind. And under the benign but iron dictatorship of the late Mayor Richard Daley, it was the Democrats who filled the city government jobs, the police, the firemen, the school superintendents, the sewage workers, the sanitation department. The only and inescapable price to be paid – by a dustman or a district leader – was to get out the district vote on Election Day.

This year, the retiring Democratic mayor, Jane Byrne, ran in the Democratic primary against the son of old Mayor Daley. A third man, with little hope, a black man named Harold Washington, challenged both of them. Byrne and Daley were, in effect, running against each other for control of the Democratic Party machine. It was a fatal error. What they did was to split the vote three ways, and, to everybody's astonishment, the black man – Washington – won and became the Democrat opposing in last Tuesday's election a Republican named Epton. From the start and till the end, the battle was an undeclared but positive race battle. The old white Democratic politicians, the city workers, the police – for one day in their lives – deserted and voted Republican. Most of the poor whites and their landlords feared that a black mayor would mean a mass takeover, and a general devaluation of their housing. But the

Chicago, 'the phenomenon of mushroom growth.'

desertion of the white Democrats was not quite wholesale. Upper-middle-class white liberals along the lakefront voted for Washington. The qualified blacks voted better than 90 percent for him.

So, Chicago has a black mayor. The Daley machine is, for the time being, a ruin. The Republicans pretend they've had a blood transfusion. As for the people, white and black, they have no better idea than the columnists and pundits what is to happen next.

Invasion of Grenada

Letter No. 1812, 4 November 1983

After the first shock of the thing itself, it developed that Americans were going to have the quite new experience of hearing about a war they were engaged in from nobody but their own government. No correspondents were allowed to accompany the invaders, and this had not happened in the two World Wars, in the Korean War, in Vietnam, or in Lebanon. For three days, anyway, we had to take on trust the battle pictures that the Pentagon thought fit to release. By then, there were already 400 correspondents of five or six nations fuming in hotels in Barbados, 150 miles away from the action, and just as dependent as the rest of us on the Pentagon's official account of what was going on. Namely, that 400 Marines helped by American Rangers and then by another 1,500 had secured Grenada in twenty-four hours, and that the American medical students there had been protected. We saw film of two or three students weeping with gratitude – students who said they were frightened and who guessed, either then or earlier, that they had been in danger.

The official accounts began to lose their confidence when, by the fourth day, there was tough resistance. They admitted that intelligence had been scanty, that the Cubans numbered not 400 but closer to 1,000; that the pacifying operation was going to take three days, then a week, or many weeks.

At that point, on the Thursday night, President Reagan went on the air to say why he had ordered the invasion: To avoid any repetition of the Iranian hostage horror by saving the Americans on the island; to restore the authority of the Queen's Governor General; and to make possible a return to free elections and a democratically run Grenada. By now, the Pentagon had recanted somewhat about press coverage. Mr Caspar Weinberger, the Secretary of Defense, was asked in a pretty rough session with the press why correspondents had not gone in. He said the invasion commander didn't want them, and he wouldn't dream of going above the ruling of a superior. That was, at best, a blunder in a country that has always believed, with the other democracies, that if war is not too important to be left to the generals, the conduct of it and the reporting of it must always be in the hands of civilians. Otherwise, as somebody said, why should Mr Weinberger and not General So-and-so be the Secretary of Defense? Soon, correspondents were allowed in, first gingerly for an official tour of picked spots,

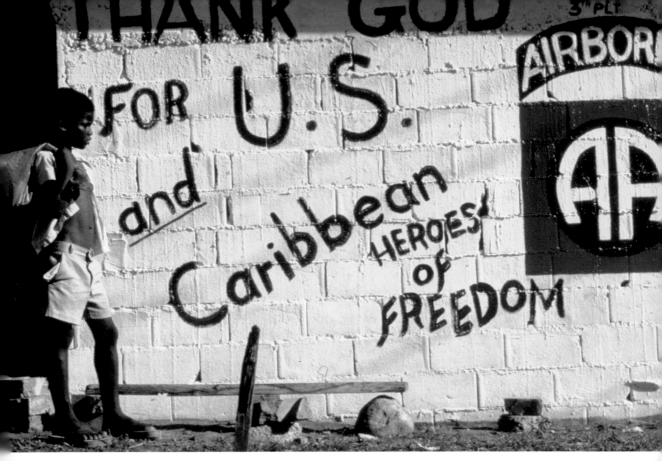

A young boy stands in front of brick wall covered with graffiti thanking the US for their invasion of Grenada to oust leftist officials.

then for six hours. By the end of the week, they were chartering boats and scrambler planes, and the television networks were let in. By last weekend the press had asserted its ancient right. By then, correspondents had interviewed refugees from Grenada, had talked to Barbadians who had come back from there, had picked up uncensored film from the French. And, if we needed any other proof of the Pentagon's initial folly in barring war correspondents, even reporters staying in Washington were so much on the hop (tapping every source they knew inside the Defense Department, inside the Marine Corps, and on the Caribbean intelligence desk) that Mr Weinberger might have wished he'd packed the whole Washington press corps off to the island at the start.

From these reporters, it came out that most of the 6,000 men – by then 6,000! – on or near Grenada had practically no prior information about the numbers, the arms of the enemy, or where it was. How 400 Cuban construction workers turned into 1,100 combat troops was put down, by the Pentagon itself, as 'weak intelligence'. The Associated Press said that Cuba had been tipped off to the invasion twenty-four hours before it began. A source in Caribbean intelligence said that the CIA had no spies in Grenada until the day before the invasion. Some invasion units had only tourist maps to go on. Throughout the week, the Pentagon pessimistically revised the prediction at its first press briefing that the whole operation would be over in twenty-four hours.

All this, of course, had to do with reports of an ill-prepared campaign and says nothing about the reason for mounting it. The legal rationale that the State Department had to elaborate on was the rather frail argument that a request for help from the tiny islands of the Organization of Eastern Caribbean States outweighed the charter of the United Nations and the charter of the Organization of American States, which ban all external intervention in an internal rebellion. The first international body to act, inevitably, was the Security Council of the United Nations. One of its fifteen members, the United States naturally vetoed the resolution being put to it that denounced the American intervention. Togo, Zaire and Great Britain abstained from a vote. And eleven nations voted for it, though it has to be said that several of them said they had voted reluctantly. They managed to soften the resolution from one of 'condemning' the United States' action to 'deeply deploring it'.

Apart from the division of public opinion here, which the President's speech apparently narrowed into a rather close division, the most striking thing domestically was something you had to search for, since it is difficult to spot something that isn't there: namely, the reaction of the Democrats in general, and the five Democratic Presidential runners in particular. They were very tight-lipped indeed for two or three days, Senator John Glenn alone saying that the President ought to have put out a warning about protecting the American medical students or have negotiated for their safekeeping. House Speaker Tip O'Neill, the President's most dependable ideological opponent, didn't want to imperil the morale of the troops until he saw how quickly they'd pacified the island. But once the Pentagon began to backtrack on its promises of an easy victory, the Democrats woke up. Speaker O'Neill said it was old-fashioned 'gunboat diplomacy' and confessed that the President's foreign policies frightened him. Mr Walter Mondale, the Democrats' leader in the Presidential primary race, openly condemned the invasion as 'undermining our ability to criticize the Russians' suppression of liberty in Afghanistan, Poland, and elsewhere.' The Senate acted very quickly after a bristling debate to give the President no more than sixty days to withdraw the troops from Grenada. The vote was 64 to 20, which is a much larger majority than the Republicans enjoy in the Senate. The House Foreign Affairs Committee voted 32 to 2 to do the same thing, a sure sign that the whole House would second the Senate.

An interesting dissenter from the majority view was not a Senator or a Congressman but former President Carter's chief adviser on national security. Mr Zbigniew Brezezinski said he must be the only Democrat who felt President Reagan did what he had to do. And that takes us to the historical background of a doctrine of American foreign policy that has not been cited much in the past few years, though President Kennedy reminded Americans of it at the height of the Cuban missile crisis.

This is the so-called Monroe Doctrine. James Monroe was president between 1816 and 1824, a time that, thanks to Monroe's benign and diplomatic character, was known as the Era of Good Feelings. The doctrine that bears his name was promulgated in 1823. It declared, for all of Europe (Spain and France in particular) to hear, that the United States would not tolerate any further colonization or intervention in the Americas – all the Americas, North, Central, and South. I'm surprised that no one in the

Administration had slipped Mr Reagan a powerful ace in claiming the Monroe Doctrine as a controlling cause in his invasion of Grenada. For what is beyond question, though it is rarely brought *into* question, is that the word, the act, of 'intervention' has undergone a radical re-definition since the nineteenth century, since, most glaringly, the successful treachery of Major Vidkun Quisling, the Norwegian who from inside his own country prepared the ground for an easy Nazi invasion and gave his name to the powerful form of intervention known as 'fifth column.' It is now granted, by the nations that were once aghast at President Kennedy's threat of invading Cuba, that the planting of Russian nuclear missiles in Cuba was a modern form of intervention in a sovereign state rather more threatening than the hovering of the Spanish Armada off the English Channel.

If it is true that the Russians and Cubans had planted an enormous cache of arms in Grenada, that the alarmingly high Russian diplomatic establishment there of sixty-nine persons, and the thousand or more Cuban paramilitary, if they were only the advance guard of forces that could have overwhelmed the island and turned it into a foreign base, then it can at least be argued that that is intervention of the modern kind and that the most persuasive passage in Mr Reagan's speech last week was this: 'Grenada, we are told, was a friendly island paradise for tourism. Well, it wasn't. It was a Soviet-Cuban colony being readied as a major military bastion to export terror and undermine democracy. We got there just in time.'

Hype

Letter No. 1816, 2 December 1983

Somebody – it may have been me – once said that a fire is easier to film than an idea. And this truth is, unfortunately, the first article of faith in the credo of all television news cameramen who are not afraid to move in for the first spurt of blood from a dying man, to remind us old film buffs of that ghastly shot of a body slumping out of a car in *Bonnie and Clyde*, which alas set the mode for a thousand subsequent blood baths.

From time to time I am overcome, like many other people I imagine, by the incessant and successful search for whatever image is most gruesome in war, and most pitiable in peace (the matchstick legs of starving children, for instance). One, perhaps the only, happy effect of this nausea is to make you recall with special vividness, even tenderness, the items innocent or comic or otherwise pleasant, with which all news programs, it seems everywhere in the world, end their evening sessions.

There was one came up a day last week. And I am not likely to forget it for a long time, because, I suppose, it struck a touching and a dignified note on a theme that is absolutely devoid of dignity or sentiment: namely, the ill will with which the two superpowers glare at each other across the map of the world. It was the story of an old American soldier who requested in his will that he be buried in East Germany. He died the other week, and his wish was respected. His name – it sounds unreal, like one of those manufactured all-American heroes celebrated in radio documentaries any day after the end of the Second World War – his name was Joe Palowski. Since then, or until he retired, he drove a taxi in Chicago. But in April 1945 he was one of the small band of soldiers – Americans and British – who made the first contact with Russian soldiers on the banks of the Elbe. His dearest wish, written down in his Will, was to have two of his buddies go to the place where the Allies joined up and bury his body there. This, of course, took money, but his friends collected it and sent off his two oldest living wartime buddies. The United States provided two Marine guards. The Russians, for their part, sent two generals. The six of them formed an honour guard, and they lowered his body into a grave down by the riverside. In the evening, there was a wake, of sorts. The last shot we saw was of the Russians and the Marines, and the two old veterans, raising glasses and embracing.

When the word of Joe Palowski's will got out, there were plenty of neighbours on hand to mutter that he must have been a Communist. Luckily, there was also on hand another cab driver, a close friend, to scorn this mischief. 'Joe was never a Communist,' he said. 'He was an Eisenhower Republican and a Reagan Republican till the day he died. He was just a man of good will, with an open heart.' That sentence alone is one we should all be worthy of. It reminds me of some of the crudely chiseled epitaphs on the plain stones that mark the graves of forty-niners or other pioneers who died along the hard way to the foothills of the High Sierras. Lines in which, every so often, simple people struggle through to a line of stark poetry. One I remember says: 'Tom Brent, died here October, 1850. He Done His Best.'

Well, the other evening, I lazed around in the bathtub and got in late for the evening news. Maybe my watch was slow. More likely, I was reacting against the prospect of more bloody battles and terrorist kidnappings and the like. Anyway, I got in late, but I was not too late to see extraordinary scenes of little mobs of women in several department stores, one in Minneapolis, one in Chicago, one in New York, literally punching the shop assistants and scratching at each other. Food riots, I wondered. Not possible. Suddenly, there was a man behind a counter, a big man with a big stick or rubber truncheon in his hand, bawling, 'So help me, I'll bash the next one who grabs at these dolls.' Dolls? That's what it was about. We were seeing desperate mothers fighting each other to adopt a doll. Not any doll. But a particular, very homely, squat doll with an oversize head, a fat face, a stubby nose, puckered lips – a pathetic monster of a baby doll. It is the product of one company. Each doll, the company promises, has a distinct personality, all of them homely to the point of repulsiveness, but in their own special way. The company calls this monstrous regiment of baby dolls – The Cabbage Patch Kids. They were introduced at a toy fair for retailers in New York last February, not that anyone noticed. The original gimmick, which the company correctly figured would set ablaze a Christmastime shopping mania, was to have the salesmen, or demonstrators, dress up as doctors offering these toy babies for adoption. Each baby comes with a birth certificate, a double name, and adoption papers. The company thought that this would encourage what they called 'increased bonding' between the child and the baby it had adopted. The company didn't collectively dream up this idea on a dull day. They employed a clinical psychologist from New York University. She says: the idea was to produce a doll 'with a quality that captures people. The Cabbage Patch Kids are very vulnerable-looking. They bring out the nurturing instinct – to protect, to hold, and cuddle.' Research has shown, she says, that if you put together certain characteristics common to the young of most mammals: 'large forehead, big eyes, tiny nose, lack of a chin, oversized head … and put them in cartoons or even abstract forms … people have warm, kindly responses. They are essentially very vulnerable.'

Well, you must have noticed that 'vulnerable' is a vogue word – especially among theatre and film critics – whose vogue has become sickening. In one biographical dictionary of the movies I happen to own, I found the word applied no less than forty times to 'vulnerables' as far apart as Marilyn Monroe and Buster Keaton. It is today always used as a compliment. It's the modish substitute for what an earlier generation

Adopting a Cabbage Patch
Kid – 'a pathetic
monster of a baby doll.'

of critics called 'sensitive'. Maybe it assumes that today nothing is more repulsive than a hero or heroine who is confident, brave, self-reliant. Gary Cooper wasn't vulnerable; he was the self-sufficient male, never more dangerous to the villain than when he just looked and said nothing. Mary Pickford wasn't vulnerable; she was the cheeky, adorable tomboy. But today, to get an Oscar nomination from the critics, you've got to be vulnerable, which is to say, sad, listless, helpless, pathetic. It was only a step for that clinical psychologist – Ms (I'm sure) Esther Buchholz – to predict that the most desirable new heroine was a doll so pathetic as to be ugly, malformed, and very much in need of adoption. Anyway, it worked. And, after these early stampedes in department stores all around the country, the manufacturing company is left groaning that it didn't make ten million of these little horrors. Their stock of two million is almost sold out.

   This mania didn't just happen. It was planned. The early publicity was mysterious. Then – before the dolls were available – the advertising hailed the early arrival of a miracle doll that you'd surely want to own. The pathos of the thing was the big selling point. And two million moms have fallen for it.

It is only the latest example of a sales triumph in the age of hype. Ten, twenty years ago it was called 'promotion'. A century ago P. T. Barnum called it 'puffery,' which took the form of huge posters advertising a circus the likes of which had never been seen, even by the ancient Romans. The modern forms of puffery or hype make the advertising campaigns of even twenty years ago seem almost charmingly naive. Those were the days when a man wrote a book, the publisher bought it, they waited for the reviews. If they were ecstatic, they then waited for Hollywood to bite. Hollywood bit, and hired writers to do a screenplay. A movie was made. Perhaps it would be a hit, perhaps not. Today, a movie company owns a publisher (as well as a soft drink firm, and an orange grove) and decides to manufacture a hit. Somebody gets out a plot line. A name writer is hired. He writes the book. Forget the reviews (which, as one distinguished publisher said to me, today count for no more than a flattering letter written to a friend). The writer flogs his book in a dozen cities, appearing on the telly and signing copies. Meanwhile, the movie company has commissioned a theme song, maybe with the movie's title, from a rock group. With this, and apocalyptic advertising for many months, the movie company boosts the coming movie, works the title into a slogan for its television orange juice ads. The actual, multimillion-dollar success of the movie is almost an anti-climax.

Or, take the case of one girl, who first appeared in a bathing suit on a sports magazine cover, was snapped up for other magazines, then had a book ghosted for her on how to stay fit. She was grabbed to do TV endorsements for beer and for lipstick. A clothing firm markets her signed swimsuits. It will spend hundreds of thousands of dollars in pre-publicity – puffery, hype – telling every girl in America she is a nerd or a wimp if she doesn't own that swimsuit. Needless to say, the innocent girl is about to become a multimillionaire.

'Hype' you may have heard is an abbreviation of 'hyperbole,' or conscious exaggeration. Not so! That's what the linguistic scholars used to call an ID (an intellectual derivation) and now call 'folk etymology'. Hype was put into print over thirty years ago by a Broadway songwriter, saying a particular movie had 'no hyped-up glamour'. He picked it up from drug users, whose aim was to be 'hyped up'. It was shortened to hype. So, think. Next time you fall for a best seller, or a pretty face, or an ugly doll, it's not your judgment that's at work. The publishers, the movie company, the manufacturer – or more likely their advertising agency – have given you the needle.

Jesse Jackson in Cuba

Letter No. 1846, 29 June 1984

I am one of those journalists who find it hard to throw anything away. The result is preposterous to anyone who dares to peek inside our apartment's many closets, where books and magazines and files never looked at and old slippers and golf shoes and even the stubs of long ago theatre tickets are stacked or balanced so precariously that it's not worth even trying to dislodge a paper, let alone a book. The resulting earthquake would certainly bring the neighbours running. But let me tell you that this ocean of flotsam does not flow out into what you might call the public channels of the apartment. My study, too, where I live and breathe and exercise my so-called brain, is also a mess until about six in the evening, when I cease pecking away on the old manual and begin the nightly clean-up. Sometimes it gets so bad that I have about five minutes to shovel the papers and notes and news magazines and memos into the one study closet and jam the door, against a possible landslide from that interior. When the guests arrive they see a neat, cool, and I like to think elegant small library, with one sharp light focused on the poteen bottle and the neighboring ice bucket. So this lamentable flaw in my character ('if only you had a system,' my father used to say) – the glaring absence of a system – is known only to my closest and dearest. So much so that years ago, when a ten-year-old friend of my son came to visit (he'd evidently been warned about the sewage dump he was about to see), he came in, looked around, and said, 'But Stephen told me you were a secret slob.' That's right, I said, and left him to figure out the discrepancy between the thing seen and the chaos unseen.

Well, from time to time, usually at the beginning of the summer, I decide to reform and shuffle through masses of papers and loads of unanswered correspondence, from, say, 1972. The one great advantage of this system or lack of same is that occasionally precious needles or forgotten nuggets of information slip out of the haystack. The other morning, as if obeying some law of extrasensory perception, a piece of brown paper, once white, fell at my feet. It was full of hasty hieroglyphics, plainly notes on a speech ('Add FDR,' it said), a presidential speech. It said, 'But all debate and dissension about foreign policy stops at the water's edge.'

What is so extrasensory about that? Well, it would be hard to find a quotation from Roosevelt or any other President more apt to something that happened this week, which shocked the Washington old-timers and a large number of the members of both Houses, but, I'm afraid, will not shock millions of Americans who have never heard of, or noticed, the old and once inviolable tradition to which all American politicians, however mad at the incumbent administration, deferred. You – you being, say, a Senator – might thunder away on the Senate floor about the sins and idiocies of the President's foreign policy, but if you ever went abroad you did not publicly criticize your own country on that count. Roosevelt's most fervent enemies, and he surely had many in the Congress, when tapped by foreign reporters gave the standard reply: 'I'm sorry but our differences on foreign policy stop at the water's edge' – the water's edge, you understand, being the shores of the Potomac River or the docks of New York.

Now, there is one very big American politician – indeed, the leading black politician of the United States – who was never told about this usage, this tradition, or scorns to pay attention to it. The Rev. Jesse Jackson went off this week as a one-man State Department, or his own Foreign Secretary, to El Salvador and Cuba. When any Congressman or Senator or Presidential candidate wants to go abroad on a fact-finding mission, he is automatically briefed by the appropriate desk of the State Department as a routine courtesy – no matter who is in the White House. The Rev. Jackson sought his own channels, corresponding directly with President Duarte of El Salvador and with Fidel Castro of Cuba. Nobody official, you understand, sent Mr Jackson. He went to

Jesse Jackson smokes Cuban cigars with Fidel Castro during his controversial visit to Havana in June 1984.

TWA Hostage Crisis

Letter No. 1897, 21 June 1985

It's only once in a very great while that I feel there's only one possible topic to talk about, that it would be irresponsible to talk about anything else. It is the episode, the outrage, the crisis – however you want to call it – that has completely monopolized the television news. Indeed, there have been hours on end, through the day and night, when it seemed that the rest of the world was permanently on hold. Certainly I can't remember a time when the newspapers performed a new function – it used to be their exclusive function – of telling you many things that were going on at home and abroad. Since Saturday June 15, not only the one-hour nightly TV summaries of the news, and the networks' half-hour summaries, and then the prior *and* the subsequent discussion programs, have been given over entirely to the crisis (and for once, surely, this word is the right word) of the hijacking of the TWA jet plane and the holding of the mostly American hostages.

We have a time problem here, one that often bugs or threatens my talk, except when I'm on about some timeless topic, like the rich vagabond spending two years looking for an island paradise, or how to make the perfect hamburger. It is no secret that some listeners are on hand on Friday evenings, others on Sunday morning, that (as I have reason to know from the mail as well as foreign journeys) Mexico and New Zealand, among other places, will not know what to think until the following Tuesday. There was a time during the agonizing last phases of the Watergate scandal that Friday's talk was meaningless on Sunday, and Sunday's talk was ancient history by Tuesday. So, I am bearing in mind, in fact I am hoping and praying that the hostages, and that indomitable, really heroic pilot, will all be safe and free by the time many people hear this talk.

And whatever happens or has happened to the hostages, or what is happening now in El Salvador, the hijacking episode has brought up in the most merciless way the whole question of international terrorism and what to do about it. 'What to do about it' is so obviously the essential, pressing, question that I notice a quite new modesty among the different schools of commentators and onlookers. I mean, there is a unique absence of cockiness, of ideological infighting, of telling us all what must be done or what is idiotically not being done, among the dogmatists of the right, the wiseacres of the left, and the 'on-the-one-hand, on-the-other-hand' pundits in the middle. For once, I hear friends, informed and uninformed, of all parties, saying, 'Well, thank God I'm not the President of the United States.'

Where to begin? Looking back over what seems an age since the first hectic news-breaks, the interruption of every sort of programme, from classical dramas and symphony concerts to golf championships, the scene that sticks in my mind is a family scene (and we have moved in on scores of them) in which a woman in the Midwest somewhere, whose son was aboard the plane and is still held, stroked her forearms in a quiet ecstasy of frustration, and said there was nothing she wouldn't do, and there was practically nothing the President shouldn't do, to have the hostages set free. She anticipated the next question, which no interviewer seems to have had the wit to ask, that up to now she'd been a gung-ho backer of the President in saying you should never give in to terrorists, don't weaken, don't negotiate, don't bargain. 'Give 'em the seven hundred men back,' she said, 'give 'em seven thousand, I don't care.'

That may have been an extreme reaction, but its extremity is the only odd thing about it. There must have been scores of families who, at the first dread word that one of their own was aboard, muffled their automatic echo of the President's proud assertion, once he was in the White House, that 'America stands tall again.' And here I must mention a cruel consequence of being President today that is quite new – new, that is, since the news networks began to amass immense television stockpiles of old Presidential campaign appearances, news conferences, and the like. In the old days, I should say any day before Jimmy Carter, a candidate on the campaign trail would have his writers bone up on the old speeches of the opponent and trot out a quotation here and there to show usually that the opponent was a hypocrite or worse. But not too many people read those campaign speeches or heard them. Now President Reagan, wherever he is – at a fundraising dinner, an airport arrival, a Rose Garden ceremony, an interview – speaks any dogmatic statement at his peril. On the evening news, he will be shown where he was today, but then they will insert an old television clip from a speech, a rally, an airport passing thought that runs directly counter to what he's say-ing now. So, and this happens several times a week, he's visibly held up for ridicule to millions of citizens. And this week, on many news programmes, the President has been the helpless victim of this trick.

I see no way that this is going to change. It feeds the self-righteousness of even the dumbest viewer. It gives mean satisfaction to the political opponents waiting in the wings for 1988. It produces an unworthy wry smile on the faces of the men who were in the White House in 1980 and wringing their hands and brains over the plight of the American hostages in Iran. Not all of them. Mr Carter's former National Security ad-viser (I guess they have clips of him too) said he could never forget the tension and the frustration of those many months in the White House. He knew what Mr Reagan was going through, and he wasn't going to second-guess him. Dr Henry Kissinger, Nixon's old Secretary of State, was on for a long interview, and he said that any policy seen from the outside is far simpler than one seen from the inside, and that he grieved for

At Beirut airport one of the two heavily armed Lebanese
Shiite Muslim gunmen aims at journalists.

the President caught in the coils of the hijacking complexity. Dr Kissinger did go on to make what one commentator called a deplorable point. It was, however, exactly what the President, the next evening, made the point of his policy. 'No negotiations with the terrorists, no concessions,' said Dr Kissinger. 'We will never,' said the President, 'make concessions to terrorists. To do so would only invite more terrorism.'

From the start, it seems that was the President's firm decision. Over the weekend, the smart word from all the Washington pundits was that plainly the three main parties – the United States, Israel, and Nahbi Berri, who then appeared to be the Shiite Muslim with the whip hand – that these three were engaged in a wriggling exercise to save face. In other words, the expectation then was that Israel could be persuaded (without any public persuasion from the White House) to release the seven hundred Shiites it held; that it must be seen to be doing this on its own accord. That Mr Reagan must be seen as not having given in. And that Mr Berri must be seen as not accepting a deal. It sounded like an impossible way out. In fact, at that point, Mr Berri was saying that he washed his hands of the whole thing; that the solution lay entirely with the White House. That was a situation complicated enough, especially since we then expected that there would be a lot of bold speeches and vows made never to surrender or yield. And then to save the American hostages, Mr Reagan would twist Israel's arm, Israel would say it was only doing what it had long ago arranged to do, would release the Shiites, and somehow the hostages would be released simultaneously, or just afterward.

The President, on Tuesday night, took on what I think was the toughest ordeal of his Presidency: a press conference at this delicate and horrible juncture, and a pitiless barrage of questions and accusations and snide reminders of his old posture of standing tall. To the surprise, I think, of the press corps, he spoke no weasel words, he prepared no Band-Aids to mask a deal. Still, right away he was asked, 'What happened to the policy of swift and effective retribution you announced four and a half years ago to deal with international terrorism?' The President's immediate answer, and his line from then on, was that in the Iran hostage crisis, it was a government that was the enemy. But that here, we don't know, as he said 'who is perpetrating these deeds, who their accomplices are, where they are located … just to strike a blow in a general direction would be a terrorist act in itself.'

Well, he may have spoken even truer than he knew then. Mr Berri, the moderate leader of the Amal Shiites, may or may not be in control. In the shantytown where the hostages are or were supposed to be hidden, radical Amal Shiites were fighting Palestinian guerrillas, and not far away Muslims and Christians were exchanging artillery. Meanwhile, Sunni Muslims were trying to destroy the Shiite television station, and at the same time, clashing with their usual allies, Druse militiamen. Another radical Shiite group (the Imam Ali Brigade) threatened to blow up the house of Mr Berri, the Shiite. And there was a time, early on, when the hijackers said they belonged to the Hussein Suicide Commando. Who can police or speak for so many warring policemen?

The word 'suicide' points to a new, grim element in terrorism. Once, terrorists did their dirty business and fled for their lives. Now, they are quite willing to blow themselves up with the victims.

Another element goes back to that frantic mother in the Midwest, an emotional switch in the minds of doughty citizens whose own kith and kin are caught: the switch from defiance to surrender. There is one other unspeakable thought: that every American who travels by air to troubled countries should be willing to die for his country. Preposterous. However, the end of air traffic would mean the end of tourism, trade, bank loans, of their economies. It's a desperate thought that no President, I believe, dare possibly act on.

Explosion of *Challenger* Space Shuttle

Letter No. 1928, 31 January 1986

'Three engines running normally. Three good cells. Three good ABU's. Velocity 2257 feet per second. Altitude 4.3 nautical miles, downrange distance 3 nautical miles … three engines now at 104 percent. Challenger, go with throttle up.' Commander Dick Scobee: 'Roger, go with throttle up.'

That was the last word from *Challenger*'s commander, and would be the last word from any of them. There came a moment that, to a normal ignoramus like me, was at the same time most beautiful and most baffling. A colossal, never-before-seen fireworks display. The puzzle was the tone of NASA's public relations officer, the man calling off the technical progress of the flight. He went on intoning, in the same professional, emotionless way: 'One minute, fifteen seconds. Velocity 2,900 feet per second, altitude nine nautical miles, down-range distance seven nautical miles.' The longest pause. Was he not seeing what we saw? This huge spray of colour against the very blue sky? He was not. It was not his job to look at the monitor. He was watching a maze of ticking numbers, the lightning calculations done from the thousand sensors, as they're called, that the shuttle feeds into the telemetry. So, while the enormous horror of the fireball was sinking into our numbed minds, he was saying his last words: 'Obviously a major malfunction. We have no down-link.' Surely the most leaden understatement of the year, for 'the shuttle has totally disintegrated in an instant, and we have no word from the crew.'

I doubt that many of us would have been watching this launch if the schoolteacher, Christa McAuliffe, had not been aboard. There have been fifty-six planned missions, and in the past few years, only the manned flights have been televised, and then not always live: the lift-off is taped at the launching and then replayed briefly on the evening news. For several years now, the work of NASA – the National Aeronautics and Space Administration – has been no big deal to the ordinary citizen. It's become a familiar subject of special articles in magazines by such famous popularizers as Isaac Asimov and Ray Bradbury; and gets into the newspapers mainly when the space-related subcommittees of Congress are arguing over the budget. But the missions have become so routine that I suspect only space buffs could call off many names, or any names, of the astronauts of the past few years. To most people, John Glenn, who has long been

Faces of spectators register incomprehension and shock as they witness the explosion of the *Challenger* Space Shuttle.

Senator John Glenn, is the one unforgettable name: the first American to orbit the earth, and that's coming up twenty-four years ago in February. And I suppose a lot of Americans know, by now, the name and face of Frank Borman, a later astronaut, but only because he is the president of and does the television commercials for Eastern Airlines, which incidentally is in dire financial trouble.

But, it was the President's idea of putting a schoolteacher in space that galvanized anew the popular interest. When the invitation went out over a year ago, there were more than eleven thousand applicants. Obviously, when you consider the rudimentary science skills required and the length of the special training, and the physical and mental stamina that's called for, I imagine they could easily knock out ten thousand of those first eager applicants. In fact, the selection committee, which combined a national council of school officers with a half dozen experts from NASA, went quickly through those eleven thousand letters and chose only 114 teachers to interview. All of them first submitted to thorough physical examinations and psychiatric screening and were reduced to ten finalists.

Christa McAuliffe was twelve years old when Alan Shepard launched America's manned space program in May 1961, with a fifteen-minute sub-orbital flight. That was inspiring stuff at the time, but was dimmed nine months later by Glenn's complete orbit of the earth. Christa McAuliffe watched the Shepard liftoff, and in her letter of application she wrote to NASA: 'I watched the Space Age being born, and I would like to participate.'

She was not, by a long shot, the most brilliant intellectually of the applicants or even of her high school class in a small Roman Catholic school in suburban Boston. She graduated seventy-fifth out of a class of one hundred eighty-one. But her teacher added a note to her graduation report. 'Tops,' it said, 'in emotional stability and seriousness of purpose.' That would outweigh the claims of many a high-strung applicant who was, say, a whizz at mathematics or physics. In school, she had been a long-distance runner, played tennis and volleyball, and was a star softball player. She went on to a Massachusetts state college, not particularly science-minded, though her father worked with an electronics firm. She took a bachelor's degree in American history and secondary education, and having married a college friend, a lawyer from Maryland, moved there and taught high-school English and American history. She then took a master's degree in education and moved back with her husband to New England when he set up a law firm in the small town of Concord, New Hampshire. She settled into teaching and had a daughter. Last Monday, all the pupils and the teachers would gather in the auditorium with whistles and blowers and little flags to watch the launch and the triumph of their Christa. She was gone from Concord on a proudly granted leave of absence for six months of training with the crew of *Challenger*. And when she went off there, she said, 'Just as the pioneer travellers of the Conestoga wagon days kept personal journals, I, as a pioneer space traveller, will do the same.'

She had, of course, to bone up on the basic mathematics, physics, and electronics involved in any space flight, while picking up, from the rest of the crew, the residue of their considerable experience of the theory and practice of flying. The only black man was a veteran test pilot. The Hawaiian was an Air Force flight-test engineer, with one space flight behind him. Three of them – a physicist who was going to launch a science platform to observe Halley's Comet, an Air Force aerospace engineer, and the other woman, Judy Resnik, who was on a space mission in 1984 and an electrical engineer – had been astronauts since 1978. This left the pilot of this mission, Michael Smith, a Navy man who had never been in space but had logged well over four thousand hours of flight time, in jets mostly, and flown in twenty-eight different kinds of civilian and military aircraft. Living and working with this crew for six months, Christa would obviously absorb a lot of practical expertise. But, of course, she had to go through the 180 hours of training manuals, of learning to manoeuvre through weightlessness in training jets, and the way the daily habits of a human being are adjusted to life in orbit, and many, many rehearsals of procedures for dealing, on the hop, with space accidents and emergency landings. She'd come through all this so well that she was going to give – from space – two science lessons over the Public Television System to schoolchildren, and meant to stay with the space agency till September as a lecturer, around the country, to schoolchildren and civic groups, and the like.

Most all of this we had learned about in the weeks before *Challenger* was to take off, and if not the space star of the crew, she became the vivid human link with all of us. For while the senator who had completed a space mission was a veteran fighter-pilot in Vietnam, Christa McAuliffe was the first ordinary citizen to go into space. No wonder President Reagan, when he heard the appalling news, was dazed for a time and said, 'I can't get that school teacher out of my mind.'

The broadcast, the telecast, began with the crew's jolly breakfast together, and went on with their being rigged up in space suits, to boarding the shuttle, the liftoff, the cataclysmic explosion, and after that on and on through the whole sad day.

Frank Borman, the ex-astronaut, the Eastern Airlines president, said, 'A thousand experts will come out of the woodwork who don't have the faintest idea what they're talking about.' Well, it didn't happen. The anchormen of the networks, and of many independent stations, were anchored to their microphones for something like eight hours, but they are not the chosen half-dozen for nothing. In this country, anchormen and women are not handsome faces with charming voices. If they are, that's incidental. They are not, and are not known as, newsreaders. They are all, even the youngest of them (in their early forties), veteran reporters. The first generation that went from radio to television, men like Walter Cronkite and Ed Murrow, were war correspondents in the Second World War. The next generation, and I'm thinking of the half dozen familiars every night on NBC, CBS, ABC and the Public (non-commercial) network, among them log up many years as war correspondents in Korea or Vietnam, and have been newspaper and/or television correspondents in Moscow, Paris, London, Budapest, Tokyo. All of them have covered many space flights and learned the elements of the game. And they were backed up by a flock of network science correspondents, and the staff correspondents each network assigns to the three space headquarters in Houston, in Pasadena, and at the launch pad itself, Cape Canaveral.

Naturally, the first thing and the second thing all of us onlookers wanted to know was what went wrong? And since NASA itself quite rightly wasn't saying, it was up to the anchormen and their back-up specialists to speculate. They didn't. They tapped experts, from former astronauts to space scientists, and John Glenn, the flying Senator, and research scientists, and nobody had a dogmatic theory. They knew too much. They all stressed that the astronauts know at the start that the perfect shuttle has not been invented; they all know (and don't talk about) the fairly certain prospect that one day what had never happened – a crew killed in space – would happen. And if there was a consensus among the old astronauts and the new, and the space experts in Congress, it was that safety first, second, and third is NASA's obsession. And that while the manned flights are frozen for the time being – no early take-off for the sun or Jupiter – the space programme will recover and push on.

To me, when the nightmare sharpness of the horror has blessedly blurred with time, there will be, I'm afraid, one picture that will retain its piercing clarity. It is the picture of an inquisitive, innocent, middle-aged woman and her affable, granity husband – Christa McAuliffe's parents – craning their necks and squinting into the Florida sky, and watching the sudden fireball and looking a little puzzled as first-time spectators might, as if this were part of the show, part of the unexpected magic.

Gorbachev and Reagan Playing Chess

Letter No. 1991, 17 April 1987

Just about the time that a very weary Secretary of State George Shultz was landing in the NATO capital of Brussels, after twenty hours of talks with Soviet Foreign Minister Eduard Shevardnadze, I was sitting down to lunch in New York with a man of venerable years and a great range of interests who is capable of talking colourfully and sensibly about cabbages and kings, politics and poetry, who is equally well acquainted with the works of Irving Berlin and Isaiah Berlin. He is also, you might say, a professional talker. Not the sort of mind for an agile reporter to interview, because the last thing he's going to give you is a direct answer to a direct question.

We did not know then what had been the outcome or the upshot or the downturn of the Shultz-Shevardnadze talks. Like everybody else in the Western world, everybody on the outside – you and me – all we'd had to go on were innumerable and interminable newspaper pieces from Western correspondents, most of whom had their minds, their choice of hero and villain, pretty well made up before they got to Moscow. I asked my companion how he felt about the general line or drift of the arms control talks so far; that means after the Reagan-Gorbachev Summit in Reykjavik and on into the latest strenuous bout. The old man looked at the slice of lime bobbing like a lifeboat amid the icebergs of his tomato juice. He swilled the drink around slowly, and he shot me a sly smile. 'Did I ever tell you,' he asked, 'about my first encounter with the Canadian chess player?' The required answer is, 'Of course not, please do tell.' I gave it. And he began.

'Well,' he said, 'I'd just arrived as a young American student at the London School of Economics, and after I'd settled in and felt confident enough to socialize, I wandered into the common room, or lounge, or whatever, and saw four or five pairs playing chess. I soon discovered that there was a permanent group of maniacal chess players. One day, a young-middle-aged pleasant man came up to me. He was a Canadian. He asked me if I'd like to play a game. I accepted at once. I suppose the first game lasted through fifteen, twenty moves. I beat him easily. Next day, we played again. This time, I beat him in a dozen moves. I was very indulgent, very kind to him. I said I enjoyed his company and was available at any time. I went off to drinks with some other students, and they greeted me as if I'd been Alekhine or Capablanca, the reigning masters of the day. 'Is it true,' they asked, 'that you twice slaughtered the Canadian?' Well, beat him, certainly. They were aghast and agog. Nobody in this place, they told me, had ever beaten him: he was the Canadian chess champion. I saw no more of him for about a month; holidays, I imagine. When I ran into him again, again he offered me a game. From then on, we played certainly once a week for the next three years. Every time I was massacred. Those first two games were the only ones I ever had a prayer of winning.'

The old man neatly rescued the lime from the bobbing icebergs, squeezed it, and looked at me sideways, expecting me to say, 'How come?' I said, 'How come?'

'Well, the first two times, the Canadian assumed he was playing with, if not a champion, with somebody within hailing distance of his standard. So he was on his guard from the start. Within two or three moves, he noticed a rather startling move or two of mine and decided I was a bold but calculating player. He promptly shifted from his, I don't know, first Rostenkowski attack to his Sicilian fall-back defence, or whatever it was. I didn't know any of these tactics; I was a simple chess player. Both times, because he was attributing to me this sophistication, his expertise was fatal. I walked in through doors he didn't even notice were open. Evidently, he talked later with some of the boys and discovered he'd been beaten by a tyro. After that, the three-year blitz. He didn't tell me till we both were about to leave London what had happened at the beginning.'

We ordered our lunch, and the old man sat back and licked his lips. No need, he implied, to point a moral. I nodded to indicate I'd got the point. I said, 'You know, I wrote a piece years ago; it must have been the first summit Lyndon Johnson ever held. If I had a thesis, it was that Russians are the best chess players in the world, and we always interpret their motives as if they were playing draughts.' 'That's it,' the old man said, 'You get it. At Reykjavik, Ronald Reagan was me, and Mikhail Gorbachev was the champion of all the Russias. He must have been totally thrown when Reagan blurted out, "Why not abolish all nuclear weapons?" What was this cunning move? It was beyond anything he'd anticipated. He jumped to the Star Wars gambit: insist on the Star Wars move and I'll force a stalemate. Which is what happened. Reagan, of course, had never dreamed of offering to abolish all nuclear weapons. He got carried away in the heat of the moment. Luckily, his dogged insistence on Star Wars, and let's talk later about how much research, when to develop, when to deploy, his insistence cut short the game. Next day, to his horror, Reagan heard that the Western Allies were even more horrified. What happens, they cried, to the defence of Europe if all we have to offer is our conventional forces against the massive Russian superiority in men, arms, tanks?'

Well, I think it is fair to say, roughly speaking, that up to Reykjavik, the Americans were dealing with the Russians hand to hand, or head to head, the main issue being the comparative deterrent strength of the Soviet and American nuclear arsenals. You'll recall it took some time before the Russians would allow the West European nuclear forces to be considered as a separate bit of arithmetic. The Americans always consulted

Iran-Contra Hearings

Letter No. 1996, 22 May 1987

I apologize. I've said several times that I am not going to bother and bewilder you with the Byzantine details of the Iran-Contra hearings, especially since they're likely to go on all summer.

But, something happened in a mere fifteen minutes during the first days of the hearings, which, I assumed, would be not only the next day's headline story but the subject of deep analysis by all the deepest minds. Nothing. An exchange of dialogue between the first witness and two Congressmen seemed to me to be crucial, perhaps, to the outcome of the whole hearings. Remember, the point of such an investigation, in this case by select committees of the Senate and the House sitting together, is not to prosecute anybody, but to discover abuses of or ambiguities in the law, and then to propose to the Congress a better one; or/and to discover criminality in the Presidential branch and pass on the evidence and leave the judgment to the House Judiciary Committee, which doomed Nixon.

All right. The subject is the secret sale of arms to Iran and the secret transfer of money from such sales to the counter-revolutionaries (the Contras) in Nicaragua. What the whole hearings are about is *the war-making powers of the President.* Did he or his staff go beyond the limits of that power as defined in the Constitution set down in 1787? I said last week that the Constitution did not create a Congress that was to be a Parliament subject to a prime minister's bidding. It was set up deliberately as a watchdog over the President's conduct of policy. Did President Reagan or his appointees find an illegal, roundabout way of giving his watchdog the slip? We have to go back and see what powers – to make war – were given in the beginning to the President, and how – if – they have been ignored or evaded.

The eighth section of the first article of the Constitution says: 'The Congress shall have power ... to declare war ... to raise and support armies ... to provide and maintain a navy ... to make rules for the government and regulations of the land and naval forces.' So, Congress decides on the money and the arms, the weapons, that will be used for the armed forces. But that first power, 'to declare war,' has been honoured in the breach for more than four decades. In 1917, in the time-honoured way, President Woodrow Wilson went before Congress to ask for a declaration of war against the

German empire, and got it with only one dissenting vote. In December 1941, President Franklin D. Roosevelt went before Congress and asked for a declaration of war against the empire of Japan, and got it. Within the next two days, he also got a declaration of war against Nazi Germany and Italy.

Believe it or not, the declaration of war against Italy was, I believe, the last one that an American President has asked for. President Truman sent Americans into action in Korea as United Nations forces, in response to a unanimous vote of the Security Council of the United Nations (Unanimous? Yes, the Russians were sulking over the exclusion of Communist China from the UN and had no delegate sitting on the Council. They have never been absent since.). President Kennedy got into Vietnam by sending technicians, so called, as advisers to the beleaguered South Vietnamese. Without any declaration of Congress, those technicians increased and turned into American fighting forces. And when President Lyndon Johnson was challenged over the expansion of those forces – they were over 15,000 by the beginning of 1964 – he appealed for half a billion dollars worth of 'aid' to South Vietnam from the Congress and got it, to finish off the job. But the American forces expanded, without much public to-do, and when, in the summer of 1964, North Vietnamese ships were reported – it's still a disputed incident – to have attacked two American destroyers, President Johnson, the superb and almost heartbreakingly persuasive politician, went before Congress not to ask for a declaration of war but to ask for a simple joint resolution by both Houses to allow him to do what he thought necessary to avenge the naval attack in the Gulf of Tonkin. It was a fatal concession. The resolution was short, simple, vague, and all-embracing of any action the President cared to take in Southeast Asia. As the war grew and grew, and the protests and riots flared around the country, and the Congress spawned furious opponents of the war, the President kept pointing to the Gulf of Tonkin Resolution. 'Look,' he'd say, 'I'm not goin' beyond my Constitutional powers. You gave me this l'il old piece of paper.' He once told me that 'I carry it with me in my pyjamas, in case of any complainin' night visitors.'

Well, as we all know, in the end, five hundred thousand American troops served and lost in Vietnam. The Vietnam disaster led Congress to pass a War Powers Act, which forbade the President to commit the armed forces to hostilities abroad without Congressional approval. You might guess that this was the beginning of a belated movement in Congress to recover its exclusive power 'to declare war'. But by that time, the day had long gone when nations delivered ultimatums and began the attack at dawn once they'd lapsed. Since the Second World War, there have been more than a hundred wars around the world – undeclared wars – not to mention guerrilla raids and terrorist rampages that turned into wars.

What Lyndon Johnson had done – and Nixon did after him, and President Reagan – is to seek money from the Congress to give economic humanitarian aid or military aid to countries whose instability the President deems is a threat to the security of the United States. So far, everything seems to be straightforward and aboveboard.

But this has become, in the past twenty years or so, the era of what we used to call

Lieutenant Colonel Oliver North is sworn in to testify
at the Iran-Contra hearings.

the secret services and today the intelligence services. In this country, it's the Central
Intelligence Agency, which in other countries is known – or not so well-known – by
initials and numbers. Because the definitions of war and threats to national security
have broadened in the wake of terrorism, plotted assassinations, military coups, and
the like, a time came when the Congress reluctantly agreed that the President might
have to take secret actions in the national security that need not be reported to Congress. The new permission was to be known as a Presidential 'finding'.

So, early as 1974, there was a law passed in Congress that required certain chosen members of Congress to be told about the CIA's operations, 'other than those

intended' solely for collecting intelligence, which would include the bombing of Libya and the invasion of Grenada. President Carter, for instance, was not required to report any secret action to free the hostages in Iran. That particular 'finding' was made disastrously unnecessary by the fiasco of his rescue mission in the desert.

So now, the President had also the secret weapon of a 'finding.' But coming to the Contras, the counter-revolutionaries fighting the government of Nicaragua, Congress passed a series of laws, not contradictory as much as changeable. They allowed financial aid to the Contras, then they allowed military aid, then only humanitarian aid, then they repented and went back to military aid. The law that is relevant to the present investigation is the so-called Boland Amendment. It was passed in 1982 and said: 'None of the funds provided in this act may be used by the Central Intelligence Agency or the Department of Defense to furnish military equipment, military training, or other support for military activities to any group or individual not part of a country's armed forces, for the purpose of overthrowing the government of Nicaragua.'

This amendment was later amended again to take effect from October of 1984 through October 1985. That is the period that all the present investigating is really about. The new amendment forbade the CIA and the Defense Department to give military or paramilitary aid to the Contras.

The question before the House and Senate committees is, did former General Richard V. Secord, a businessman, Mr Robert McFarlane, as head of the National Security Council, and his subordinates, Lt. Colonel Oliver North and Vice Admiral John Poindexter, break the law, the Boland law?

It seemed to me that the crucial session of the hearings so far happened while Mr Secord was on the stand. Massachusetts Congressman Edward Boland read the law he sponsored and asked Mr Secord, 'Who do you think is prohibited by this amendment?' And Secord replied: 'The agencies you have just ticked off.' Then Mr Boland asked something that I have not seen reported in any paper or on any radio or television report. 'Don't you think,' Boland asked, 'that the National Security Council is an intelligence agency?' 'Certainly not,' said Mr Secord. 'No?' 'No, they use intelligence, of course, but they are not in the collection business.' I felt Mr Boland thought he had him. But then, and this passage also I never saw reprinted or quoted, another Congressman asked Mr Secord if he knew of a 1981 statute that 'specifically excludes the National Security Council' from being defined as an intelligence agency. 'Yes,' said Mr Secord, he knew there was such a statute. That was all.

This struck me at the time as the first glaring sign that not only Mr Secord, as a businessman, but Poindexter, McFarlane, and North might very plausibly be let off the hook of the Boland Amendment. It may, at any rate, explain the sudden and confident switch in the defense tactics of the White House, and President Reagan's almost boastful assertion that he has always been in favour of people raising money for the Contras (he calls them 'freedom fighters') and that his advocacy, even of arms supplied by groups, individuals, and foreign sympathizers, broke no law.

New Anxieties

Letter No. 2000, 19 June 1987

My mother-in-law came from the Deep South, her family having come, long ago, from France and gone to New Orleans and then on to Galveston, Texas. She used to shake her head over the many peculiar habits of her three daughters, all born in the North. She was mildly offended by their slang, by their use, way back there in the 1930s, of words like 'OK' and 'lousy'. She simply tolerated their accents, which she thought harsh. 'They say *mother-err*,' she would complain. Of course, they didn't say '*mother-err*,' but they didn't say, '*motha*' – eitha.

Most of all, though, she used to go on to me about the insane new fashion that came in in the 1920s, and has remained, of lying prostrate on the beach or in the parks in order to pick up a suntan. It's true that in her youth, around the turn of the century, a lily-white pallor was the preferred complexion among young Southern ladies. But my mother-in-law, though she was elegant and fetching, was much too earthy to be a prey to fashion. Her prejudice was acquired in childhood. In the South, where the sun burns pitilessly from April to November, there are verandas on ordinary houses, and often whole streets of offices and shops are shaded from the noonday sun by overhangs supported by a row of slender columns. In short, the sun was something you stayed out of. In the old lady's time, a suntan would have been not merely unbecoming but bizarre, like a punk hairdo.

Well, it takes time for every ingrained social habit to be dropped. The 'cigar-eet', so called, came in in the 1870s, just after the Civil War, and now seems to be slowly on its way out. And the news that would have cheered my mother-in-law is that the government, the environmentalists, and the skin doctors agree with her. The suntan may have had its day.

The skin doctors' offices are packed these days with nervous youngsters and panicky oldsters who have been looking in the mirror and seeing small, small moles and blotches of various shapes and colours. They have been reading the papers and watching the tube and hearing the dread word: *Melanoma*.

This new anxiety has come about because, finally, governments and industrialists have had to listen to the environmentalists. They have shown that among the horrendous effects of all the pollutants that rise into the air, due in particular to the general

AIDS demonstrators in front of the City Hall in New York City, 1988.

use of aerosol sprays, the ozone layer is becoming contaminated. In a word, we are more and more becoming exposed to the most damaging of the sun's rays, so that skin cancer is dramatically on the rise. The old wives' tale was right: the sun is a good thing to stay out of.

New Yorkers now have another threat to worry about. The government's Environmental Protection Agency sets national standards for what we now know as 'air quality.' The standard sets levels of carbon monoxide and ozone in the atmosphere that are considered safe for humans. Last week, the Agency announced that New York City is way above the acceptable national standard. And the Agency's director in this part of the country has blandly announced that the safe standards are not going to be met for some time. Carbon monoxide, he thinks, might be controlled in the next five years. Realistically, he adds, we can't expect the ozone to cease to be toxic until the year 2000! I don't have at hand the figures for London or Manchester, but they must be at least as bad.

All this reminds me of a similar scare that happened sometime in the 1930s, when a Dr Shastid, an eye doctor of Duluth, Minnesota, announced that the time was coming when Man (today he would have to say 'persons') would have only one eye, which would be situated in the center of the face at, I quote, 'the spot where the bridge of the nose appears.' Robert Benchley was, I believe, the first journalist to face this threat to our ideas of a normal human face. He was relieved, as weren't we all, by Dr Shastid's assurance that this radical change might take, as he put it, 'countless ages'. But Benchley was not entirely reassured. 'My eyes,' he wrote, ' are so close together as they are that I bet I win. I bet I'm the first one-eyed man in the world.'

Americans are, I suppose, more subject to, or alert to, threats to health than any other people, because they are, unlike the Latin nations, not stoical about the inevitability of death. They may say that nothing is more certain than death and taxes. But Mr Reagan has already declared, and proved, that taxes are a bad thing. And the Americans were the first to make a specialty of gerontology, the study of aging, and then to go into furious research to see if it can't be delayed. The notion that one day everybody may live to be a hundred is one that exhilarates more Americans than it frightens. It could never have been an American poet who wrote: 'Grow old along with me: the best is yet to be.'

So, it's understandable that no threat to mortality that has come along in years has so alarmed this country as what is being called the plague of AIDS. For a year or two, the whole epidemic was so repulsive, touching as it did on the most intimate clinical details of sex, that the federal government looked the other way. First, it shared a common view that AIDS was restricted to homosexuals and mainline drug addicts, what are now called the high-risk groups. For a time, there were people who wanted to believe it was a divine judgment on San Francisco for its raunchy ways. Then cases were reported, puzzlingly, from Haiti. Then, we heard about an alarming spread of the disease – and among heterosexuals – in Africa. Then, it began to be reported here among heterosexuals. Now, the President is alarmed. 'AIDS,' he said the other day, 'is surreptitiously spreading throughout our population.' And he's talking about testing not only the armed services, federal employees, but all immigrants – that last precaution, fair or not. The Immigration Service, from the earliest days, tested immigrants for contagious diseases. And there are sad photographs, taken during the tidal wave of European immigration between 1900 and 1914, of men and women being deported from Ellis Island with marks painted on their backs signifying tuberculosis. But, after a period of listless indifference, the administration has now gone into a sort of hysteria about the Black Death running like wildfire throughout the country. The mayor of New York City actually proposed testing all incoming visitors. He's said no more about it since the Chamber of Commerce went into delirium at the thought of no more tourists.

The facts about the present spread of the virus have been stated simply, clearly, and without hysteria, by a man who has kept expert track of the disease longer than anybody has. He is Harold Jaffe, who is in charge of AIDS research at the Federal Centers for Disease Control. He says, 'We really have not seen much evidence for the spread of the virus outside high-risk groups. For most people, the risk of AIDS is essentially zero. Why it isn't getting out beyond the immediate sexual partners of the risk group members, I don't know. Is the disease going to sweep into the heterosexual population, like Africa? I don't see it.'

Well, on this – I'm told – special occasion, is there no good news? There is another trend, another fashion, that is on its way out. And a great many more Americans than you're likely to hear about are happy that it's on the wane. It's nothing less than the disappearance of the American flag from television commercials. That's a little too cryptic, a little too literal. What I'm talking about is the steady decline, over the past year, of commercials that turn everything good, everything tasty, chewable, desirable, buyable, into something exclusively American. A beer, not advertised as a product of fine brewers but a beer 'made the American way'. A bread advertised as 'a little slice of America'. A motorcar advertised 'as American as apple pie'. Banks, of all suspect characters, that promised no prudence but the special virtue of 'American prudence'. This trend really began as an echo of President Reagan's insistence, in his first term, on America 'standing tall'. It really got under way with the Olympics of 1984. It began to wane in the late fall of last year, and I don't doubt that the Iran-Contra revelations had something to do with it. Anyway, it was not an accident. The main advertising agencies noted a waning response to the Red, White, and Blue, and without apology have dropped it. We even now have an automobile advertisement that makes outrageous claims for the car – you can buy it for three dollars – they throw in a suburban house, and the cheerful, brazen narrator is contradicted with subtitles that repeat: 'He's lying.' I think this is a good thing. It will soften or muffle for the rest of the world the old American reputation for 'foolish boasting'.

I have to mention what many of you may already know, that this is the two-thousandth edition of a series of talks that were meant, when they started in the spring of 1946, to go on for thirteen weeks, twenty-six weeks at the most. Since President Truman's abrupt suspension of Lend-Lease aid in the wake of the Japanese surrender plunged Britons into a harder year than any they'd endured during the war, there was trouble converting sterling into dollars. But somehow, the Treasury heroically squeezed out my modest fee. And here I am. I was urged to deliver some missionary message. But missions are for bishops. I am a reporter. And I can't say where America is going. I am a hopeless prophet. One book I will never write is: *Whither America?* As it is, the most memorable line, or bit of philosophy, from an American this week came from a ninety-nine-year old man in Gilroy, California. He and his wife of seventy-eight years were congratulated by the Governor. The man was asked his recipe for a happy marriage. He said: 'Frequent separations, and a growing loss of hearing.'

The New, New Bush

Letter No. 2082, 13 January 1989

Now is the time for all good men to come to the aid of the party. That seems to be the proper slogan or marching song in a Washington that is beginning to deck itself out in its best bib and tucker and welcome hordes of lobbyists and their wives from all over the country, and chill the champagne, and agree for the moment to turn away from the dark side of things and accentuate the positive. If it is understood that 'the party' is not a political party but the Washington party, the glittering shindig that will be thrown for George Herbert Walker Bush for about three days of next week, beginning on Thursday, going through the Inauguration on Friday, and winding up with a final blowout on Saturday. Let the new hero be paraded and cheered through the fair city, before next week we set him up at the coconut shy and start to knock him down.

This is the standard procedure, a tradition of civility and good will toward anyone about to be inaugurated President, no matter who he is, from whichever party. I recall, with a wince, my introduction to this tradition, though there was no Inaugural festival. It was only a few days after Franklin Roosevelt had dropped dead in Georgia, and suddenly a man from Missouri, whom nobody outside Washington knew very much about, was President of the United States. This man, who for some time was called in the press 'the little man', said himself: 'I felt as if the moon and the stars had fallen on me.' He was Harry S. Truman. In those days, the White House press corps, the journalists who had credentials to cover the White House, was no more than about sixty, seventy. Hardly so many attended press conferences, of which Roosevelt held regularly two a week. I don't suppose more than forty of us shuffled into the Oval Office of the White House when the Secret Service gave us the signal to enter for President Truman's first press conference. As we were moving in, I remember expressing what I assumed was a shared mood – of anxiety verging on alarm – about the qualifications of the new man. Here we were about to sit at the feet of a man already being dubbed 'a failed haberdasher from Missouri', and it did seem then that a midget was trying to fill the footprints of a giant. I said something of the sort to the man next to me, the Washington bureau chief of one of the national weekly news magazines. To my astonishment and embarrassment, he turned on me. 'That's no way to talk,' he said, 'about a new President. This is the time to build him up, not tear him down.' It doesn't ease the memory of my embarrassment to recall that within a year or two of Mr Truman's reign, this magazine devoted its best talents to tearing him down. Anyway, Truman (it was clear after that first press conference) didn't need our sympathy or condescension. He turned out to be about as diffident as a sergeant major; he snapped and crackled at the press with much good humour but also with occasional slaps at people whose questions, he thought, showed that they ought to go away and read over the Constitution.

Well, today in Washington, this capital of mischief, vortex of rumour, cooking pot of gossip and malice, you can't hear or read a bad word about George Bush. It takes an actual effort of memory to recall how all the press, in the early spring, was rollicking in the fun and games of George Bush's unfortunately preppy manner, his accent, his incurable habit of, in moments of bafflement or temper, stammering out such lurid epithets as 'By Golly!' or 'Darn it'. The now forgotten Don Regan, Mr Reagan's all-powerful chief of staff, wrote in his memoirs that when he told Vice President Bush that the President's appointments calendar was controlled by Mrs Reagan on the advice of her astrologer, 'When I finished,' the Vice President 'uttered what was a strong expletive for George Bush: 'Good God!' he said.'

Mr Bush was being written off as a candidate after he lost the Iowa primary. He was shown, mockingly, wearing blue jeans and a windbreaker driving a truck through the snows of New Hampshire – a last, pathetic effort (it seemed) to appear as a man of the people. But his primary opponent Senator Bob Dole, the recent winner, was too witty, too mean to poor old George Bush in New Hampshire, and Mr Bush leapt back again. The preppy stigma was plucked away once and for all when he borrowed the most artful and gifted of President Reagan's speech-writers, a lady not to be forgotten in the history of President-making: Peggy Noonan. And she wrote Mr Bush's acceptance speech for the New Orleans Convention. It was simple, gutsy, very eloquent, and set a surprising new tone with its hopes of a 'kinder, gentler nation.' I don't know if Mr Bush copied the Churchill habit of rehearsing a speech before a mirror for hours on end, but George Bush, the Republican nominee, looked like a new man, a new voice, a new type. We rarely heard the word 'preppy' after that.

And then, during the Presidential campaign, a new Bush was fashioned by the producers and writers of the Bush commercials: a downright, glib, scolding, mean Bush, hammering away to the distress of a lot of people at two themes. A Massachusetts convict who, out on a weekend pass, had committed rape and murder; and the dreadful fact that his Democratic opponent Massachusetts Governor Michael Dukakis carried a dreadful letter on his forehead but wouldn't admit it. The letter was the dreaded 'L' – Liberal. That touched the lowest depth of Mr Bush's campaign but also, it appeared, the most effective part. In the wake of the election, most Democrats and many moderate Republicans were saddened and embarrassed by the public image of the Bush who had won. But then, once the interminable campaign is over, the people heave a great sigh. Let bygones be bygones. The American people have a short political memory. They didn't have to forgive the mean, jabbing George Bush of the campaign. They

President George H. W. Bush in the Oval Office escorting the two
springer spaniel puppies delivered by the infamous Millie.

simply forgot. That character is now as dead as the laughable preppy.

There is yet another new George Bush, and the people who know him best and
have worked with him say that the two former Bushes were both false fronts: the first,
an invention of the media, and the second, a ferocious battle-dress that Mr Bush was
only too glad to shed. So now, he is the traditional incoming new man and given the
benefit of every doubt. His Cabinet is complete and pays no dues to the far right, or
to the television evangelists who gave him hefty support. It is a collection of moderate
Republicans, and it is entirely a Cabinet of insiders, of Washington veterans. This is
odd, almost to the point of hilarity when you consider that both Jimmy Carter and
Ronald Reagan campaigned and won their presidencies on the theme that government
was the big culprit, Washington insiders were the villains, and that what the country
needed was new blood from the outside, men from the country uncorrupted by the
machinery and the machinations of power. So, first arrived the Georgia Mafia, as it
was called, and then the troop of Californians new to the capital city. True, George
Bush has brought in, and will bring in, some old buddies from Texas, but none of them
is a newcomer to Washington and its ways. And for the most part, they are moderate
conservative Easterners.

Easterners. That again is an extraordinary reversal of a movement we have written
about for twenty years and long ago decided was irreversible. For the first fifty years of

this century, the Republican Party drew its strength from Eastern money and Midwestern idealism: rural, independent Republicanism. No later than 1964, when Senator Goldwater of Arizona was the Republican candidate, we all reported as a great new lurch of American history that the power of the Republican Party had gone to the West and Southwest, and then added the new generation in the Deep South that had once and for all deserted its ancient links with the Democrats. From now on, we said, the money is banked in Los Angeles and San Francisco, and the ideology comes from the Sun Belt: from Florida all the way to California.

So, not at all remarked on, so far as I've seen, is the geographical set-up of the Bush Administration, which quite quietly, without protest or excuse, has moved the power of the party back to the old boys of New England and the Northeast, plus a little infusion of new blood from Texas. It's remarkable, and I wouldn't dare say just now what it signifies, or will come to signify.

And if it is traditional to think no evil of the new man, and wish him nothing but the best, it is even more proper to think only on what is lovely and of good report in the Presidency of the man who is leaving it. The columnists and television pundits are getting busy this week getting in their brief, historical surveys of the Reagan years. A national paper printed on Wednesday a page-sampling of one-liners, final crisp opinions from a cross-section of Americans. They go all the way from a twenty-six-year-old in Massachusetts, from thanks to God for bringing America a saviour at a time when the nation was unsure of itself, to a sixty-seven-year-old man in Oregon who says, 'I see Ronald Reagan as a stubborn ideologue who has led an administration filled with lies, dishonesty, deceit, and corruption. He will be remembered for having led a nation into a moral, ethical, and financial and industrial decline.' In Omaha, a seventeen-year-old: 'He restored patriotism; he strengthened the economy and lowered unemployment ... one of the greatest Presidents.' I could go on and on, spanning a gamut from idolatry to disgust. But those short quotations record the actual balance of opinion, by two to one. He came in, in early 1981, with 60 percent of the people taking a good view of him. His popularity dipped down into the forties twice, once after the Marines were murdered in Lebanon, and then during the Iran-Contra revelations. But it was soon up again, and at the end he leaves it in unparalleled popularity. Sixty percent of Americans are for him.

San Francisco Earthquake

Letter No. 2122, 20 October 1989

Sometime in the middle of the First World War – it must have been toward the end of the dreadful year of 1916, after the nightmare slaughter of the Somme – an aunt of mine, whose husband was a soldier in France, announced that she didn't believe a word of what she read in the papers. She was going to write to her husband to find out for real what was going on on the Western Front. This showed, first, a touching ignorance of the censorship of letters, both ways. But eventually he replied. All he could tell her about the way the war was going was what life was like in a muddied trench he'd been living in for a month or two. And what a blasted two-hundred yards looked like between him and the German trenches. The whole war for him shrank to dampness, lice, chilblains, rats, bully beef, the sight of two ruined trees, and would she please send him some chocolate and cigarettes.

On Tuesday night and Wednesday of this past week, it struck me that the constant irony of the San Francisco earthquake, in this wonderful age of worldwide communication, was that compared with the people of Europe, Australia, India, wherever – the only people who hadn't a clue as to what was going on were the people of San Francisco and other neighboring cities without power. From the first rumble and shudder of those wracking fifteen seconds, and on for a couple of days, they had no power, no television, no radio, no newspapers. A reporter who had flown in from the East on Wednesday wrote that it was a strange, embarrassing feeling to stand in almost any part of the city and tell those gaping natives about Candlestick Park, the Nimitz Freeway, the damage in the Mission district, the collapsed shopping mall ninety miles away in Santa Cruz, the buckled highways, the astonishing range of pictures she'd seen on television overnight. Mainly they were transmitted from that station in Atlanta, Georgia – CNN – which the irrepressible Ted Turner started years ago and that pulls in through innumerable saucers live coverage from everywhere on earth, and broadcasts without a pause, twenty-four hours a day. On Tuesday night in the East when the scene jumped to President Bush at a dinner, the CNN anchor people, to give us the latest word, charitably left him as soon as possible: he was already well behind the times. He had not been at home watching CNN Atlanta.

It was an eerie break for millions of Americans settling down across the country at

Cars wedged in the collapsed section of Bay Bridge after
the San Francisco Earthquake.

5:00 Pacific time, 8 p.m. in the East, that they were about to have the privilege of getting a vast panorama of the scene below, of the baseball stadium and the surrounding
city, as seen by a blimp that is always on hand, on high, for such sporting occasions.
All these fans were settling in, as I was, with a friend and a beer, to watch the third
game of the baseball championship of the World Series. It was eight o'clock, and we'd
seen the 62,000 rustling away down there, and inevitably they always like to set the
stage, long panning shots of the enchanting bay and the great bridges glistening in the
falling sun. We saw the pitchers warming up in the bullpen, the managers and teams
chewing away, gum, perhaps, more often tobacco, in the dugout. We were ready for
the introductions, the national anthem, then all but one of the batting team would
trot back to the dugout, and the fielding team would spread out for the first pitch, and
there'd be a raucous roar of the Oakland fans who had come to see the Christians, the
Giants that is, mauled.

Back to three anchor men in their booth. They chatter. One of them looks behind
him and down, as if a friend had called. Then he looks up. Then the second deck of
the stadium at Candlestick Park – well, the camera must have been clumsily handled,
the deck seemed to sway and sag a little. I don't believe we knew this as a fact till it
was over. And, providentially, the huge crowd didn't seem to catch on either. In fact
after the first rolling wave there was a cheer, and a big cry of 'Play Ball.' And then a

stranger wave, of a vast human sigh or gasp. And then the players broke up, their wives appeared on the field, and soon they were cradling bewildered children or walking quietly off with arms around their wives. To this day, the blessed, the unexplained truth is the absence of panic. I thought for a time the umpires had not turned up, some other failure of the usual arrangements. And then we heard. And in no time the great blimp took off and, as the night came on, soared and was seeing the incredible sight of a collapsed span of the Bay Bridge over the huge blacked-out city, with smoke plumes rising there down toward the bay, and then the plumes turning into flames and the beginning of the fire. The pictures, picked up now from all around the bay, swam with menacing slowness all through the night, till at daybreak we saw, as I'm sure you did, wherever you were, the collapsed upper deck of the Nimitz Freeway on the Oakland side, the sudden ghastly appearance of what somebody called the concrete sandwich. Hasty guesses were made about the numbers of cars and people trapped in there, and overseas papers grabbed at a figure – 250 – which the police here first deplored, saying that after many hours only seven bodies had been dragged out. But on Thursday morning a reporter close by pointed to the compression of the upper deck of the highway onto the lower and banished any hope of survivors by remarking that the visible space between the two decks was at most eighteen inches high.

Apart from the strange, almost casual, departure of the sixty thousand baseball fans, it must be said that the other great and unanticipated blessing was the comparatively minute damage done to the city of San Francisco itself; accordingly little loss of life compared, that is, with April 1906. This reading on the Richter scale, as you'll have heard, was 6.9, exactly the measurement of last year's earthquake in Armenia, which took 25,000 lives. That difference is easily explained. Since 1906, California, northern California especially, has lived always with the prospect in mind of another great quake, and in 1907 drafted its first new building code, devised for the first time by structural engineers working with architects. It required bracing systems and reinforced masonry. And until the Second World War, the city has withstood innumerable shocks, minor by Tuesday's reckoning. In 1946, another, tougher code went into effect. By 1965 we had a wealth of new building materials, and by then, also, San Francisco was, lamentably, about to put up its first high-rises and downtown skyscrapers. So another more elaborate and stricter code was made to apply to all new building. In the early 1970s, by the way, they decided that the concrete decks on the two-tier bridges might, in an earthquake, be too heavy for the vertical supports. They reinforced them. The Golden Gate Bridge and two others across the bay held firm this time, though engineers now suspect that the sustaining verticals on the Bay Bridge proved too skinny. One expert in earthquake engineering went so far – after the Nimitz disaster – as to doubt whether any more two-decker highways should be built.

As I speak, only days after the event, what is most impressive is the speed and harmony that marked the mobilization, within the hour, of the National Guard, the Army Corps of Engineers, the California state authorities, the city fathers, the police, engineers, the Red Cross, and a resource that San Francisco is unique in being able to call on: a permanent, steady earthquake medical team. Not to forget the heartening sight of thousands of ordinary citizens up from their beds in the middle of the night, helping the teams at the collapsed highways or forming human ladders with buckets at the Marina fire, before they were able to rig up the system of pumping water from the Bay itself. All these volunteers, in San Francisco, were warned to go home and stay there; the great fear, once the fire started from burst gas mains, was the fear that was devastatingly fulfilled in 1906, the gas leaks from other mains and the eruption of hundreds of other fires. When I first went to San Francisco, fifty-six years ago, and for several decades thereafter, old San Franciscans would wince at a gaffe regularly committed by visitors: any mention of the Earthquake. It was always the fire – the great fire. And it's true that while immense damage was done by the initial shock –8 points on the Richter scale – that April morning, the ravaging of the heart of the city was done by fire. So insatiable was the fire's appetite, raging over four square miles, that to save the northwestern part of the city, the Army was called out from the Presidio to dynamite the whole cross avenue of Van Ness, and that held the fire.

Well, this time, there were no aftershocks to burst other mains (aftershocks can happen days or weeks or months after the first jolt). And all these helpers, expert and amateur, came together under the government's central authority: The Federal Emergency Management Agency, which it so happens held a simulated earthquake drill throughout the city only two months ago. FEMA's main job is the granting of low-cost loans to people who have suffered loss of property or injury. FEMA just now suffers from a cruel disability: most of its national team is off in Puerto Rico, the Virgin Islands, and South Carolina, working sixteen hours a day helping to repair the wrecked lives of over a quarter million victims of Hurricane Hugo. A disaster insurance expert with FEMA brought us a timely, if grisly, reminder on Wednesday, that Hugo is a far greater human catastrophe than the earthquake. At this moment, FEMA is trying to handle 20,000 applications for help in the Virgin Islands, 45,000 in and around Charleston, South Carolina, 200,000 in Puerto Rico. FEMA's resources have touched bottom, and the insurance man stressed, for all of us who feel compassionate about San Francisco, that cash for Hugo – from people, anywhere – is still the main burden of their appeal.

The Berlin Wall

Letter No. 2126, 17 November 1989

In the forty-odd years that these talks have been going, I don't remember another time when the political commentators of this country have been lost for words, at least lost for the proper superlative to match the shock and scale of the popular upheaval in Eastern Europe. Many great names have been invoked, of men who in the past suddenly or gradually turned the world upside down: Martin Luther, the French Revolutionists, or Thomas Jefferson. One writer, a temperamental sceptic if ever there was one, wrote: 'In the forty years since the Soviet behaviour provoked a reluctant America to stop disarming, defence has cost $10.4 trillion. It has been history's biggest bargain. It held the line, while Jefferson's ideas sowed their wholesome disorder.'

In sifting around the other morning for a word that would be grand yet sensible enough to salute the collapse of the Berlin Wall, I found myself reaching not for a word but a recording, by massed choruses, of the 'Hallelujah Chorus.' It sounded wonderfully right. It seemed to declare, with sublime simplicity, that people everywhere, once they get a glimpse of liberty, begin to crave it, and sooner or later will demand it.

Well, in the morning after the euphoria, the pundits took over, and we've already had a heavy dose of analysis and explanation. There are two ingenious explanations that may not have been aired in your part of the world, and that are different from the predictable, automatic responses of professional liberals and conservatives. Who ordered the opening of the Wall, and why?

One theory is that Mikhail Gorbachev alone was responsible for firing the old Eric Honecker regime in East Germany; that he's gambling on a united Germany that will invest heavily in the Soviet Union, that will in time request the gradual withdrawal of American troops: a Germany that, permitted by Russia to become a nuclear power, could, as the ally of the Soviet Union, keep in line any and all of the threatening rebels, like Hungary, Romania, and Czechoslovakia.

The second theory, from a German historian with impressive credentials, is very different. It sees in the opening of the Wall a daring bluff, and one called by Mr Egon Krenz, the new East German leader, who hopes to overwhelm West German Chancellor Helmut Kohl with an unmanageable flood of refugees that the Chancellor will eventually have to stop, by revoking the Easterners' right of automatic citizenship.

This presumes that Mr Krenz is determined to persuade the mass of his people to stay put and (with Mr Gorbachev's ready approval) to 'repackage a legitimate government responsive to its people's needs.'

In the coming weeks, and months, the turn of events will doubtless throw up new theories. For the moment, and for the great mass of Americans, the tumbling of the Wall was an occasion like the victory of the American Revolution, the end of an old regime to be celebrated with general rejoicing. What we've been celebrating this time is the collapse, if not the death, of Communism (counting Albania, if at all, as a historical relic).

I suggest, very gently in the surrounding din of joy, that these hosannas may be premature, not unlike seeing in Henry VIII's dissolution of the monasteries the collapse of Christianity in England. Christianity was a faith powerful enough to have retained a hold on Europeans, the great and the humble, for fifteen hundred years; and renouncing it in its established form by no means meant the end of it. Democracy and Communism, too, are faiths, very much younger, but both of them, I believe, are powerful enough not to succumb to the first counter-revolution. Faiths change their form and practice, and we ought not to forget how drastically democracy has changed since the days of its early pretensions. The American founding fathers, who abandoned six years of a chaotic Confederation to invent a new nation, had no intention of setting up a democracy. Indeed, in the first days of the Convention that wrote the Constitution, George Washington reminded them that 'of all forms of government, democracy is the least accounted by civilized nations.' Other leaders, notably James Madison and Alexander Hamilton, concluded that, at best, democracy was only possible 'in a small spot,' not in a large republic. So, they moved on to found a republic, of men of property.

But many symptoms of democracy had already invaded the governments of the new States, and a delegate from Massachusetts bemoaned the fact as 'the source of the evils we experience.' Once the new nation got under way, and thanks to a radical Virginian known as 'Mad Tom' Jefferson, the juices of what Hamilton called the poisons of democracy began to seep into the lives of the common people who pushed over the mountains into the interior and took more and more of their government into their own hands.

Yet, democracy as we know it barely appeared before this century. Not until 1850 did adult males, (white, of course) have the vote. It is only in the past seventy-five years that the United States Senate has been chosen by the voters. Only since the 1920s have British and American women had the vote at all. Today, American democracy is buffeted between two opposing forces: to 'get the government off our backs' and to make the government more and more responsible for more and more people: for minorities, for the children of working women, for poor women wanting an abortion, for a health service that will cover everybody.

Communism, also, is a powerful faith. In the form the Soviet Union established it, it was maintained like Christianity for the longest time by torture, imprisonment for

Celebrating freedom on top of the Berlin Wall on the
morning of 10 November 1989.

heresy, censorship. And, in spite of the abundant and appalling Soviet record of suppression, from purge trials in the 1930s to military oppression in Eastern Europe in the
1950s and 1960s, and at all times censorship, the ubiquitous watchdog of the secret
police, the denial of anything like free elections; in spite of all this, the original theory,
the faith ('faith from each according to his abilities, to each according to his needs') is
surely still very powerful. Whenever a Western leader (usually an American President)
lectured a Soviet General Secretary about human rights, the General Secretary –
Khrushchev, Brezhnev, Gorbachev – did not shuffle with the embarrassment we expect.
Instead, they lectured us about their view of fundamental human rights: a guaranteed
home, a job, an education, medical care from the womb to the tomb. I seriously question whether the peoples of Eastern Europe have been seething for years with demands
for open elections and more individual liberty. May not the sudden explosion have
been due to the grim, non-ideological fact (which has spurred many another revolution) that food was beginning to give out for too many people?

No question that the televised scenes of hundreds of thousands of young families
tumbling joyously across the borders and finally hacking away at the Bastille of the
Wall have presented us with an exhilarating spectacle, a 'Hallelujah Chorus' of the op-
pressed yearning to be free. In the months, and years, ahead we shall learn what sort
of freedom they had in mind. They may find themselves moving into democracies less

perfect than they'd been led to believe. There will be much disillusion: of young idealists who are delighted to find that they are free to speak their minds, travel where they please, pick their own job, elect their own governors, but will find also that as the United States Supreme Court pronounced not too long ago (in ruling on child labour) that they are as free to work twelve hours a day as their employers were free to hire them. How many of the spirited young looking for those famous streets paved with gold will find them paved with 'crack'? How many of the new immigrants will exchange a bare, safe home for a tenement in a neighbourhood wracked with crime?

For all of us who do crave the collapse of Communism, it was sobering to hear from the current Western hero, Mr Gorbachev, that it is 'useless to shout about victory in the Cold War and the collapse of this or that social system.' This, he told the French Foreign Minister, is no time to gloat or believe that what inevitably will follow on the tumult is 'the exporting of capitalism'. It cannot have been bluster on his part to maintain that Communism is alive and changing, so that, in a sudden, remarkable change of emphasis, the West shouldn't get too excited about breaking up the Warsaw Pact or re-unifying Germany. Interesting that while we've been emphasizing trade and free speech and free markets, he should have reverted to the defense of the East. It was a reminder that however desperate is his domestic economy, the Soviet defence budget is only now beginning to shave its massive percentage of the gross national product, and billions in military aid still pour into Cuba and Nicaragua. If we in the West uncomfortably feel once more the old fear of Germany as the dominant power in Europe, the Russian leaders have never forgotten their nine million casualties in the First World War, the fourteen millions of the Second.

No doubt we shall all cool off, remembering in the meantime those similar jubilant scenes on the nights, in India, in Africa, in Indonesia, when the flag of the old imperial ruler went down and the flag of the new independent republic went up, to the crackle of fireworks, the changing of anthems, and the full-throated cry of 'Uhuru!' Freedom! Within a year or two, more than half of them were rent by murderous civil wars or under the rule of a dictator.

Yet, it must be said that the East European tumult does signify a counter-revolution at least. And that somebody started it. So it was a happy, a moving, coincidence that the night the Wall came down, the President of the United States was awarding the Medal of Freedom, the highest American civilian honour, to the man who, eight years ago, sparked the new revolution. Usually, the triggerman has been a defiant monk, or a cloistered philosopher, or a scholar brooding in a public library. This time, it was a shipyard electrician. President Bush hung the shining medal round the cherubic neck of – Lech Walesa, the leader of Poland's insurgent Solidarity movement.

When he had a series of small heart attacks, his pace slowed considerably. In the last four years of his life he was no longer able to visit us in Vermont, travel to San Francisco or London, or even, the last summer, to go to Nassau Point for a few days a week. But though his body was failing, his mind was astonishingly clear. His memory never wavered, and he worked at keeping it tuned by reciting the plays of Shakespeare every night as he drifted off to sleep.

The constancy of the *Letter* was his anchor to the world. What originally had been an afternoon's endeavour was now the focus of his week. The luxury of more time and the fact of his advancing age led to pieces that were more reflective in nature. No longer was he necessarily commenting on the latest news or the random cabdriver or Christmas dinner or whatever caught his fancy, he was viewing events and people with a more seasoned perspective, not just of history but also of a life long lived. It seemed that he was more interested in cultural tides, perhaps even enduring truths, than in flashing news stories. He resisted, however, all entreaties to write a credo of some sort, a W. Somerset Maugham *The Summing Up*. The only time he ever came close to such an endeavour was when he was interviewed for an introduction to a book called *America Observed*, a collection of his pieces from the *Guardian*. What strikes me is that despite his concern about America's love of decadence, he still had faith in the energy, spunk and generosity of its people. 'In general, then, there doesn't seem to be any decline in curiosity, inquisitiveness, enlisted in the dogged belief that things can be made better, that tomorrow ought to be better than today. The stoic and fatalist are not yet familiar American types' (*America Observed*, p.17). Never for a moment stoical in nature, he did on occasion lean into a fatalist view. Perhaps one reason he loved America was because it saved him from himself, from what, as a small boy in Blackpool, he had feared would be his lot. Raised in a culture of stoicism and humble acceptance of limited circumstances, his passionate nature, curiosity and inquisitiveness won out against a certain inculcated fatalism against which he would always be on guard.

Perhaps he was so good at what he did because, as he interpreted America for Great Britain and the rest of the world, he endeavoured to reconcile and balance his own character and life, a life steeped in centuries of tradition and history, and then dramatically injected with the vitality, youth, and exuberance of a new nation. His love for both countries was the secret of his wisdom and the inspiration for his work.

S.C.K.

Reagan's Achievement

Letter No. 2134, 12 January 1990

We give labels to decades – The Gay Nineties, The Roaring Twenties – despite the fact that God didn't invent decades. We did. And usually there's no good reason to think that the tides of history rise and fall every ten years. But for once, 1980 just happened to mark the first year of something we never expected but now can see was an American revolution: a drastic turn in the direction of American government, for the first time since 1933. And before we look at the social changes that flowed from it or happened to go along with it, we must, I think, this time, take a new look back to the Mover and Shaker himself. None other than Ronald Reagan.

I don't think any of us thought during that heady summer of 1980 of Mr Reagan as anything remotely like a revolutionary. Sure, he promised to slash taxes. He promised what Franklin Roosevelt promised during his first presidential campaign, to decentralise the government and give much of it back to the states. But the moment Roosevelt got into the White House he performed a 180-degree U-turn, seized the executive power of the federal government, and ran a central government like no other president in peacetime history. Well, Reagan was a new-born Republican; he'd voted for Roosevelt four times, and surely he would do the same as F.D.R. had. He would say and act in the reluctant belief that Washington *is* the place that is primarily responsible for jobs, relief, insurance, housing, healthcare, the works.

So, when Mr Reagan arrived in the White House, very few veteran politicians expected him for a minute to try to legislate his soaring campaign promises. Promises, promises are the stuff of campaigns. Once you're elected, you have to liquidate your campaign rhetoric and get down to the humdrum, un-dramatic business of government, which is to say who gets what.

But he had up his sleeve, and in his heart, too, a shocking surprise. 'Now,' said the Democratic leader, House Speaker Tip O'Neill, 'now you are in the big leagues.' That was not only a patronising remark, it was thoughtless. Reagan had been Governor of California for eight years. California has been called 'the great microcosmic national state', which had confronted Reagan with just about every domestic issue that confronts a President.

The first, minor shock was the discovery that Reagan was not a political tyro, the

A dazzling moment in the Reagan presidency, with Frank Sinatra
and Nancy at a birthday party for the President.

aw-shucks B-film actor who would have to be nursed into the ways of Washington.
In his first hundred days, he held sixty-nine private meetings with four hundred Congressmen. (In Mr Carter's first hundred days, he barely got to know the majority and
minority leaders in the Senate.) Mr Reagan dazzled and dazed these men by announcing his Boy Scout's fidelity to the gaudier slogans of his campaign. He meant what he
said. And with an energy and an audacity that took all the breath out of the opposition, he bulldozed through a bigger defence budget. More, to the delight of the people
who'd voted for him (and the secret pleasure of the people who hadn't), he slashed
the income tax in half and began to abolish or trim a lot of the government bureaus.
More money, he said, is going to come from lower taxes than from higher taxes. How
could that be? Well, by broadening the tax base, having more people pay some taxes,
it came true.

The balanced budget was an obvious impossibility and was forgotten. The tax deal
produced a recession, which Reagan said would be temporary. It was. He then started
cutting social services, producing howls of protest from the poor, from welfare depen-
dents, from minorities, students, from all the Democrats and the liberals. But once the
recession lifted, employment kept going up and up to record levels, and, against all the
doctrines and the warnings of the liberal economists, inflation went down and down,
from Carter's 13 percent to 2 percent. Of course, there were lots of new, hidden taxes;

he'd learned this trick in his eight years as Governor of California. Not income taxes, they were called 'revenue enhancements', user fees, indexing repeal, contingency surcharges, and certainly the general public either didn't think of them as taxes or didn't care. What people mean by taxes is income taxes.

What Reagan did was to bring about the absurdity he'd promised: to reverse the movement of American government, of the New Deal, welfare, central government's spending and taxing movement; to change the direction of government that had been steady from Roosevelt to Carter. His best biographer, Mr Lou Cannon, pictured this idealistic Midwestern youth as 'intuitively keen but intellectually lazy', who for all his rigid self-help doctrines and his nostalgia for small-town America, 're-defined the ground of political discourse and set the nation on a course of change.'

For better or worse. We may not know for some time. The demoralized Democrats warned us in the early 1980s that there would be a dreadful price to pay, that soon there would be a bitter harvest. But we didn't reap it, and they said, well, in the long run. Well, as the man said, in the long run we'll all be dead. In the long, short run of the 1980s, more people were employed, more people than ever before had more money, the huge middle class had never been better off. It was a decade of unprecedented prosperity – for the great majority. To this, the Democrats responded, at the end of Reagan's first term, by noticing that all these remarkable gains had been bought at the price of a massively growing federal deficit. The voters didn't seem to care; they sent Reagan back to the white House in another electoral landslide. The Democrats went on dooming and glooming through the next four years about the deficit. It still didn't seem to weaken the economy. George H. W. Bush came along, and surely now the country would heed the Democrats' omens. They didn't. Bush won forty states to ten. And today, the United States is riding the longest stretch of prosperity it has known, of record employment across almost all the regions.

By last year, the Democrats gave up publicly mourning the deficit. Top economists in several Western countries outrageously said it didn't matter. That what did matter was the deficit in relation to the gross national product. And by that test, the United States was better off than some other economic giants – Japan, for instance, and Germany.

So, the Democrats pointed rightly to the decay of the cities, to constantly rising crime, to the grim, undeniable fact that one American child in five lives in poverty. Do the people in the mass care? Of course they care. But the Democrats insist, imply at least, that these are the symptoms of 'a sick society'. The Republicans and most of the voters see them as nasty stains on an otherwise successful society. Only the occasional commentator of no particular stripe notes the equally undeniable fact that in the past twenty years no matter who was in the White House, the people go on demanding more government services than they are prepared to pay for. That's the bill that sooner or later will have to be paid – in the long run, perhaps.

Fighting for Oil

Letter No. 2179, 16 November 1990

The big story remains Saddam Hussein and the Persian Gulf. Suddenly, within one week, another figure has been unwillingly shoved into the limelight, as if into the dock of a court of law, and challenged to defend himself. And he is, President George H. W. Bush. Within two weeks, approval for his Gulf policy has dropped from 68 percent to 49 percent, and it is slumping more every day. Why now? What set off this popularity avalanche was the President's announcement last week that not only had he cancelled the plan for rotating the forces that go on duty in the Gulf but he was ordering another 150,000 troops to Saudi Arabia. This is going to build the American fighting force, by Christmas or thereabouts, into 380,000. That's only forty thousand less than the entire American force that, in the end, served in Korea.

Served, of course, meant *fought*. And so far, in the Gulf, not a bullet has been fired. The President said he was sending that extra 150,000 to provide 'an adequate offensive military option'. You'll have noticed that in all the political announcements, the UN resolutions, the ambassadorial pronouncements, we stagger through thickets of jargon and always come out with something like 'offensive option.' And what does that mean? Of course, it means war. On the day that President Bush announced the huge increase in the number of 'offensive option personnel' (that means soldiers), he also let drop the casual, irritated aside that he'd 'had it' with Saddam Hussein. Well, I'm sure that he and the other Allied leaders have said such a thing (as also 'fed to the teeth' and 'had it up to here') in private. But when the President of the United States says it in public, and then orders up another 150,000 troops, what's that meant to do? Frighten Saddam Hussein? Well, to paraphrase the Duke of Wellington, it frightened *us*, it frightened the disbanded Congress. So much so that many Democrats said out loud in public what they've been muttering in private; and two leading Republicans, normally dependable Bush lieutenants Senator Robert Dole and Senator Richard Lugar, came out and asked the President to revive the dead Congress, call it back into special session now, and frankly say what he has in mind. In fact, the urge has taken hold of Congress (about a month after being felt in the country) to force the President to answer the original elementary question: why are we in the Gulf, and what are we going to do there?

This seems an extraordinary question to ask at this late date, almost four months after the President's so swift response to the invasion of August second. He said then that we are opposing naked aggression. Saddam Hussein must get out of Kuwait. We can't have dictators walking into little countries. This aggression will not stand. The first fifty thousand, and rising every week, were sent off to defend, the President said, Saudi Arabia; for, if Hussein conquered coastal Saudi Arabia, he would control over 40 percent of the world's oil supply. I should think, for any Western nation, that was in itself an intolerable prospect. It was odd and unfortunate, however, that the administration, the President especially, didn't stress this dire prospect and emphasise that it represented a threat to the economies, the actual prosperity of, among others, Western Europe. Fight for oil? Yes, indeed, the President might have said, and gone on to quote vivid and memorable instances from history of great wars fought down the centuries, from the Egyptians to the Indochinese, for some raw material whose denial would impoverish your country. But neither the President nor his Secretary of State came out firmly at the start and said there was nothing dishonorable in fighting for oil. (The awkward fact that may have inhibited this line was that the United States is far less dependent on oil from the Gulf than most other Western countries and, most glaringly, Japan.)

As the American forces gathered through August and September, I must say that many thoughtful Americans began to feel nervous about the President's apparent assumption that everybody knew why America was in the Gulf, and that there was no further need to define the cause more clearly and put it up to the people. Of course, there was no pressing popular objection to make him do this. For a month or so, more than 80 percent of the American people backed him on what they took to be American policy in the Gulf. Nevertheless, I felt at the time that the country was in a sort of trance. It was proud of all those thousands of troops being deployed in Saudi Arabia. A nightly high was available in the TV shots of men thundering through clouds of sand in tanks or toasting their families and saying things were fine. The country got a lift from seeing the first big dramatic exhibition of its strength, to be used, surely, if at all, in a good cause. But once the United Nations Security Council passed that unanimous resolution and voted sanctions, it was noticeable with what relief a lot of political leaders, and surely millions of ordinary citizens, decided that the U. N. decision was an actual insurance policy against war. All those precious American boys weren't going to fight after all. The Administration expected, I think, that the troops would then settle down for the long haul, living in the desert till March or April, maybe into the blazing summer, to see if sanctions worked. But the TV microphones soon amplified the awkward fact that many of the troops weren't at all prepared for a long haul. They wanted action, or they wanted out. Realising this, and getting disturbing reports about the morale of all those thousands, President Bush said he'd had it with Hussein and ordered up another 150,000. Suddenly it occurred to the complacent homebodies – you, me, and the Congress – that perhaps, after all, the President meant all those soldiers actually to fight. Sooner than later. So, suddenly the *New York Times* and many other

Saddam Hussein practises
launching a rocket
propelled grenade.

fine institutions begged for patience; let the sanctions work. Demonstrators took to the streets: 'No Blood for Oil'. The Congress, roused from its deathbed, says that under the Constitution the President cannot go to war; only the Congress can declare war. That is absolutely correct, but they hesitate to remark that the Constitution has been blandly ignored for forty-nine years. The last Congressional declaration of war was against Italy in December 1941.

In the meantime, at least six presidents have committed American forces abroad without even a nod to Congress. The question now emerges: does the President have emergency powers that transcend the Constitution? For nearly fifty years, Presidents have assumed those powers. A noisy confrontation seems to lie just ahead. All this preliminary noise – the war drums, the street protests, the sulking troops, the weeping TV wives, the angry liberals in Congress, the rebellious Senators Dole and Lugar – all this must be music to the ears of Saddam Hussein. He must be leaning back, sitting it out, and loving it.

The Passing of the Blue Blazer

Letter No. 2282, 6 November 1992

When I became Chief American Correspondent of a paper whose mission, way back then, was to prompt and protect the thinking of one city, Manchester, I was disturbed at the thought that I was going to have to move myself and my family from New York to Washington. Washington, of course, was where all the chief foreign correspondents were based. To my great relief, I soon had a letter from my editor – a small, canny, spiky-haired, bespectacled imp of a Lancashireman. He wrote quite simply: 'No, I don't want you to move to Washington. I don't want you to report Washington, except from time to time. I want you, *all* the time, to report America. New York is the best news base, and the best home base for travel.'

That wise and wily sentence is one that might not only be passed on to editors of papers around the world. It would serve a useful purpose if it could be engraved or done up in needlework, framed, and hung in the Oval Office of the White House. It would remind every President of a truth that every President, especially in his second term, is in danger of forgetting: that the White House is not home or anything re-motely like the homes of the two hundred million people he is there to represent. The White House is a temporary Versailles and not the best place in which to maintain what Teddy Roosevelt called 'a sense of the continent'.

You have to have been in the White House as a guest to appreciate its elegance and patrician comfort, and to be treated like some venerated old monarch in luxuri-ous exile in order to feel the benign truth behind the phrase coined by the historian Arthur Schlesinger, Jr.: 'the Imperial Presidency'. He was referring to the White House – I almost said the Court – of Richard M. Nixon. And certainly there's been no Presi-dency in our time, or perhaps in any time, when the White House more resembled a royal palace. Mrs Kennedy had done the place over into an eighteenth-century French mansion more exquisite than most royal palaces. Mr Nixon added some folderols of a monarch's office as imagined by Hollywood. He summoned for ceremonial occasions a row of trumpeters in uniform, with tight, white rumps and knee britches, looking for all the world like the wedding guard of honour designed for Rupert of Hentzau (Ronald Colman) and Madeleine Carroll.

The television pictures of this absurdity evoked such hilarity and mirth (not least in the British Royal Family) that these yeoman of the guard were soon disbanded. But what Mr Nixon had revealed, in exaggeration, was a perception of himself to which a President, after a year or two, is in danger of succumbing. That he is in charge of – that he rules – a nation and that the word is handed down from the White House, not up from the people. It may be said that every Prime Minister probably feels the same in his official residence. I doubt it. Once, at a White House dinner, I sat next to the son of the British Prime Minister, who was at that moment the President's guest of honour. The son had been received, as everyone is, by a young marine officer in a spanking dress uniform. His lady companion took the marine's proffered arm. They were led through a small suite with a small orchestra playing waltzes by Strauss. Other beautiful rooms or galleries they passed through were ablaze with gilt and glass. On into the main reception room. More marines, more impeccable manners – the reception line – the shaking hands with the king – I mean the President – and the First Lady. Cocktails and smiling chatter. And on into two linked dining rooms – and a splendid banquet sparkling with a hundred candles. A soothing fountain of music showered from another room. 'Home,' said the Prime Minister's son, 'was never like this.' And, in truth, by comparison, No. 10 Downing Street is a modest upper middle-class townhouse.

Apart from this beautiful protective shell in which the President lives, there is the constant human situation, in which he is surrounded by people who defer to him and who pass on to him every day their own view (which might be as blinkered as his) of what is happening, what is being felt and thought, on the Great Outside. The outside is the United States and its people. Only in the past month or so did Mr Bush attempt to listen to their troubles, to emerge from his cocoon of complacency. ('Yes, there are people having a bad time, but the economy's growing, 93 million at work – things are getting better all the time.') This reminded me of the fatal 1932 assurance Herbert Hoover issued from the White House to millions shivering in tar-paper shacks down by the rivers, and to the one-quarter of the working people of America who had no work: 'Prosperity is just around the corner.'

Some of you may have expected me to talk about the failures of the Bush campaign, for, only two days after the election, the papers are full of reasons and excuses and explanations by Republicans about failures of *technique*: he should have had sharper figures, he should have been more insulting earlier, he should have used more women, he should have hired as mean a man as the one who invented the infamous Willie Horton television commercial last time. (He was the Massachusetts black man who, given parole by Democratic Governor Michael Dukakis, promptly raped a woman.) One bitter intimate who could enjoy the frankness of having left the administration came a little closer to the central truth when he moaned: 'He surrounded himself with second-rate talent and clones. He was only comfortable with a white-bread crowd, a bunch of white male Protestants and number-crunchers.' I can sympathize with that man's view. I and my generation *are* probably more comfortable with WASPs (and a Catholic friend or two) than with the polyglot (white-black-Latino-brown-Asian), multicultural society that America has increasingly become. But Bill Clinton has reached out to it,

President Elect Bill
Clinton hugs his mother
Virginia after visiting
some neighbours in
Arkansas.

listened to it, and is at home with it, his generation is a link with it.

This was never clearer than on Thursday morning, when the *New York Times* carried a front-page photograph of the President-elect with his mother and pals at a friend's house. Clinton in threadbare jeans, a checked wool shirt, unzipped windbreaker, bulging Reeboks. Mostly young pals in laughing bunches similarly dressed, or undressed. Not a suit, not a necktie, not a button-down shirt in sight. 'Well,' I said to my wife, 'Can you believe this? There is the next President of the United States and his buddies.' I wasn't suggesting that Mr Clinton was putting on an act, as poor Mr Bush had to do when he wolfed a hamburger at the local lunch counter and said, 'Gee whilikins, this is great.' 'Clinton,' said my wife sternly, 'is the President of those people and he dresses like them.' Quite right. Unbuttoned, one way or another, is his natural style. Along with the passing of George H. W. Bush, we shall see, I fear, the passing of the blue blazer.

The O. J. Simpson Case: Preliminaries

Letter No. 2368, 1 July 1994

There used to be a rule in England that, so far as I was concerned, might have been the eleventh commandment handed down by Moses. The rule carried a warning, in two words only, for any journalist who, when a crime had been committed, felt like stretching himself. The warning phrase, as pronounced by English judges, was 'sub joodissi' or 'soob oodikay.' Either way, it meant that the crime you were interested in was at the time under consideration by the court, and until some authority decided there was a case to be tried, it was none of your business commenting on or speculating about it. In fact, there were strict, sometimes expensive, penalties that could be levied against any journalist or any newspaper that broke this rule.

Anyway, as a fledgling journalist, I was brought up on that *sub judice* rule, as well as several others that protected the citizen from being unfairly criticized. The laws of libel and slander were also something you had to know a little about. One rule I learned very early was never to write anything that brought a man into 'ridicule with his fellow men'. That pretty much would have deprived English literature of just about every satirist you can think of, from Geoffrey Chaucer to Alexander Pope to Evelyn Waugh to Groucho Marx, not to mention the satiric TV puppet show 'Spitting Image.'

Mention of that last, like a bomb dropping on a tea party, will tell you in a flash that all these legal niceties and concern for what the United Nations Charter calls 'the dignity of the individual' have been trodden underfoot in the roughshod march of human curiosity, as demonstrated by the daily parade of those gallant defenders of free speech, the tabloid press. The tabloid telly is growing fast and flourishing in programs that once would have had their producers behind bars.

So, you may have gathered why I have not, at any time during the past few weeks, made even a mention of the name and sudden notoriety of O. J. Simpson, and why even now I am loath to talk about him. People have been saying to me, 'I suppose this week you had your fill of comment about the shocking case of O. J.' And, I've said, 'No, when it's decided there's a case against him, and he comes to trial, then we'll go into it.' And people say, 'Oh, really?' I'm afraid it's no longer possible to stay with the old rule without sounding prim and fussy. Prissy, in fact.

If it is possible that anyone listening to me at this moment has not heard the name and the case of O. J. Simpson, I'd better say that he is probably the most famous, the most handsome, certainly the most greatly gifted of modern American athletes in my time, your time, or the time of anyone interested in American football who is now alive and sentient. Just as once Americans, and not only Americans, automatically referred to Bobby Jones as the greatest golfer who had ever lived, so Americans repeat, as in a catechism, the answer to the question: who is the greatest running back in the history of American football? O. J. Simpson. He's in his mid-forties now, long retired, but the memory of him weaving, feinting, slicing through the plunging opposition is dazzling still. And the recollection of his grace, his elegant good humour, his looks, has been preserved by some clever television commercials he did for a car rental agency, and then a raft of movies that were never going to win any Oscars but didn't demean either the remembrance of one of the most admired men (and also one of the most admired blacks) of our time.

Imagine, then, the unhappy early morning of Monday 13th June,when the telephone rang in O. J. Simpson's room in a Chicago hotel (he'd gone there for a business meeting with his car rental sponsor). The call was from the Los Angeles Police to tell him that his wife had been found stabbed and murdered just outside her house, along with a murdered man.

Even that bare account, the first we heard, was brutally shocking, and the first impulse was to grieve for Mr Simpson. Within hours, it came out that O. J. had been in his Chicago hotel room only about two hours – he had checked in, I believe, at about four a.m. Chicago time. He said he had taken a plane from Los Angeles airport at a quarter to midnight. He had been, his lawyer came to say, waiting in his own Los Angeles home, a mile or two away from his separated wife, waiting for a limousine to take him to the airport, when the crime, according to the police, could have been committed. There, the first doubt was sprung. A day or two later, the district attorney's office charged him with premeditated murder of both victims. Then we learned that, the day before, O. J. and his wife had taken their two children to a school performance of some kind, that O. J. had gone home, and Mrs Simpson had gone off to dinner at a favourite restaurant. She was described by friends as happy and much relieved at her decision to divorce O. J. She left her glasses at the restaurant, and in the evening telephoned the manager. He said not to worry; a waiter who was a good friend of Mrs Simpson's would drop them off on his way home. He did so. He was the murdered man.

To that point, the case (the public knowledge of it) was within the normal restrictions of the law. But the moment O. J. was charged, the television networks and the cable networks and the independent city stations and, of course, the tabloids went ape with impatience to know the worst, or to assume it. In no time, even the most serious American papers and the television were printing as news, rumours and rumoured leaks they said they had from the police, or from those most useful informers (when you haven't much to go on), 'observers'. There was a big to-do about a ski mask having been found (which would suggest premeditation and do away with the early idea that Mr Simpson's defence would be one of insanity). It turned out, by confession of

In the 1995 trial, O. J. Simpson tries on a leather glove allegedly used in the murders of Nicole Brown Simpson and Ronald Goldman.

the prosecutor, there was no ski mask. Then lots of unproved assertions about blood-stains, drops, a glove in one place that was said to match a glove in O. J.'s house. And so on.

Mr Simpson has by now fortified himself with three lawyers who have an impressive record of getting acquittals for defendants whose cases looked hopeless at the start. The lawyers first complained that some of these rumours were coming from the police. In the arraignment session, they said they would ask for a hearing at which the prosecution would be challenged to say whether this rumour or that was correct. The chief prosecutor responded with what amounted to an apology: there was never any ski mask.

The rumour mill ground on. Meanwhile, a grand jury had been sitting, summoned the day after the bodies were found. Grand juries, abolished sixty years ago in England, are famously the creature of the district attorney, the prosecutor. The defence plays no part, is allowed no witnesses, no cross-examination, so nine times out of ten (if not more often still) the grand jury, hearing at length the prosecution's case, brings in a bill of indictment. Yes, they're saying, there is a case against the man or woman charged, and it should go to trial.

Now, we were being told every day after the murders that the grand jury was on the verge of indicting Mr Simpson. Then, one evening about a week ago, it seemed to me that nearly every television program on the air was suspended for the time it took to play over (with subtitles) an unseen but shocking scene, a desperate, sometimes sobbing wife begging the police to come and arrest her husband, who could be heard in the background raving and storming and spouting obscenities. The shocker part was the realization that the wife was Mrs Simpson, and the raving man was Mr Simpson. This tape had not been filched. It had been released by the Los Angeles City Police without permission from anyone. The DA's office, the prosecutor, was furious. But so was the judge who'd presided over the arraignment, for the same reason. The airing of that tape, the ugly brutal scene it fed into our imaginations, was about as prejudicial a piece of evidence as you could dream up.

On that ground, the judge closed down the grand jury hearing (an extremely rare practice, but one a judge is qualified to do), saying that it was almost inconceivable that the jurors had not heard or would not hear about the police tape. Incidentally, the solidly planted prejudice was dug deeper by the correct report that Mrs Simpson had, over the last year or two, called the police nine times to save her from her husband's beatings. Once, he was brought to court for a specific offence and lightly punished. Somehow, this never got out to the media at the time.

So, instead of a grand jury indictment, the defence requested and got a preliminary hearing before a judge, at which the prosecution was to lay out its positive case, on the understanding that the defence lawyers would be allowed to see, and independently test, every bit of evidence brought in to support the charge of a double murder. That began on Thursday, the first development being that the judge ordered ten hairs to be taken from the head of O. J. Simpson, to be matched against hairs found in a cap left near the murdered bodies. The first hit for the defence was scored when it urged that all the evidence – skid marks, blood, caps, whatever – picked up by the police in the early morning of the 13th should be excluded from the case, because the police had secured the evidence by illegal entry. They did not have a warrant. Which they didn't.

The press and other media are, of course, within their most respectable rights in reporting that hearing. So, the networks were prepared to lose millions of dollars to sponsors by stopping the soap operas, even going to the extreme of abandoning coverage of the World Cup and sacred Wimbledon. Why, why so impatient, little man? Because everyone wants to know the verdict now, before we've heard the facts, the case charged, the case defended, before in fact, the trial, which is the point at which we, the media, should decently come in.

Microsoft and Monsters

Letter No. 2571, 22 May 1998

It's not hard to imagine as the theme of a James Bond movie that a man acquires the power to control the Internet worldwide. He could, before long, control the world's economies, knowledge, food, transport, all the services that more and more will be done over the Internet.

Well, such a monster is inconceivable in life, but the United States government is acting as if the lives of nations, as well as you and me, would be disturbingly affected if one man controlled everybody's access to the Internet.

This week the government – not the Clinton Administration but the cavalry division of the government, namely the Department of Justice – came down like a wolf on the fold of one famous young man way off there in Seattle, on the Pacific Coast, in the Far West. The name of the case on the docket is USA v. Microsoft Corp.

Not only the federal government, but riding alongside were the supporting troops of twenty states, commanded each by its own attorney general, each bringing its own charge (against Mr Bill Gates's corporation) of *monopoly*. Why should there be so many additional guns brought into action? Why isn't the federal suit enough? The answer is simple, though tedious and maddening to a corporation (a company) being sued. In the United States, a business corporation is set up and licensed not by the federal government but by one particular state it means to do business in. It may go off and get licensed in another state as well. And another, and so on. The original idea was sound: it was to prevent any one company, let alone any one man, from getting control of a single product, or a national resource: coal, say, or oil, or, heaven help us (as heaven did), the railway systems.

Let's remind ourselves what these twenty-one legal assaults on Mr Gates are all about. I talked about him first when he appeared before a special Senate investigating committee at the beginning of March. For newcomers, or innocents, let it be said that Mr Bill Gates is forty-two years old, has a baby face and large wire-framed glasses (don't let them fool you), and, it is generally admitted, is a genius of an innovator with computers to whom millions owe their livelihood. He is the king of software manufacturers; some say the dictator. One of his struggling competitors said he is 'the most dangerous and powerful industrialist of our age.'

However, let's cut out the fine writing and stick with the facts. As I hope everybody knows by now, you navigate through the Internet's World Wide Web and choose your program or font of information on anything and everything. You do this with one essential software tool: a 'browser'.

Now, Mr Gates's company, Microsoft, manufactures a browser known as the Explorer. In theory (the theory of free or competitive trade), you should be able to buy one man's computer and somebody else's browser, the one you find most compatible. However, the government charges (and so do those twenty states' attorneys general) that Mr Gates's Microsoft forces makers of personal computers to load his Explorer for browsing. But since Mr Gates integrated Explorer with the Microsoft operating system, if you don't accept Explorer, then you can't use Microsoft's operating system.

At Mr Gates's Senate hearing, there were several heads of rival computer companies present, very angry men I can tell you. When Mr Gates was disputing the use of the word 'monopoly', one of them swivelled round and put a question to the astonished audience at the hearing, 'How many people own personal computers?' About three quarters of those present. 'How many have a computer that's not fitted with Microsoft's Explorer?' Not a hand raised. 'That,' shouted the rival, 'is a monopoly.'

The burden of the government's complaint is the bruising fact that by forcing rival systems to use his browser and his operating system, he controls about 95 percent of the whole personal computer business and exercises a stranglehold on his competitors, which amounts to a sin precisely defined in the famous anti-trust law, the Sherman Act, which the government has resurrected from the grave. 'Every contract, combination in the form of trust or otherwise, or conspiracy, in restraint of trade or commerce among the several states, is hereby declared to be illegal.'

The very first big government campaign against monopoly – the first and incidentally the last – was famously undertaken by President Theodore Roosevelt at the beginning of the century against the so-called Robber Barons, the handful of men who each cornered some single material resource – coal, coke, steel, oil, the railroads – by crushing his competition. A simple, dramatic example is that of one John D. Rockefeller, a twenty-two-year-old very humble clerk in Cleveland, Ohio, sent by the produce company he worked for to Pennsylvania to see if there was anything to the rumour of a messy oil that somebody had made gush up from the farmland, land where the farmers for two centuries had complained about their streams being muddied with a kind of black glue. It was oil all right, and young, neat Mr Rockefeller saw it might grow from being a smelly lamp oil into oil for heating, for steamships, for power. But he went home to Cleveland and with a straight face told them there was no future in it. But on the quiet, he pooled his small savings with another young man and invested them in a candle-maker who had refined lard oil and was moving on to petroleum. To end your suspense, let me say that within nine years young Rocky owned 90 percent of all American oil refineries and all the main pipelines, and the oil cars of the Pennsylvania railroads. Then he got secret low rates from the railroads for the huge business he could give them, and a bonus from the regular rates that small oil producers had to pay. Need I say that within a year or two he'd either bought out the small rivals or killed them off. When he was only thirty-three, in one stretch of six weeks, he took over twenty-two of twenty-six competitors. One of these unfortunates said, 'If we didn't sell out, we'd be crushed out.' They all would belong to Mr Rockefeller's supreme monopoly: The Standard Oil Company. When all this came out, the Supreme Court, hearing the government's case against Standard Oil, broke up the monopoly in 1911. It looked like a whopping success for the Sherman Act. But wait!

There is a short phrase in the Sherman Act that a non-American may be forgiven for paying little attention to. It is this: ' … in restraint of trade among the several states.' Three years before the Sherman Act was passed, the Congress tried to regulate trade 'between the states' by making price-fixing, railroad freight-rate fixing, pooling of companies illegal. It was called the Interstate Commerce Act, and from then on these sharp practices were to be watched over by a permanent, non-party, Interstate Commerce Commission. But very soon the Sugar Trust, which controlled 98 percent of the sugar-refining business of the country, appealed against its prosecution under the Sherman Act, and the Supreme Court held that that a 98 percent grip on sugar refining (the raw material came from Cuba) did not violate the law because it was not an act 'of interstate commerce'. It was a single corporation monopolizing the processing of a foreign product.

Bill Gates, owner of Microsoft, '42 years old, has a baby face and large wire framed glasses (don't let them fool you)'.

I imagine that the main purpose of having twenty states bring separate charges against Mr Gates's Microsoft is to foil any attempt (which succeeded ninety-odd years ago) to say that the federal suit doesn't address a problem of 'interstate commerce'. Well, the Supreme Court's upholding of the Sugar Trust dealt the 'death blow' to the legality of the Sherman Act. But what truly killed it in practise, what soon arrested every attempt to use it, was the ingenious invention of a gentleman named Mr Dodds (I know no more about him): the invention of the holding company.

A holding company was a pure (or not so pure) financial company formed simply to hold the stock of operating companies. For instance, American Electric Power owns, or owned, eight companies. But it itself did not generate any electricity or mine any coal. It just held the stock of the people who did. Maybe the old cowboy comedian Will Rogers had a pithier definition of a holding company: 'The people you give your money to while you're being searched.'

So, when Mr Rockefeller's infamous monopoly, the Standard Oil Company, was dissolved under the law, it was dissolved into several theoretically competing units in different states. However, they were still a consolidation of the old oil companies, under the control of a holding company. And Mr Rockefeller got richer.

Time alone will show whether the resurrected Sherman Act is more potent today than it was ninety years ago in controlling what Teddy Roosevelt called one of the 'mighty industrial overlords'. Even in his time, when there was popular outrage at the totalitarian control of oil, sugar, railroads, and beef by the Robber Barons, even then, one of the most upright justices of the Supreme Court, and its most formidable intellect, Mr Justice Oliver Wendell Holmes, called the Sherman Act 'an imbecile statute that aims at making everyone fight but forbids anyone to be victorious.'

The last big business monopoly case that the government brought spent seventeen years in the courts before an outside settlement was reached. So, don't expect this mighty case to be done with tomorrow, next week, or even perhaps by 2100. If you're around then, please tell me the result in an E-mail, sent to Cooke. Dot com. Valhalla.

Bill and Monica

Letter No. 2585, 28 August 1998

Last Wednesday evening, just when those of us whose job is to keep one eye peeled for the news feel free to close it and listen in relief to what E. B. White called 'the most beautiful sound in America: the tinkle of ice at twilight,' a bulletin came in. President Clinton would make a public speech on Thursday, 27 August, in Worcester, Massachusetts. Let me put you in the mood – the very wary, watchful, the almost morbidly suspenseful mood in which we heard about that coming speech.

Only eight days before, a very chastened President had made what everybody hoped would be a full, liberating confession about the squalid Lewinsky affair. Yet, it was, to all but a handful of senators and politicians and the media and other public figures, deeply disappointing – tricky, legalistic, evasive. For Mr Clinton the social aftermath was grim. He was going away for a holiday on Martha's Vineyard, up in Massachusetts, a small triangular island off the elbow of Cape Cod. That surely would provide a blessed haven, only half a century ago it was described as 'a small land of old small towns, new cottages, high cliffs, white sails, green fairways, saltwater, wild fowl, and the steady pull of an ocean breeze.' The tumbling centre of this island paradise was Edgartown, population 1,399. Very old residents possibly dream of this sanctuary, but when they wake up they see the sort of reality that has overtaken similar heavenly islets everywhere: as many people as cobblestones, a summer invasion of tourists who suffocate as they jostle each other through the quaint old showplace houses. Luckily, for Presidents in retreat, there are people rich enough to swipe and buy as much as fifty acres and make them their own. To such a borrowed place, on the Tuesday morning after the sad Monday evening, the Clintons repaired. Trudged would be better. They approached the Presidential plane not as usual waving at the crowd, if any. They were photographed from behind, young Chelsea Clinton holding her mother's right hand, her father's left. He holding on to his dog's leash. They ambled into the plane. No waving. No waving at the other end. The President embraced his old and firm ally Mr Vernon Jordan, suspected by Prosecutor Kenneth Starr of having arranged a job for Miss Lewinsky so as to get her out of the White House and, what you might call, 'out of harm's way'. Mrs Clinton was not seen, then or for days. Nor was the President. All that the press corps, bedded down in various spots on the island, most on the mainland,

President Clinton seen hugging Monica Lewinsky among supporters
after his re-election victory.

could report was nothing: no golf, no swimming, no sign of the almost compulsory ritual for a President on holiday, a walkabout through the quaint old streets pressing the flesh with one and all. The general surmise about this odd decision to go into seclusion was perhaps incorrect, but it was fairly understandable: Mrs Clinton was surely trying to get over the shock of having heard, only the day before the President's confessional, that he did after all have a thing with Monica Lewinsky. This inference has been firmly denied by the many people who remember how Mrs Clinton went off round the country to speak up for her husband, right after his January sworn declaration that he'd never had a sexual relationship with Ms Lewinsky. How, therefore, the confession, after more than six months, must have been a cruel emotional blow to Mrs Clinton. I've heard more people say 'I don't believe for a minute she didn't know.' This was not a vicious rumour. It was a plain statement from Mrs Clinton's own press secretary. A sympathetic Senator, an old ally of Mr Clinton's, mused, 'What a vacation this is going to be. I'm sorry for both of them.'

Then, swift as an incoming tornado that can take your mind off anything, came the cruise missile attacks on the Sudan and Afghanistan. Only a momentary pause here, I must say, for the unworthy thought that the President had invented a mighty distraction from his troubles. This idea never really got going, even on the sleazier talk shows. Most such gossip seemed to come from abroad, from Muslim countries. The allies, to a

President Clinton whispers to First Lady Hillary Clinton at the White House in 1999.

man, seconded the attacks, and nobody here paused to doubt the rightness or wisdom of this tactic. Effectively, whether by luck, design, or the grace of God, the name of Lewinsky vanished from the front pages, the top TV spots, for the first time in months. The full-throated support went up from the Congress (they're scattered on holiday just now) but they cried in harmony with all the unison of a Hallelujah Chorus.

In a few days, of course, since there were no more exploding missiles there were no more exploding headlines, just what they call 'investigative' pieces about the likely suspects – profiles of the handsome, diabolical chief suspect (now reported captured). Meanwhile, the White House press corps, heard a new sound, a new hunch was launched, from where I don't know. The President was thinking of responding to the shabby notices he'd had for the first confessional by going before the public once more to make a second. That precious fount of news known as 'sources' kept saying that the White House staff were, weren't, advising the President to make the grand gesture now, while our minds were on the Sudan and hurricanes.

Then, Wednesday evening, the President is going to make a speech tomorrow, at high noon, in Worcester, Massachusetts. The President had made up his own mind and would bare his soul. And, we learned, he would be introduced by the last of the old-style liberal Democrats, the famous Senator from Massachusetts who had had similar troubles of his own and weathered them all, except the first: the fatal drowning of a girl off a tiny island off the coast of Massachusetts – Chappaquiddick. Still, who more fitting than Senator Ted Kennedy to stand in for a penitent President?

So – came Thursday noon – and heaven alone knows how many people skipped the lunch hour, how many oldsters delayed the golf game, how many journalists in how many states sat with pen and paper or tape recorder to hear a confession.

The speech, the occasion – a Massachusetts town, the joyous, stunning reception by a small audience of parents – was the shock. Mr Clinton did not deign to mention Whitewater, the FBI, Ms Lewinsky, or any other inappropriate houri. A young news editor, coming on the tape of this speech twenty years from now, could have dated it 1993; or, since it gave a breathtakingly impressive recital of all the splendid things the Clinton administration had done, maybe it was a triumphant speech at the end of his *first* term; maybe it was a campaign speech delivered in October 1996, just before he went thundering back into the White House. And that same editor, looking at the tape would have said, 'No wonder they re-elected him. What bounce, what confidence, what intelligence, what a range of knowledge tossed off quickly and lightly – on top of all the detail.' Then he'd see the date: Thursday, 27 August, 1998. Impossible. This a marooned, a besieged President. Where? How?

Do you remember the film, *The Three Faces of Eve*, for which Joanne Woodward (oh, forty years ago) won the Oscar? I hope some people recall it – not, of course, because I introduced it and did the running commentary. It was about a famous case reported by two doctors in Georgia, of a young woman who had two separate personalities and woke up each day to be, and act out for the day, one of them: an austere, painfully shy, hesitant young puritan and next day, say, a saucy hoyden sashaying around nightclubs and raunchy young men. This famous case established the fact of people with two or more personalities that emerge and subside at different times.

Well, in a totally non-clinical way, Mr Clinton gives the impression of having two characters, the tricky, sly, deceptive, engaging con man, and the public, conscientious, truly concerned, engaging, eloquent, sympathetic statesman.

So, the unreal spectacle on Thursday, which for an hour or more made me think we were living on two planets at once: there was this ruddy-faced, engaging, cheerful, funny, eloquent President – reeling off impressive stuff about a balanced budget, lowest unemployment ever, more home ownership, smaller government bureaucracy, determination to make every school in the country safe for children, to free every parent from the haunting menace of guns, robbers, drugs. The small audience gave the cue to all of us and rose with a collective shout of praise and wonder.

Meanwhile, Russia was stumbling into bankruptcy, Islam was starting protest marches against the outrage of American attacks on their soil, Saddam Hussein was chucklingly telling the United Nations inspectors to get lost – and Secretary of State Madeleine Albright was almost saying, 'Yes, sir.' The stock market, as Mr Clinton spoke so rapturously, so cheerfully, was plunging down 300 points, as deep a drop as any since the Black Monday of 1987. Surely, in the hour we need him, he will survive.

Our Long Holiday from History is Over

Letter No. 2610, 19 February 1999

It is the morning after, when the hung over gentleman shakes his head like a puppy throwing off fleas, takes the shot of bicarbonate of soda, and looks back on the dreadful experience. And his friends and family moralize. In other words this is sermon time. Everybody who ever said a public word about the affair – from politicians of every stripe, clergymen of every denomination, commentators of every age and medium, men and women in the street, in the desert, in mountain villages, roaring city squares – now that it's all over, why do we have to hear, all over again, from everybody who had talked so often while it was going on? Because of television. Because television, like Mount Everest, is there. I propose quickly and simply to list the themes of these sermons, what might have been their titles, and then we'll guess at the likelihood of the truth of any of them. And there's, if you don't mind, an end to it.

If you could scan or surf all or most of the people who sounded off, here are most of the judgments you'd read or hear about: that the Constitution was the winner; that there were no winners; that the grounds on which the impeachment articles were voted will make it all the easier in the future to impeach a President; that the Presidency has come out strengthened; that the Presidency has been seriously weakened; that the authority of the Senate was strengthened by the seriousness with which they finally debated, away from the cameras, behind closed doors; that the House prosecutors never made the case for 'high crimes and misdemeanours'; that the whole show further weakened the already feeble public confidence in Congress; that the popular judgment was upheld; that, although the President lied under oath many times, his behaviour did not constitute 'high crimes and misdemeanours'; that if 75 percent of the people think his behaviour was immoral and appalling but still wanted him to stay, it only goes to show that they're as bad as he is, and the nation is in moral decline. There are thoughtful people of every type and place who think one or more of these things.

Now you may have noticed that several, if not most, of these judgments imply a prophesy. Because of this trial, this is what's going to happen: more risk of impeachment trials, less trust in Congress, etc., etc. However, within half an hour of the Chief Justice's tapping his gavel and saying, 'The impeachment trial of William Jefferson Clinton stands adjourned,' we had swift and punishing proof that the gift of prophesy

Multiple television monitors broadcast President Clinton's
Grand Jury testimony, 21 September 1998.

is one denied to human beings. For weeks, for months in fact, ever since an actual impeachment trial seemed likely – that's before the House had voted the two damning articles – the Democrats were busy floating a very conspicuous trial balloon they hoped would fly and actually persuade the Senate to forego an impeachment trial altogether. It was the trial balloon of a motion of censure. The Democrats stood solid from the start, saying, 'You'll never find him guilty of high crimes.' In this the Democrats were not wiser or more far-seeing than the Republicans; they just saw and stressed with irritating frequency that a guilty verdict was impossible, that in the Senate trial they would require a two-thirds majority, and there was no way the Republicans could ever get that without twelve Democrats going over.

So, a couple of months ago, three or four Democrats got together and started drafting the language of a censure motion, and later on, of course, brought in some Republicans, including Senator Trent Lott, the Republican leader in the Senate. Obviously, to get a censure motion passed, the language would have to be agreeable to the Republicans as well.

By the way, from the first session of the House to study the possibility of impeachment to the last days of the Senate's vote, what most depressed some of us looking on was the total unwavering partisanship of both sides, while all the time each party kept congratulating itself on its high sense of non- or bi-partisanship. For the longest time it seemed not one Republican, not one Democrat, had the independence, the moral guts, to desert his Party.

In the end, did you notice, ten Republicans found the perjury charge not good enough and voted with the Democrats. And on 'obstruction of justice', five Republicans went over and joined the Democrats in saying 'Not guilty'. It was the Republicans who were supposed to be the locked-tight, hidebound partisans, united by prejudice and hate, but in the end not a single Democrat spoke up for himself. All they, like sheep, went trotting into the fold.

Well now: censure. As I say, during many weeks, night and day, small knots of Democrats and Republicans have met and composed language: 'immoral', 'degrading', 'unworthy', 'unacceptable', 'loathsome', on and on. And by the time the Senate was coming to the last days, no censure motion had been composed that satisfied both sides. But one Senator, a Democrat, the often valiant Senator Dianne Feinstein from California, had a censure motion all prepared to offer after acquittal, to prove to the world that the Democrats did not condone the President's behaviour.

So, the Chief Justice taps his gavel. He is escorted out; it's all over. But wait. The cameras go hurtling back to the Senate. Another gavel sounds. 'The Senate will come to order'. So it does. And up rises the beautiful and gallant Senator Feinstein. There are to be two votes: one a procedural vote to admit consideration of a motion of censure of the said William Jefferson Clinton, and when that's passed the motion itself to be read aloud, debated, and voted on. 'And how long would that take?' asked a random reporter of a veteran Senator. 'Ooh, could take a day, a week, a month, who knows?' So Senator Feinstein proposes the consideration of censure. The vote is taken electronically – it took seven minutes and was hopelessly outvoted. They're not even going to discuss it. End of three months' rumour, labour, negotiation, prophesy.

Somebody got to Senator Lott, the Republican leader. 'Well,' he said, glancing at his watch, 'it's outside the Constitution, and anyway, time's giving out.' As if this motion had been one of those casual, trivial motions offered at the end of every session: 'That this House deplores the rumour that Elvis Presley is still alive.' The line that struck me about as casually as a bolt of lightning was Senator Lott's 'it's outside the Constitution.' Of course, but it always was.

Once again, I have to say that the crucial phrase in the Constitution that tells you how far you can go by way of punishment once you've voted the impeachment verdict (to the end nobody quoted it), the last word in the Constitution on impeachment is this: 'Judgment in cases of impeachment shall not extend further than removal from office.' What could be more brutally plain? Vote him free or remove him, but don't then fiddle around, add some other charge, dream up motions of censure or something by way of ameliorating the tough judgment.

Anyway, it does finally seem to be over, which means, however, that as George Will puts it, 'Our long holiday from history is over.' And most of the people in the Senate and the House seem to know it. They're already drawing up responses to the President's beautiful painting of a government-paid utopia that he unveiled in his State of the Union Address. His promise that, with the outlay of a few billion dollars, in a year or two America will have the best public educational system in the world, was brought quickly to earth by his own man in New York, the formidable Senator Daniel Patrick Moynihan, saying, 'Never mind being the best. How about getting to be fairly good?' Instead of eighteenth in maths, fifteenth in history, twelfth in general science, the Senator said that with hard work all round, and the raising of elementary and high school standards of teaching, the United States might expect to show a radical improvement in its public education in about three generations.

Apart from getting back to the business of government, there's a public issue that's been swept under the rug but is not going to stay there, and could inflame labour relations in this country. The pilots of a leading airline, the second largest in the country, downed the joysticks and stayed home in protest against the company's absorbing a small airline that does connecting flights and hires pilots at half the salary of the regular pilots. The scary point is that the pilots didn't strike; they called in sick, which meant they didn't work but they still got paid. They stayed out four days, and the company lost $70-odd millions. A federal judge ordered them back to work. Two-thirds refused. Another judge came in and fined the pilots' union $10 million. So all the rest went slinking back to work, and the media forgot about it as if the whole issue were solved. It isn't. The pilots are working but fuming at their company, and the mighty powerful labor union has discovered a new technique: the general sick call. No strike. Many pilots are talking about the union's refusing to pay any fine imposed by the courts. This technique, if picked up by other national industrial unions, could cause unguessed-of mischief between the public and organised labour – two forces that, for fifteen, twenty years or more, have been so strangely passive. 'Pilots refusing to serve under any circumstances? They can't do that,' is a popular reaction.

It recalls the Boston police strike of 1919, which brought chaos to the government and the streets of the famous old city and much of New England. The Governor of Massachusetts was as horrified as the people. He said: 'There is no right to strike against the public safety by anybody, anywhere, anytime.' And people hoped so desperately that this would come true that they had that Governor, one Calvin Coolidge, run for President – and elected him.

'These are my times and I must know them'

Letter No. 2621, 7 May 1999

The old Roman poet Martial, or 'Mar-tee-al' (he was a Spaniard who went to Rome in his twenties, in about 64 AD, and spent the rest of his life there), was once chided by a friend for going to the Colosseum and watching lions fight and devour slaves. Martial said he would hate the scene as much as anyone could, but he must go once. 'These,' he said, 'are my times and I must know them.'

I feel very much the same way about the atrocious shootings at the small-town school in Littleton, Colorado. I've not talked about them because I've always said I see no point in talking about great natural disasters – earthquakes, tornadoes, even assassinations – unless a commentary can help in some way. Nothing we say now can help those dead children and the well-liked teacher. But these horrors keep happening far more often in this country than anywhere; and since the dread day in Littleton, everybody from the President and the Congress down (or up) to the psychiatrists, prison commissioners, clerics, Parent-Teachers Associations, has had his or her say. And lots of good people have agonised over two questions: why did it happen and how can it possibly be prevented? Apart from one overriding topic, everything that you or I have thought and said has been thought and said. And mostly it amounts to laying down what ought to happen. For instance, parents ought to stay closer to their children and their pastimes at home. The two boys plotted for a year and spent months building a bomb in their garage. Surely somebody upstairs might have noticed. But surely, also, there's no way of making parents pay attention by act of Congress. There is one state, the far-western state of Oregon, which has a law that punishes parents for any crime committed by a child of theirs, with a fine going up to a stiff prison sentence according to the severity of the crime. But apart from that, every sort of idea has been offered as a preventative. Every school in the country ought to have metal detectors at every entrance, bullet-proof vests, an ever-ready counselling group, trouble watchers who wonder if this boy might play with a gun at home or if that girl is likely to think of suicide, and so on and on. There are imaginative and well-meaning suggestions about what ought to happen, but not much consideration is given to the how, except on the main topic. The main, indeed the seething argument all over the country swirls around gun control.

A Columbine High School video shows Dylan Kleybold and Eric Harris on the day they killed twelve students and one teacher before killing themselves.

The pros and cons are about evenly split. The fight between gun controllers and the National Rifle Association, which maintains that all Americans have a right to carry a gun, has been going on for so long and so exhaustively that by now it has all the subtlety of two drunken sailors at the end of a saloon brawl. I should tell you that every state has its own gun control laws – light or heavy, simple, complicated – and the nation has two, three laws, the first of which (the Brady Law) passed against Herculean resistance in the Congress after twelve years of lobbying by Sarah Brady, the wife of James Brady, who was President Reagan's press secretary and was with him and was shot and paralysed during the assassination attempt on the President.

The bill is called The Brady Handgun Violence Prevention Act. It requires a five-day wait and a computer check on the background of anyone who wants to buy a handgun at retail. I stress retail because thousands of handguns are bought privately and from unlicensed dealers at gun shows. It's not much of a bill, is it? Any intelligent crook of any age can easily fake his identity as a purchaser. In the following year, 1994, President Clinton put up a new federal bill that made it a crime for any adult to sell or pass on a handgun to a juvenile. And then the possession of a concealed weapon became a federal crime.

Well now that's much better, or it would have been, if the Justice Department had started catching and prosecuting and jailing offenders. However, of over two thousand adults caught passing on guns, the Department of Justice prosecuted five one year, six last year. Over two hundred thousand felons have tried to buy handguns; nine were prosecuted and convicted.

The solid core of the National Rifle Association's membership are the country people of America, especially in the South and West, who started as toddlers following their fathers at weekends on hunting expeditions. 'Hunting' in America means always and everywhere 'shooting' and is not remotely a class – that is to say, upper class – sport. On the contrary, it has flourished since the earliest colonial days among poor people whose food was the animals that roamed the woods and the mountains, and no President, no Party, is ever going to prohibit the ownership of rifles. You'd think once that was understood, that the argument would end there. But about once a year there's a murderous school shoot-out, and automatic weapons are used. How can anyone justify anyone's right to own an automatic assault weapon? If you have the luck – or the misfortune, according to taste – to attend a meeting of the National Rifle Association, you will hear a phrase constantly quoted, chanted as reverently as a prayer: 'Our constitutional right to bear arms shall not be infringed.'

What constitutional right?

On the façade of the National Rifle Association's headquarters building in Washington there is or was chiselled in the stone a phrase enclosed in quotation marks. It says: ' … the right to keep and bear arms shall not be infringed.' That is the mantra, the watchword, the rationale for the NRA's conviction that the Constitution gives them a sacred right to keep guns. But it doesn't, and the simple reason is in those three dots, the first part of the sentence in the Constitution they didn't print and chisel. This is what the Second Amendment to the Constitution says in full: 'A well regulated militia being necessary to the security of the free state, then the right of the people to keep and bear arms shall not be infringed.' The one condition of having that right was to be able to spring to attention and help to form a militia whenever it was called into being.

A militia? One prejudice the New England settlers brought to America was a fear of standing armies. Kings could seize control of an army overnight and enslave the people. So this nation, when it was created, absolutely rejected the idea of a standing army. A militia was the alternative thought indispensable to a republic. And militiamen would form, be summoned by the President in an emergency – an Indian uprising, a whisky rebellion (there was such a thing) – and then disbanded once the trouble was over. So, as Adam Smith wrote: 'All men joined in some measure the trade of a soldier to whatever trade or profession they happened to carry on.'

Of course the militia is long gone. We do have, you may have heard, a standing Army, Navy, Air Force, Marine Corps, and they take care of all the shooting that may be necessary for the security of the state. So the only point in the Constitution that sanctions a citizen's right to own a gun is his willingness to join an institution that vanished a century and a half ago. There is no Constitutional right to own a gun to go out and shoot a rabbit, let alone to stick up a school or kill the President.

As for the root cause of the two boys' murderous spree in Littleton (if there was a root cause), there are as many theories as there are religions, atheists, social scientists, and people who live by hunches. One of the most popular is the addiction of those two boys to video war games and especially to the notorious 'Doom', which can, by constant practice, teach kids to pick off single targets quickly and accurately. This was a very persuasive line until some sociologist pointed out that no nation's children are more insensate in their addiction to war and murder games than the Japanese, who have fifteen homicides a year against America's ten thousand.

It all sends me back, I'm afraid, to an evening over thirty years ago in Fort Worth, Texas, where in a hotel suite the President of the United States was having a late-night chat with two or three of his closest pals. Not statesmen, not Cabinet men, but old school and college and early campaign pals who now constituted, we used to say, his Irish Mafia. They were discussing ways, technologies, precautions, whereby the absolute personal safety of the President could be guaranteed. Pretty soon the President grew weary of what he took to be a pointless discussion. He got up. He said: 'Look, if a man is determined to kill the President of the United States, he'll make it. Now I'm off to bed. Goodnight.'

Early next afternoon, while driving along a street in Dallas, he was shot and killed by a sniper in a sixth floor window overlooking the route.

Rosa Parks: Freedom in America

Letter No. 2627, 18 June 1999

When you see on television some protest rally, I mean a spontaneous protest – people suddenly taking to the streets, brandishing fists, howling insults, waving posters – do you ever wonder who planned the spontaneousness of it all. We long ago accepted that in totalitarian countries, whose tyrannical system is disguised from the start by calling it a 'people's republic', that in tyrannies we know that a people's uprising is as well planned as a coronation. But I'm always surprised after forty, fifty years of television why commentators on riots and demonstrations still use the phrase 'the people took to the streets', when from the evidence of the posters they flourish, somebody must have ordered them to appear on the double, or else. The posters? A genuine spontaneous uprising has single nasty words scrawled in paint on random sheets or has no posters at all. The regular popular protests – anti-abortion, anti-war, anti-hunting, whatever – usually have professionally printed placards in coloured lettering, the order for which must have gone out weeks in advance of the 'spontaneous uprising'.

This struck me with new force this week when we saw everywhere – on television, the front pages of every newspaper, the cover stories on magazines – the face of a sweet old lady with golden spectacles, her white hair swept up and topped off with a ropey knot, sitting alongside the President of the United States and Speaker of the House. She is the heroine of a ceremony in the Capitol Rotunda, where, before an audience of about a thousand and the Congress (including a Senator in his nineties who, forty-four years ago, was the old lady's bitterest enemy), Miss Rosa Parks was awarded a rare honour, the Congressional Gold Medal. It goes back to George Washington, and it is awarded only to national heroes, the last two of whom were Mother Theresa and Nelson Mandela, and it was voted two months ago by Congress to Miss Rosa Parks as a 'living icon for freedom in America'.

Let us, to use the Victorian novelists' fancy phrase, turn back the pages of history to see how and when and why this old black lady, now eighty-six, earned this singular honour. The pages of any history of America that I might have recorded lie, as you might imagine, in the files of a newspaper reporter. And if I were a more orderly man than you are, Gunga Din, I would keep files, but I don't. However, by the grace of my beloved, long-gone editor there is on my shelves a little pamphlet, brown-edged with age, a collection of re-printed daily dispatches of mine from the South, written from various towns in the spring of 1956 – two years after the Supreme Court abolished the segregation of the races and one year after a bus boycott in the capital city, Montgomery, State of Alabama. If you don't already know the facts of that famous boycott, they are simply told.

On a December day in 1955, four blacks went aboard a city bus and sat where they'd never sat before, in the forward section reserved always for whites. The bus driver, following the city law, asked them to move to the back. The three men complied. The fourth, a woman, refused. A firm, upright little woman of forty-two, she was asked again, and once more said no. If the bus driver had decided to make nothing of it and let her stay, he could have been prosecuted for flouting the city law, and the company could lose its license. This was well understood on both sides. The bus driver called two policemen, and still refusing to budge, she was arrested and taken off, charged and released. I put this down just as flatly as that in my piece. I didn't even print her name. It was, of course, Rosa Parks. And the legend has grown and shone and blazed, of one coloured woman who took it upon herself on a whim to stand out at last against the separation of blacks and whites on a Southern bus. And so, down the years, the *fame* of Rosa Parks has grown, and her courage has been burnished with each new telling.

In that original piece, and right after that humdrum recital of the facts, I find this sentence: 'That same afternoon, thousands of printed handbills mysteriously dropped on the doorsteps of the coloured homes in the neighborhood urging a boycott of the bus line, to begin to start two days later,' at an appointed time. And so it did, and went on for over a year, till the blacks got more reforms than they had protested and sued for. In shorter words, Miss Rosa Parks's decision to stay in a forward seat in the bus was the first move in a planned boycott of the bus company and the city law, a campaign organized long before by the NAACP (National Association for the Advancement of Colored People) and run by a young, bland, handsome black parson, name of Martin Luther King, Jr., who while I was in Montgomery, flew in and out from Atlanta twice a week to buy little vans and station wagons for use by the boycotters.

We could leave it there, having made the seemingly mean point that Miss Rosa Parks just happened to be chosen as the cat's-paw or dupe of a boycott campaign well planned beforehand; or that some official of the NAACP looked over a list of the regular users of the bus on that route and decided a woman would serve their purpose best, since the arriving cops would have to treat her fairly civilly if they didn't want to trigger a scandal. Well, it's not so. Miss Parks was not chosen arbitrarily. *She* did the choosing. She was not just another bus rider. She was the secretary of a city chapter of the NAACP twelve years before she stood, or sat, her ground in 1955. The first time she was thrown off a bus was for using the white entrance – at the front. That takes us back to 1943, the middle of the Second World War, in which her brother had served both in Europe and in the Pacific. He came home unhurt, but she watched in disgust, helpless disgust, to see her brother, in uniform, picked out by rednecks, or white trash,

for especially bigoted treatment. From that time on, she was a prominent civil rights activist (this is all, remember, ten or more years before the Supreme Court's ruling abolishing segregation). May 1954 is always given, and rightly, as the Bastille Day – the day that started the revolution for equal black rights.

Well, back in 1945–46, once the war was over, Miss Parks, among other audacities, tried to register to vote just like any other citizen. She tried three times, and some discrepancy in her residential record, or something, had her turned away. From long practice, the returns officers, as you'd call them, of Southern election districts were experts at finding some sort of discrepancy in any black person's qualification to vote, especially in those states in the Deep South where blacks were a majority.

Miss Parks, soon after the war, began to draw up a record of cases of actual violence against her fellow blacks in the state of Georgia, and, here's an interesting oddity, became chief adviser to the Youth Council of the NAACP on how to, as she put it, 'maintain one's dignity' before situations of insufferable insult, cruelty, contempt. I can't conceive now, looking back on it, how any black person would have the gall, the simple courage, ever to do anything but walk away as fast as possible from the jeers and insults of street-corner rednecks. That's what all the most sensible blacks, young and old, did. So you didn't see much of the beatings and home burnings and violence. It was done mostly in quiet private places, and after dark.

Well, only a couple of months before Rosa Parks chose to be the cat's-paw on that bus, she heard the sickening news (it sickened this country) of a black teenage boy from Chicago who had been murdered just for being found, a Northerner, walking through a town in Mississippi. The white men who killed him on a lark were acquitted by an all-white jury, in Mississippi. Rosa Parks, the eighty-six-year-old lady, so belatedly honoured, now recalls: 'It was not that I was just fed up in December 1955. I'd been fed up my whole life, as far back as I can remember, with being treated as less than a free person.' So, she stayed put on that bus, knowing there'd be unpleasant treatment, and nasty telephone calls. She didn't know she and her husband would receive death threats for another twelve years, which forced them, eventually, to move up North, to the Middle West, to Detroit. It wasn't the end of her activism. She joined the 1963 March on Washington, was on the frightening but now famous march from Selma, Alabama, to Montgomery, the city of her notoriety and her persecution and, now her glory.

So, after all, Rosa Parks was no accidental heroine. For her, December 1955 was not the start of anything. It was the end of her rope, the last straw of her tolerance of harassment and shaming and white beastliness. That gold medal and that resolution of Congress passed in April were little enough compensation for a lifetime's crime – of being black.

Above, Rosa Parks sits on a bus in Montgomery, Alabama 1956. Below, receiving from President Clinton the Congressional Gold Medal for her act of defiance.

Y2K Alert

Letter No. 2654, 31 December 1999

Notice from the landlord to all tenants: 'In anticipation of any potential Y2K problems, the four elevators in your building will be brought down to the lobby and kept out of service for thirty minutes beginning at 11:45 p.m. on 31st December, 1999.'

If ever there was a talk that ought to be heard the moment it's being spoken, this is the one. I have a problem that has never come up in fifty-three years of broadcasting and plainly will never come up again. I'd better begin explaining it by saying that I'm recording these words on Wednesday, 29 December, in deference to – how shall I put this delicately? – the fairly recent European custom of stretching what used to be a two-day holiday into something more like a two-week break. As I understand it, many millions of people in Europe, including Britain, will be taking (or have taken) things a little easier than usual on Friday, New Year's Eve, perhaps even leaving work early. When I mentioned this to an American friend who happens to be in broadcasting, he reeled visibly in disbelief. 'You've got to be kidding.'

I think that would have been the reaction of most other Americans, simply because on Friday, millions of Americans will have stayed at work or come on to an all-night shift, from the whole federal government down to every kind of office worker, people who work in hospitals, airports, banks, factories, and companies that have never before been open through New Year's Eve into the dawn of New Year's Day, all of them on, of course, a Y2K alert. The suspense that built up in the weeks before New Year's Eve was nerve-shattering, scary, also often funny, and I had meant to recite the drama of it, not to mention the nationwide fear of terrorism, until I realised that it would be like retelling a gripping whodunit when you already knew who 'dunit' – *you* being the majority everywhere that hears this talk on Sunday or Monday. By now you'll know the worst and the best. Either chaos has come to Russia and millions of small businesses in Latin America and the Third World, possibly even to little Piddletrenthide and Tombstone, Arizona; or nothing at all happened, and the wise guys (that's to say the know-it-alls who know absolutely nothing about the history of the computer) are going to be able to chant: 'I told you so. Tremendous fuss about nothing.'

Well as I must remind you, I'm talking more than forty-eight hours before the great revelation. If all is well and a whirlwind sigh of relief passes throughout our world, there is one human being more than another to whom we should give the credit. He will deserve the Nobel Prize for Peace, for Physics, and perhaps a newly created one: the Nobel Prize for Survival. It was a United States Senator, one Robert Bennett, from whom we first learned of a technical glitch that any computer mechanic could fix but which, after deeper thought, turned into what one expert called 'the most ominous threat to human life since the discovery that e=mc2.' Before we come to our blessed watchdog, I'd like to go back to the experts' first awareness of the problem and the recollections that have only now been told.

The problem first occurred to a young expert on systems development about – as he recalls – 1978. In a joking moment with some colleagues, at a time when there was a subdued but general fear about the possibility of a nuclear war, one man said, 'Just imagine: the world is going to end when somebody presses a button.' The systems development man, one Richard Reagan, said in response, 'No, the world's going to end when the clock ticks over to 2000 and all the computers will erase all the data.' Now this was not shouted aloud to the multitude as a threat to anybody. It was more or less of an in-joke, 'shoptalk'. Mr Reagan says: 'We could have fixed it then, but it would have meant re-creating all our customers' existing programs. And at that time no responsible programmer would have been anticipating a problem twenty-two years away. Also at that time there were not too many computers, and they had a large number of uses.' Another systems developer touched the crux of the matter: 'The problem of Y2K isn't an internal computer problem, it's in the connection between business computers and the reliance on data transfers.' That's about as simply as it can be put. I think the point for lay persons to appreciate is that even way back in the 1970s, to fix Y2K would have meant recalling all the private computers or junking them and creating new ones. 'The main point,' says another expert, 'is none of us was so arrogant as to think any of the code we were writing then was going to be around in twenty, thirty years.'

That prospect, of making all the private computers obsolete at a stroke, reminds me of a trip I took about fifty years ago into the Adirondack Mountains in upstate New York. In an old phonograph store (in England, a gramophone shop), the owner, an old man, beckoned me to a phonograph and played me a record. It was a Beethoven symphony. The recording was tinny but the orchestra was on pitch. But the record, instead of spinning around at the usual 78 revolutions a minute, was crawling. 'We thought,' said the old man, 'everybody would soon have one of these at the time.' It was what would come to be called 'a long-playing record.' Now the point of this harmless story is that the machine the old man played for me had two switches and a fine-grooved record. They had been manufactured in 1906, but because everybody would have had to buy a new player (the idea of a cheap attachment didn't occur) and somehow to come by these fine-grooved records, the manufacture of two-switch machines was abandoned and the patent or patents on long-playing records were frozen for forty years. The old man was right. By the early 1950s, the standard, universal record playing at 78 rpms was dead. It is a crude analogy, but I hope it's a useful one

President Clinton discusses the computer glitch 'Y2K'
at the National Academy of Science, 1998.

that stresses the extreme unlikelihood of any computer expert in 1978 guessing that
the code of 1999 computers would not be able to cope with that almost comical hy-
pothesis of the clock rollover problem of 2000 AD. All this about the first gleanings of
the problem has come out only in the past few weeks. But when did we wake up to the
imminence of the rollover as a menace to the whole world? That takes us to the summer of 1997, when Senator Robert Bennett of the State of Utah called into session a
Senate subcommittee of which he was the chairman: the Senate Banking Subcommittee
on Technology and Financial Services. Senator Bennett brought up for the first time in
public the strange puzzle of the year 2000.

I don't believe any of us had heard of a disturbing episode that happened that spring in the warehouse of a frozen-food factory. A supervisor doing his rounds happened to notice something he'd never seen before. The expiration date of a shipment of food that was just going out said that the food was already forty years old, an absurdity since forty years ago the firm didn't exist. The supervisor consulted his boss, and it was decided, considering the one chance in a hundred, say, that the printed note might be right, they dumped the whole shipment. Senator Bennett had heard about this and other freaks, and he knew then why this had happened. Mainframe computers more than ten years old, which most around the world were, had not been programmed to handle a four-digit year, as in AD 2000. To make an immense saving in storage space in all the memory banks, two digits only had been allocated to any given year, so 1978 was 78, 1993, 93, and so on. Same with chips and software. So when 1999 was to turn over to 2000 the chips and the software would go back to 1900. Senator Bennett presented to his subcommittee a necessarily blunt and graphic picture of what this could mean. Government services everywhere could be partially paralysed, the electric grid of towns and cities would be out (no light, no power, no water supply, telephones, railroad traffic – all computerised), food transport would stop, and hospitals would go back to the most primitive care. And especially troublesome to this banking committee, the international banking system would be crippled. Maybe you'd wake up, in the dark, to find among other annoyances that your bank deposits registered zero.

Senator Bennett went on holding hearings, and he woke up the world in June of last year. 'It is not a computer problem simply,' he said, 'it is the responsibility of management of businesses big and small around the world to reprogram their product to fix things now. When people say to me, 'is the world coming to an end?' I say I don't know whether this will be a bad bump in the road (the most optimistic assessment) or whether it will trigger a worldwide recession with absolutely devastating economic and social consequences.' After that committee rose, the government of the United States – beginning with the White House and then on down to both Houses of Congress – redoubled their work on fixing, as we put it, the Y2K bug.

All the Allies were consulted to see how far along they were with the necessary work. Some weren't along at all. Russia was the most notable laggard. And in no time the United States lent a couple of billion dollars to Mr Boris Yeltsin to get busy killing the bug. As of New Year's Eve, the President assured us that, as for the federal government anyway, everything was A-OK. The work that had to be done in every country around the world would be prodigious if January 1, 2000, was to be only a bump in the road.

If you are listening to me anywhere in comfort, I can only say God bless your government, your businessmen and computer doctors, most of all Senator Bennett – and happy, happy New Year.

The Scandal of Pardons (and White House furniture)

Letter No. 2714, 23 February 2001

'The president shall have power to grant reprieves and pardons for offences against the United States.' This little-regarded and rarely quoted sentence in the Constitution defines a topic that has been shocking our senses during the past few weeks to the exclusion, to put it brutally, of much of public interest and the doings and proposed policies of the new president – a situation I've never ever known before. Well, even though the shock hit us a month ago about the manner of the Clintons' departure from the White House, the scandal of several pardons, the looting of the White House furniture, I had been reluctant to talk about it, walking around it, in the hope, which the Democrats, indeed the Democratic Party as a whole, share, the hope that it would go away. My reluctance to talk about it springs honestly from a fact that very rarely confronts a reporter who tries to tell a story that's fair to all sides. The trouble with this story is that there doesn't seem to be more than one side.

You must have guessed by now that I'm talking about what has variously been called 'the squalid Clinton exit', 'the shrinking ex-presidency', and about which the *Washington Post*, which has been a steady admirer of Mr Clinton for most of eight years, wrote, regretfully, last week: 'The defining characteristic of the Clintons is their incapacity to feel embarrassment.'

Before we go into what is so shocking or bizarre about the Clintons' exit, it might be useful to look at the normal procedure, the normal behaviour of a President leaving the White House on the day of the Inauguration of his successor. I've looked through the comings and goings of the Presidents for the past hundred years, for the twentieth century only. Briefly then, in that time, during that century, there were seventeen Presidents before Clinton. Looking for the norm, you have to discount quite a few of them. Two were assassinated, two died in office, three – Coolidge, Truman, Lyndon Johnson – announced early on that they would not seek another term, so they had no further ambition to nurse or promote. One was threatened with impeachment and resigned, rather than face a trial he knew he would lose. Two retired to their homes but remained the titular leaders of their party until a new one would emerge. Two had served the maximum terms under the new two-term rule and so joined the remaining five, who went home to a dignified or unpublicised retirement. They, I believe, established

Outgoing President Clinton and First Lady Hillary Clinton receive
US President-Elect George W. Bush and his wife Laura Bush at the White
House on 20 January 2001.

the norm. And they include in our time Presidents Eisenhower, Carter, and Ford.

What they did on the election of the incoming man was to do what had been done since the middle nineteenth century: They accompanied the new man to the Capitol (until thirty, forty years ago, in an open car), saw him sworn in, and quietly left with their wives and went back to the homes they had left. So really, the normal behaviour comes down to what the majority of the people expect or have come to expect about how a President leaves the White House.

The best thing I can do is to recall a memory of the most typical presidential exit I can remember. A bright, mild day in 1953 in Washington. The usual date: 20 January. The day of the Inauguration of the former General, Dwight D. Eisenhower. The departing President was Harry Truman. It was a simple story. By the afternoon about a hundred people of every sort had gathered on a street in Georgetown, the old Georgian suburb, where the departing President was the guest of his former Secretary of State, Mr Dean Acheson. The small crowd simply waited till the lunch was over in order to watch Mr Truman and his wife come out of Mr Acheson's house and leave for the last time. He came out, his large glasses glinting in the sun. He shaded his eyes, saw the small crowd, put his hand up for quiet, and said two sentences. He said: 'Your coming out here means more to me than many enthusiastic greetings I had as President. Now

I'm Mr Truman, private citizen.' He got in a car with his wife, and he left for the railroad station. And there he stood on the observation platform of the train and waved and smiled, and the train pulled out.

The next thing we learn is from his diary. After he arrived in Independence, Missouri, where he was born, he went to the only house he'd ever owned, a modest, two-storey house on a side street, and he wrote: 'First thing I did was to take the suitcases upstairs, like the old days.' And that was it.

The first misgiving, shall we say, about Mr Clinton was that when he left President George W. Bush to the Inaugural luncheon in the White House and the following parade, he went to the airport and spent two hours with a crowd of friends and supporters, complete with microphones and television cameras. He flew to New York, in a White House plane for the last time, where it turned out he'd invited 10,000 people to see him land at Kennedy. The weather was atrocious, only about a thousand came to hear him, but mainly to hear the new New York Senator – Mrs Hillary Rodham Clinton – make a political speech. What Mr Clinton was doing was swiping the limelight, not only from the new President but from the forgotten former Vice President Al Gore, and proclaiming himself still leader of the Democratic Party. Next day he appointed a friend and big money-raiser as Chairman of the Democratic National Committee, not by custom the privilege of an ex-President. There was a pervasive mutter in the media that this performance was immodest. Well, not in the best of taste. And then only days later we heard that the Clintons had walked off with something like $190,000-worth of White House furniture. At first this was not to be believed; but then came the stupefying, the more incredible story of the pardoning of Mr Marc Rich.

All Presidents, in the last days of their term, exercise this constitutional privilege of pardoning people who, one way or another, have committed offences against the United States, usually people who violated ethics rules of Congress, prisoners whose guilt is dubious, rarely if ever, I believe, men indicted, as Mr Rich was, or convicted of trading with the enemy, or, as with other Clinton-pardoned felons, of drug dealing or money laundering. Presidents routinely check with the Department of Justice to judge the seriousness of the offence. Mr Clinton did not. But he said that three lawyers approved Mr Rich's pardon. Next day all three said they had never approved any pardon for Mr Rich. and all three, it turned out, had been Mr Clinton's defense lawyers in his previous troubles.

So what had Mr Rich done? He'd been indicted seventeen years ago for a raft of criminal charges, here in New York, by Mr Rudy Giuliani, now New York's mayor, but then the United States Attorney. Mr Rich, apart from charges of massive tax evasion and money laundering, had traded with Libya in defiance of the embargo; with Iran while the American hostages were held there; with Iraq through the Gulf War; and with South Africa in defiance of the United States embargo against the apartheid government. Then the news came out that Mr Rich's former wife had given $450,000 to the coming Clinton Library, $3,000,000 to Democrat fundraising lunches, $10,000 to Mr Clinton's legal defense fund.

Well, there once was a time in the long ago when even civil servants, in several Western countries, were not only expected to do no wrong; they could be fired for giving the appearance of doing wrong. Today a great majority of Americans, including many Democrats in and out of Congress and a host of liberal commentators, believe that Mr Clinton has given the appearance of doing wrong. Stronger language has been used most recently. Even an ex-President and Democrat, Mr Jimmy Carter, has called the Clinton behaviour 'simply disgraceful'.

Every day it gets worse. The United States Attorney in New York has instituted a criminal investigation into the history and circumstances of Mrs Rich's gifts, and that is where, I think, for the moment, we ought to leave it.

A public question that was asked almost two years ago, and comes up again, is: Did Mr Clinton degrade the Presidency? Well certainly we can say now that he degraded *his* Presidency. But we should remember that during the long Roman decadence, there was from time to time the interruption of a virtuous emperor. The Presidency is there, and new and decent men will come to inhabit it. And then there is the curious evidence of the polls that still about 40 percent of the people can see no fault or flaw in Mr Clinton as President.

How about as a man? Ah, well, the polls say almost 70 percent now agree he is, and this was put to them, 'dishonest and untrustworthy'. But doesn't this affect his standing as President? To many people, apparently not. Such people certainly don't believe, with Franklin Roosevelt, that: 'The President is assumed to be the moral leader of the nation.'

There's finally the fatalist view that Mr Clinton is not a noticeable sinner but merely reflects the morality of our time. Such a fatalist was Edward Gibbon, who could write about Rome in decay what might well have been his epitaph on the Clinton Presidency: 'The people became insensitive or indifferent to the debauches of the emperor provided he repaired the roads and remitted taxes.'

9/11 America's Day of Terror

Letter No. 2743, 14 September 2001

Last Monday I woke up and, as usual on Monday mornings, I began to ponder what I might talk about this time. I was out of touch, you might say, with what they now call the real world after two weeks' absorption in the fantasy world of the United States Open Tennis Championships. But first, as the anchor men say, the weather. (I like to know if it's cool enough for me to venture around the block.) So, first, I turned on the Weather Channel, and within ten seconds knew all too well what this talk would be about. The man was pointing to a blurry circle just north of Bermuda. The circle had a bull's eye, and it had a name. Its name was Erin, the fifth tropical storm up from the Caribbean this season, and it was said, by the hurricane center in Miami, to be the most lethal in a quarter century, its winds swirling at 120 miles an hour. And, the point that hit me literally where I live, it was headed due northwest and expected to make landfall on Wednesday at Suffolk County, the eastern end of Long Island. Not since 1986 have we had to retire from a hurricane to the underground bunker my wife designed twenty-five years ago.

I had breakfast and thought about when I might take off for the Island to join my wife and my daughter over from London. Then I went back to the weather man, who was mysteriously in a very cheery mood. He pointed to the whirling circle and then across the Atlantic waters inland to Pennsylvania, to show a vertical line of arrows pointing east. They marked a cold front that the experts positively declared would move swiftly east and not merely block the oncoming hurricane but push it rudely due east to expire in the mid-Atlantic. For once, the experts were dead right. No more was heard about Erin, and, waking on Tuesday morning, I was free to ponder again.

But not, you'll understand, for long. I turned on a 24-hour news station and saw a kind of movie I detest, of the towering inferno type: a roaring image, of a monolith collapsing like a concertina in a vast plume of smoke. Just as I pressed my thumb to switch to 'the real world', I caught the familiar voice of a newsman and realised I was in the appalling real world of Tuesday 11 September, 2001, a date that for Americans will live in infamy, along with the memories of Pearl Harbor, 7 December, 1941, and

The second hijacked plane moments before striking the second tower of the World Trade Center on 9/11.

22 November, 1963, the grievous day of President Kennedy's assassination.

Before nightfall, an old United States Senator was to call it 'the most tragic day in American history.' And by that time, numb from the apocalyptic images, not even a historian was going to question the Senator's definition by bringing up, say, the Civil War and a million dead. But in our time, in my time certainly, the most awful, startling, morning I can remember, not because this was the most awful domestic disaster ever, but because, for the first time in the American experience, an act of war aroused, and television pulverized, our senses in a way we'd never known. Before the eleventh of September, most of the Americans who had seen and felt war on their own shores were nearly a century in the grave. The first word I had from my wife, who was a hundred miles away in that so nearly fateful Suffolk County was, 'To think, all these years, I've been saying we were the luckiest people alive, never to have known war in our own country.'

For myself, after the first mere announcement, I thought back to another September, by a fluke of memory, to another eleventh of September. The date is confirmed by the books, but my boyhood memory of the newspapers is sharper. You must bear with me in this. The point will emerge. The first great battle of the First World War was over, the Battle of the Marne, on the eleventh, and in the following days the newspapers hailed the German retreat as a triumph. The subheadings printed: 'Heavy casualties on both sides.' I didn't at first know what that meant, but soon learned, as during the next four years it became a standard phrase. We often suggested the German casualties – at 60,000 in one day. We didn't print numbers of our own. Later, when the Battle of the Somme was over, Britain had lost a quarter of a million men in that battle alone. We never knew nor read that. Many years later, I wrote: 'Is it conceivable that if the British could have been a population of *viewers* – of television viewers instead of newspaper readers – is it conceivable they would have just shaken their heads and gone to the railway stations, as they did, to wave their boys off on the troop trains?'

So, the first thing I felt was, 'This is a war. It's here, it's happening to us.' It is the first thing, I think, for people outside the United States to realize. It is the same feeling of bewilderment and secret fear (What next?) that Londoners felt after the first night of the Blitz, in September 1940.

What next, now? I have reams and reams of notes, made over four days and three nights. But most of them recount heartbreaking scenes and awful facts you yourself will have seen and heard much of. If there is one note, one small note, in this whole monstrous story that can be called heartening, it is the act on Wednesday of the NATO ambassadors in Brussels. For the first time in the history of the alliance, the council voted to invoke Article 5 of the original treaty, which says plainly (something that has been quietly and blandly evaded): 'An armed attack against any of the allies in Europe or North America shall be considered an attack against them all.' This was far and away the best news for the White House and the Pentagon in many a year, for it gave strength and credibility to the President's promise of punishment for the perpetrators.

The word perpetrators points at once to the mystery that has maddened everybody, the military especially, since last Tuesday morning. Since the first microphone was pushed in front of an official of any kind, the line I remember best was that of General Norman Schwarzkopf, the commander of the alliance in the Gulf War: 'That's our main problem: how and where to respond to an enemy we can't identify.'

While he was talking, the FBI had organized around its counter-terrorist squad four thousand agents and two thousand others: scientists, forensic lawyers, weather men, aviation experts, architects, engineers. They have been very busy all around the country, and already from an avalanche of data have learned enough to alert the entire continental American air defense system, and to discover with careful speed the prime suspect to be Osama bin Laden. From now on it would be wise not to believe the welter of rumors that are bound to flood us and credit only what is confirmed by the American and European intelligence services. Attorney General John Ashcroft and his FBI chiefs have been remarkably patient with the media, most conspicuously with the younger television reporters – as with the dense, super-stupid question of the year from a young girl reporter: 'Sir, do you think this attack had been planned?' It gave an FBI terrorist expert the chance to respond dryly. 'I should say it would be brilliant if it had been planned in less than one year.'

Talking of patience before the interminably inquisitive and often stupid press, the Mayor of New York City, Rudy Giuliani, has stood out as a hero, a hero who apparently has to get along without sleep.

And as for the unseen heroes, I recall most vividly a doctor who had been in combat in Vietnam. He emerged from this Hieronymus Bosch inferno in a blizzard of ash and rubble and said, 'Never saw anything like this – this is hell.' And there was a young television cameraman, a simple (late twenties I should guess), all-American boy with ropey hair and good looks, wiping the ghostly ash from his face and talking of the nurses among the hundred-odd doctors there, the nurses: helping survivors, staunching wounds, day and night on the move, calmly saying, 'Please make way.' The boy said, 'People – are unbelievable.'

What is more unbelievable than the enormous wasteland of downtown New York is the stamina and courage of the firemen rescue workers (over 300 lost by now), the thousand or more on their sixteen-hour shifts before they nap for a couple of hours and begin again, slogging through, so far, 100,000 tons of ash and rubble and tangled steel, pointing dogs into dark tunnels of wreckage, on and on, looking for the shape of a life or a corpse.

There is an old song, what we knew as a spiritual, which goes: 'Sometimes, I'm up, sometimes I'm down – sometimes I'm almost to the ground.'

Well, today, tonight, America is down. But between the deeds of the rescue men and the words of NATO – if they mean what they say – America is not 'almost to the ground.'

Iraq and Foreign Policy

Letter No. 2842, 8 August 2003

Iraq *is* the central problem of *foreign* policy not only for the United States but for Western Europe and – since I am not one who shares the fashionable belief that Europe is dead, or the contagious popular nonsense that under President George W. Bush the United States is going into the empire business – I believe also that the closest unity of principle and action between the United States, the United Kingdom, France, and Germany is essential to their future, both as self-respecting nations and as a powerful and influential alliance. The terrorist enemy is widely scattered in its operations, but *it* is a worldwide alliance. The opposition to it cannot afford, for our survival, to be split into two or three conflicting blocs: the United States, United Kingdom, Spain, Italy, and twenty-odd smaller nations against France, Germany, and Russia. For anyone with a glimmer of imagination, the prospect of a terrorist triumph riding high among a jungle of dictators is too horrible to go into.

I once was asked in some interview what was my mission in life. I said if you have a mission, you should become a bishop not a journalist. On government and politics I am and continue to be a reporter, collecting facts, however awkward or contradictory, and leaving you to arrange them into an opinion. But, for once, I have to admit a secondary purpose – I mean other than reporting. It is the hope of playing a small part in the healing – which *must* happen – between the Anglo-American alliance and Germany and France.

For the time being, I have two items that ought to be brought up, the first particularly because it has lain on my desk for months. I have not seen it mentioned anywhere, and it might have a bearing on the German and French votes in the UN Security Council that fired the whole uproar about the Anglo-American invasion and started the apparently unending controversy about the actual legitimacy of the war.

I am holding in my hand a map printed in the *New York Times* after the invasion of Iraq. It shows the countries that, in the 1980s, sold to Iraq 'chemical agents, equipment, and munitions', which were declared by Iraq to United Nations inspectors. Iraq had declared 17,600 tons of sensitive chemicals. Most of the sarin, Tabun, and mustard gas came from the Netherlands, Singapore, Egypt, and India. The interesting category is 'equipment'. Iraq reported 340 pieces of equipment 'used for making

An Iraqi soldier guards a convoy of UN weapons inspectors as
they resume searches of suspect sites in December 2002.

chemical weapons.' A small fraction came from Spain and Austria. But from France:
21 percent. Germany: 52 percent. So between them, Germany and France provided,
by Saddam's own declaration, 73 percent of the then existing equipment with which
to manufacture chemical weapons. If I had been a member of the German or French
delegations, I think I should have been in a quandary: whether to want the UN inspections to go on and on fruitlessly, or whether I should share the suspicion of the
Americans and the British that maybe they'll never be discovered, because they had
very likely been hidden away in a neighbouring country.

You must bear with me on the second item. It came as a shocker to me, even though
it is a piece from my own hand and mouth. It is a *Letter from America* that more than
suggests we were on the verge of going to war in Iraq. The United States Secretary of
State had just said – after a tour of the Middle East to recruit allies for America: 'We
should prefer to act multilaterally, but if necessary we shall act unilaterally.' So, which
Secretary of State said that? Madeleine Albright, that's who! I shall re-do for you the
gist of this old talk (dated second weekend in February 1998), because I came upon,
the other day, a good cause to look up this five-and-a-half-year-old talk. The cause was
a survey of popular European opinion. The simple, appalling (to me) result was that
an actual majority of ordinary people in Europe is under the delusion that the whole
problem of Saddam and chemical weapons started last autumn!

Here is the gist of that talk: 'On the eve of what turned out to be a fruitless talk-fest at the United Nations, President Bill Clinton defined the problem and his policy simply and truly: all the sites of Saddam's chemical and biological weapons, the laboratories and the materials of their production, must be discovered and destroyed. If Saddam resists the UN inspections team or otherwise hampers the inspectors' work he will have to be punished by the United Nations.' The existence of these ghastly materials was known, and the elements were spelled out: the anthrax, botulin and VX, the hideous muscle-paralyzing gas. 'The use of at least one of these on his own people, on the Kurds, is well authenticated.'

That speech was given just before the Security Council met in November, 1997, to go through the formality of a resolution condemning Saddam Hussein and a vote to take action against him. However, the Council debate was hardly under way before it became painfully plain that France, Russia, and China had no intention of punishing Saddam with war, a word never used then or subsequently. So then Secretary of Defense William Cohen and Secretary Albright went off on a recruiting tour of Europe and the Middle East looking for allies. Saudi Arabia refused to serve as a base this time. The whole Arab world was against giving any help. Egypt thought things over and decided that military action would be 'inappropriate'. Britain alone was ready to join. From most delegations to the UN came the parrot cry: 'Seek a diplomatic solution.' The Secretary General, Kofi Annan, urged everybody to be 'more flexible' and announced, for quotation, 'we should not insist on humiliating Saddam Hussein.' Still, the United States went on preparing. Another aircraft carrier went to the Gulf. Tense discussion at the Pentagon about the tactics of the new war – the efficacy of new, more precise, 'smarter' aerial weapons, followed by a controversy about the peril of an air strike on a biological van or tub releasing a nerve gas that could destroy a whole population. The message was: 'Think twice before you bomb the very materials you mean to destroy.' Then the debate started about ground forces. How many hundred thousand? Then Saddam, who had thrown out the UN inspectors – after seven years' search – recanted and said they could come back for two months, only if the team contained no Americans.

So, the UN fell back into a wobble or 'diplomatic solution'. In this hopeless stalemate, President Clinton was ready to give up on the UN and go into Iraq with Britain. So, what happened? My talk was given, as I say, the second weekend in February, 1998. I did not mention the fateful thing that had happened only three weeks before. President Clinton had been called to testify in a long-hanging sexual harassment suit and, on television before the whole nation, denied that he had ever been sexually intimate with a young White House intern and/or that he had ever covered it up. Within days, it became manifest that the President had lied. By then, as a warrior leader, as a President of the United States, he had lost every shred of moral authority.

So, he talked on and on about Iraq, and the need to act, and the United Nations blushed and settled back into an onlooking position, or what Secretary General Annan called 'a more flexible mode.'

Temperatures Drop

Letter No. 2864, 16 January 2004

Sunday morning last: clean, blue, blue sky from the midtown skyline all the way north to the needle-sharp George Washington Bridge. A wonderful day, they tell me. *They* being a frosty-nosed, panting, twenty-odd-year-old couple – grandchildren – who've just, I presume, taken a quick mad jog 'round the reservoir. Well, bully for them! They who don't know that the inventor of jogging died at age fifty-two, after a healthy jog. They're all I'll see of that wonderful day, and positively all it'll see of me. Central Park temperature, from the official weather station: 3 degrees. Fahrenheit. Or what in my time (it if had ever happened in London) would have been called 29 degrees of frost.

Meanwhile, the word comes in from Vermont that my daughter, bundled up a little more than usual, went off to preach in – steady now! – 59 degrees of frost, or to put it more usually, 27 below zero. Being bundled up in such brilliant but Arctic weather means ear flaps and some sort of tight shawl worn up to the nose, making women young and old look like Yankee Muslims.

The Weather Bureau tells us that, for once, the word Arctic is to be taken literally. In other words, this weather system does not, as usual, come blowing in from the Pacific across the Rockies, then due East across the prairie, and then into New England. It was born in the Arctic and swept down through Canada and fanned out across a five-hundred-mile stretch through New England to the northern tip of the South. Of course, this west wind coming across 3,000 miles of dry land is cracklingly dry. We love it in the fall because it's cooling, and it chases away all the humidity and smog over the coastal cities. This time, receiving no opposition (in the form of a damp or warmer system), it was much too cold for snow.

So, what did the city – New York City – do? We have a mayor, Mr Michael Bloomberg, a Republican who has never claimed (as the party does every other day) to be 'compassionate conservative', but he has his own urbane, droll way of practising it.

I look out, as you know, straight ahead over the Central Park reservoir. I turn an inch or two more to the right and there is a great meadow, appropriately called The Meadow. So, on Saturday – through the night – Mayor Bloomberg had a fleet of his juggernaut machines at it, making snow, and pouring it over The Meadow. Sunday morning, there was a compact, isolated playground of the deep and crisp and even.

And by the time I looked out, the scene was like a big canvas out of Breughel – with a score or two of little black imps sliding and waving and skiing. It was a merry Christmas card indeed – and a comical one, for you had only to turn your head a fraction either way and see the whole extent of a brown winter park, not a flake of snow, the leafless trees a forest of feather dusters.

However, sooner or later, I had to cease my nostalgic meditations, while watching the happy kids at play, and turn on the telly, to immediately become aware of New England and New York State and New Jersey as a vast Disaster Area. You began to see pictures, shots of old people being lifted into ambulances, others rescued from cars whose doors had to be opened with hammers and axes. As the week went along, the general outlook for the poor, and the homeless especially, was grim. The temperatures eased up a touch, to twelve, sixteen (still below freezing) and for one blessed day almost touched a scorching 38 degrees. But it was merely a blip. As I talk now, the Weather Bureau pronounced it to be the longest stretch of extremely cold weather in fifty years. And there is no end in sight. Record lows all through the region – a small town in upstate New York: 33 below zero. The mayors of many cities are mobilizing firemen, police, and willing volunteers to rescue the homeless and the thousands of families that, if you can believe it, have no heat. 'It's like,' said one old woman in a hospital, 'like waking up in a snowbank.'

So, Tuesday, Wednesday, I try to banish these grim thoughts by turning at once to mail. Encouraging letters from New Zealand, from Gloucester, a sad letter from a girl in Africa who is an orphan and wants me to pay for her college education. I try to cheer up on a late but welcome Christmas card from Wales, hoping that these *Letters* will go on – as the lady optimistically writes, 'for a very long time to come.'

My spirits were truly revived, though, when I came to the last letter. It's an offer to go to a college for a six-month course and no initiation or registration fee. The tuition fee was, they implied, ridiculously low. Still, what they offered, if you graduated, was something practically everybody would like to have. But, I regret to say, that the two women who rule my life – my wife and my secretary – told me it was too late. The secret the college promised was one I would never know. I tossed the letter into the wastebasket, after a short wistful look at the long envelope and its beautifully embossed title. It was from 'The College for Successful Ageing'.

Well! By midweek, sure enough, there came sliding under the back door another reaction to the frozen north that is always dependable: jokey postcards from friends in Florida, a letter enclosing a blazing headline from a Miami newspaper: 'New England, New York paralyzed by record cold.' A recording engineer who tapes these talks has moved to Florida, and of course he calls to tell me he has just emerged from the pool and is stretched out on his little lawn snorting fresh – not concentrated – Florida orange juice.

I try to sniff and despise these juvenile communications, but, I have to admit, I pause and recall longingly the last winter break I had in Palm Beach. At this time, mid-January over forty years ago, I was doing a piece on the history of that island strip of

A wintry view across the Reservoir in Central Park taken by
A.C. from his apartment window.

sand lying in a turquoise sea, from its first days as a haven for draft-dodgers from the Civil War. A dozen years later, a Spanish ship was wrecked nearby and spilled a cargo of coconuts on the beach. The nuts took root, and within a few years it looked like the backdrop for a Bob Hope–Bing Crosby–Dorothy Lamour 'road' picture. In the 1880s, a tycoon from Philadelphia, who owned the railroad down the Florida peninsula, liked the look of Palm Beach, as a fetching winter playground for his friends. So, in those spacious Robber Baron days, he threw a bridge across from the mainland, built a private track, and simply carried his fellow millionaires over in a private train! A famous architect friend built a whole lush settlement of Spanish villas with Martello towers and large gardens and luxurious appointments. For the next forty years or so, new money moved in, provided it was possessed by the right sort – that is to say, WASPy Anglo-Americans. It was quietly but firmly understood, 'no Jews' and, of course, NINA (no Irish need apply).

In the Roaring Twenties, there moved in one winter the son of a poor Irish refugee from the Irish potato famine, who, in America, became a saloon-keeper. His son made himself an immense fortune through projects both respectable and dubious. He bought a house in Palm Beach, but he knew the rules and actually scorned trying to break down any barriers. He did not strain to hobnob with the established WASP nobility.

Well, that is only the early part of my story. The end is better. On a January Friday afternoon, I, along with a half dozen or so other reporters, had an assignment to watch the departure of some visiting big shot at the Palm Beach airport, which in those days, the very early 1960s, was no more pretentious than a country railway station. What was odd about its functioning this time was a series of reconnaissance raids by men in blue suits, of searching and waving away and huddling, even, coveys of the very rich and their chauffeurs into a guarded lounge. A general appeared, and more men in blue suits who had also in common a mechanical habit of looking first over one shoulder and – click – then over the other. The control tower closed the airport to all incoming and outgoing planes for twenty minutes. Suddenly on a private field there slid in a black limousine. Out of it jumped two bodyguards. A big plane we had barely noticed on the horizon came swishing down the tarmac. It stopped, and as the blue suits lined up by the limousine, the general saluted an emerging, slim, tall, youngish man with light brown hair and shoulders hunched. Soon the engines roared and the plane hurtled screaming down the runway. Multimillionaires shaded their eyes against the sun and no doubt mused on the many aspects of fame and fortune. The grandson of the Irish immigrant saloon-keeper was airborne. He was John Fitzgerald Kennedy, thirty-fifth President of the United States.

Was Saddam a Threat or Not?

Letter No. 2866, 30 January 2004

If I wanted to catch your attention at once, I should say that not since a lanky, un-known, young American aviator dropped his rickety plane by night into the Paris airport, climbed out and said 'I am Charles Lindbergh', has a totally unknown Ameri-can hurtled overnight into the limelight of more countries than his own. I'm talking about the lightning arrival on the scene of David Kay. Only time and history will tell if that comparison is hopelessly melodramatic or a colourful reflection of the truth. Of one thing I'm certain: while Charles Lindbergh's act was one of great personal courage it did not affect the political fate of any nation. Dr Kay's single Reuters agency news-paper interview has deeply embarrassed the Bush administration and could prove to be the first strike to wound it.

David Kay was, until last week, the chief weapons inspector of the Central Intel-ligence Agency, a man who, you might say, as much as any American in government, keeps his secrets to himself. However, Mr Kay resigned last Friday and made public the findings of his long association with the task of searching through Iraq for biologi-cal and chemical weapons, and the materials, projects, and objects that might suggest a forthcoming nuclear arms programme. The whole argument about the extent and imminence of Saddam's threat has been reduced or simplified in most countries to the question: Did he or did he not have, in being or hidden away, weapons of mass destruction?

I've asked various people: What comes to mind with the mere utterance of that phrase? And without exception, the unconscious fact of the word 'mass' creates a picture of some fairly massive weapons – a van or a truck – yes, something like those two famous trailers that were reported. At the time I suggested that a vial of nerve gas the size of a beer bottle could also – could it not? – be defined as a weapon of mass destruction since it could paralyse the population of a capital city. But in the language of the intelligence people, biochemicals were identified as a separate threat.

Now, what did Dr Kay conclude in the findings he reported to the Reuters agency? First he said that throughout both the Clinton Administration and the present one, the intelligence experts in America and many foreign countries were sure that Iraq had illegal weapons, but that in his experience the Bush administration used no pressure to exaggerate Saddam's threat or prejudice the work of the CIA's inspectors. But, he said that the CIA and United Nations inspectors uncovered all there was of a nuclear programme, and that after the Gulf War further nuclear efforts to make a crude bomb were a failure. Also, well before the invasion of Iraq, Saddam had abandoned his bio-chemical weapons programme.

The day before Dr Kay appeared on the scene, Mr Dick Cheney, the Vice President of the United States, asked of the administration's critics: how about those two trailers that were found in Iraq? Surely they were conclusive proof of mobile, biological weapons. Dr Kay, on the day of his retirement, immediately answered the Vice President. The trailer story was, he said, a fiasco. They were intended to produce hydrogen. And before the invasion of Iraq there were no stockpiles of biological or chemical weapons.

To report Dr Kay's findings as briefly and starkly as this is to leave the impression of a whistle-blower – a government employee resigning and telling a tale to humiliate his former employer. Quite wrong. Dr Kay is an amiable, solid, middle-aged man with a greying moustache, who is so vastly experienced in his field and therefore so comfortable with himself that none of his answers showed a trace of irritation with mean or loaded questions.

On Wednesday morning Dr Kay appeared before the Senate Armed Services Committee to discover the rightness or wrongness of the intelligence information that led to America's preemptive invasion. By the way, at one point Dr Kay, making a general lament, thought that the whole technical language of war was obsolete. He doubted that 'preemptive' had much meaning in a world of technology, when a war could start and end overnight. What were very much in the forefront of the anxieties of both the Clinton and the present administration were the intentions of a likely attacker and the immediacy with which he could carry them out. Dr Kay wondered if we'd noticed the chemical protection suits the men invading Baghdad were wearing. No choice of the soldiers (they were very uncomfortable, especially in 115 degrees) but they vividly reflected the fear of an unheralded use of chemical and biological weapons by an enemy who, he said, had lied and cheated for decades and had used them with devastating results twice on his own neighbours. Dr Kay was asked: If Saddam was in power today, how fearful would he be as a threat to the United States and its allies? The same, he said. Of course, he added, what he was reporting might well be repudiated when the right historian comes along. There have always been intelligence failures in war, big and little. For example, he said, in the Second World War American and British intelligence were fully agreed that the heavier the bombing of German cities the swifter was the decline in civilian morale. After the war it was made quite clear that exactly the opposite was the truth: the more the bombing, the more morale strengthened, until, alas, the war could only be ended by continuous massive bombing of cities by two countries whose leaders, at the beginning, had sworn as much as possible to avoid civilian targets.

I have greatly simplified as accurately as I can the actual language in which this Senate investigation was being conducted. There were times when we were befogged with jargon, not merely technical but the daily jargon of politicians and lawyers who were very verbose while actually being incapable of plain English. Not, thank the lord, Senator John McCain. Do you remember the naval hero who survived five years of torture in Vietnam, ran for President, soundly defeated George W. Bush in New Hampshire but lost out in the Southern primaries? At one point Senator McCain, plainly fed up with the buffet of jargon on hand, said firmly: if Saddam were in power today would he be considered a threat to the United States? Yes, said Dr Kay. And wouldn't that be an intelligence failure? It would, said Dr Kay.

Several times, both in the Reuters interview and again in his Senate testimony on Wednesday, Dr Kay quite calmly rejected the notion, which one or two Democrats were understandably eager to have him confirm, that granting Dr Kay's recital of failures by his team in the field – the vast field of Iraq – he would agree that the primary responsibility rested with President Bush. Dr Kay would not say so. Time and again he said that the United States and its allies did not in any way press the CIA and the foreign agents to find a good cause for war. I'm just saying, he insisted, that these are facts on the ground. There was no evidence of a biochemical weapons programme, and the very primitive nuclear programme had been abandoned.

At the same time, we must not forget that there had been biochemical weapons and raw material found and declared during the United Nations inspections through the 1990s. Dr Kay had no doubt that since 1998, perhaps even after the Gulf War, Saddam had shipped war-making materials to Syria. Dr Kay finally said there were persuasive reasons for finding Saddam a serious threat, but to justify the war on his possession of weapons of mass destruction was false, because such information was false. In the end Dr Kay said it all in seven words: 'It turns out we were all wrong.' *All* meaning the American and British and other allied intelligence. Dr Kay thus gave the President the escape hatch that the Hutton report opened to Prime Minister Tony Blair.

Directly asked by a reporter next day if he would now withdraw the 'weapons of mass destruction' excuse, the President looked dazed; and after six seconds simply dodged the question. He said he had regarded Saddam as a serious threat to the security of the United States. Why he turned down a golden opportunity to claim rightly that he was misled is a mystery. He just doesn't want to blame anybody, including the CIA.

Do you remember the movie *Casablanca*, about a cynical American played by Humphrey Bogart who sets up a nightclub in Casablanca during its occupation by France's Vichy government? He pretends to be indifferent to either side's winning the war but is secretly helping refugees from Hitler get to America. Asked, 'Why did you come to Casablanca?' lazily he replied: 'I came for the waters.' 'Meester Rick, there are no waters in Casablanca.' 'I was misinformed.' When will the President quote Bogart?

Overleaf, the day after US troops entered the centre of Baghdad –
the toppled Saddam Hussein statue.

Postscript

From *America Observed: The Newspaper Years of Alistair Cooke*
(1988), selected and introduced by Ronald A. Wells

WE WHO HAVE in this century seen the rise of many forms of tyranny, from both right
and left, know that to have survived at all with some semblance of a free and democratic society is no mean achievement. The American 'experiment', begun more than
two centuries ago, can be declared moderately successful. Nevertheless, as Alistair
Cooke said in concluding his television history of America, 'In this country – a land
of the most persistent idealism and the blandest cynicism – the race is on between its
decadence and its vitality.'

That sentence has been widely quoted since. The reader is bound to wonder how, in
Cooke's opinion, the race is going after all that time. In late February 1988, he agreed
to sit down and make the following comments in a taped conversation, prefaced – as
always – by a reminder of his temperamental reluctance ever to write a piece called
'Whither America?':

'Well, to begin with, let me say my reluctance to predict the future of this country,
or any country, is based on more things than my own poor record as even a short-
range prophet. It has to do also with sharp recollections of the long-range predictions
of some very eminent prophets, among them Shaw, Wells, Count Keyserling, Ortega
y Gasset, Spengler.

'But beyond – or before I'd read – these cautionary tales, I think I picked up from
my father a distrust of dogma. Not by precept, but by the example of his behaviour.
He was a religious man and lived, quietly, privately – with absolutely no evangelical
fife and drum – by the Ten Commandments as much as anyone I've ever known. But
if someone broke any of them, and the church elders began to fish out the statutory
punishment, he'd admonish them by nervously noting the way Christ treated sinners.
Forgiveness was all. It was something in those days, in a strict Methodist chapel, to go
on acting as if there were just as many good people outside the church as in it. He felt
the same way about politics. He was a staunch Manchester Liberal (to the constant
grief of my mother – she always voted Conservative) but even there you never knew
who, from any party, he'd decide was a good man. I think – I hope – this habit of
mind passed over to me. So dogmatic opinions were always shadowed by what I later
learned was called 'the cloud of unknowing'. This may be a character flaw, though reli-

gious people say it's the steady companion – or, guardian, perhaps– of Faith. However, I now think it may have moved me early in life, before I ever guessed it, to become a reporter – to leap to a seat on the fence and develop the habit of swivelling from one view of things to another, a habit fatal to the care and feeding of an ideology.

'During an evening I once spent with Pandit Nehru, I mentioned to him one of the problems of reporting to a country – and from a country – whose people have been brought up to believe that 'there's much to be said on both sides.' I found so often that going after a story on, say, racial discrimination, hospital care, the arms race, the drug problem, women's rights – any really serious matter – as often as not there were not two sides to the story but five! 'Ah,' he said, 'you have discovered the Hindu view of truth.' Very flattering. But if you're going to govern a country, instead of simply re-porting it, that view can lead to at least five different parties and, I suppose in the end, to proportional representation. Which, on paper, is wonderfully fair, but can produce what my old headmaster called (a propos of the many parties in the French govern-ment in those days, and the constant reshuffling of power) the sort of chaos produced by a streetcar that has to run on six or seven different levels of track.

'Well, enough of reluctance. You want me to say what I see as signs of decadence or vitality in the life of America today – it would be better to say in the life of the West – because most of these symptoms are at least as lively in Western Europe as in the United States. Let's put them down and call them trends, which I can't help seeing as other than characteristic or decisive one way or the other. (You remember Justice Holmes's definition of the truth as 'what a man can't help believing must be so.')

'I have several times sat down to check what I take to be present symptoms of deca-dence on the model of Gibbon's remarkable and penetrating diagnosis of the decline of Imperial Rome. Let's mention first some of the nagging constants, in our social life. First, no doubt about it, money mania, that is, money sought as power. Our business schools are graduating fewer and fewer people who are going into manufacturing and more and more who are going into investment banking. Fewer people making things, more making money.

'Of course, the money mania is nothing new. It comes at us in waves, riding on a tide of unusual prosperity. It partly explains Jefferson's distrust of inherited wealth, and Andrew Jackson's detestation of banks. And in the 1870s, Mark Twain saw the hog-wild gallivanting of the money men as the main symptom of 'an era of incredible rottenness.' But I do think it's as bad now as at any time since then.

'The collapse of public education, due, I think to the constant setting of – you might say, revisionist – standards that are easy and dithering. The gross over-commercializ-ing of all sports. Child actors in television commercials. The arts – in theatre, music, painting, especially – going the way Gibbon astutely described: 'freakishness pretend-ing to originality, enthusiasm masquerading as vitality.' The widespread persistence of a phoney counterculture: the replacement of thrift, work, minimum social duties, by what Philip Larkin called the new hippie syllabus: sex, not working, drugs. I suppose, not to beat around the bush, that much of what I take to be the social sickness of the time – beginning in the Sixties and exacerbated in the Eighties – could be attributed by a moralist to a clutch of certain deadly sins: namely, greed, envy, lust, covetousness. Not to leave anyone with the pious feeling that he/she is out of 'the mainstream', I'd say that the conservative sin is secret greed (holding on to what you've got); whereas the liberal sin is self-righteousness ('Why aren't you more like me?'). I guess lust is no respecter of class, gender, colour, or party – just epidemic.

'Now, for government, and disturbing trends which may or may not have a moral root. Once a year, the self-defeating, elephantine Congressional budget process: the stuffing of a five-thousand-page budget – which nobody has time to read –with every pet pork barrel project of every Congressman who has a bridge to repair, a defense plant to build, a soybean subsidy to maintain, and so on. Maybe it's an inevitable concomitant of the two-year Congressional term: the only budget a Congressman has any say in is the one to be spent in his reelection year.

'Then, there's the apparently unavoidable need, in a much advertised democracy, for political candidates to solicit millions of dollars in order to run any campaign at all. There is the shameful fact of a bare fifty percent turnout of eligible voters in national elections – much the lowest of any democracy.

'In foreign policy, there's the attempt to extend American influence beyond the reach of American power. It could be argued, I think, that this is, on an international scale, the same urge as that of corporations, big and small: the urge to live beyond one's means. I'm taken with Paul Kennedy's thesis, which he supports by tracing the rise and fall of the great empires, that they all in the end are the victims of what he calls 'imperial overstretch', of the Romans' effort to maintain their power far beyond the borders they were able to discipline or contain. I think America falls into line with this thesis in three stages. First – and you could call it the first fatal declaration of intent – was President Kennedy's inaugural, which was wonderful as rhetoric and hair-raising as policy. To give a guarantee to forty-three nations. What was it? We shall 'pay any price, bear any burden, meet any hardship,' et cetera, 'to support any friend, oppose any foe.' Wonderful! The fact was that few Americans were ever going to give up their automobiles or dishwashers to help Zambia or Angola or a whole raft of countries whose names they could barely pronounce and which – it now comes out – about sixty percent of their high school and college students couldn't place on a map.

'The second stage was Vietnam, when we acted on the promise – against the warnings of Generals Eisenhower and MacArthur. Not only did we not – at home – bear much of a hardship, but it was the only war Americans didn't have to pay for – there were no extra taxes. The payment was to come later, in the form of a whacking national deficit. Which, to maintain the social services already established, and a defence programme each succeeding president has felt bound to increase, leads us to Ronald Reagan and the compounding of the deficit. In his first five years, Reagan added 950 billions to the budget, Congress about seventy. Of course, it's true that while all Presidents are blamed for their budgets, it's Congress that approves the final figure, so it must share the blame. And I'm afraid that given the unpaid debt of Vietnam, the guaranteed growth of Social Security, and our enormous loans to Third World countries, it was probably impossible to lower the ceiling drastically. I doubt that a Democratic President would have managed it, without a stiff tax increase that the country was not ready for. As for knowing any feasible way out of the deficit, that is something that certainly boggles my mind, and which I have to leave to the Volckers, Greenspans, Rohatyns, Galbraiths, and other competing wizards.

'Well, that's quite a lot of decadence, or, say, decadence and decline. Now, against this jeremiad, we have to set the vital signs, and they are easier to define because, whereas sickness has a series of symptoms, health can usually be summed up in a word: vivacity, humour, courage, serenity.

'In general, then, there doesn't seem to be any decline in curiosity, inquisitiveness, enlisted in the dogged belief that things can be made better, that tomorrow ought to be better than today. The stoic and fatalist are not yet familiar American types.

'There is now more concern for the poor, even when there are proportionately fewer of them than ever this century . Most people believe that whatever else the government should or shouldn't do, it has the primary responsibility for children, for the poor and the old, the sick and the disabled. And, government or no government, I'm constantly impressed by the restless experimenting that's being done all over the country, and the self-sacrifice of ordinary men and women, with disabled and sick people once given up as hopeless wards of the community.

'Most of all, three things: First, the unflagging energy of the media in digging out and facing all the nastiest problems of the country, not shunning the worst that's happening, by way of crookedness or incompetence or injustice or default, both in the nation and in the local neck of the woods. Second, very many rich Americans, far more than the rich of any other country, do go on making great fortunes in order to give a good deal of them away to worthy causes of every kind. Europe may have its dozens of philanthropists, but America has its many thousands. And, third, among the people at large, an unsleeping passion for liberty, even when it slops over into forms of licence absurdly defended by the First Amendment.

'Well, the odds may seem to be on the side of decadence. I suppose I'd have felt much the same way, about most of our sins, if I'd been writing in 1929, never anticipating the crash or the arrival of a Roosevelt to summon up reserves of stamina and work and courage we didn't know were there, which showed, dramatically, that the President, whoever he is, sets the moral tone of the country. I have written elsewhere that, in many matters, which should require an administration to avoid even the appearance of wrongdoing, the Reagan Administration has been too often notable for moral numbness. Perhaps, in every period of affluence and self-indulgence, America needs a national crisis – a depression, a collapse of the money market – to throw up a benevolent leader (he had better be benevolent if the system is to hold) who mobilizes the best of America instead of the worst. At the moment, I do not see one. As it is, if I were filing daily pieces today, instead of in the Forties, Fifties, Sixties and Seventies, I don't think I could be – shall we say? – so sprightly without guilt.'

Index

Acknowledgements

On behalf of the Estate of Alistair Cooke, I would like to thank those who have made the publication of this book possible: Colin Webb, my father's book editor and literary executor, who selected and edited this collection ready for publication; Dr Ronald A Wells, who provided his experience as consulting editor, having edited the collection of *Guardian* articles published under the title *America Observed* in 1988; Patti Yasek who took on the onerous task of transcribing all of the original scripts into electronic copy, worked beyond the call of duty and provided much sound advice; Walton Rawls, who once again has copy edited with sensitivity and understanding; George Perry who provided his advice on the selections for the early sections; Victoria Webb, who diligently helped with the editing and picture research; Helen Smith for the index; Adam Scoville for advice and help with images; Matthew Robertson, the art director at Other Rooms, for his elegant layout and efficiency; Alex Rankin, at the Howard Gotlieb Archival Research Center, for the provision of information and photographs; Susannah Jayes for the picture research.

S.C.K.

Picture credits

Corbis: 15, 31 (Bettmann), 34 (Bettmann), 37 (Bettmann), 40 (Bettmann), 43 (Bettmann), 46 (Hulton-Deutsch), 50 (Bettmann), 52 (Bettmann), 59 (Bettmann), 61 (John Springer Collection), 63 (Bettmann), 70 (Sunset Boulevard), 73 (Bettmann), 76 (Bettmann), 79 (Bettmann), 83, 91 (Bettmann), 93 (Bettmann), 98 (CinemaPhoto), 103 (Bettmann), 106 (Bettmann), 108 (Bettmann), 112 (Bettmann), 115 (Bettmann), 119 (Bettmann), 120 (Bettmann), 121 (Bettmann), 124 (Bettmann), 127 (Yoichi Okamoto), 136 (Bettmann), 140 (Bettmann), 143 (Bettmann), 146 (Ted Streshinsky), 149 (Ted Streshinsky), 153 (Bettmann), 161 (Bettmann) 162 (Bettmann), 165t (Bettmann), 165b (Bettmann), 174 (Wally McNamee), 178 (Buzz Aldrin), 180 (Neil Armstrong) 183 (Arnie Sachs/CNP), 191, 202-203 (Bettmann), 204 (Bettmann), 207 (Wally McNamee), 212 (Bettmann), 218 (Owen Franken), 221 (Bettmann), 225 (Bettmann, 233 , 236 (Bettmann), 243 (Wally McNamee), 246 (Kaveh Kazemi), 250 (Brownie Harris), 255 (Bettmann), 260 (Bettmann), 263 (Bettmann), 266 (Bettmann), 270, 283 (Bettmann), 285 (Bettmann), 292 (Lawrence Manning), 395 (Jacques M Chenet), 303 (Bettmann), 312 (Wally McNamee), 334 (Bettmann), 338 (INA/Handout/Reuters), 348 (Robert Sorbo/Sygma), 352 (Reuters), 359 (Reuters), 364t (Bettmann), 375 (Masatomo Kuriya), 379 (Reuters), 388 (Peter Turnley). **Courtesy of the Estate of Alistair Cooke:** 15, 87, 88, 330. **Getty Images:** 8 (Leonard Mccombe/Time Life Pictures), 12 (Leonard Mccombe/Time Life Pictures), 26 (Leonard Mccombe/Time Life Pictures), 28 (Leonard Mccombe/Time Life Pictures), 66 (George Tames/New York Times Co), 68 (Tony Vaccaro), 131 (George Silk/Time Life Pictures), 157 (Joseph Louw/Time Life Pictures), 169 (CBS Photo Archive), 195 (Popperfoto), 199 (Co Rentmeester/Time Life Pictures), 229 (Dirck Halstead), 279 (Diana Walker/Time Life Pictures), 287 (Francois Lochon/Time Life Pictures), 300 (Joel Robine/AFP), 308 (Dirck Halstead/Time Life Pictures), 315 (John Chiasson/Liaison), 320 (Time Life Pictures/White House), 323 (Chuck Nacke/Time Life Pictures), 326 (Tom Stoddart Archive), 341 (Tim Clary/AFP), 344 (Lee Celano/WIreImage), 351, 355 (Porter Gifford), 364b (George Bridges/AFP), 368 (Richard Ellis), 371 (Stephen Jaffe/AFP). **Mary Evans Picture Library:** 55. **NB Pictures:** 253. **Topfoto:** 24-25 (David Gamble). **Penny Tweedie:** 2, 18, 186.